Docker

Rheinwerk Computing

The Rheinwerk Computing series from Rheinwerk Publishing offers new and established professionals comprehensive guidance to enrich their skillsets and enhance their career prospects. Our publications are written by leading experts in the fields of programming, administration, security, analytics, and more. Each book is detailed and hands-on to help readers develop essential, practical skills that they can apply to their daily work. For further information, please visit our website: *www.rheinwerk-computing.com*.

Philip Ackermann
JavaScript: The Comprehensive Guide
2022, 982 pages, paperback and e-book
www.rheinwerk-computing.com/5554

Sebastian Springer
Node.js: The Comprehensive Guide
2022, 834 pages, paperback and e-book
www.rheinwerk-computing.com/5556

Christian Ullenboom
Java: The Comprehensive Guide
2022, 1126 pages, paperback and e-book
www.rheinwerk-computing.com/5557

Johannes Ernesti, Peter Kaiser
Python 3: The Comprehensive Guide
2022, 1036 pages, paperback and e-book
www.rheinwerk-computing.com/5566

Bernd Öggl, Michael Kofler
Git: Project Management for Developers and DevOps Teams
2023, 407 pages, paperback and e-book
www.rheinwerk-computing.com/5555

Bernd Öggl, Michael Kofler

Docker

Practical Guide for Developers and DevOps Teams

Rheinwerk
Computing

Editor Meagan White
Acquisitions Editor Hareem Shafi
German Edition Editor Christoph Meister
Translation Winema Language Services, Inc.
Copyeditor Julie McNamee
Cover Design Graham Geary
Photo Credit Shutterstock.com: 304298384/© Yann Hubert; iStockphoto.com: 165958933/© anilyanik
Layout Design Vera Brauner
Production Graham Geary
Typesetting SatzPro, Germany
Printed and bound in Canada, on paper from sustainable sources

ISBN 978-1-4932-2383-1
© 2023 by Rheinwerk Publishing, Inc., Boston (MA)
1st edition 2023
3rd German edition published 2021 by Rheinwerk Verlag, Bonn, Germany

Library of Congress Cataloging-in-Publication Control Number: 2022950845

Contents at a Glance

Dear Reader,

One line from Docker's mission statement has always stood out to me: "We handle the tedious setup, so you can focus on the code." I like to think that we do something similar here at Rheinwerk.

Having been internet-dwellers for a few decades now, most of us have had the experience of picking up a new skill solely from web content. We've cobbled together an education in, say, sourdough baking, via YouTube videos, blog posts, and how-to articles. However, online learning has its drawbacks: you've got to sift out misinformation, you don't always know *what* you don't know, and content isn't always tailored to your needs (as anyone who has tried to bake at 8,000 feet above sea level using a standard recipe can testify)!

So perhaps our version would be: "We curate the content, so you can focus on learning." With all our books, our goal is always to present our reader with vetted information that's been thoughtfully organized and meets their needs. My first piece of advice to new authors is this: keep your reader in mind and write what they need to know.

What did you think about *Docker: Practical Guide for Developers and DevOps Teams*? Your comments and suggestions are the most useful tools to help us make our books the best they can be. Please feel free to contact me and share any praise or criticism you may have.

Thank you for purchasing a book from Rheinwerk Publishing!

Meagan White
Editor, Rheinwerk Publishing

meaganw@rheinwerk-publishing.com
www.rheinwerk-computing.com
Rheinwerk Publishing · Boston, MA

Contents

3   Basic Principles

4 Custom Docker Images (Dockerfiles)

7   docker Command Reference

PART II   Toolbox

8   Alpine Linux 177

9   Web Servers and Company 185

17   Continuous Integration and Continuous Delivery

18   Security

19 Swarm and Amazon Elastic Container Service 411

20 Kubernetes 435

Appendices

Preface

In the early 2000s, virtualization software turned the daily lives of many developers upside down: suddenly it was possible to run Linux *and* Windows on one machine, to easily try out programs in different environments or web apps in old versions of web browsers, to install and test different software stacks in virtual machines in parallel, and much more.

Of course, virtual machines continue to play a major role for developers; moreover, the cloud in its current form isn't even conceivable without virtualization. Nevertheless, a shift away from virtual machines to containers began a few years ago and seems to be accelerating more and more.

Containers allow certain software components (web servers, programming languages, databases) to run without the overhead of a virtual machine. Why install an entire operating system (usually Linux) on a virtual machine for just *one* very specific function?

Rarely does the paradigm "less is more" apply as well as it does to container technology. The concept of "less" expresses itself in countless advantages: containers are much faster to set up than virtual machines, are easier to replicate across different development systems, use fewer resources, and offer much better scaling and load balancing capabilities. Not only are containers a blessing for development teams, but they also provide entirely new methods of deployment, that is, in the productive operation of the developed solution.

Docker

Docker is *the* container software par excellence. While there are now certainly interesting alternatives, Docker has created the container market as such. In a survey of thousands of developers by the Stack Overflow website (*https://insights.stackoverflow.com/survey/2020*), Docker was the most important platform after Linux and Windows. Docker was even number one in the "Most Wanted Platform" question. So, Docker is the tool most developers want to familiarize themselves with. And among developers already using Docker, Docker ranked number two in the "Most Loved Platform" question. (Linux had a few percent higher approval in this case.)

However, the Docker Inc. company got into financial trouble in 2019. Then, in November of that year, cloud provider Mirantis bought Docker's enterprise division, turning *Docker Enterprise* into a new product called *Mirantis Kubernetes Engine*. Since then, the remaining company has been more concerned with the needs of "ordinary" developers and development teams that aren't part of huge corporations.

Fortunately, we don't need to be concerned that Docker might just disappear due to financial issues. Almost all components of Docker are available as open-source software. Some Docker interfaces have also been standardized by the Open Container Initiative (OCI), making it easier for other vendors to offer products compatible with Docker. That's why, in this book, we'll also take a look at the most interesting competitor product for Linux users, *Podman*.

Docker has set a standard that, in all likelihood, will endure. Just how agile Docker continues to perform was most recently seen with the introduction of Apple's new ARM-based ("Apple Silicon") CPUs. Within a few months, Docker has ported all of its tools to ARM. No other container system can keep up in this respect.

About This Book

This book provides an introduction to using Docker and an overview of the most important components (images) that you can use to assemble your own container worlds. Based on several large-scale examples, we'll show you how to use Docker in real-life projects, and we'll go into detail about cloud deployment.

The book is divided into three parts:

- Part I introduces Docker. On the basis of numerous examples, you'll learn how to use the docker and docker-compose commands in a meaningful way and what the syntax of the *Dockerfile* and *docker-compose.yml* files looks like.
- Part II presents important images that can serve as a basis for your own projects. These include the following:
  - Alpine Linux
  - Apache and Nginx web servers (including proxy setup with Traefik and Let's Encrypt configuration)
  - Database servers, MySQL/MariaDB, Mongo Database (MongoDB), PostgreSQL, and Redis
  - Programming languages, JavaScript (Node.js), Java, PHP: Hypertext Preprocessor (PHP), Ruby, and Python
  - Web applications, WordPress, Joomla, and Nextcloud
- Part III demonstrates the use of Docker in practice. We'll show you both how to develop modern web applications with Docker in a particularly efficient way, and how to transform existing projects with all their legacy issues into more maintainable Docker projects.

  Two chapters on using GitLab with Docker and on *continuous integration* (CI) and *continuous delivery* (CD) demonstrate new paradigms and tools for developing software in teams.

The topic of deployment won't be neglected either. With Docker *Swarm* and *Kubernetes*, you can take your Docker projects to the cloud and benefit from the scaling capabilities there. A collection of tips ensures that safety doesn't get overlooked in the process.

Finally, we'll briefly introduce the *Podman* program developed by Red Hat in the appendix. It adopts many ideas and the syntax of Docker, but breaks new ground in regards to its implementation. However, Podman is only relevant in the Linux world.

Brave New Docker World

Once you've tried Docker and gotten to know it, you'll never want to do without its features again. Let us guide you into a new world!

Bernd Öggl (*https://webman.at*)
Michael Kofler (*https://kofler.info*)

Book Resources

The following resources are available for you to download from the website for this book:

- All project files
- All code examples

Go to *www.sap-press.com/5650*. Click on the **Resources** tab. There you'll see a list of downloadable files along with a brief description. Click the **Download** button to start the download.

GitHub

We use Git to manage our sample files. For this reason, you can also find (possibly already updated or corrected) sample files on GitHub (*https://github.com/docker-compendium*).

The repository *https://github.com/docker-compendium/samples* contains an overview of the individual chapters with the links to the corresponding repositories with Git submodules. This means you can use the following commands to download all the examples from GitHub to your computer:

```
git clone https://github.com/docker-compendium/samples.git
cd samples
git submodule update --init -recursive
```

If you have any suggestions for improvement, we are happy to receive pull requests from you.

Test Platforms and Linux Distributions

Our main test platform for this book was Ubuntu Linux. In parallel, we also tried many examples on Windows and macOS, as well as Debian, Fedora, and Oracle Linux.

One more thing about Red Hat: When this book refers to RHEL, it doesn't mean only Red Hat Enterprise Linux; rather, the information also applies to all distributions compatible with it. This is especially true for AlmaLinux, CentOS Stream, Rocky Linux, and Oracle Linux.

PART I
Introduction

Chapter 1
Hello World

The three Hello World examples for Docker presented in this chapter are intended to do a little more than just output the much-quoted string to the screen: We want to start one web server at a time, which will provide a web page that displays the current time and a value for the server's utilization. In this context, we use three different programming languages.

To keep the program code that's independent of Docker and unimportant for this example as short as possible, we'll refrain from separating frontend and backend code, as a modern web application would do. You can consider this chapter rather as a *proof of concept*. Examples of modern web applications can be found in Part III of this book.

1.1 Docker Quick Install

The first step is to install the Docker software on your computer. For detailed installation instructions, see Chapter 2. At this point, we want to provide a quick-start option for all those whose fingers are already tingling with anticipation.

1.1.1 Windows

For Docker installation on Windows, you need a 64-bit installation of Windows 10/11 Home, Pro, or Enterprise. Docker uses the Windows Subsystem for Linux version 2 (WSL2) and activates it if needed. To install Docker, simply download and run the setup program from the following address (no need to register with Docker Hub to do this):

https://hub.docker.com/editions/community/docker-ce-desktop-windows

1.1.2 macOS

The installation file (DMG) for macOS can be found at the following address:

https://hub.docker.com/editions/community/docker-ce-desktop-mac

Note that there's a version for the Intel chip here and a version for the new Apple chips (M1) that have been in use since 2020.

1.1.3   Linux

For a common Debian-based Linux distribution (Debian, Ubuntu, etc.) and a computer with a 64-bit processor, it's usually sufficient to enter the following four commands in the command line:

```
sudo apt -y install apt-transport-https ca-certificates curl
curl -fsSL https://download.docker.com/linux/ubuntu/gpg | \
  sudo apt-key add -
sudo add-apt-repository \
 "deb [arch=amd64] https://download.docker.com/linux/ubuntu \
  $(lsb_release -cs) stable"
sudo apt update
sudo apt -y install docker-ce docker-ce-cli containerd.io
```

Concerning other Linux distributions (Fedora, CentOS, etc.), have a look at Chapter 2, Section 2.4.

To try and reproduce the following sections, you'll need the relevant permissions for Docker in addition to the installation. If you're having trouble on Linux, simply run the Docker commands as root on your computer. Windows and macOS take care of the necessary permissions during the installation process. In addition, a fast internet connection is helpful, as the base images you need to download are several hundred megabytes in size.

1.2   Apache with PHP 8

We'll describe three different variants to implement the specifications for this example (a HTML page provided by a web server) using Docker. The first Hello World variant is programmed with the well-known combination of Apache web server and PHP as the programming language.

It's very useful to create a separate directory for each Docker attempt. For this example, the project directory is *hello-world-php*. The PHP/HTML code is pretty straightforward. Following, you can see the *index.php* file that's placed in the project directory:

```
<!DOCTYPE html>
<!-- File index.php -->
<html>
<head>
  <title>Hello world</title>
  <meta charset="utf-8" />
</head>
<body>
<h1>Hello world: apache/php</h1>
```

```
<?php
  $load = sys_getloadavg();
?>
  Serverzeit: <?php echo date("c"); ?><br />
  Server utilization (load): <?php echo $load[0]; ?>
</body>
</html>
```

The PHP call `sys_getloadavg` provides a measure of the current utilization of the system. Among Unix-related operating systems, this is a common benchmark, usually represented by three average values. They describe the CPU utilization as an average of the last minute, the last five minutes, and the last 15 minutes, respectively. In the Hello World example, we use only the first of these three values: the average utilization for the last minute (the array index is 0, hence `$load[0]`).

For this file to be delivered from a Docker container running Apache and PHP 8, you must first create a Docker image using the aforementioned software. A Docker container is then derived from this image to do the actual work.

> **Terminology**
>
> Don't be put off now by perhaps unfamiliar terms such as *Docker image* and *Docker container*. Chapter 3, Section 3.1, describes these terms in greater detail.

To create a Docker image, you must create the following *Dockerfile* file and save it in the project directory. This file contains what can be regarded as the instructions for creating the image.

```
# File: hello-world-php/Dockerfile (docbuc/hello-world-php)
FROM php:8-apache
ENV TZ="Europe/Amsterdam"
COPY index.php /var/www/html
```

So . . . three almost self-explanatory lines are sufficient to install an Apache web server and PHP in the current version and make the *index.php* file available to the world? Actually, it's three lines and two commands, to be exact. Now you need to enter these two commands in the command line to get the magic started:

```
docker build -t hello-world-php .
```

This will create the desired Docker image from the *Dockerfile* and tag it `hello-world-php`. The first time you call this command, Docker will attempt to load the base `php:8-apache` image from the internet, which you referenced in the first line of the *Dockerfile*. More specifically, the image gets downloaded from the *Docker Hub*, a platform provided by the company behind Docker that maintains a variety of prepared images (see Chapter 3, Section 3.1). All future docker build commands that are based on the php:8-apache image will use your local copy of it.

Finally, from the Docker image, you must launch a container with which the application is executed:

```
docker run -d --name hello-world-php -p 8080:80 hello-world-php
```

The -d parameter causes Docker to run the program in the background, while --name provides the running container with the name hello-world-php, allowing you to easily address it later. The -p parameter connects port 80 of the container (that's the 80 after the colon) to port 8080 of the executing system (that's the 8080 before the colon). You can now access the application via *http://localhost:8080* (see Figure 1.1).

Figure 1.1 Hello World Web Server with PHP Container in the Browser

1.2.1   Dockerfile

Let's finally take a brief look at the three lines of the *Dockerfile* shown previously (see also Chapter 4):

- FROM php:8-apache
  You use the Docker image for PHP 8 provided by the PHP developers as a base.

- ENV TZ="Europe/Amsterdam"
  To output the time in the correct time zone, you need to set the environment variable (ENVironment) TZ (for TimeZone) to the appropriate value.

- COPY index.php /var/www/html
  The Apache web server in your image has set the default directory for documents to path */var/www/html*. That's exactly the position in the image to which you copy the *index.php* file.

With that, your first Docker image is completed. You can use it on any computer running a recent Docker version.

That was amazingly simple, wasn't it? You didn't have to search for and download the latest Apache version on the internet, find and install the appropriate PHP 8 module, and then copy *index.php* to the right place on your computer. In addition, you don't exactly have countless files scattered in different locations on your computer's file system, which will be hard to find if you uninstall one of the components. So, among other things, Docker helps you get started quickly and keep your computer clean.

Speaking of clean, the web server is probably still running in the background on your computer now. Stop the container by calling docker stop hello-world-php, and then delete it with docker rm hello-world-php.

1.3   Node.js

The second Hello World variant is implemented using the popular JavaScript runtime, *Node.js*. For this purpose, you need to create a new directory named *hello-world-node*. The *Dockerfile* is again kept very short:

```
# File: hello-world-node/Dockerfile (docbuc/hello-world-node)
FROM node:16
ENV TZ="Europe/Amsterdam"
COPY server.js /src/
USER node
CMD ["node", "/src/server.js"]
```

In this example, your Docker image is based on node:16. This is again an official image maintained by the Node.js developers. As in the first example, the default time zone is set to ensure the correct time. Then the *server.js* file is copied from the local file system to your image.

Because you don't want to run the server as the root user, you need to switch to the unprivileged user node in the subsequent step. The final line containing the CMD statement is also new here. It starts the Node.js interpreter with the server.js parameter. To learn why the call is written as an array construct, please refer to Chapter 4, Section 4.1.

The *server.js* file contains the code to start a web server that responds to incoming requests:

```
// File hello-world-node/server.js
const http = require("http"),
  os = require("os");

http.createServer((req, res) => {
  const dateTime = new Date(),
    load = os.loadavg(),
    doc = `<!DOCTYPE html>
<html>
  <head>
```

```
    <title>Hello world</title>
    <meta charset="utf-8" />
  </head>
  <body>
    <h1>Hello world: node</h1>
    Server time: ${dateTime}<br />
    Server utilization (load): ${load[0]}
  </body>
</html>`
  res.setHeader('Content-Type', 'text/html');
  res.end(doc);
}).listen(8080);
```

The Node.js runtime also provides a call for the Unix load, `os.loadavg()`. This call works in the same way as the PHP function described in the previous section (see Figure 1.2).

Figure 1.2 Hello World Web Server with Node.js Container in the Browser

To run this variant, you must first create a new Docker image:

```
docker build -t hello-world-node .
```

If no errors occur during the process, you can start a container based on your new `hello-world-node` image:

```
docker run -d -p 8080:8080 hello-world-node
```

If the `docker` command is responded to with a somewhat cryptic error message, for example, ending with the following:

```
Bind for 0.0.0.0:8080 failed: port is already allocated.,
```

In this case, the container from the first example is most likely still running and occupying the port. Linux systems allow only one service per port. Who else should answer the query: the PHP container or the Node.js container? To successfully start the Node.js container, you need to stop the PHP container as described previously (`docker stop hello-world`).

This time, you didn't assign a name to the container at startup. How do you still get access to this container? The Docker command line can help here as well, as `docker ps` lists all running containers. The output could look something like this:

```
CONTAINER ID    IMAGE                    COMMAND
3fdb675f68f7    hello-world-node         "docker-entrypoint.s..."

CREATED         STATUS
12 seconds ago  Up 11 seconds

PORTS                                    NAMES
0.0.0.0:8080->8080/tcp, :::8080->8080/tcp    beautiful_hypatia
```

The outputs have been distributed across several lines in the preceding listing to save space. At this point, only the first column, CONTAINER ID, is of interest to us. This hexadecimal string allows you to stop the container and delete it afterwards:

```
docker stop 3fdb675f68f7
docker rm 3fdb675f68f7
```

For productive work, you probably wouldn't program a web server this way. All requests, no matter to which URL on this server, receive the same response. In the Node.js environment, web servers are usually created using the well-developed `express` library. (Details on this library will follow in Chapter 9.).

1.4 Python

To make sure the Python community doesn't get shortchanged, we now want to demonstrate a third variant of the Hello World example in Python. No matter which Python version you've installed on your computer (or if you have Python installed at all), this *Dockerfile* will launch `python` in the latest version 3:

```
# File hello-world-python/Dockerfile (docbuc/hello-world-python)
FROM python:3
ENV TZ="Europe/Amsterdam"
COPY server.py /src/
USER www-data
CMD ["python", "/src/server.py"]
```

The Python code for the web server is very similar to the previous Node.js example:

```
#!/usr/bin/env python3
from http.server import BaseHTTPRequestHandler, HTTPServer
import os, datetime

class myServer(BaseHTTPRequestHandler):
  def do_GET(self):
    load = os.getloadavg()
    html = """<!DOCTYPE html>
<html>
  <head>
    <title>Hello world</title>
    <meta charset="utf-8" />
  </head>
  <body>
    <h1>Hello world: python</h1>
    Server time: {now}<br />
    Server utilization (load): {load}
  </body>
</html>""".format(now=datetime.datetime.now().astimezone(),
                  load=load[0])

    self.send_response(200)
    self.send_header('Content-type','text/html')
    self.end_headers()
    self.wfile.write(bytes(html, "utf8"))
    return

def run():
  addr = ('', 8080)
  httpd = HTTPServer(addr, myServer)
  httpd.serve_forever()

run()
```

Friends of Python will know their way around right away: The run function starts the web server on port 8080. The do_GET function in the myServer class handles the HTTP GET call made by the browser when the address *http://localhost* is called. The HTML framework in the html variable is filled with the current date and *load*, which you already know from the previous sections. Once the headers have been set, the html variable gets converted to utf8 and sent to the browser (self.wfile.write).

To launch this service as a Docker container, you must first create the image, as in the previous examples:

```
docker build -t hello-world-python .
```

Then you create and start the container with the port mapping to 8080 on the local port (refer to Figure 1.3):

```
docker run -d --name hello-world-python \
  -p 8080:8080 hello-world-python
```

Figure 1.3 Hello World Web Server with Python 3 Container in the Browser

Don't forget to tidy up after the experiments. The aforementioned `docker stop hello-world-python` followed by `docker rm hello-world-python` will stop the execution and delete the container. If you want Docker to tidy up for you, you can use the `docker system prune` command. This command deletes all stopped containers (and other resources, which we haven't used yet).

Chapter 2
Installation

This chapter provides a detailed description of how you can install Docker on Windows, macOS, and Linux. Although Docker actually originates from the Linux environment, it's much easier to install on Windows and macOS. Regarding Linux, depending on the distribution, there are countless variants and special cases that make a compact description difficult. In this book, we cover the distributions Debian/Ubuntu, Fedora, Oracle Linux (representing the whole Red Hat Enterprise Linux [RHEL] family), and Raspberry Pi OS.

Podman as a Docker Alternative

We'll also take a look at the Docker alternative, Podman, which is becoming increasingly popular on Linux. If you run a Red Hat–related operating system (e.g., Fedora or RHEL, as well as any clones), you might consider using Podman instead of Docker. Although there are only a few functional differences, Podman scores with its deep integration into the distribution as well as its particularly simple installation. In our view, the biggest disadvantage of Podman is that the `docker compose` command, which is enormously important in practice, is rather poorly supported. You can find Podman-specific installation instructions in Appendix A.

2.1 Docker Variants

The Docker website (*https://docker.com*) provides you with various Docker subscriptions to choose from, ranging from *Free* to *Pro* to *Team* to *Large*. For many developers, the free variant is absolutely sufficient. All examples in this book have been implemented using the free Docker version.

This is not to say that commercial Docker offerings are unattractive to professional development teams, as paying customers get better support, unlimited access to container images, the ability to set up private image repositories on Docker Hub themselves, and much more.

Even if the design of the Docker website suggests the opposite, neither the installation nor the use of Docker requires registration. You don't need a Docker account or a so-called Docker ID until you want to provide images in Docker Hub yourself. A Docker account also increases the number of permitted accesses per hour to images in the hub.

> **What Is the Docker Desktop?**
>
> Docker provides the *Docker Desktop* for Windows, macOS, and Linux. This is a complete package that includes the Docker infrastructure as well as a graphical user interface (GUI).
>
> On macOS and Windows, Docker Desktop simplifies the installation process. However, the additional functions of the GUI aren't absolutely necessary. Whether you run macOS, Windows, or Linux, you'll be controlling Docker predominantly via commands. These commands work the same on all platforms. Docker Desktop provides platform-specific configuration options and, in some cases, more ease of use, but no significant additional features.

> **Caution**
>
> Docker Desktop, unlike the Docker core components, isn't an open-source product! Its free use is intended only for home users and small businesses. Large companies need to purchase a license. (Using Docker on Linux without the Docker Desktop, on the other hand, is unrestricted and free.)

2.2   Version Numbers

Docker is made up of several components that have different version numbers. Docker Engine decides which functions are available. When we revised this book, version 20.10 was the latest one. When we refer to a version number in individual sections without any additional information, we always mean that of Docker Engine.

A completely different numbering applies to Docker Desktop, which we tested in version 3.5. The important `docker-compose` command also has its own version number for now. In spring 2021, version 1.29 was the latest one. In the near future, `docker-compose` is expected to be replaced by Docker's built-in subcommand, `docker compose` (no hyphen). Then there'll be no need for a separate numbering for this component.

2.3   Installation on Windows

The first versions of Docker for Windows used Hyper-V as a backend. Then, in 2019, Docker moved to the *Windows Subsystem for Linux* (WSL). Hyper-V is still supported, but only for compatibility with older versions of Windows. In this book, we assume that you use Docker in combination with WSL2. For this, you need a reasonably up-to-date 64-bit installation of Windows 10/11 Home, Pro, or Enterprise. Your computer needs at least 4 GB RAM. (For everyday development use, however, we rather recommend 16 GB.) Furthermore, the virtualization functions of the CPU must be enabled.

You can download the latest version of Docker Desktop here:

https://docs.docker.com/docker-for-windows/install

The installation is usually absolutely uncomplicated. You don't need to set a single option! During the installation process, WSL2 gets activated automatically if that hasn't already happened on your computer. Once the installation process has completed, you'll find an entry to start Docker Desktop on the desktop or in the **Start** menu. This program provides the opportunity to take an initial introductory tour.

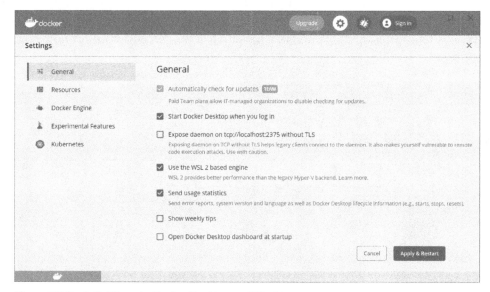

Figure 2.1 Basic Settings in Docker Desktop on Windows

Alternatively, you can use PowerShell, `cmd.exe`, or Windows Terminal to verify that the installation was successful. You just need to run the `docker version` command, which provides an overview of the installed Docker components and their version numbers. The result should look similar to the following (abbreviated) listing:

```
docker version

  Client:
    Cloud integration: 1.0.14
    Version:           20.10.6
    API version:       1.41
    ...

  Server: Docker Engine - Community
    Engine:
      Version:         20.10.6
      API version:     1.41 (minimum version 1.12)
```

```
...
containerd:
  Version:        1.4.4
runc:
  Version:        1.0.0-rc93
docker-init:
  Version:        0.19.0
```

To test that Docker really works, you can start the mini Linux system, *Alpine*, as a container. Using ping, you can test if the network connection to the external world is working. exit terminates the container, which is also deleted immediately due to the --rm option:

```
docker run -it --rm alpine

  Unable to find image 'alpine:latest' locally
  latest: Pulling from library/alpine
  540db60ca938: Pull complete
  Digest: sha256:69e..cf8f
  Status: Downloaded newer image for alpine:latest

ping -c 1 -q google.com

  PING google.com (142.250.186.142): 56 data bytes
  1 packets transmitted, 1 packets received, 0% packet loss
  round-trip min/avg/max = 20.318/20.318/20.318 ms

exit
```

VirtualBox

Previously, the interaction between Docker and VirtualBox on Windows constituted a problem. Today, however, the biggest problems seem to have been overcome. In our tests, Docker with WSL2 and VirtualBox ran stably side by side.

2.4 Installation on macOS

To install Docker Desktop, including all accompanying tools, you need to download the correct DMG file version (there's one for Intel CPUs and one for ARM ["Apple Silicon"]) that matches your CPU architecture from the following website: *https://docs.docker. com/desktop/install/mac-install/*.

We tried out many examples on a Mac mini M1 for this book. Here's a brief summary: The support for the new CPU architecture is excellent! However, because Docker uses a relatively large amount of RAM, a model with at least 16 GB RAM is highly recommended!

To start the installation process, you should simply move the image file to the *Applications* directory. When Docker starts for the first time, you need to provide your password again so that Docker can set up various drivers. Docker Desktop then runs as a background process and makes itself noticeable in the panel by means of a small icon. This icon takes you to the Docker Desktop (see Figure 2.2).

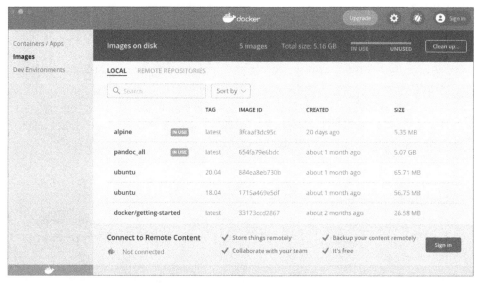

Figure 2.2 Docker Desktop on macOS

By default, Docker will be started automatically in the future. Docker Desktop periodically checks for available updates and, if necessary, asks you whether it should install them. In the settings dialog, you can specify how much memory (both RAM and on the SSD) and how many CPU cores Docker is allowed to use. Docker must be restarted after each change to these settings. Any running containers will be terminated in the process.

2.5   Installation on Linux

Docker was originally developed for use on Linux, which makes it quite surprising that a Docker installation is easier on Windows or macOS than on Linux. However, there are a couple of reasons for the various variants or additional configuration work required:

- **Distributions**
  There's only *one* Windows and *one* macOS, but there are numerous Linux distributions. Interlocking Docker with the specifics of each distribution isn't always trivial.

- **Security**

  On Linux, Docker can be run in two ways, namely with or without root privileges. Depending on which variant you choose, different installation instructions must be followed. This section covers the currently more common system-wide installation. However, if you want to go *rootless*, you can install Docker in your local account (see Section 2.6).

Irrespective of that, it only takes a few commands to get Docker running on most Linux distributions.

Use Docker Package Sources Whenever Possible!

Some Linux distributions provide Docker packages as part of the distribution's own package sources. However, these Docker packages are often outdated.

Regardless of which Linux distribution you use, you should always prefer the official packages. During the installation process, a Docker-specific package source is set up in each case from which you subsequently obtain all Docker updates automatically.

Docker Desktop for Linux

Docker Desktop has also been available for Linux since mid-2022. This complete package consists of all necessary Docker components and an additional GUI as on macOS/Windows.

Unfortunately, Docker Desktop on Linux comes with significant drawbacks. Specifically, Docker now uses a virtual machine to run Docker containers, as it does on macOS and Windows. This contradicts the lean concept of Docker, which runs containers (almost) like normal processes. In addition, Docker Desktop for Linux can't be used when Linux itself is running in a virtual machine. (The result would be a nesting of virtual machines: one for Linux and, within it, one for Docker.) Amazingly, installing Docker Desktop is even more cumbersome than a traditional installation.

Long story short: The relatively new offer didn't convince us. The few additional features of the Docker Desktop are dispensable and don't outweigh the drawbacks. You can find more details about installing Docker Desktop for Linux here: *https://docs.docker.com/desktop/install/linux-install/*.

2.5.1   Installation on Ubuntu

If necessary, you should remove previously installed packages from the Ubuntu package sources:

```
apt remove docker docker-engine docker.io containerd runc
```

Next, you need to first install a few base packages and then use `curl` to download the key for the new Docker package source, which you can set up using the `echo` command. After installing Docker via `apt install`, the program gets started automatically. (All commands must be executed with `root` privileges. You should therefore put `sudo` in front, or first switch to the `root` mode via `sudo -s`.)

```
apt install apt-transport-https ca-certificates curl gpg

curl -fsSL https://download.docker.com/linux/ubuntu/gpg | \
  gpg --dearmor -o /usr/share/keyrings/docker-archive-keyring.gpg

echo "deb [arch=amd64 \
     signed-by=/usr/share/keyrings/docker-archive-keyring.gpg] \
     https://download.docker.com/linux/ubuntu \
     $(lsb_release -cs) stable" > \
  /etc/apt/sources.list.d/docker.list

apt update

apt install docker-ce docker-ce-cli containerd.io
```

Tip

Instead of an error-prone copying and pasting of the preceding commands, you should copy them from the official installation guide:

https://docs.docker.com/engine/install/ubuntu

If you want to install a trial version of Docker instead of the current stable version, you need to replace `stable` with `test` or `edge` in the `echo` command given previously. Sometimes this is also necessary if you use a brand-new Ubuntu version. It often takes a few weeks for Docker to provide a stable Docker version for the latest Ubuntu release.

If you use the Uncomplicated Firewall (UFW) on Ubuntu (by default, you aren't), Docker containers can't use a network bridge. The culprit is the default setting of UFW, which prevents IP packets from being transferred. A solution to this could be to make the following change in /etc/default/ufw, and then restart the firewall via `ufw reload`:

```
# File /etc/default/ufw
...
DEFAULT_FORWARD_POLICY="ACCEPT"
```

> **Debian**
>
> The installation process on Debian is similar to that on Ubuntu; the only difference is the name of the package source. (This affects the echo command.) You can find more details on this here:
>
> *https://docs.docker.com/engine/install/debian*

2.5.2 Installation on the Raspberry Pi Operating System

Surprisingly, Docker also runs on Raspberry Pi. However, the Docker documentation indicates that this platform isn't currently intended for production use. Regarding the installation on Raspberry Pi OS, the best way to proceed is to use a script provided by Docker for this purpose:

```
curl -fsSL https://get.docker.com -o get-docker.sh
less get-docker.sh
sudo sh get-docker.sh
```

We've only briefly tested Docker on Raspberry Pi OS and didn't notice any problems in the process. Due to its rather limited speed, however, we don't consider Raspberry Pi to be an ideal platform for software development apart from electronics projects. However, Docker can help to easily get programming languages or other tools running in versions that Raspberry Pi OS doesn't yet provide or no longer provides, which can definitely be a big help for tinkering projects or Internet of Things (IoT) applications.

2.5.3 Installation on Red Hat Enterprise Linux 8 and Fedora

If you use Fedora, RHEL 8, or a distribution compatible with them, such as Oracle Linux 8, AlmaLinux, or CentOS Stream, you should consider using Podman (see Appendix A). Of course, installing Docker is no problem either. We ran our tests on Oracle Linux 8 and Fedora 34.

Before you begin, you should make sure Podman and its container build system Buildah are uninstalled:

```
dnf remove podman buildah
```

Then you need set up a new package source and install Docker using the yum-config-manager from the yum-utils package. The following commands are valid for RHEL and Co:

```
dnf install dnf-plugins-core
dnf config-manager --add-repo \
    https://download.docker.com/linux/centos/docker-ce.repo
dnf install docker-ce docker-ce-cli containerd.io
```

The same commands can be used on Fedora. However, you'll need a different package source. For this reason, the `dnf config-manager` command must be changed in the following way:

```
dnf config-manager --add-repo \
    https://download.docker.com/linux/fedora/docker-ce.repo
```

Unlike the installation on Debian/Ubuntu, Docker won't start automatically right away here, but the following two commands can help you in this context:

```
systemctl enable --now docker.service
systemctl enable --now containerd.service
```

2.5.4   Other Installation Variants

We'll cover running Docker containers in the cloud in detail in Chapter 19 and in Chapter 20. Installation instructions for other Linux distributions or for trial versions of Docker can be found here:

https://docs.docker.com/engine/install/

2.5.5   Troubleshooting and Logging

To test whether Docker is running, you must execute the `docker version` command. It should show the version numbers of the Docker client and Docker server (see also the listing in Section 2.3). By using `journalctl -u docker`, you can read the logging messages of the Docker daemon.

Depending on the kernel version, the Docker daemon may provide warnings that certain features aren't available:

```
journalctl -u docker  | grep warning
  warning: Your kernel does not support CPU realtime scheduler
  warning: Your kernel does not support cgroup blkio weight
  warning: Your kernel does not support cgroup blkio
          weight_device
```

You can safely ignore these warnings. The missing features would give Docker a finer control over how containers are run. On a development computer, these functions are completely irrelevant. Even in production use, the functions are only of secondary importance.

2.5.6   Working without "sudo"

By default, almost all Docker commands must be executed with root privileges on Linux. Instead of `docker run ...` you need to run `sudo docker run ....` The following command provides an uncomplicated solution to this and adds the specified user to the docker group:

```
sudo usermod -aG docker <username>
```

The group change won't become effective until after a new login. However, you should take into account that the seemingly harmless group assignment indirectly assigns root privileges to the user in question (see Chapter 6, Section 6.6).

As far as security is concerned, it's better to run Docker containers entirely without root privileges. The following section describes how you can do that.

2.6 Rootless Docker

The concept of *rootless Docker* is that both the Docker service (the *daemon*, as it's referred to in Linux jargon) and the Docker command are executed with the privileges of an ordinary user. This has a fundamental advantage: if a tampered or malformed Docker container manages to break out of its environment and access the host machine, the code executed in the process will have only your ordinary privileges and no root privileges.

There are two ways to use rootless Docker:

- If you've already installed Docker as in the previous section, almost all requirements are already met. You should just stop the Docker service running at the system level and run that service in your own account instead.
- If Docker hasn't been installed yet, you must run a Docker installation at the user level. This is even possible if you don't have any root privileges (e.g., for a student account on a university computer).

The following sections describe both variants. Note that rootless Docker is only possible on Linux.

Limitations

Rootless Docker comes with certain limitations; otherwise, this type of use would have become the default mode long ago. Most of the limitations are related to network options. For example, container ports can't be assigned to local ports smaller than 1024—this requires root privileges. Likewise, ping doesn't work in the containers.

In some cases, you can even work around these restrictions by changing kernel options or giving additional permissions to the docker command. However, these measures have the disadvantage that Docker then has more rights than an ordinary command despite being in rootless mode—with all the associated security concerns. In that case, it's easier to work in normal mode, that is, with root privileges.

In practice, the limitations caused by rootless Docker have proven to be surprisingly small. Many of the examples presented in this book work rootless right away or with tiny adjustments (e.g., to the port numbers used). However, rootless Docker is largely unusable when the vfs driver is used. This is the case if the kernel version of your Linux distribution is lower than 5.11.

2.6.1   "newuidmap" and "newgidmap"

Regardless of which of the two presented installation paths you choose, you'll need the Linux package uidmap (Debian/Ubuntu) or shadow-utils (Fedora/RHEL) in any case. It provides the two commands newuidmap and newgidmap, which are a basic requirement for using the rootless Docker mode.

```
apt install uidmap          # Debian/Ubuntu
dnf install shadow-utils    # Fedora/RHEL
```

The newuidmap and newgidmap commands enable a user to reserve local user and group IDs. However, this requires that the */etc/subuid* and */etc/subgid* files contain entries that assign an ID range to the user. For example, if the user name is maria, the corresponding lines must look like the following patterns:

```
# File /etc/subuid
maria:100000:65536
```

```
# File /etc/subgid
maria:100000:65536
```

This means that the user Maria may have UIDs and GIDs between 100,000 and 165,535. Depending on the setup, it may be that suitable entries were automatically created for your personal account with the installation of uidmap or shadow-utils. If this isn't the case, you must add a corresponding line in each of the two files, where the first number indicates the starting point, and the second number indicates the number of IDs. Instead of maria, of course, you should enter your own account name.

2.6.2   Using a System-Wide Rootless Docker Installation

If you've already installed Docker on your entire system (Section 2.5), then all the prerequisites for using rootless Docker are already in place. First, you should disable the system-wide Docker service to avoid any misunderstandings:

```
sudo systemctl disable --now docker
```

Then you need to run the script dockerd-rootless-setuptool.sh to set up rootless Docker for your account. This script doesn't require you to have root privileges. (If

Linux doesn't find the script, you must first install the package, docker-ce-rootless-extras.)

```
dockerd-rootless-setuptool.sh install
```

```
  Creating /home/kofler/.config/systemd/user/docker.service
  starting systemd service docker.service
  systemctl --user start docker.service
  ...
  Make sure the following environment variables are set (or add them to ~/
.bashrc):
  export PATH=/usr/bin:$PATH
  export DOCKER_HOST=unix:///run/user/1000/docker.sock
```

In the subsequent step, you need to paste the last output export command into the *.bashrc* file (or into *.zshrc* if you use zsh instead of bash). You can omit the export PATH=... statement. /usr/bin is contained in the environment variable anyway.

For these settings to take effect, you must log out and log in again. Afterward, docker version (now without sudo!) should return the usual result:

```
docker version
```

```
  Client: Docker Engine - Community
    Version:           20.10.6
  Server: Docker Engine - Community
    Engine:
      Version:         20.10.6
  ...
```

To verify that the Docker service is indeed running rootless, you can use systemctl --user status docker:

```
systemctl --user status docker
```

```
  docker.service - Docker Application Container Engine (Rootless)
  Loaded: loaded (/home/kofler/.config/systemd/user/\
      docker.service; enabled; vendor preset: enabled)
  Active: active (running) since ...
```

To return from rootless Docker back to the "ordinary" Docker mode when needed, you need to uninstall the local Docker service and reenable the system-wide service:

```
dockerd-rootless-setuptool.sh uninstall
sudo systemctl enable --now docker
```

2.6.3   Installing Rootless Docker

The following instructions apply if you haven't yet installed Docker system-wide in the form of packages. In this case, you can use a script from the Docker website to install Docker locally within your home directory only. (It's also assumed in this case that newuidmap and newgidmap are available.)

```
curl -fsSL https://get.docker.com/rootless > docker-install.sh
less docker-install.sh          # briefly check setup script
sh docker-install.sh

  Creating /home/kofler/.config/systemd/user/docker.service
  starting systemd service docker.service
  systemctl --user start docker.service
  ...
  Make sure the following environment variables are set
    (or add them to ~/.bashrc):
  export PATH=/home/kofler/bin:$PATH
  export DOCKER_HOST=unix:///run/user/1000/docker.sock
```

The Docker files are installed into the local bin directory. You then need to put the last two commands issued by the setup script into *.bashrc* or *.zshrc*, depending on which shell you work in. After logging out and logging in again, you can try using Docker.

A disadvantage of this installation variant is that it doesn't install man pages. This means you can't use man docker run to quickly look up the syntax of the docker run command.

Another disadvantage is that a deinstallation hasn't been provided for. For this purpose, you must delete the affected commands as well as the *.local/share/docker* directory via rm. To do this, ironically, you need root privileges because rootless Docker creates numerous files with UIDs or GIDs that don't match the UIDs/GIDs of your own account:

```
cd ~/bin
rm containerd* ctr docker* rootlesskit* runc vpnkit
cd
sudo rm -rf .local/share/docker
```

2.6.4   No "ping"

Depending on the distribution you use rootless Docker in, the ping command may not work in the containers. To check if the network connection to the outside world is working, you can use the commands httping, wget, or curl. (Of course, this assumes that a web server is running on the contacted computer. For *google.com*, you can bet on that.)

```
docker run -it --rm alpine

wget google.de

  Connecting to google.de (172.217.16.131:80)
  ...
  'index.html' saved
```

The documentation for rootless Docker suggests two methods to allow ping after all. For this purpose, you must either add a line to */etc/sysctl.conf* or use setcap to change the permissions of the *bin/rootlesskit* file. In tricky cases (e.g., in our tests on Debian 11), however, both measures remain ineffective.

https://docs.docker.com/engine/security/rootless/#routing-ping-packets

2.6.5   Local Docker Files

Depending on whether you run Docker as a system service or rootless, the images, containers, and so on created by Docker end up in different directories:

```
/var/lib/docker      # system-wide Docker files
.local/share/docker  # Rootless Docker
```

2.6.6   Problems with the Virtual File System Directory

In our experiments with rootless Docker, we found that the space required in the *.local/ share/docker/vfs* virtual file system (VFS) directory quickly takes on insane dimensions, depending on the distribution. Even after installing a few containers on a beta version of Debian 11, the directory took up more than 10 GB of space, while the same containers in the corresponding directory on Ubuntu 21.04 (*.local/share/docker/overlay2*) took up less than 2 GB of space.

The vfs driver is primarily designed for testing purposes. It combines different layers of the file system of an image or a container (see also Chapter 6, Section 6.6).

Typically, Docker uses the much better overlay2 driver. In rootless mode, however, this driver requires a current kernel version (at least 5.11). You can determine which storage driver is in use via the following command:

```
docker info | grep Storage
  Storage Driver: overlay2
```

If the result is vfs, we recommend you don't use rootless Docker. Then you'll have the following two options: you can either run docker with root privileges or switch to Podman, which caused far less trouble in this regard during our tests.

Chapter 3
Basic Principles

This chapter describes the concepts and basic principles of Docker, and it addresses numerous fundamental questions:

- What are images and containers?
- How do they differ from each other?
- How can you redirect network ports of a container to the host?
- Where is the variable data of a container stored?
- How do containers communicate with each other?

To avoid this chapter becoming too theoretical, we'll answer these questions on the basis of concrete examples. These examples will demonstrate how you can interactively operate an Ubuntu container, how you can start Docker containers in the background and use them in your computer's web browser, how you can operate a database server so that other containers (e.g., with WordPress) can access it, and more.

The foundation for all these examples is the docker command. This command is used to manage Docker images and containers. A systematic reference of all docker commands follows in Chapter 7.

3.1 Basic Principles and Terminology

This section explains the most important terms used in the Docker world and provides an overview of how Docker works.

3.1.1 Images and Containers

The starting point for the execution of each container is an *image*. You may already know the term from virtual machines, where a disk image is a file presented to the virtualization system as a hard drive. The virtual machine can set up partitions and file systems there.

With Docker, on the other hand, an image provides the basis for the container as a read-only file system. Unlike virtual machines, the running container never changes the image. Instead, any files modified or added by the container end up in a separate overlay file system, which is mapped by its own directory within the Docker base directory on the host.

The separation between immutable image files and mutable container files makes it possible to derive any number of containers from an image, which can certainly be executed at the same time.

A lot of images are available for download on the internet, especially on Docker Hub, and the vast majority are free of charge. You can help yourself to these images as you would a toolbox: you can derive your own containers from them and even combine them into new images yourself.

Part II of this book provides an overview of the most important standard images for programming languages, database and web servers, and complete web applications.

Docker Hub

Docker Hub is operated by the Docker company, but the images provided there predominantly originate from the Docker community. Having set up a login, anyone can publicly provide images here for free. Although this is a fantastic offer, there's a lot of junk on Docker Hub in addition to a multitude of great images: test projects, software that's no longer maintained, and the like. In this respect, you should exercise some caution when selecting images on Docker Hub. Usually, "official" images maintained by Docker are unreservedly recommended.

https://hub.docker.com

3.1.2   Volumes

A basic concept of Docker is that when images are updated (e.g., because of a new software version), the running container simply gets stopped, and a new container is set up to replace the old one. (Neither the update nor the container restart occurs automatically. You'll have to take care of that yourself.)

As far as the program code contained in the image, this concept is as simple as it is ingenious—but what about the files created during the operation of the container? After all, it's not acceptable that they'll all be lost when a new container gets set up.

To avoid this, Docker provides *volumes*, which are directories in the host file system that are separate from the container. Files are stored there that will be preserved when switching from one version to the next, that is, from one container to the next. For example, in the case of a container with a database server, all database files are located in such a volume; in the case of a container with a web server, the HTML documents, PHP scripts, and so on are located there.

By default, when you create a new container, Docker automatically sets up an associated volume directory (in the */var/lib/docker/volumes* directory or in *.local/share/docker/volumes* on Linux) and names it with a universally unique identifier (UUID). For the purpose of better management, you can assign volumes their own name or even specify the location of the directory. This way, you avoid long path names that are impossible to remember. If you don't know where a container's volume is located, you can use docker inspect to determine this information.

3.1.3 Services, Stacks, and Clusters

As long as you run Docker on *one* machine, the concept of containers is sufficient. However, as soon as it comes to distributing services across multiple machines (via multiple Docker hosts), the administrative overhead increases significantly. To make Docker more scalable in such cases, as well as to implement load-balancing and high-availability features, the concept of services was introduced.

A *service* describes a service or a task. Similar to a container, when you define a service, you specify which image you're referencing and which command should ultimately be executed. The main difference with containers is that you don't need to bother about running services yourself as Docker takes care of that. In particular, Docker uses rules to decide on which Docker hosts the service is supposed to be run. (Behind the scenes, of course, to run a service, a container must be set up and started. Services don't replace containers, but form an additional management layer.)

In Docker practice, multiple services are often combined. Only the overall product resulting from this combination can be meaningfully tested or used. *Stacks* simplify the management of such service groups. The corresponding docker stack command can set up, start, or stop multiple related services together.

The basic requirement for using services and stacks is that you assemble a cluster of Docker hosts up front. In Docker terminology, however, we don't speak of a *cluster*, but of a *swarm*. A swarm consists of multiple Docker instances connected by a relatively simple configuration using docker swarm init and docker swarm join. In extreme cases, a swarm can even consist of only a single Docker instance. This is sufficient for initial tests; however, the advantages of a cluster system can't manifest themselves in the process, of course.

For initial examples of using services and stacks, see Chapter 5. That chapter deals with *docker-compose.yml* files, which describe a whole group of containers or services. More extensive examples of using Docker clusters follow in Part III, in particular, in Chapter 19.

An alternative to Docker Swarm is *Kubernetes*, which is an open-source program developed by Google for managing containers. Kubernetes also supports other container systems, but it's often used in combination with Docker. Kubernetes is currently much more widely used than Docker Swarm. For more details about Kubernetes, see Chapter 20.

3.1.4   docker Command versus Docker Daemon (dockerd)

Docker is implemented as a client-server model. The Docker daemon running in the background is responsible for executing the containers. The name *Docker Engine* is also commonly used for this program. On Linux, this is the dockerd process. On macOS or Windows, on the other hand, the functions are distributed across several processes whose names begin with com.docker or Docker. In particular, a virtual machine with a tiny Linux distribution must additionally be run on macOS or Windows to provide the functions required for Docker.

To control the daemon or Docker Engine, you should use the docker command. It often happens that the Docker daemon and docker run on the same host. However, it's also possible to use docker to establish a network connection to an external Docker daemon.

3.1.5   Linux versus Windows

In a production environment, Docker is most commonly used to run programs from the Linux world on a Linux server (Docker host). Before a program can run productively, however, it must be developed, and you can do that just as well on macOS or Windows, with few restrictions. In other words, you can choose to develop your new web application on a Linux desktop distribution, macOS, or Windows. When everything is running satisfactorily, you can operate the Docker container on a Linux server or in a cloud. For tips on switching from test to live operation, that is, *deployment*, see Chapter 17.

While Docker has been established as a tool for Linux-savvy developers for years, the range of Docker images specifically intended for Windows is growing at the same time. These include, for example, a minimal version of Windows Server (the so-called *Nano Server*), the Internet Information Server (IIS), or ASP.NET. However, such images can only be run with the Docker version for Windows. In some cases, the operating system variant of the host is also checked for licensing reasons. Thus, you can't try out Nano Server on Windows 10; rather, you need a Windows server instance.

From Microsoft's point of view, this is understandable: Among other things, the company earns its money by selling server licenses. It would be counterproductive to allow a Windows server container to run on a machine that's not a Windows server. On the other hand, it's precisely this kind of restriction that makes life arduous for developers and almost forces them into the Linux segment.

In this book, we describe Docker across different platforms as far as the host is concerned. For containers, on the other hand, we focus on open-source software, mostly from the Linux world.

Switching the Docker Engine between Linux and Windows Containers

A Docker host running on Windows can run both Linux and Windows containers (see Table 3.1)—but not simultaneously! By default, the Windows version of Docker is also configured to run Linux containers.

	Linux Host	Windows Host	macOS Host
Linux-based containers	OK	OK	OK
Windows-based containers	—	OK	—

Table 3.1 Linux-Based Containers Run on All Docker Hosts, Whereas Windows-Based Containers Run Only on Windows Docker Hosts

If you want to use Windows containers instead, you need to run **Switch to Windows containers** from the Docker menu (which you can access via the icon in the info area of the taskbar). After the obligatory Windows restart, you can then run Windows containers.

Switching back to the Linux world works similarly via **Switch to Linux containers**, and surprisingly without another Windows restart. Switching between the two worlds is done without any loss of data. As a result, images that have already been downloaded, containers that have been set up, and so on are retained.

3.1.6 Virtual Machines versus Containers

Even though virtual machines and containers pursue similar goals, such as running various test programs or server applications on a physical computer as isolated from each other as possible, the way they work is fundamentally different.

In each virtual machine, the entire hardware of a PC is replicated by means of software. The virtual machine has the impression of running on a real computer. But this requires a huge number of resources (RAM, disk space, CPU cycles).

Containers, on the other hand, directly use the infrastructure of the host system, in particular, its file system and a common kernel. On Linux, this is simply the kernel of the host computer. If, on the other hand, Docker is run on macOS or Windows, a Linux kernel optimized for Docker runs separately from the actual operating system. On Windows, the Windows Subsystem for Linux (WSL2) is used to run this kernel.

In a sense, Docker containers run like isolated processes (similar to *sandboxes*) directly in the host system. The space requirements of containers are usually much smaller than those of virtual machines because the substructure can be reduced to a minimum. Containers also start up much faster.

The advantage of virtual machines is that they are better and more securely separated than Docker applications. Docker can only keep up to a limited extent in this respect because the kernel in particular, as a central shared resource, makes complete isolation impossible.

On the other hand, the greatly reduced overhead speaks in favor of Docker. In addition, Docker applications can be created and configured within a few seconds on the basis of a script. When it comes to setting up applications in an automated manner, whether for testing or scaling, Docker provides huge advantages over the comparatively cumbersome virtual machines. While with virtual machines it's usually expedient to combine several related services in one virtual machine, each function can get its own container with Docker. In this context, we often speak of a *microservices architecture*.

Virtualization and containers are by no means mutually exclusive. In practice, for example, it often happens that the Docker Engine itself runs in a virtual machine again.

3.2   Running Containers

To become familiar with Docker and its terminology, we recommend you spend a few hours playing around and experimenting. The following sections will give you some ideas on how to do this. We explicitly point out that the goal of these examples isn't the launch of a real development system or even the productive use of Docker. Concrete instructions on how to use important Docker images will follow in Part II. At this point, it's more about getting to know the concepts of Docker through examples—learning by doing.

For the very first tests, which are even simpler in their functionality than our Hello World example from Chapter 1, there's a special Hello World image in Docker Hub (*https://hub.docker.com*). To try out this image and start the container derived from it, you need to run `docker run hello-world` in a terminal. This command first checks whether the `hello-world` image is already available on the local computer. If it isn't, it will be downloaded from Docker Hub and stored locally. Docker will then create a container from it and finally run the container:

```
docker run hello-world
  Unable to find image 'hello-world:latest' locally
  latest: Pulling from library/hello-world
  b8dfde127a29: Pull complete
  Digest: sha256:f226...d519
  Status: Downloaded newer image for hello-world:latest

  Hello from Docker!
  This message shows that your installation appears to be working
  correctly.
```

From the second time onward, `docker run hello-world` will be executed at lightning speed because then a local container of the Hello World app will be available.

The official Hello World image is an atypical Docker example in that the app packaged within it runs once and then immediately terminates. A large number of Docker containers, on the other hand, contain programs that can process input, run continuously, or be used interactively.

The docker Command on Linux

You can basically try out the examples presented in this chapter on Linux, macOS or Windows. But while you can run the docker command in an ordinary user account on macOS or Windows, it requires root privileges on Linux (unless you use *rootless Docker*, see Chapter 2, Section 2.6).

Since it's annoying to constantly work with root privileges or to prepend sudo to every docker command, there's a way out: You can add your user account to the docker group:

usermod -aG docker <accountname>

For this change to take effect, you must log out and log back in. After that, you can easily run docker on Linux as well. Note that the seemingly innocuous group assignment indirectly gives the user in question root privileges (see Chapter 6, Section 6.6).

3.2.1 Status Information

docker ps -a returns a list of all Docker containers that are running or have run in the past. The strange names in the NAMES column result from Docker assigning each container not only a random ID number but also an easier-to-remember (but equally random) name.

```
docker ps -a
  CONTAINER ID   IMAGE         COMMAND      ...   NAMES
  f5269c759b7d   hello-world   "/hello"           nervous_lamarr
  c6770e95fdd3   hello-world   "/hello"           kind_wright
```

docker images lists the locally installed images:

```
docker images
  REPOSITORY    TAG      IMAGE ID       CREATED       SIZE
  hello-world   latest   48b5124b2768   7 weeks ago   1.84 kB
```

3.2.2 Tidying Up

There's always the risk of quickly accumulating countless containers that have been executed once but are no longer needed. For this reason, you should immediately delete such containers:

```
docker rm nervous_lamarr kind_wright
```

If you're more or less sure that you don't need the underlying image anymore either (in this case, because you don't plan to run `hello-world` more often), then you can also delete the image. If you need `hello-world` again later, `docker` will have to download the image again.

```
docker image rm hello-world
```

> **Starting a Container Once and Deleting It Immediately**
>
> If you know right from the start that you want to execute a container only once and then delete it immediately, you can pass the additional option `--rm` (preceded by two hyphens):
>
> `docker run --rm hello-world`
>
> This way, you can avoid having to clean up later.

3.3   Using Containers Interactively

While the `hello-world` container, once executed, terminates immediately after outputting a few lines of text, many other containers can be used interactively. The official *base images* of common Linux distributions, such as Alpine, CentOS, Debian, Fedora, openSUSE, Oracle Linux, or Ubuntu are very well suited for first experiments.

The name base image originates from the fact that these images are intended as a starting point for custom developments. So, for example, if you want to create a container for a web server, you can start with the base image of your distribution of choice and install Apache in it. From the perspective of Docker, a completely new image won't be required then, but the base image can be supplemented by a (comparatively small) image with your extensions.

The following examples use the Ubuntu image as a starting point. In this context, it doesn't matter which distribution you use for the Docker host. So, you can run containers of the Ubuntu image also on Debian, Fedora, and even macOS or Windows!

There are several versions of the Ubuntu image. If you simply run `docker run -it ubuntu`, you'll get the version Docker has provided with the `latest` attribute. As a rule, this is the most up-to-date long-term support (LTS) version. If you want to use a different version, you need to specify it explicitly, for example, `docker run -it ubuntu:21.04`. You can find more information on the configuration of this Docker image here:

https://hub.docker.com/_/ubuntu

The `-i` and `-t` options further describe the function of the `run` command:

- -i means that the container should be executed interactively and connected to standard input.

- Because of -t, Docker uses a pseudo-terminal emulator (pseudo TTY) and connects it to standard input.

The combination of these two options is required if a container is supposed to be operated interactively in a terminal or PowerShell window. As a rule, -i, and -t are abbreviated to -it.

Thus, the following command downloads the current Ubuntu LTS image, creates a container based on it, and finally executes it. You'll automatically land in an instance of the bash shell, which is common on Ubuntu, where you can then execute commands with root privileges:

```
docker run -it ubuntu
```

```
root@f8fec4640176:/# cat /etc/os-release
  NAME="Ubuntu"
  VERSION="20.04.2 LTS (Focal Fossa)"
  ...

root@f8fec4640176:/# df -h | grep -v tmpfs
  Filesystem      Size  Used Avail Use% Mounted on
  overlay         20G   11G  7.6G  59% /
  /dev/sda1       20G   11G  7.6G  59% /etc/hosts
  shm             64M    0   64M   0% /dev/shm

root@f8fec4640176:/# ps ax
  PID TTY      STAT   TIME COMMAND
    1 ?        Ss     0:00 /bin/bash
   11 ?        R+     0:00 ps ax

root@f8fec4640176:/# exit
```

Here are some brief explanations:

- f8fec4640176 is a randomly generated host name assigned to the container by Docker.

- cat /etc/os-release outputs information about the distribution that serves as the basis for the container.

- df -h lists how much space is free in the container's file systems. The results depend on the Docker host. On Linux, the entire file system containing the */var/lib/docker* directory is shared with Docker containers. On macOS and Windows, a limited amount of storage space is provided for all containers together, usually about 60 GB.

grep -v eliminates all temporary file systems that aren't relevant from the df out-puts.

- ps ax returns a list of all running processes. Note that unlike an ordinary virtual machine, there are no other processes running in the container: no SSH server, no cron daemon, no systemd daemon, no logging service—nothing!

- exit terminates the execution of the container. All further commands are then valid again in the context of the terminal or the PowerShell.

Image Names

Docker image names are composed of three parts:

source/imagename:tag

Here, source is the name of the person or organization that compiled the image and uploaded it to Docker Hub. If the source is omitted, the docker command assumes that you're referring to one of the official Docker images.

Needless to say, imagename specifies the name of the image.

If multiple versions of the image exist, the optional tag specification explicitly selects the image marked with this tag. If the version specification is omitted, docker decides to use the image marked with latest.

If you repeat the docker run -it ubuntu command after a few months, the Ubuntu image downloaded at the first attempt will still be used, even if a new version has been available for a long time. You'll have to initiate the download of a more recent image version yourself if necessary:

```
docker image pull ubuntu
  Using default tag: latest
  latest: Pulling from library/ubuntu
  ...
```

Ubuntu versus Alpine Linux versus Other Distributions

Ubuntu is one of the most popular Linux distributions in the desktop and server area, but that doesn't make Ubuntu the ideal starting point for Docker! The main drawback of Ubuntu is that even its smallest version is a relatively large distribution. With Docker, lean distributions are preferable. Alpine Linux is therefore particularly popular in the Docker world, for example, as a basis for images with a web server or a programming language. Chapter 8 provides an introduction to Alpine Linux.

3.3.1 Network Connection

Using hostname -I, you can determine the IP address of the container:

```
root@f8fec4640176:/# hostname -I
  172.17.0.2
```

However, the familiar commands `ip addr` and `ping` don't work because they aren't included in the Ubuntu image for space reasons. But that can be changed very quickly:

```
root@f8fec4640176:/# apt update && apt install -y \
                     iproute2 iputils-ping

root@f8fec4640176:/# ip addr
  1: lo: ...
       inet 127.0.0.1/8 scope host lo
 41: eth0@if42: ...
       inet 172.17.0.2/16 scope global eth0
```

`ip addr` shows that the network connection leads to a private network that Docker provides by default. Docker assigns unique IP addresses on this network to containers at startup. In contrast to using virtual machines, however, Dynamic Host Configuration Protocol (DHCP) is not used.

`ping` proves that the containers can also access the internet (otherwise, `apt update` wouldn't have worked earlier either):

```
ping -c 1 google.de
  PING google.de (142.250.186.35) 56(84) bytes of data.
  64 bytes from fra24s04-in-f3.1e100.net (142.250.186.35):
  ...
  1 packets transmitted, 1 received, 0% packet loss, time 0ms
  rtt min/avg/max/mdev = 19.221/19.221/19.221/0.000 ms
```

Ping Problem

We've already referred to this in Chapter 2, Section 2.6: if you use rootless Docker, `ping` doesn't work with some host distributions. To test whether an internet connection to a known web server is possible, you can use `wget <hostname>` or `curl <hostname>` instead. This allows you to download the start page of the respective website (often *index.html*).

3.3.2   Containers versus Images Again

Now it's time to experiment a bit with `docker` so you can understand the difference between an image and its containers. If you exit the Ubuntu container with `Ctrl`+`D` or `exit` and then restart it via `docker run`, you may notice that the container has been assigned a new host name. That's weird!

Now try to create a new file using touch. Stop the container, run docker run again, and look for the file. You won't find it. Can't Docker save file system changes consistently?

```
docker run -it ubuntu
  root@168a2ec648f0:/# touch abc
  root@168a2ec648f0:/# exit

docker run -it ubuntu
  root@26a4a5f5b281:/# ls -l abc
  ls: cannot access 'abc': No such file or directory
```

Things become a little clearer if you try running docker run concurrently in multiple terminal windows. That's not a problem for Docker! The reason for this strange behavior at first glance is that Docker creates a *new* container for this image every time you run docker run imagename!

Each container is automatically assigned a random UID, whose short form is reflected in the host name, and its own file system. (Strictly speaking, a read-write file system of the container is superimposed on the read-only file system of the image—see Chapter 6, Section 6.6.)

```
docker ps -a | grep ubuntu
  CONTAINER ID   IMAGE    STATUS                 NAMES
  26a4a5f5b281   ubuntu   Exited (2) 6 seconds ago  wizardly_...
  168a2ec648f0   ubuntu   Exited (0) 6 minutes ago  musing_kilby
  f8fec4640176   ubuntu   Up 36 minutes             naughty_borg
```

3.3.3 Running the Container Again via "docker start"

To reuse an existing container later, you must explicitly specify from the second launch onward which container you mean. You can choose to use the random container ID or the equally random but easier to remember container name (see the result of docker ps -a).

Note that to restart an existing container, you must use docker start, not docker run! To use the container interactively, you must again specify the -i option. -t, on the other hand, isn't permitted. Most options you specify when creating a container with docker run are stored permanently in the container. -i is one of the exceptions.

The following two examples show that Docker did indeed save the *abc* file. The only thing that matters is that you specify the correct container ID or container name at the next startup.

```
docker start -i musing_kilby
  root@168a2ec648f0:/# ls -l abc
    -rw-r--r--. 1 root root 0 Mar 10 15:27 abc
  root@168a2ec648f0:/# exit
```

```
docker start -i 168a2ec648f0
  root@168a2ec648f0:/# ls -l abc
    -rw-r--r--. 1 root root 0 Mar 10 15:27 abc
  root@168a2ec648f0:/# exit
```

Autocompletion

When typing docker start, you may be able to complete the container ID or name by pressing [Tab]. Note, however, that this function is only available on Linux and macOS. If you use zsh with the Oh-My-Zsh extension, you need to add the docker and docker-compose plug-ins to the plugins line in *.zshrc.* Additional configuration tips are provided here:

https://docs.docker.com/compose/completion

3.3.4   Custom Container Names

The random container names are handier than the IDs, but it's even better to assign custom names to containers. To do this, you need to specify the desired name using --name when you create the container with the docker run command. Optionally, you can also assign a host name to the container via -h, which can be identical to the container name, but doesn't have to be.

```
docker run -it --name myubuntu -h myubuntu ubuntu
  root@myubuntu:/#  ...
  root@myubuntu:/# exit
```

To restart the container later, you can use myubuntu instead of hexadecimal codes or confusing name compositions:

```
docker start -i myubuntu
```

Options with One and Two Hyphens

In the preceding docker run command, there are options with one hyphen (-h) and with two hyphens (--name). Why's that?

Traditionally, it's common for Linux commands to specify most options in two variants: as a short form with one letter and a hyphen in front, and in a variant with detailed option names and two hyphens. Instead of -h, --hostname would also be permissible. We prefer the abbreviated notation for the most part in this book due to space restrictions. However, there's no short notation for --name. This option must be passed in the long form.

A special case is -it. In this case, *two* short options have been combined so that -it is an abbreviation for -i -t. Likewise, -abc would be short form of -a -b -c.

For a complete reference of all options for a given Docker command, you can use man on macOS and Windows. For docker run, you can thus use man docker run. Windows users will instead need to look for the documentation in the Docker manual, which is located here for docker run:

https://docs.docker.com/engine/reference/run

3.3.5   Running Other Processes in Parallel via docker exec

It often happens that only one process is running in a Docker container, be it an interactive shell in the foreground as in the previous examples, or a server service in the background. docker exec enables you to start any other processes in parallel to a running container. docker exec is primarily intended for debugging, but it can be used universally.

The following command, to be executed in a second terminal or PowerShell window, starts the top command in parallel with the already running myubuntu container. It's executed until terminated by pressing Q.

```
docker exec -it myubuntu /usr/bin/top
```

You can also run multiple shell sessions concurrently:

```
docker exec -it myubuntu /bin/bash
```

3.3.6   Tidying Up

Presumably, various Ubuntu containers are now left over from experimenting. docker ps -a provides an overview of all containers. In another command, you can now use docker rm <name1> <name2> to delete all the containers in question. In Section 3.9, we'll show how you can use a single command on macOS and Linux to delete all containers that use a particular image.

Basically, you could now also delete the Ubuntu image by using docker image rm ubuntu. However, it's quite possible that you'll need this image more often at a later point. If you refrain from deleting now, you won't have to initiate another download later.

3.4   Port Redirection

In addition to the hello-world image already presented, there's another image in Docker Hub which is intended for first experiments. macOS and Windows users are unmistakably advised to try out this example after installing Docker Desktop. If you decided against it after the installation or if you want to try out the example on Linux, this section is for you!

3.4.1 Connecting Container Ports to Local Ports

`getting-started` is exciting compared to the previous examples in this chapter in that it brings another aspect of the Docker application into play, namely, integrating containers into the local network. It's a simple web server whose container runs as a background service. Provided that you connect port 80 of the container to a free port of your host computer (option -p), you can use a web browser to read the HTML documents provided by the web server.

You can start it in the typical Docker fashion with a nondescript, short command:

```
docker run -d -p 80:80 docker/getting-started
```

Here's a brief explanation of the options: -d (*daemon*) means that Docker should run the container in the background. Because of -p 80:80, Docker connects port 80 of the container to port 80 of the local machine.

Official Images

Unlike the previous examples, in this example, it won't suffice to simply specify getting-started as the image name. This short notation is intended only for "official" images that provide base images or basic programming languages, servers, or other tools.

Official images must adhere to certain rules of the game, but in return are given preferential treatment within Docker Hub:

https://docs.docker.com/docker-hub/official_images

For all other images provided by developers or companies via Docker Hub, the image name must be prefixed with the company or developer name, in this case: docker/getting-started.

After a few status messages (usually Docker has to download the image first), nothing apparently happens. `docker` has executed the command, but in contrast to the previous examples, there's no visual feedback in the console. `docker ps` at least proves that the container is actually running:

```
docker ps

CONTAINER ID    IMAGE                   PORTS              ...
6f3f1d532659    docker/getting-started  0.0.0.0:80->80/tcp
```

The PORTS column tells you that port 80 of the container is connected to port 80 of the Docker host (i.e., your machine!). To see what's happening on port 80, you need to open *localhost* in your web browser. (You may have to enter "http://localhost" to prevent the browser from understanding your input as a search prompt.) This will take you to a website provided by the container that's run by Docker—a web server, to be precise (see Figure 3.1).

The website consists of a whole range of pages that takes you through another example of how Docker is used. This involves launching another container based on a previously created local image. Quite confusingly, this image is also called getting-started, albeit without the prefix docker/. We recommend that you first read Chapter 4 before following the getting-started example.

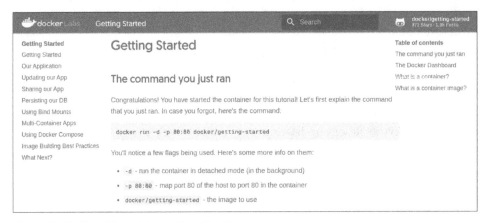

Figure 3.1 Getting Started App in the Web Browser

3.4.2   Problems with Port 80

The docker run command specified earlier doesn't lead to success in every case. A possible cause of the error may be that port 80 is already taken because a web server is already active on your computer. This isn't unusual, especially on development computers. In this case, you should change the options of docker run a bit and specify a different destination port (here, 8080).

Note the syntax -p hostport:containerport! The first port number refers to the host (to your computer), and the second refers to the container. This order contradicts the source-destination logic of most Linux commands. Basically, for all Docker options that specify a mapping between host and container (ports, volumes, etc.), the host data is specified first, followed by the container data.

```
docker run -d -p 8080:80 docker/getting-started
```

If this works, then you must now use port 8080 also in the address you specify in your web browser, that is, *http://localhost:8080*.

A second cause of the error may be that you're running rootless Docker on Linux. Without root privileges, Docker can't have the "privileged" ports smaller than 1024. The solution here is the same as before: you just use a port number greater than 1024, such as 8080. (Any number between 1024 and 65535 will work unless the port has already been reserved for another function.)

3.4.3 Tidying Up

The `getting-started` container continues to run in the background until you explicitly terminate it or restart your computer. (If you run rootless Docker, a logout will cause the container execution to stop as well.)

To delete the container, you first need to determine its name or ID number via `ps`. After that, you can stop the container:

```
docker ps

  CONTAINER ID   IMAGE                     ...      NAMES
  3c8ac71262b8   docker/getting-started             nervous_williams
```

```
docker stop 3c8ac71262b8
```

If you want to start the same container again later, you can run `docker start <id>` or `<name>` accordingly. You can get the ID number using `docker ps -a` if needed. The `-a` option makes `docker ps` list all containers, even those that aren't currently running.

`docker rm <id>` deletes the container. But this only works if the container isn't running. If necessary, you must run `docker stop` first or pass `docker rm` the `-f` (*force*) option to both stop and delete the container.

You can delete the image using `docker image rm docker/getting-started`. Again, this is only possible after you've previously deleted all containers derived from it.

3.5 Data Storage in Volumes

This section deals with the question of how and where containers store data. The best way to answer these questions is to take a look at a container with a database server. For this purpose, we've chosen the MariaDB database system, which is compatible with MySQL. You'll see that you don't need to be a database expert to follow the example. (More tips on the practical use of MySQL and MariaDB will follow in Chapter 10, Section 10.1.)

In Docker Hub, there are various images for the MySQL and MariaDB database servers. For this section we've used the official MariaDB image which is documented on the following page:

https://hub.docker.com/r/_/mariadb

When setting up the container, the root password for the database server gets passed as a parameter. This mechanism isn't ideal because the password is briefly visible for everyone in plain text in the process list.

We'll present a better approach in Chapter 5, Section 5.5. The content of MYSQL_ROOT_ PASSWORD can also be read later with docker inspect mariadb-test, but only by users who have the permission to run docker themselves.

Instead of MYSQL_ROOT_PASSWORD, you can also use the equivalent variable, MARIADB_ROOT_ PASSWORD. We'll stick to MYSQL_xxx in this chapter because these variable names work universally for MariaDB and for MySQL images.

```
docker run -d --name mariadb-test \
        -e MYSQL_ROOT_PASSWORD=secret mariadb
```

The docker run command outputs the ID number of the new container, but apart from that, it doesn't display any status information indicating a successful start. You can use docker ps to make sure the container is actually running:

```
docker ps
  CONTAINER ID ...  COMMAND    CREATED        NAMES
  02f5b1017abb      mysqld     52 seconds ago  mariadb-test
  ...
```

If docker ps doesn't return any output or if mariadb-test is missing from the list of active containers, it's best to use docker logs to determine the cause of the error. For example, if you forget to pass the desired password with the -e option, docker logs will return the following error message:

```
docker logs mariadb-test
  Entrypoint script for MySQL Server maria~focal started.
  Switching to dedicated user 'mysql'
  Database is uninitialized and password option is not specified
  You need to specify one of MYSQL_ROOT_PASSWORD,
  MYSQL_ALLOW_EMPTY_PASSWORD and MYSQL_RANDOM_ROOT_PASSWORD
```

Note that prior to restarting, you need to delete the container that was created last; that is, you must run docker rm mariadb-test.

If the start was successful, the database server continues to run in the background because of the -d option until the container is explicitly stopped again:

```
docker stop mariadb-test
```

Multiline Commands

In this book, when we need to spread commands across two lines for space reasons, we mark the end of the wrapped line with the \ character. On Linux and macOS, you now have the choice of simply entering the command in one line or entering the command in multiple lines, including all \ characters, as printed in the book.

Note, however, that multiline commands in PowerShell on Windows must be separated with the ` character! For this reason, you'd need to enter the preceding command either in one long line in PowerShell or as follows:

```
docker run -d --name mariadb-test `
 -e MYSQL_ROOT_PASSWORD=secret mariadb
```

3.5.1 Storing the Database in an Automatically Created Volume

MariaDB basically stores all database files in the */var/lib/mysql* directory. However, in the MariaDB *Dockerfile*, that is, in the description of the image, */var/lib/mysql* is marked as a *volume*. This means that this directory is created *outside* of the container, as follows:

- On Linux, Docker does this by creating a subdirectory within */var/lib/docker/volumes* on the host machine. If you use rootless Docker, the subdirectory will be placed in *.local/share/docker/volumes* accordingly. You can determine the exact directory name via `docker inspect mariadb-test1` when searching for `mounts` in the multipage output of this command.

- On Windows and macOS, the functionality is quite similar, but the volume directory isn't set up directly in their file systems, but in the file system of the Linux kernel, which is responsible for running the Docker Engine. This reinforces the "black box character" of such volumes.

For now, you don't get much from Docker differentiating between data stored in the container and data that ends up outside (i.e., in a volume). Both the containers and the volumes end up in a Docker-managed directory (e.g., */var/lib/docker*), the contents of which you should never access directly. But volumes enable you to transfer the data of one container to another container later. This is useful, for example, if you want to delete the existing container after a MariaDB update and replace it with a new container with the latest MariaDB version. Of course, you don't want to lose your data during such an update.

In addition, in the next section, you'll learn how you can connect volumes to their own local directories and thus, in a sense, detach them from the Docker black box.

3.5.2 Analyzing Volumes

The `docker inspect` command provides countless details about a particular container in a listing more than 100 lines long. At this point, we're mainly interested in the volume data:

```
docker inspect mariadb-test

  ...
```

```
"Mounts": [
    {
        "Type": "volume",
        "Name": "d19f5b86...",
        "Source": "/home/kofler/.local/share/docker/volumes/\
                    d19f5b86.../_data",
        "Destination": "/var/lib/mysql",
        "Driver": "local",
        "Mode": "",
        "RW": true,
        "Propagation": ""
    }
],
...
```

Thus, the `mariadb-test` container is assigned to a volume with ID `d19f5b86`.... This volume is physically located in the following directory:

/home/kofler/.local/share/docker/volumes/d19f5b86.../_data

Instead of laboriously extracting the volume data from the listing, you can pass a format option to `docker inspect` and filter out only the data that is relevant to you—in this case, all *mounts*:

```
docker inspect -f '{{ .Mounts }}' mariadb-test

[{volume d19f5b86...
  /home/kofler/.local/share/docker/volumes/d19f5b86.../_data
  /var/lib/mysql
  local
  true }]
```

Once you know the name of a volume (here, `d19f5b86...`), you can use `docker volume inspect` to obtain more information.

> **Note**
>
> You must specify the entire 64-character hexadecimal code when doing this. We show only the first 8 digits in each of the listings in this section for clarity.

```
docker volume inspect d19f5b86...
  [
      {
          "CreatedAt": "2021-05-14T18:06:16+02:00",
          "Driver": "local",
          "Labels": null,
```

```
        "Mountpoint": "/home/kofler/.local/share/docker/\
                      volumes/d19f5b86.../_data",
        "Name": "d19f5b86..",
        "Options": null,
        "Scope": "local"
    }
]
```

Unfortunately, docker volume inspect won't reveal the size of a volume. docker system df does provide this information, but not specifically for one volume; instead, it's provided globally for all images, containers, volumes, and so on managed by Docker. Accordingly, the output of docker system df is usually quite long. In the following listing, we've removed all information that has nothing to do with our volume:

```
docker system df -v

  Images space usage: ...
  Containers space usage: ...
  Build cache usage: ...
  Local Volumes space usage:
    VOLUME NAME       LINKS     SIZE
    d19f5b86...        1        136.8MB
```

You may wonder why the volume is so large. After all, we haven't created any databases and filled them with data. The volume size has to do with a peculiarity of the MariaDB server: at the first startup, files are set up where later databases, transactions, and so on will be stored. The minimum size of these files is already quite considerable.

3.5.3 Calling the MariaDB Client

Before we go into detail on how you can handle volumes efficiently in the next section, we want to briefly demonstrate what you can see or analyze from the MariaDB container. This isn't quite trivial because an interactive use of the container isn't provided for. However, you can use docker exec inside the container running in the background to launch the interactive mysql command. (mysql is a command you can use to execute SQL statements on a MySQL or MariaDB server.)

```
docker exec -it mariadb-test mysql -u root -p
  Enter password: ******** (root password for MariaDB)
  Welcome to the MariaDB monitor.
  Server version: 10.5.10-MariaDB-1

  MariaDB [(none)]> show status;
```

```
...

MariaDB [(none)]> exit
```

3.5.4   A Look Inside the Container

If you're curious and want to find out more details about the container, you can start a
bash process for the container concurrent with the MariaDB server via docker exec:

```
docker exec -it mariadb-test /bin/bash
```

```
root@34de866bff12:/# cat /etc/os-release
  PRETTY_NAME="Ubuntu 20.04.2 LTS"
  ...

root@34de866bff12:/#  ps -ax
  PID TTY       STAT    TIME COMMAND
    1 ?         Ssl     0:00 mysqld
  147 ?         Ss      0:00 /bin/bash
  218 ?         R+      0:00 ps -ax

root@34de866bff12:/#  mysqld --version
  mysqld  Ver 10.5.10-MariaDB-1:10.5.10+maria~focal for
  debian-linux-gnu on x86_64 (mariadb.org binary distribution)

root@34de866bff12:/#  exit
```

Due to cat /etc/os-release, you now know that MariaDB uses Ubuntu as its base image.

3.5.5   Logging

Because the MariaDB container runs in the background, you won't see any error messages or logging output in the terminal. You can read those via docker logs:

```
docker logs mariadb-test
```

```
mysqld (mysqld 10.5.10-MariaDB-1:10.5.10+maria~focal)
  starting as process 99 ...
InnoDB: Uses event mutexes
InnoDB: Compressed tables use zlib 1.2.11
InnoDB: Number of pools: 1
  ...
```

3.5.6 Tidying Up

When a container gets deleted, the associated volume is always preserved. This is useful because volumes contain data you may need in other containers.

However, this isn't the case with our current example. Here, we want to delete both the container *and* the volume. For this reason, you should definitely determine the name of the mapped volume via `docker inspect` prior to using `docker rm`! This allows you to subsequently delete the volume as well:

```
docker inspect -f '{{ .Mounts }}' mariadb-test

  [{volume d19f5b86...  ...  /var/lib/mysql local  true }]

docker stop mariadb-test

docker rm mariadb-test

docker volume rm d19f5b86...
```

If you've already deleted the container without first determining the associated volume ID, it will be difficult to delete the volume. `docker volume ls` lists all known volumes, but it doesn't reveal which container these volumes are associated with.

After all, you can use `docker volume prune` to delete *all* volumes that aren't associated with any container. If you've merely experimented with Docker so far, this isn't dangerous. `docker volume prune`, however, involves the risk that you might delete volumes whose data you might need later.

3.6 Named Volumes

In the previous section, you learned about volumes as a mechanism to swap out mutable data of a container to store it separately from its own container. Provided the image has been configured appropriately, Docker takes care of almost everything itself. However, the automatically created volumes have a serious disadvantage in that they are given a random, 64-digit hexadecimal number as their name. The previous examples have shown that this makes further management or deletion of volumes pretty unclear.

Fortunately, there's a simple way out in the form of an option that allows you to assign custom names to volumes. In the following examples, we'll continue to use MariaDB. The `-v <vname>:<containerdir>` option assigns a volume name to a directory of the container:

```
docker run -d --name mariadb-test \
        -v myvolume:/var/lib/mysql \
        -e MYSQL_ROOT_PASSWORD=secret mariadb
```

Nothing changes concerning the use of MariaDB. However, the administration of the volume becomes easier. docker inspect and docker system df display the name of the volume instead of an ID:

```
docker inspect -f '{{ .Mounts }}' mariadb-test

  [{volume myvolume
    /home/kofler/.local/share/docker/volumes/myvolume/_data
    /var/lib/mysql local z true }]

docker system df -v

  ...
  VOLUME NAME    LINKS     SIZE
  myvolume       1         136.8MB
```

3.6.1   Container Update without Data Loss

The benefits of volumes become clear when you want to perform a container update (e.g., after a new version of the MariaDB image has been released in Docker Hub). To do this, you need to stop and delete the current container, download the current image using docker pull, create a new container, and mount it to the already existing volume.

Note that for docker run, you can then omit the -e option for setting the password. myvolume not only contains all databases you've set up when using the container so far but also the MariaDB password. For this reason, it doesn't need to be reconfigured.

```
docker stop mariadb-test
docker rm mariadb-test
docker pull mariadb
docker run -d --name mariadb-test \
        -v myvolume:/var/lib/mysql mariadb
```

3.6.2   Tidying Up

The task of tidying up is also much easier with named volumes. Of course, you should only delete the volume if you no longer need the data it contains. (For the remaining examples in this chapter, the volume isn't needed—we'll create a new one at the next opportunity.)

```
docker stop mariadb-test
docker rm mariadb-test
docker volume rm myvolume
```

3.7 Volumes in Custom Directories

Whether with a custom name or with a random ID number, by default, all volumes end up in Docker-managed directories and, on macOS and Windows, in the space reserved for Docker in a virtual machine and WSL, respectively. However, it's also possible to store volumes in a separate directory in the local file system. This has the advantage that you can access the contents of the directory detached from Docker. The following commands show the command sequence. The first command sequence sets up the container with a local volume directory. Again, the -v option is used, but this time as -v <localdir>/<containerdir>:

```
mkdir /home/<username>/varlibmysql
```

```
docker run -d --name mariadb-test \
  -e MYSQL_ROOT_PASSWORD=secret \
  -v /home/<username>/varlibmysql/:/var/lib/mysql mariadb
```

On Linux and macOS, the path to the local volume directory must start with /. A relative path such as ./*name* won't be accepted. If you specify only name, docker run considers the string as the volume name. It will then create a volume itself as in the previous section and name it with name.

Volumes versus Mounts

The Docker documentation sometimes talks about volumes and then again about mounts. But what's the difference?

Mounts refers to a mechanism for embedding an external file system in the container's directory tree. There are three types of mounts: bind, volume, and tmpfs. This means that a volume is a variant of a mount—a variant that is particularly important in practice.

Instead of the -v or --volume option of the docker run command, which is often used in this book, you can also use the --mount option. As a result, -v <hostdir>:<container-dir> then becomes the following:

--mount type=bind,source=<hostdir>,destination=<containerdir>

The lengthy syntax of --mount is the reason we prefer -v.

3.7.1   Problems with Security-Enhanced Linux

For Fedora, RHEL, and compatible distributions, Security-Enhanced Linux (SELinux) doesn't accept volumes that aren't in Docker's designated directory (e.g., */var/lib/ docker/volumes*). When you specify your own location, an error will occur. The solution here is to add the additional flag `:z` or `:Z` to the volume option (e.g., `-v /home/<user-name>/varlibmysql/:/var/lib/mysql:z`).

Both flags cause the files created by Docker to be automatically assigned the required SELinux context. The difference is that `:z` allows files to be used by different containers, while `:Z` assigns files to one specific container. You can find more details and background information on this here:

https://stackoverflow.com/questions/44139279

The `:z` or `:Z` flags must also be used if you're using Podman instead of Docker, regardless of whether you're working with or without `root` privileges.

3.7.2   Problems on Windows Hosts

Basically, using the `-v` option to specify a local volume directory is also allowed on Windows hosts. However, there are three limitations to this which you need to keep in mind:

- The path can be specified with the / character, which is unusual in Windows, or it must be enclosed in quotation marks like the following, for example:

```
-v C:/Users/name/dir:volumedir
-v "C:\Users\name\dir":volumedir
```

- Local volume directories come with limitations due to the different internal structures of Windows and Linux file systems. Some file operations work, while others don't.

- File operations in local directories are significantly slower than with volumes managed directly by Docker.

You can find numerous threads in the Docker forums from users having issues with volume directories in Windows. In a nutshell, life can be much easier for you if you avoid volumes in local directories in Windows.

3.7.3   Tidying Up

Nothing changes when you stop and delete the container. However, you must now take care of deleting the volume directory yourself, running `rm -rf dir` or `rmdir /s dir`, depending on your operating system.

```
docker stop mariadb-test
docker rm   mariadb-test
```

```
rm -rf varlibmysql        (Linux, macOS)
rmdir /s varlibmysql      (Windows)
```

If you work on Linux without root privileges, the rm command may fail. The containers run by Docker create files that aren't always associated with your own account. Deleting these files therefore requires sudo:

```
sudo rm -rf varlibmysql
```

3.8   Communication between Containers

For many Docker applications, the following holds true: a container rarely comes alone! However, as soon as several containers are running at the same time, the question arises as to how they can communicate with each other. The easiest way to make this happen is via an internal network, which you can set up via docker network.

The commands presented in this section demonstrate the combination of three containers with MariaDB, phpMyAdmin, and WordPress. The examples also work identically with rootless Docker and with Podman.

> **Greater Comfort with docker compose**
>
> At this point, we'll show you how you can manually set up a Docker network as well as several containers primarily for didactic reasons because we want you to understand the way Docker works.
>
> In practice, it's much more efficient to accomplish this type of setup using the docker compose command. You'll learn how to do that in Chapter 5.

3.8.1   Setting Up a Private Docker Network

Setting up a Docker network is simple:

```
docker network create testnet
```

3.8.2   MariaDB

Starting the database system is much more complicated. Basically, you already know how to use MariaDB from the previous examples. This time, however, a few details must change:

- We want MariaDB to create an empty database (wp) and a new account (wpuser), including a password, upon the first startup. Later on, phpMyAdmin and WordPress will get access to this account. The MariaDB image takes care of the necessary initialization work when you pass the MYSQL_DATABASE, MYSQL_USER, and MYSQL_PASSWORD variables to docker run with -e.

- The example doesn't require that the root password of MariaDB be known to the other containers. Thanks to -e MYSQL_RANDOM_ROOT_PASSWORD=1, MariaDB simply uses a random password.

- What's also new is the --network option, which connects the container to the network created earlier.

This results in a somewhat more complex sequence of options for starting the MariaDB container:

```
docker run -d --name mariadb-test --network testnet \
  -e MYSQL_RANDOM_ROOT_PASSWORD=1 \
  -e MYSQL_DATABASE=wp  \
  -e MYSQL_USER=wpuser \
  -e MYSQL_PASSWORD=secret \
  -v myvolume:/var/lib/mysql \
  mariadb
```

3.8.3   phpMyAdmin

phpMyAdmin is a popular web interface for the administration of MariaDB (see Figure 3.2). Starting a corresponding container isn't complicated at all:

```
docker run -d --name pma --network testnet \
  -p 8080:80 \
  -e PMA_HOST=mariadb-test \
  phpmyadmin/phpmyadmin
```

Following are a few notes about the options:

- The --network option also connects this container to the private network of this example.

- -p causes the web interface (port 80 in the container) to be accessible on the host system at port 8080.

- Thanks to the PMA_HOST variable, the phpMyAdmin container knows under which host name the MariaDB server is running on the network. (Docker networks automatically take care of the network-internal name resolution, using the names specified with --name.)

Like MariaDB, the phpMyAdmin container runs in the background (-d option). To test if everything works, you need to open the address *localhost:8080* in your web browser. You must log in to the database server with the account name wpuser and the password that has been set via the *mysql-pw.txt* file. After that, you can use the web GUI to set up new databases, query the data they contain, and so on.

> **Root Access in phpMyAdmin**
>
> If you want to see in phpMyAdmin not only the database wp but also all databases of MariaDB, you need to set a root password (`-e MYSQL_ROOT_PASSWORD=entirelysecret`) when starting the MariaDB container as in the previous sections. Then, in phpMyAdmin, the login with root and the corresponding password will succeed. In this example, this isn't possible because the root password was randomly determined due to the variable, `MYSQL_RANDOM_ROOT_PASSWORD=1`.

Figure 3.2 phpMyAdmin and the MariaDB Server Are Running in Two Separate Containers

3.8.4   WordPress

How long did it take you to install WordPress on a server the last time? If you do it regularly, probably only a few minutes, but the first time it often takes much longer to install and configure the foundation, which consists of Apache, PHP, and MySQL or MariaDB, with all its additional packages.

That's significantly faster with Docker. Assuming you've already set up a MySQL or MariaDB container, then all that's required to get WordPress up and running is the following, admittedly not very short, command:

```
docker run -d --name wordpress-test \
  --network testnet \
  -h wordpress-test \
  -v wp-html:/var/www/html/wp-content \
  -p 8081:80  \
  -e WORDPRESS_DB_HOST=mariadb-test \
  -e WORDPRESS_DB_USER=wpuser \
  -e WORDPRESS_DB_NAME=wp \
  -e WORDPRESS_DB_PASSWORD=secret \
  wordpress
```

Then you use the address *http://localhost:8081* to put the website into operation (see Figure 3.3). The initial configuration is limited to two dialogs. On the first page, you select the desired language, while on the second page, you set up the WordPress administrator. The often-tricky configuration of the database server's access data is no longer necessary because a WordPress container script has already taken care of it.

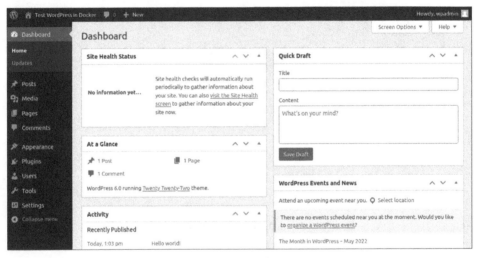

Figure 3.3 WordPress Completes the Example in a Third Container

Following are a few words on the docker-run options:

- -d causes the container to be started as a background service.
- --name gives the container its name.
- --network testnet makes sure that the WordPress container runs on the same network as the MariaDB server and phpMyAdmin.
- -v turns /var/www/html/wp-content into a volume named wp-html. In this directory, uploaded images, plug-ins, and so on are stored—in other words, all the data that has nothing to do with the actual WordPress installation. The volume name facili-

tates the further administration of the container, for example, for updates or deletion. All uploaded files and extensions remain in the volume.

- You can use -p to specify the port through which the WordPress installation on the
Docker host can be accessed. Because port 8080 was already used for phpMyAdmin
in the previous example, we've now used 8081. Provided you're running Docker with
root privileges, and port 80 is available on your host machine, you can of course also
specify -p 80:80.

- The variables WORDPRESS_DB_HOST, _USER, _PASSWORD, and _NAME specify the host name
the MySQL or MariaDB server is running under, the login name and password that
should be used when connecting, and the name of the database, respectively. This
database must already exist. (Unlike previous versions of the WordPress image, the
database won't be created.)

  You must specify the name (--name option) of the MariaDB container as the host
  name. The login and database names must match the ones you used when starting
  MariaDB with the MYSQL_USER, MYSQL_PASSWORD, and MYSQL_DATABASE options.

Other environment variables of the official WordPress image are documented here:

https://hub.docker.com/_/wordpress

Docker Building Kit

At this point, our only goal has been to present simple examples that demonstrate the
use of Docker. Numerous additional details on the practical use of web servers
(Apache, Nginx), database systems (MariaDB, MySQL, etc.), web applications (Word-
Press, Joomla, Nextcloud, etc.) will follow in Part II of this book, where we'll introduce
you to a large number of Docker images. These images are like a building kit from
which you can then assemble your own applications.

3.8.5   Stopping and Restarting Containers

If you temporarily no longer need the three containers, you can stop and then restart
them as needed. Fortunately, you can pass multiple container names to docker stop or
docker start at once:

```
docker stop  mariadb-test pma wordpress-test
...
docker start mariadb-test pma wordpress-test
```

3.8.6   Updates

If new images of MariaDB, phpMyAdmin, and WordPress are available, you can perform a fresh installation as follows:

81

```
docker stop mariadb-test pma wordpress-test
docker rm   mariadb-test pma wordpress-test
docker pull mariadb
docker pull phpmyadmin/phpmyadmin
docker pull wordpress

docker run -d --name mariadb-test --network testnet \
  -v myvolume:/var/lib/mysql \
  mariadb

docker run -d --name pma --network testnet \
  -p 8080:80 \
  -e PMA_HOST=mariadb-test \
  phpmyadmin/phpmyadmin

docker run -d --name wordpress-test \
  --network testnet \
  -h wordpress-test \
  -v wp-html:/var/www/html/wp-content \
  -p 8081:80  \
  -e WORDPRESS_DB_HOST=mariadb-test \
  -e WORDPRESS_DB_USER=wpuser \
  -e WORDPRESS_DB_NAME=wp \
  -e WORDPRESS_DB_PASSWORD=secret \
  wordpress
```

Compared to the initial installation, docker run for MariaDB is significantly shorter because the existing database and all passwords are still used. This data is located in myvolume.

With phpMyAdmin, docker run remains unchanged. Surprisingly, this also applies to the start of the WordPress container. Here, you could have assumed that the configuration data would also be permanently stored in the volume. But, in fact, the crucial configuration file *wp_config.php* contains code that evaluates the environment variables. If the environment variables are missing, the connection between WordPress and the database server fails.

Thanks to the reuse of the volumes, all data (i.e., wp database tables, blog posts in WordPress, etc.) will be preserved during the update.

3.8.7   Tidying Up

If you want to delete all components of this example, that is, the network as well as the containers, volumes, and images, you need to execute the following commands:

```
docker stop mariadb-test pma wordpress-test
docker rm   mariadb-test pma wordpress-test
docker volume rm myvolume
docker volume rm wp-html
docker network rm testnet
docker image rm mariadb wordpress phpmyadmin/phpmyadmin
```

3.9   Administration of Docker

This section provides an initial overview of docker commands you can use for the administration of your Docker system. Such administration tasks include listing and deleting images, containers, and volumes. A detailed description of all important docker commands will follow in Chapter 7.

3.9.1   Determining Space Requirements of Images and Containers

How much space is actually required for images or for the container layer (i.e., for the data of a container that deviates from the original image)? This question is answered by the docker images and docker ps -a -s commands.

docker images returns a list of all downloaded or custom images, including size information:

```
docker images
  REPOSITORY              TAG       ...   CREATED        SIZE
  wordpress               latest          17 hours ago   550MB
  mariadb                 latest          7 days ago     405MB
  phpmyadmin/phpmyadmin   latest          2 months ago   477MB
  ...
```

By default, docker ps lists only the running containers. The -a option extends the output to all containers that have ever been set up. -s adds the SIZE column. It indicates how much space those files take up that have been changed in comparison to the image. Provided that most of the mutable data is stored in a volume, the additional space required is often tiny. However, when there are changes, the actual space required in the local file system is often noticeably larger than docker ps suggests. This is due to the overhead of the file system when many small files are stored.

The information in parentheses (virtual) refers to the total size of the container, including the read-only images. This data is virtual in that multiple containers can share common images, as it were.

```
docker ps -a -s

  CONTAINER ID   IMAGE            ...   SIZE
```

```
2bf9e954b4b7    wordpress          20.1MB (virtual 571MB)
3af937080228    phpmyadmin/...     70B (virtual 477MB)
ac98aca37f7a    mariadb            2B (virtual 405MB)
...
```

3.9.2   Deleting Containers and Images

docker rm <id> or docker rm <name> deletes the specified container. If necessary, you can determine container IDs and names with docker ps -a.

```
docker rm ac98aca37f7a
```

Caution

docker rm has a lot of similarities with the classic rm command on Linux: it deletes without confirmation and without the option to undo the operation!

The following command first uses ps to generate a list of all IDs of containers derived from the image, ubuntu. This list is then passed to docker rm to delete all containers. So, if you've experimented with docker run ubuntu for a while, you can delete all the created containers on this occasion. Note that this command works only on macOS and Linux, not on Windows. The concatenation of two commands presented here assumes that a shell such as bash or zsh is used, as is the case by default on Linux or macOS. On Windows, the command works as well, as long as you use PowerShell.

```
docker rm $(docker ps -a -q -f ancestor=ubuntu)
```

The next command is even more radical as it deletes all existing containers!

```
docker rm $(docker ps -aq)
```

docker rmi imagename deletes the specified image. This is possible only if there are no containers derived from the image. The following commands first delete all hello-world containers and then the hello-world image:

```
docker rm $(docker ps -a -q -f ancestor=hello-world)
```

```
docker rmi hello-world
```

Note that docker rmi only runs locally. If you've uploaded your own image to Docker Hub, the image will remain there. You can delete it in the web GUI of *https://hub.docker.com*, if necessary.

3.9.3   Managing Volumes

Volumes are stored separately from containers and images in their own directory, for example, in */var/lib/docker/volumes* on Linux. When you delete containers, Docker generally doesn't touch any volumes. However, you can determine a list with the names or IDs of all volumes for which the associated container no longer exists, as follows:

```
docker volume ls -q -f dangling=true
  4df85efbf1240b7429f7bf554e2ead52b90a1934875d57773c1c80c405d64a
  6eec952744a21b55c71b8e6dc28da822bf3c8147ed54351dcb88c30094eb1b
  ...
```

The size of the volumes can be determined by passing the preceding result to du. However, this only works in this way on a Linux host. On Windows and macOS, Docker files are stored in a separate file system inside a virtual machine, which you can't access directly from the outside.

```
du -h --max 0 \
  /var/lib/docker/volumes/$(docker volume ls -q -f dangling=true)
```

You can delete all orphaned volumes with the following command if necessary. The query that would pop up can be suppressed using -f.

```
docker volume prune
  WARNING! This will remove all volumes not used by at least
  one container. Are you sure you want to continue? [y/N] y
```

3.9.4   General Overview

A compact overview of the space requirements of all images, containers, volumes, and the build cache is provided by docker system df:

```
docker system df
  TYPE            TOTAL     ACTIVE    SIZE       RECLAIMABLE
  Images          18        11        10.72GB    1.854GB (17%)
  Containers      33        4         496MB      495.9MB (99%)
  Local Volumes   2         1         169MB      119.8MB (70%)
  Build Cache     0         0         0B         0B
```

If you also pass the -v option, the command will list all images, containers, volumes, and so on.

3.9.5   Releasing Unused Space

Instead of searching for images, containers, and volumes and deleting them one by one, you can use docker system prune to help you with your cleanup tasks. This command deletes all containers that aren't currently running and all images that aren't needed by other images (*dangling images*).

The large-scale cleanup becomes even more intensive with additional options:

- `-a` or `--all` also deletes images that aren't used by containers.
- `--volumes` also deletes volumes that aren't associated with any container. (Caution: Data in non-associated volumes will be lost and cannot be reused in another container!)

```
docker system prune -a --volumes

  WARNING! This will remove:
    - all stopped containers
    - all networks not used by at least one container
    - all volumes not used by at least one container
    - all images without at least one container associated
      to them
    - all build cache

  Are you sure you want to continue? [y/N]
```

Chapter 4
Custom Docker Images (Dockerfiles)

When getting started with Docker, your first experience is usually based on ready-made images from Docker Hub. From this, you derive your own containers to work with. However, it often happens that the prefabricated images largely meet your requirements, but not entirely. Of course, every time you set up a container, you can do the necessary extra work manually, such as installing some packages or changing some configuration files, but it's much more efficient to create your own image in such cases. To do this, you need to enter the required changes into a file called *Dockerfile* and run `docker build` to obtain a new local image. If you have an account on the Docker website, you can also share your image with other users and upload it.

This chapter describes the *Dockerfile* syntax and how you can upload images, as well as some usage examples. A large number of other examples will follow later in Part II and Part III.

4.1 Dockerfiles

In a nutshell, the procedure for creating a new image looks like the following: You set up the *Dockerfile* file in a separate directory. There you write the properties of your image using keywords. `docker build` creates the local image. Using `docker push` (see Section 4.3), you can eventually upload it to the public image collection of Docker, if you want to.

GitHub Builds, Private Images, and Custom Repositories

At this point, we'll only cover the simplest variant for setting up and uploading Docker images. In this case, all files are located in a local directory, and you manually upload the finished image to Docker Hub.

Alternatives include using a GitHub project to store the *Dockerfile* and other files if necessary (this enables automated builds), using private image repositories in Docker Hub (requires a paid account), and setting up your own Docker repository. You can find more information at the following addresses:

- *https://docs.docker.com/docker-hub/builds*
- *https://docs.docker.com/docker-hub/builds/link-source*
- *https://docs.docker.com/registry*

4.1.1   Dockerfile Syntax

The *Dockerfile* determines the features of custom images. Table 4.1 summarizes the most important keywords.

Keyword	Meaning
ADD	Copies files to the file system of the image
CMD	Executes the specified command at container startup
COPY	Copies files from the project directory to the image
ENTRYPOINT	Always executes the specified command at container startup
ENV	Sets an environment variable
EXPOSE	Specifies the active ports of the container
FROM	Specifies the base image
LABEL	Sets a character string
RUN	Executes the specified command
USER	Specifies the account for RUN, CMD, and ENTRYPOINT
VOLUME	Specifies volume directories
WORKDIR	Sets the working directory for RUN, CMD, COPY, etc.

Table 4.1 Important Dockerfile Keywords

Numerous other keywords and details can be found in the official documentation: *https://docs.docker.com/engine/reference/builder*.

In addition, it's certainly worth taking a look at the *best practices* for dealing with *Dockerfiles*: *https://docs.docker.com/develop/develop-images/dockerfile_best-practices*.

An easy way to familiarize yourself with the *Dockerfile* syntax is to go to Docker Hub and look at the *Dockerfiles* of images that perform similar tasks to your own image.

4.1.2   Introductory Example

A minimal *Dockerfile* that extends the Ubuntu base image with the package of the joe editor looks like the following:

```
# Dockerfile file
FROM ubuntu:20.04
LABEL maintainer "name@somehost.com"
RUN apt-get update && \
    apt-get install -y joe && \
```

```
    apt-get clean && \
    rm -rf /var/lib/apt/lists/*
CMD ["/bin/bash"]
```

You can use RUN to specify commands that will be executed once when the new image gets created. These commands are executed in the container that has been temporarily set up for image creation, that is, in the guest system, not in the host system. Often these are commands for installing packages or compiling/configuring programs.

4.1.3 Specifying the Source Image ("FROM")

Custom images are mostly derived from other images. You can specify the image name using FROM. If possible, you should use official, well-maintained images.

4.1.4 Adding Files ("ADD" versus "COPY")

At first glance, the ADD and COPY commands seem to perform the same task: You copy files to the file system of the image you want to create. ADD is the more flexible command, which differs from the simple COPY in three aspects:

- As a source parameter, ADD not only accepts a local file but also a URL. This allows for downloading files from the internet and copying them to the image file system.
- If the source parameter of ADD is a directory, the entire contents of that directory will be copied to the image.
- If the source file with ADD is a local TAR archive, it will be unpacked automatically. This also works for archives compressed with the gzip, bzip2, or xz methods.

The *Dockerfile* documentation recommends using ADD only when one of these additional features is used. For the simple copying of a local file, you should use the COPY command instead.

For both ADD and COPY, you can use --chown=user:group to specify which account and group the file should be associated with in the image file system.

4.1.5 Container "start" Command ("CMD" and "ENTRYPOINT")

The question of which program will be executed when a container is run for the first time using run or later on with start has a bewildering number of answers:

- You can specify a default command in the *Dockerfile* using the CMD and/or ENTRYPOINT keywords.
- When setting up the container, you can specify an alternate command for the CMD variant or add further parameters to it for the ENTRYPOINT variant.

- If necessary, you can also replace the ENTRYPOINT command with your own command if you pass it to docker run with the --entrypoint option.

- While a container is running, you can use docker exec to execute any other command.

The recommended syntax for ENTRYPOINT or CMD is to put the complete file name of the command and its parameters in double quotes each and pass them in square brackets separated by commas:

```
CMD ["/bin/ls", "/var"]
```

CMD and ENTRYPOINT seem to perform the same task. However, there's one major difference:

- **CMD**

  The command you pass to docker run after the image name is executed *instead* of CMD.

- **ENTRYPOINT**

  The parameters passed to docker run are added to the ENTRYPOINT.

A multiple specification of CMD or ENTRYPOINT isn't intended. If that does happen, the last statement of that kind will apply.

In practice, the ENTRYPOINT isn't defined for many base images, which means it's empty. CMD contains the name of a shell, that is, /bin/sh or /bin/bash. Similarly, with images for programming languages, ENTRYPOINT is mostly undefined, while CMD either starts a shell of the programming language or is also empty.

For images for server services, on the other hand, ENTRYPOINT often refers to a shell script that first takes care of various initialization tasks (see Table 4.2). Once these have been completed, the command specified with CMD gets executed, which means that usually the server service gets started. If no initialization work is required, ENTRYPOINT is empty.

Image	ENTRYPOINT	CMD
Alpine Linux		["/bin/sh"]
Apache		["httpd-foreground"]
Debian		["/bin/bash"]
Nginx		["nginx", "-g", "daemon off;"]
MySQL/MariaDB	["docker-entrypoint.sh"]	["mysqld"]
Nextcloud	["entrypoint.sh"]	["apache2-foreground"]

Table 4.2 ENTRYPOINT and CMD Settings for Some Popular Images

Image	ENTRYPOINT	CMD
Node.js		["node"]
OpenJDK (Java)		["jshell"]
Oracle Linux		["/bin/bash"]
PHP	["docker-php-entrypoint"]	["php", "-a"]
Python		["python3"]
Ubuntu		["/bin/bash"]
WordPress	["docker-entrypoint.sh"]	["apache2-foreground"]

Table 4.2 ENTRYPOINT and CMD Settings for Some Popular Images (Cont.)

Table 4.3 shows how different specifications for ENTRYPOINT, CMD, and the docker run parameter result in the command to be executed. Note that the RUN keyword has nothing to do with CMD and ENTRYPOINT! RUN specifies commands to be executed once when the image is created. CMD or ENTRYPOINT, on the other hand, specify the command to be executed later when the container is started.

ENTRYPOINT	CMD	RUN Parameter	To Be Executed
["script.sh"]			script.sh
["script.sh"]		/bin/bash	script.sh /bin/bash
["script.sh"]	["mysqld"]		script.sh mysqld
["script.sh"]	["mysqld"]	/bin/bash	script.sh /bin/bash
	["/bin/sh"]		/bin/sh
	["/bin/sh"]	/bin/bash	/bin/bash

Table 4.3 Individual Components of the Command Executed by "docker run"

Shell Variant of CMD and ENTRYPOINT

The Docker documentation recommends passing the command to be executed and its parameters to CMD and ENTRYPOINT, respectively, in square brackets and double quotes, as in the preceding examples. However, there's a second type of syntax according to which you simply pass the command without brackets and quotes, such as CMD ls /etc/*. In that case, the command will be executed via a shell. When that happens, it's not the command that receives process ID 1, but the shell.

The shell variant has its pros and cons. The advantages include the fact that the substitution mechanisms known from the shell work without a problem. For example, * is replaced by file names, $VAR is replaced by the contents of the environment variable, and so on. In addition, you can omit specifying the full path of the command—the shell will find the command if it's located in one of the PATH directories.

The biggest drawback is that there's no signal redirection: `Ctrl`+`C` for an interactive container or `docker stop` for a noninteractive container stops the shell, but they don't allow the actual command to be executed to perform the signal processing itself.

4.1.6   Running Commands (RUN)

The commands specified with RUN are executed when the image gets created. Often these are commands for installing packages. Because the process is automated, you need to avoid interactive queries. For many package-management commands, the -y option is sufficient for this (*yes,* that is, answer all queries in the affirmative).

```
RUN apt-get update -y && \
    apt-get install -y --no-install-recommends \
        subversion \
        joe \
        vim \
        less && \
    apt-get clean && \
    rm -rf /var/lib/apt/lists/*
```

Tip

Each RUN command adds another layer to your image, that is, a file system layer. (We'll describe how images are assembled from multiple layered file systems in Chapter 6, Section 6.6.) However, a large number of layers will make images inefficient. For this reason, it's recommended to combine as many statements as possible in one RUN command, as in the preceding example.

To prevent images from becoming larger than necessary, all cache files should also be deleted immediately (here, with `apt-get clean` and `rm`). If these files end up in a layer, they'll unnecessarily inflate the image.

4.1.7   Volume Directories (VOLUME)

VOLUME specifies which directories are to be mapped as volumes in the file system of the host. As with CMD, you can specify multiple directories in square brackets and each in double quotes:

```
VOLUME ["/var/lib/mysql", "/var/log/mysql"]
```

Where the volumes actually end up in the host file system depends on how the container is set up. If you run docker run or docker create without the -v option, Docker sets up a directory with a random UID for each volume (*/var/lib/docker/volumes/uid*). The user of the image can also specify the desired location in the host by using the -v option:

```
docker run ... -v /myvolumes/mysql:/var/lib/mysql \
   -v /myvolumes/log:/var/log/mysql  imagename
```

Fedora and Red Hat Enterprise Linux (RHEL) users must note that Security-Enhanced Linux (SELinux) doesn't typically allow volumes outside of */var/lib/docker*. The solution in such cases is the additional flag :z, which you add to the volume option (i.e., -v /myvolumes/mysql/:/var/lib/mysql:z).

4.1.8 Creating and Testing an Image

You usually run docker build in the directory where the *Dockerfile* is located. As a parameter, you can pass a dot that you use to point to the directory containing the *Dockerfile*. Using -t, you can specify the desired image name. For accountname, you should use the name of your Docker account (see Section 4.3). If you haven't set up an account yet, you can enter any name for the time being or omit the account name altogether.

```
cd project directory
docker build -t accountname/imagename .
```

We'll use the account name koflerinfo and the image name ubuntu-joe in the further course of this example:

```
docker build -t koflerinfo/ubuntu-joe .
```

If errors occur while running docker build, you must correct the *Dockerfile* and repeat the build process. Docker takes a fairly intelligent approach to this by creating an interim image in a cache directory for each statement in the *Dockerfile*. If statements remain unchanged after the *Dockerfile* has been modified, docker build can continue to use the corresponding images from the cache. (You can prevent this with the --no-cache option if necessary.)

In this respect, it's recommended for debugging to avoid a complicated and error-prone RUN command and instead to provide multiple RUN commands for each substep.

This approach can unfortunately lead to images that are larger than absolutely necessary. This is especially the case when something is installed or compiled in one RUN command and cleanup is performed in a second RUN command. Docker isn't able to reasonably clean up files added in one delta image and deleted in another delta image. So, if your *Dockerfile* works fine, you should run all the commands together in *one* long RUN command, as in the *Dockerfile* of Section 4.2.

docker history imagename provides a list of the interim images and the commands executed for them:

```
docker history koflerinfo/ubuntu-joe
```

To try out the successfully created image, you should create a container from it and test it—in this tiny example, you can do that by calling the jmacs editor from the joe package:

```
docker run -it --rm koflerinfo/ubuntu-joe
  root@b1c2c0a04f47:/# jmacs /etc/os-release
  ...
  root@b1c2c0a04f47:/# <Strg>+<D>
```

"docker build" versus "docker buildx"

The docker build command provides the easiest way to create custom images. In parallel, Docker provides the docker buildx command, which, in turn, contains various subcommands where docker buildx build is largely compatible with docker build.

Among other things, using docker buildx is recommended if you want to create images in parallel for multiple CPU platforms. It also provides various optimization features that are missing in docker build. More details about docker buildx can be found here:

- *https://docs.docker.com/buildx/working-with-buildx*
- *https://docs.docker.com/engine/reference/commandline/buildx*
- *https://github.com/docker/buildx*

4.1.9   Tidying Up

It often takes several attempts before the new image works as it should. Keep in mind that every now and then, you should delete all containers and images that are no longer needed. (In the following commands, you need to replace accountname/imagename with your designations, of course. If the commands return error messages, then there was nothing to delete.)

```
docker rm $(docker ps -a -q -f ancestor=accountname/imagename)

docker rmi \
  $(docker images accountname/imagename -f dangling=true -q)
```

4.2   A Custom Web Server Image

The purpose of this example is to create an image for a simple web server. The following lines show the *Dockerfile*:

```
# Dockerfile file
FROM ubuntu:20.04

LABEL maintainer "name@somehost.com"
LABEL description "Test"
# Set environment variables and time zone
# (saves interactive queries)
ENV TZ="Europe/Berlin" \
    APACHE_RUN_USER=www-data \
    APACHE_RUN_GROUP=www-data \
    APACHE_LOG_DIR=/var/log/apache2

# Set time zone, install Apache, remove unnecessary files
# from package cache immediately, enable HTTPS
RUN ln -snf /usr/share/zoneinfo/$TZ /etc/localtime && \
    echo $TZ > /etc/timezone && \
    apt-get update && \
    apt-get install -y apache2 && \
    apt-get -y clean && \
    rm -r /var/cache/apt /var/lib/apt/lists/* && \
    a2ensite default-ssl && \
    a2enmod ssl

# Release ports 80 and 443
EXPOSE 80 443

# copy entire content of project directory
# samplesite to /var/www/html
COPY samplesite/ /var/www/html

# Start command
CMD ["/usr/sbin/apache2ctl", "-D", "FOREGROUND"]
```

The preceding file describes an image based on Ubuntu 20.04. The Apache web server is additionally installed in it and also configured for HTTPS operation with a2ensite and a2enmod. Accordingly, ports 80 and 443 of the container should be accessible to the outside. Setting the time zone will prevent an annoying interactive query when you run docker build.

The local samplesite directory, located in the same directory as the *Dockerfile*, contains the *index.html* and *style.css* files. The COPY statement in the *Dockerfile* copies the entire contents of this directory to the */var/www/html* directory of the container.

4.2.1   Creating and Testing an Image

docker build now creates the image. Using the -t option, you can assign the desired name and possibly a tag to the image right away. Of course, you must replace koflerinfo with the name of your Docker account.

```
cd project directory
docker build -t koflerinfo/testwebserver .
  Step 1/8 : FROM ubuntu:20.04 ...
  Step 2/8 : LABEL maintainer "name@somehost.com" ...
  Step 3/8 : LABEL description "Test" ...
  ...
  Successfully built 37e3a605b0eb
  Successfully tagged koflerinfo/testwebserver:latest
```

docker run enables you to create a container from the local image and run the web server in it. Due to the -d option, the container runs in the background until you terminate the process via docker stop. docker start name restarts the container if necessary. docker run requires that ports 8080 and 8443 are free on the local machine.

```
docker run -d -p 8080:80 -p 8443:443 \
  --name testwebserver koflerinfo/testwebserver


...
docker stop  testwebserver     (stop container)
docker start testwebserver     (restart)
docker rm    testwebserver     (or delete)
```

In a web browser on the Docker host, you can now visit *http://localhost:8080* to view the test website. The address *https://localhost:8443* redirects to the HTTPS variant of the website. An automatically generated, self-signed certificate is used for HTTPS encryption. This will cause a corresponding warning to be displayed in the web browser. You may need to set up a proper certificate (see Chapter 9).

The previously presented docker run command is suitable for initial tests, but not for the permanent operation of the web server. For the latter, it's convenient to separate the container from the variable data. On the one hand, this involves the website itself and, on the other hand, the logging files of the web server.

The workaround here is to have two local directories, one that stores the HTML and CSS pages for the local site, and another one that stores the logging files. These directories are then passed to the container as volumes via the -v option, replacing its local directories, */var/www/html* and */var/log/apache2*. In the following example, we assume that the local directories are located in the home directory—but any other location is just as well conceivable.

```
docker run  -d -p 80:80 -p 443:443 \
  -v /home/kofler/webdir:/var/www/html \
  -v /home/kofler/logdir:/var/log/apache2 \
  -h webtest --name webtest koflerinfo/testwebserver
```

On Fedora and RHEL, you need to add :z to the two volume options to make SELinux accept the volumes outside */var/lib/docker*.

The key benefit of this container configuration is that it's now possible to set up a new container based on an updated image at any time. So, if there's a new Apache version, you create a new image, stop the running container, set up a new one, start it as described previously—and your server update is complete!

4.3 Uploading Images to Docker Hub

Prior to creating an image based on a *Dockerfile*, you should create an account on the *https://hub.docker.com* website. If you choose a *free* account, all you have to do is enter an account name, an email address, and a password.

4.3.1 Login

After clicking the confirmation email, you can log in to your Docker host using docker login:

```
docker login
  Login with your Docker ID to push and pull images from
    Docker Hub.
  Username: accountname
  Password: secret
  Login Succeeded
  WARNING! Your password will be stored unencrypted in
  /home/<name>/.docker/config.json. Configure a credential
  helper to remove this warning.
```

On Linux, docker login stores the account name and password in a string encoded using the base64 method in the *.docker/config.json* file. The corresponding command looks as follows:

```
echo -n '<accountname>:<password>' | base64
```

`docker login` warns you that the password will be stored in plain text. This isn't quite true, but the password can be very easily determined from the string with `base64 -d` in any case. Docker recommends using a *credential helper* for security reasons. This is easier said than done because no procedure or program has been properly established for this on Linux. (The best we can recommend is `pass`; see *www.passwordstore.org*.)

It's much easier to generate an access token in the web user interface of *https://docker.com* in the **Security** dialog of your account settings (see Figure 4.1). After that, you can use this token instead of the password for login:

```
docker login --username <accountname>
  Password: <your-secret-token>
```

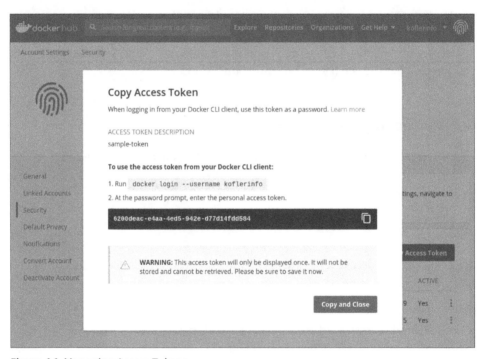

Figure 4.1 Managing Access Tokens

This will store the token in *config.json* instead of the password. Should a stranger gain access to it, this would be far less serious. If necessary, you can delete the token in the Docker web user interface to block further use of the token.

On macOS or on Windows, the easiest way to perform the login is in the *Docker Desktop* program. The authentication data is stored in the keychain or credential manager. In that case, *config.json* contains only one entry that references the location, for example, `"credsStore": "osxkeychain"`.

4.3.2   "push" Command

Once you've tested the image locally, you can upload it for public distribution:

```
docker push accountname/imagename
```

4.3.3   Image Description

After the successful upload, you'll find the image in Docker Hub. In the web UI, you can edit a short description and a *README* file using the **Manage Repository** button (see Figure 4.2).

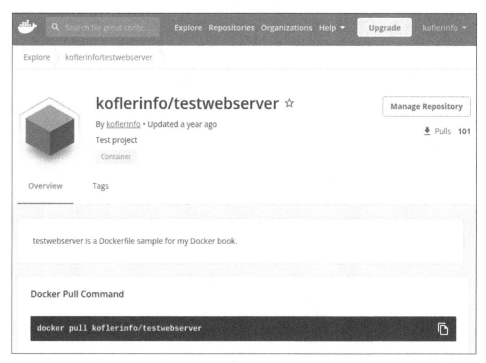

Figure 4.2 Presenting a Custom Docker Image on Docker Hub

Unfortunately, there's no way to specify these texts in the *Dockerfile*. However, for automated builds where Docker adopts the *Dockerfile* and all other project data from GitHub, you can provide the *README.md* file in the project directory. The contents of this file will then appear in Docker Hub as the **Full Description** of your image. (However, the mechanism we've described here doesn't work for local builds!)

4.3.4   Image Tags

By default, the latest image created with docker build is assigned the *tag* latest. In this case, docker push overwrites the last image designated this way.

You can optionally set tags that differ from this directly when running docker build or via docker tag:

```
docker build -t account/image:tag
docker tag account/image[:oldtag] account/image:newtag
```

4.3.5   Deleting Uploaded Images

If you want to delete images once they've been uploaded to Docker Hub, you need to switch to the **Tags** dialog, select the images you no longer need, and run **Actions • Delete**. The **Settings** dialog also contains the option to delete the entire project (the web UI speaks of a *repository*).

4.4   Setting Up a Pandoc and LaTeX Environment as an Image

As a final example in this chapter, we want to show you the *Dockerfile* for our working environment. We've written this book in Markdown syntax. The pandoc command and a whole collection of custom-built scripts generate an HTML version (for the ebook editions) as well as LaTeX files from which PDFs for printing the book will subsequently be generated.

This setup has the advantage for us as authors to each use our favorite editor without dealing with Microsoft Word. However, the downside is that it's extremely tedious to manually set up the plethora of tools necessary to generate a finished PDF file.

Fortunately, this problem can be elegantly circumvented using Docker. A comparatively tiny *Dockerfile* is sufficient to build an image that contains all the necessary programs. The explanations will follow after the listing.

```
# Dockerfile file
FROM ubuntu:20.04

# Install packages, set time zone (avoids
# interactive query)
ENV TZ="Europe/Berlin"
RUN ln -snf /usr/share/zoneinfo/$TZ /etc/localtime && \
    echo $TZ > /etc/timezone && \
    apt-get update -y && \
    apt-get install -y -o Acquire::Retries=10 \
                    --no-install-recommends \
      texlive-latex-recommended \
      texlive-latex-extra \
      texlive-fonts-recommended \
      texlive-lang-german \
```

```
      texlive-pstricks \
      texlive-fonts-extra \
      imagemagick \
      unzip \
      python3 \
      ghostscript \
      locales \
      joe \
      vim \
      curl \
      wget \
      ca-certificates \
      less && \
    apt-get clean && \
    rm -rf /var/lib/apt/lists/*

# Install Pandoc
RUN curl -L https://github.com/jgm/pandoc/releases/download/2.14/pandoc-2.14-1-
amd64.deb \
    -o /tmp/pandoc.deb && \
    dpkg -i /tmp/pandoc.deb && \
    rm /tmp/pandoc.deb

# Install fonts
ADD myfonts.tgz /usr/local/share/texmf
RUN texhash

# Connect volume /data for docker run with the working
# directory, so: docker run -v $(pwd):/data
# Fedora, RHEL:    docker run -v $(pwd):/data:z
VOLUME  ["/data"]

# Start command
ENTRYPOINT ["/bin/bash"]
```

Sorry, Incomplete Sample Files

There are only incomplete sample files available for download for this example. The fonts associated with the example can't be passed on, and this example fulfills rather didactic functions in other aspects. Although the practical benefits for us as authors are great, this won't be true for most readers.

4.4.1 Installation Work

As an entry point, we used Ubuntu again. The first step in the preceding *Dockerfile* is to install various packages and set the time zone. To keep the *Dockerfile* easy to read, it's recommended to specify the required packages line by line.

The next step is to download Pandoc as a ready-made package and install it with dpkg. (Pandoc is also provided in the Ubuntu package sources, but the version found there is rarely up to date.)

Finally, various fonts are installed so that different LaTeX commands as well as dvips can access them. ADD unpacks the archive automatically. After that, the texhash command must be executed using RUN. This way, a file index is updated so that LaTeX and Co can find the fonts.

4.4.2 Working Directory and Volume

The containers derived from the image should have access to a local working directory. Inside the image, */data* serves as the working directory. It's automatically the active directory after starting a container. To the outside, the connection is made via a volume (see also the following docker run command).

Because the image contains not just one command but multiple commands (latex, pandoc, dvips, ps2pdf, etc.), it doesn't make sense to prefer one of these commands by default. Rather, ENTRYPOINT makes bash the default command.

4.4.3 Creating the Image

To create the image, you need to go to the directory where the *Dockerfile* and the font archive are located and run docker build there. Using -t allows you to assign a name to the image that you can freely choose:

```
docker build . -t pandoc_all
```

Note that the creation process takes about 10 minutes because of the extensive downloads and installation work. The resulting image is huge—about 2.1 GB—and thus not an example of a lean container service.

> **Tips for Developing Your OwnDockerfiles**
>
> For small images, the trial-and-error method of development works well. However, if creating an image takes longer, as in this example, it can be annoying if an error occurs at the end of this process.
>
> We proceeded in such a way that we first tested the basic functions as well as the commands to be executed manually in an Ubuntu container. The installation commands that proved successful there were then transferred to the *Dockerfile*.

4.4.4   Running the Container

To try out the image, you must go to the directory where the Markdown files are located and create a container derived from it. This associates the current directory with the /data volume. The container is assigned the name mypandoc.

```
cd <directory-with-markdown-files>
docker run -it -v $(pwd):/data --name mypandoc \
         -h mypandoc pandoc_all


  # pandoc --version
    pandoc 2.14
```

If you want to use a container in multiple terminals or terminal tabs concurrently, you must use docker exec from the second terminal onwards:

```
docker exec -it mypandoc bash
```

If you exit the main container via exit or ⌜Ctrl⌟+⌜D⌟ and thus terminate it, you can always start it again later with the following command. The -a and -i options allow interactive use (equivalent to -it for docker run and docker exec).

```
docker start -ai mypandoc
```

4.4.5   Troubleshooting

The *Dockerfile* assumes that you're using a machine with x86 architecture. If that's not the case, you need to change the command for installing the binary package:

```
# Pandoc for M1/ARM architecture
RUN curl -L https://github.com/jgm/pandoc/releases/download/2.17.0.1/pandoc-
2.17.0.1-1-arm64.deb \
    -o /tmp/pandoc.deb && \
    dpkg -i /tmp/pandoc.deb && \
    rm /tmp/pandoc.deb
```

Depending on which files you edit in Pandoc, a second problem may occur: LaTeX searches in vain for *lmodern.sty*. To solve this issue, you can either add lmodern and fonts-lmodern to the package list, or remove the --no-install-recommends option. However, the resulting image will then become larger.

Chapter 5
docker compose

Setting up Docker containers with docker run is straightforward, but if you need the same kind of containers over and over again, there is an even more convenient way: the docker compose command evaluates the *docker-compose.yml* text file in the current directory and then sets up the appropriate containers. This is especially useful if you want to combine multiple containers in one setup.

To use docker compose, you just need to learn the syntax of *docker-compose.yml*. This is the syntax we'll focus on in this chapter. Countless usage examples will then follow in nearly all the other chapters of this book. (You can tell we're big fans of docker compose!)

---

docker compose versus docker-compose

In the past, docker-compose was a command independent of docker. In current versions, however, compose is implemented as a subcommand of docker and can thus be called without a hyphen. In Spring 2022, the new docker compose command was built in to Docker Desktop by default. Linux users with older Docker installations, on the other hand, had to install the old docker-compose command separately (details will follow momentarily).

Regarding their functionality, docker-compose and docker compose are almost completely identical (see also the following link with a very short list of incompatibilities). What has changed, however, is the internal implementation: like the entire docker command, docker compose was developed in the Go programming language and should run noticeably faster than the older docker-compose command, which is actually a Python script.

https://docs.docker.com/compose/cli-command-compatibility

5.1 docker-compose versus docker stack

As if the differentiation between docker compose and docker-compose wasn't enough, docker stack opens up another way to bring a setup formulated in *docker-compose.yml* to life, so to speak:

- The traditional way is to use the docker compose or docker-compose command to set up and start the containers.

- Alternatively, you can use docker stack deploy to create and run equivalent services. Just as docker compose saves you from running docker run or docker exec multiple times with countless parameters, docker stack deploy replaces various commands of the docker service ... type.

Although the end result is ultimately very similar (you can use the setup described in the file), the differences behind the scenes are significant: docker compose works directly with containers.

docker stack deploy, on the other hand, sets up a group (a *stack*) of services. Services were designed to make Docker services distributable and scalable. However, you absolutely don't need to set up a Docker cluster (or *swarm*, to stick with the official terminology) for you to use docker stack deploy. It suffices to run docker swarm init once, which turns your Docker instance into a mini swarm consisting of just one member.

So, the initial hurdle for docker stack deploy isn't high. Nevertheless, you must be aware that the use of services brings an additional layer of abstraction into play. For Docker beginners, this makes the application more confusing without providing any immediate benefits. In this respect, it's advisable, especially for beginners, to give preference to docker compose for the time being.

Advanced Docker users, on the other hand, consider services to be the better containers. "Docker service is the new docker run," was once said at a Docker talk. docker stack deploy is then the more versatile alternative to docker compose. We'll describe the options for deploying Docker applications across multiple computers or in the cloud in Chapter 19 and Chapter 20.

> **Version Numbers**
>
> docker stack deploy requires that the *docker-compose.yml* file conform to at least version 3.0 syntax. This is the case with all the examples in this book.

5.2   Installing "docker-compose"

On macOS, Windows, as well as recent installations on Linux, docker compose is an integral part of Docker. You proceed as follows to check that yourself:

```
docker compose version
  Docker Compose version 2.11.1
```

For older Linux installations, you should test to see if you can run docker compose without a hyphen. Only if it comes to the error message **compose is not a docker command** will a manual installation of the conventional command docker-compose be required. To do this, you need to run the following command, replacing 1.29.2 with the current version number:

```
sudo curl -L "https://github.com/docker/compose/releases/\
  download/1.29.2/docker-compose-$(uname -s)-$(uname -m)" \
  -o /usr/local/bin/docker-compose
```

```
chmod +x /usr/local/bin/docker-compose
```

```
docker-compose  --version
  docker-compose version 1.29.2
```

The installation command for the latest version of docker compose can be found on the following pages:

- *https://docs.docker.com/compose/install*
- *https://github.com/docker/compose/releases*

If the /usr/local/bin directory isn't included in the PATH environment variable, you can either modify PATH accordingly (e.g., to .bashrc or .zshrc) or perform the installation directly in /usr/bin. To do this, you want to replace /usr/local/bin/docker-compose with /usr/bin/docker-compose twice in the preceding commands.

If you work with rootless Docker, you can simply install docker-compose into the local bin directory. This doesn't require any root privileges.

5.3   YAML Ain't Markup Language Syntax

Before you can run docker compose or docker stack deploy, you must create a file named *docker-compose.yml*. The extension *.yml* denotes the *YAML Ain't Markup Language* (YAML). We've briefly summarized the syntax rules of YAML for you here:

- --- introduces a new section.
- # starts a comment that extends to the end of the line.
- Strings can be expressed as "abc" or 'abc'. However, this is only mandatory in exceptional cases, for example, if the string contains special characters or can be interpreted as another YAML expression.
- Several expressions introduced with - form a list:

  ```
  - red
  - green
  - blue
  ```

  Alternatively, lists can be enclosed in square brackets:

  ```
  [red, green, blue]
  ```

- Associative lists (key-value pairs) are created in the key: value format:

  ```
  name: Howard Hollow
  age: 37
  ```

  Here, too, there's a space-saving variant, but this time in curly brackets:

  ```
  {name: Howard Hollow, age: 37}
  ```

- | introduces a text block in which the line breaks are preserved:

```
codeblock: |
  Line 1
  Line 2
```

- > introduces a text block in which line breaks are ignored, but empty lines are kept:

```
textblock: >
  Text that
  belongs together.

  Here begins the
  second paragraph.
```

All presented elements can be nested within each other. The structure is created by indentations. Note that spaces must be used here (no tabs!). When accessing the elements, the identifiers (keys) are strung together.

```
# sample.yaml file
data:
  list:
    - item1
    - item2
  key1: >
    This text is assigned to the
    'data.key1' key.
  key2: |
    code line 1
    code line 2
```

Some advanced syntax elements of YAML, which usually don't play a role in *docker-compose.yml* files, are documented in Wikipedia:

https://en.wikipedia.org/wiki/YAML

To read YAML files, you can use the Python script shyaml. On Ubuntu, you can install the command as follows:

```
sudo apt install python-pip
sudo pip install shyaml
shyaml get-value data.list < sample.yaml
  - item1
  - item2
```

When you experiment with YAML files, the YAML validators or parsers on the following websites are also quite useful:

- *www.yamllint.com*
- *https://yaml-online-parser.appspot.com*
- *https://codebeautify.org/yaml-validator*

5.4   Hello Compose!

The following introductory example for the syntax of *docker-compose.yml* describes a Docker setup that consists of two services: a database server (MariaDB in the current version) and the WordPress content management system (CMS).

Most of the settings for the two services should be readily understandable:

- Named volumes are used to store the database files and HTML files, respectively. (The names of the volumes must be specified *twice*, once in the description of the respective services and a second time—usually at the end of the *docker-compose.yml* file—in a separate volumes section.)
- In MariaDB, the wp database and the associated user wpuser are to be set up with the password secret. A random string can be used as root password because it's not relevant for the setup.
- For WordPress to access the database, the corresponding WORDPRESS variables must be initialized. DB_HOST references the service name db and the default port number of the MariaDB server.
- The web server responsible for WordPress uses port 80 in the container. This port should be connected to port 8082 of the host computer.

```
# file test/docker-compose.yml
version: '3'

services:
  db:
    image: mariadb:latest
    volumes:
      - vol-db:/var/lib/mysql
    environment:
      MYSQL_RANDOM_ROOT_PASSWORD: 1
      MYSQL_DATABASE: wp
      MYSQL_USER: wpuser
      MYSQL_PASSWORD: secret
    restart: always

  wordpress:
    image: wordpress:latest
```

```
    volumes:
      - vol-www:/var/www/html/wp-content
    ports:
      - "8082:80"
    environment:
      WORDPRESS_DB_HOST: db:3306
      WORDPRESS_DB_USER: wpuser
      WORDPRESS_DB_NAME: wp
      WORDPRESS_DB_PASSWORD: secret
    restart: always
volumes:
  vol-www:
  vol-db:
```

5.4.1 "docker compose"

To try out docker compose, you must first go to the directory containing the file *docker-compose.yml*—here, the wordpress-example directory. Note that the directory name is used to name the containers, volumes, networks, and so on.

docker compose up -d then searches for the *docker-compose.yml* file in the current directory, downloads the required images (only if they aren't already available, of course), creates the containers, connects them in a specifically created network, and starts them as background processes (option -d). The entire process takes only a few seconds (plus the time to download the images, if necessary). Note that because of restart: always, the containers are restarted automatically even after a reboot of the computer.

```
cd wordpress-example        (directory with docker-compose.yml)
docker compose up -d
  Creating network wordpress-example_default" with the default
    driver
  Creating wordpress-example_wordpress_1 ... done
  Creating wordpress-example_db_1        ... done
```

The docker ps command displays the two running containers (the output is heavily abridged due to space limitations). After a few seconds required to initialize the container, you can start using WordPress at the address, *localhost:8082*.

```
docker ps
  ID       PORTS                    NAMES
  5211...  0.0.0.0:8082->80/tcp  wordpress-example_wordpress_1
  d9dc...  3306/tcp                 wordpress-example_db_1
```

To stop the execution of all related containers, you need to run docker compose stop. Similarly, docker compose start continues the execution. These commands each require *docker-compose.yml* to be in the current directory.

You can use docker compose down to stop and delete all the containers of the setups, while the volumes will remain intact. If necessary, you can redeploy the containers and keep the previous data using docker compose up:

```
docker compose down          (stop and delete containers)
...
docker compose up -d         (set up new containers)
```

If you want to delete the containers and their associated volumes, you should run the following commands for this example:

```
docker compose down
docker volume rm wordpress-example_vol-db \
              wordpress-example_vol-www
```

5.4.2   "docker stack deploy"

Instead of using docker compose, you can also process the *docker-compose.yml* file via the docker stack deploy command. docker stack requires that the computer is a member of a Docker swarm. However, you absolutely don't need to create a Docker cluster to use docker stack. It's perfectly sufficient to run docker swarm init once on your machine. This way, your computer creates a swarm that consists of only one member. (We'll show you how to use "real" Docker clusters composed of multiple computers in Chapter 19.)

```
docker swarm init
  Swarm initialized: current node (eqbx...) is now a manager.
  To add a worker to this swarm, run the following command:
    docker swarm join --token SWMTKN-xxx 10.0.0.1:2377
  To add a manager to this swarm, run
  'docker swarm join-token manager' and follow the instructions.
```

To deploy the containers described in *docker-compose.yml* along with a network, you must pass the file name of the compose file to docker stack deploy with the -c option and the name of the setup or stack as another parameter. This name will be prepended to the network, volume, and service names. (docker compose uses the name of the directory where *docker-compose.yml* is located instead of this name by default.)

```
docker stack deploy -c docker-compose.yml stacktest
  Creating network stacktest_default
  Creating service stacktest_wordpress
  Creating service stacktest_db
```

docker stack ls proves that the new stack has been set up and consists of two services:

```
docker stack ls
  NAME         SERVICES   ORCHESTRATOR
  stacktest    2          Swarm
```

You can now use docker service ls to verify that the services have actually been created and are up and running. As before, the output had to be shortened by a few columns:

```
docker service ls
  ID             NAME                   REPLICAS  PORTS         ...
  skz4ab9p71va   stacktest_db           1/1
  ghdrn0z2gi5n   stacktest_wordpress    1/1       *:8082->80/tcp
```

The REPLICAS column is decisive here. If it reads 0/1, an error occurred during startup. Information about the cause of the error can be obtained from the ERROR column of the output of docker service ps <sid/stackname>, where you pass the service ID or stack name as a parameter. The command specifies which tasks are executed in a service. The ERROR column is usually truncated to the point of being unrevealing. Then, the --no-trunc option can provide help:

```
docker service ps sometest --no-trunc
  ... NAME              ... ERROR
      stacktest_db.1        starting container failed: Invalid
                            address 10.0.1.14: It does not belong
                            to any of this network's subnets
```

With docker ps, you can verify that a corresponding container has been created and launched for each service.

Unlike containers, there's no way to stop and later restart stacks. However, you can delete the entire stack with all its services and networks using docker stack rm:

```
docker stack rm stacktest
  Removing service stacktest_db
  Removing service stacktest_wordpress
  Removing network stacktest_default
```

The volumes specified in *docker-compose.yml* are preserved in this process. For this reason, you can set up and rerun the stack later without losing any data:

```
docker stack deploy -c docker-compose.yml stacktest
```

When you no longer need the setup, you can delete both the stack and the mapped volumes:

```
docker stack rm stacktest
docker volume rm stacktest_vol-db stacktest_vol-www
```

5.4.3 Debugging

Ideally, when the containers are started by docker compose up, everything goes well. But what happens if errors occur? A first means of troubleshooting is to run docker compose up without the -d option. This way, all logging output of all containers occurs directly in the console. So, to a certain extent, you can follow what's going on in the containers.

Alternatively, you can use docker ps to take a look at the container list. There, you can usually tell immediately if there are containers that aren't running as planned or that are constantly being restarted. You can then use docker logs <cname> to read the logging output of the affected containers. docker compose logs shows the combined logging of all containers in the group.

As usual, you can use docker exec to start an additional interactive shell process to look inside a running container:

```
docker exec -it test_wordpress_1 /bin/sh
```

```
ps -ax
  PID TTY      STAT  TIME COMMAND
    1 ?        Ss    0:00 apache2 -DFOREGROUND
   66 ?        S     0:00 apache2 -DFOREGROUND
  ...
   78 pts/0    Ss    0:00 /bin/sh
   83 pts/0    R+    0:00 ps -ax
```

5.4.4 Interactive Use

It's not a good idea to specify an image in *docker-compose.yml* where no process is running permanently:

```
# File docker-compose.yml
# Container/service ends immediately because
# there is no background process
version: '3'
services:
  myservice1:
    image: alpine
```

If you now run docker compose up, the container in question will be set up and started, but the execution will again terminate immediately. The result looks similar when you run docker stack deploy, as the service gets set up and started, but due to the lack of a background process, its execution ends immediately. The swarm logic of Docker then keeps trying to start the service—but of course that doesn't help either. The REPLICAS column of docker service ls shows 0/1, and docker service ps lists various startup attempts but shows no error messages:

```
docker stack deploy -c docker-compose.yml test4

docker service ls
  ID              NAME           REPLICAS    IMAGE
  1t8cfulkpxoz    test4_myservice1    0/1           alpine:latest

docker service ps 1t8cfulkpxoz
  ID              ...   DESIRED STATE    CURRENT STATE              ERROR
  kolqn5wnzgp2          Ready            Ready 4 seconds ago
  yrzb2d0g4arc          Shutdown         Complete 10 seconds ago
  y3ojrkgfv6sw          Shutdown         Complete a minute ago
  y54o8unhqf8s          Shutdown         Complete a minute ago
  xayg2njehiyj          Shutdown         Complete 2 minutes ago
```

It will probably be an exceptional case, but it *is* possible to create a container for interactive use with docker compose. To do this, you must use docker compose to execute the run <servicename> command instead of up. The additional option --rm causes the container to be deleted after exiting the shell.

```
docker compose run --rm myservice1

  cat /etc/os-release
    NAME="Alpine Linux"
    PRETTY_NAME="Alpine Linux v3.13"
    ...
  exit
```

There's no comparable interactive usage variant for docker stack deploy because docker stack is based on the concept of services, and the interactive operation of a service doesn't make any sense.

5.5   The docker-compose.yml File

This section provides an overview of the major keywords that can appear in the *docker-compose.yml* file. You can find a complete reference here:

https://docs.docker.com/compose/compose-file

docker-compose.yml starts with the version number, and, in this book, we're using version 3, which has been valid since 2017. Strictly speaking, version 3.8 has been in effect since 2019, and by the time this book is published, there may be another minor version. If you use new features in *docker-compose.yml*, you must also specify the corresponding version number.

This is followed by the `services` identifier, which is indented and followed by the names of several services that can be freely selected. The features of each service are specified (again indented) by various keywords:

```
# Basic structure of docker-compose.yml
version: "3"

services:
  servicename1:
    keyword1: setting1
    keyword2: setting2
    ...

  servicename2:
    keyword1: setting1
    keyword2: setting2
    ...
```

In some cases, the `services` section at the top level is followed by other top-level sections, such as `volumes`, `networks`, or `secrets`. These are usually associated with keywords of the same name within a service. Corresponding examples will follow in the coming sections.

5.5.1   Image or Dockerfile?

The `image` keyword specifies which base image is to be used. Image names in all variants (`reponame/imagename:tag`) and image IDs are permitted.

```
image: ubuntu:20.04
```

Unless you use `docker stack deploy`, you can also specify the path to a directory where the *Dockerfile* is located instead of an image:

```
build: directory
```

`docker compose` then takes into account the information in this file, creates an appropriate image, and uses it as a base. If you saved the *Dockerfile* in the same directory as *docker-compose.yml*, you merely need to specify a dot instead of the path.

5.5.2   Networks

`docker compose` or `docker stack deploy` automatically sets up a separate network for the containers or services to be executed. If you also want to set up additional networks and use them in your services, you must define your own `networks` with the top-level keyword networks and reference them in the services section with another networks keyword.

In the following example, the web service can communicate with the myownnet network. This is the host network that's always available in Docker (see docker network ls).

```
services:
  web:
    ...
    networks:
      - myownnet

# Top-level section for defining additional networks
networks:
  myownnet:
    external:
      name: host
```

5.5.3 Network Ports

The ports keyword is followed by a list of port mappings in the syntax, portnumber (simply forward the port) or local:service (redirect a service port to another local computer port). The following setting makes ports 80 and 443 of the Docker container or service accessible on ports 8080 and 8443 of the Docker host:

```
ports:
  - "8080:80"
  - "8443:443"
```

If you want to share a port only within the network that docker compose or docker stack deploy creates for the project's containers or services, you can specify these ports using expose:

```
expose:
  - "7500"
  - "7501"
```

5.5.4 Volumes

The volumes keyword is also followed by a list where you specify the local locations in the Docker host where the image's volume directories should be stored. The following entry causes the /var/lib/mysql volume of the image to be stored in the /data/db directory of the Docker host. This directory must already exist when docker compose or docker stack deploy is run.

```
volumes:
  - /data/db:/var/lib/mysql
```

The path for the local volume directory may also be specified relative to the location of the *docker-compose.yml* file in the form `./<name>`. On Fedora and RHEL, you must specify the additional `:z` flag for volumes that aren't to be stored inside `/var/lib/docker`.

Volumes in the Home Directory

The local volume path (i.e., the part before the colon) is evaluated relative to the *docker-compose.yml* file. If you want a path relative to the active user's home directory, you can start the path with ~.

`docker compose` doesn't interpret the mere specification of `<name>` as a relative path, but as a name for a named volume! `docker compose` expects an additional `volumes` section at the top level in this case, where the details of the `<name>` volume are defined. A corresponding example follows in the next section.

Note that individual files are also considered volumes. In this case, the local file in question must already exist. But be careful not to mix directories and files. For example, you can't map a local file to an image directory or a local directory to an image file.

```
volumes:
  - ./default.conf:/etc/nginx/conf.d/default.conf
```

5.5.5   Named Volumes

To define named volumes, you simply need to prefix the volume directory with the desired name (`webdata` in the following example). However, you must specify the volume a second time in the top-level `volumes`. There you can set special properties of the volume if necessary:

```
# File docker-compose.yml in directory test2
version: '3'
services:
  nginx:
    volumes:
      - webdata:/var/www/html/
    ...

volumes:
  webdata:
```

Docker takes care of setting up the volume. The volume name is composed of the current directory name, the name specified in *docker-compose.yml*, and `data_`. Provided you run Docker with root privileges and the current directory is test2, the following path will result:

```
/var/lib/docker/volumes/test2_webdata/_data
```

> **Volumes for Services**
>
> In a Docker swarm, the swarm manager decides on which node to run a service. This means the location can change at any time. When using volumes, this will cause problems: after all, a volume set up on node A during the first run doesn't exist on node B, where the service might run the next time.
>
> To work around this problem, you can use deploy.placement.constraints in the deploy settings to specify rules about which node the service should run on.

5.5.6   Environment Variables

The environment keyword is optionally followed by key-value pairs or list items in the form var=value. The environment variables defined in this way apply when the command is executed in the container. The following two listings are equivalent:

```
environment:
  WORDPRESS_DB_HOST: mariadb
  WORDPRESS_DB_NAME: dockerbook

environment:
  - WORDPRESS_DB_HOST=mariadb
  - WORDPRESS_DB_NAME=dockerbook
```

If you need to set many environment variables, you can also read the settings from a file via env_file: filename.

5.5.7   Command Execution

Typically, the command that's specified in the image by ENTRYPOINT and/or CMD is executed in containers or services (see also Chapter 4, Section 4.1.5). For an Apache image, this will be a start command for the web server; for a MySQL image, it will be the service of the MySQL server; and so on.

If a different command is to be executed, you must specify it using the entrypoint and/or command keywords. Note that you must pass commands that are composed of multiple parts either as a list or in the form ["part1", "part2", "part3"].

```
entrypoint: ["some-script.sh"]
command:    ["/bin/bash"]
```

```
# multi-part command
command: ["php", "-a"]

# equivalent
command:
  - "php"
  - "-a"
```

5.5.8   Restart Behavior

For containers created with `docker compose`, you can use the `restart` keyword to specify whether they should be restarted automatically on a machine restart or after an error. The default behavior is `no`. The other permitted settings are `always`, `on-failure`, or `unless-stopped`. (For a detailed explanation of the keywords, see Chapter 6, Section 6.5.)

```
restart: always
```

The `restart` keyword is ignored by `docker stack deploy`. For stack services, the default is to automatically restart the services when needed. You can specify different settings with `deploy.restart_policy`, as discussed in the next section.

5.5.9   Deploy Settings

The `deploy` keyword controls how services are `deployed` through `docker stack deploy`. These settings only apply to Docker Swarm mode. `docker compose` ignores the `deploy` keyword and all settings derived from it!

The following list summarizes the most important keywords:

- `deploy.mode` specifies how the service is executed. The default setting is `replicated`. This can be used to specify how many instances will be executed. The swarm manager then decides on which Docker machines to launch the instances.

  The alternate setting `global` determines that exactly one instance of the service should be executed on each node in the swarm.

- `deploy.placement.constraint` specifies a list of rules that determines on which node the service is supposed to run. The following lines provide examples of possible rules:

  ```
  - node.id==<xxxx>
  - node.hostname==<name>
  - node.role==manager|worker
  ```

- `deploy.replicas` specifies how many instances of the service must run concurrently (usually only one instance).

- `deploy.resources.limits.cpus` limits the CPU usage of the service. The setting `0.25` indicates that the service is allowed to utilize a CPU core up to 25% on average.
- `deploy.resources.limits.memory` sets an upper limit for the memory requirements of the service.
- `deploy.restart_policy.condition: any|on-failure|none` specifies under which circumstances a service should be restarted automatically (any by default).
- `deploy.restart_policy.delay` determines how many seconds Docker should wait before restarting a service (0 by default).
- `deploy.restart_policy.max_attempts` limits the number of restarts (no limit by default).

In *docker-compose.yml*, the settings must be formulated using indentations as usual:

```
version: '3.1'

services:
  nginx:
    image: nginx:alpine
    deploy:
      placement:
        constraints:
          - node.hostname == "dockerhost7"
      replicas: 5
      resources:
        limits:
          cpus: '0.25'
          memory: 50M
      restart_policy:
        condition: on-failure
        delay: 2s
```

5.6   Passwords and Other Secrets

In Section 5.4, we passed the MySQL password as an environment variable to the two containers or services. In terms of safety, of course, this isn't perfect. It's better to transfer passwords, Secure Shell (SSH) keys, Secure Sockets Layer (SSL) certificates, and comparable data as so-called *secrets* between Docker containers or services.

For this purpose, docker compose provides the secrets keyword, which you need to specify in *docker-compose.yml* at least twice: once within the service you want to define, and a second time as a top-level section. In *docker-compose.yml*, you must specify at least version number 3.1 because secrets are supported only from this version onward.

In the following example, the contents of the local *./top-secret.txt* file (where the path is relative to *docker-compose.yml*) are accessible in the container via the path */run/secrets/password*. The file contains the string very secret :-).

```
# File docker-compose.yml
version: '3.1'

services:
  secrettest:
    image: alpine
    secrets:
      - password
    command: ["cat", "/run/secrets/password"]

secrets:
  password:
    file: ./top-secret.txt
```

If you try out the example, you can use cat to output the contents of the */run/secrets/password* file. After that, the container execution will terminate.

```
docker-compose up
  Recreating alpine-secret_secrettest_1 ... done
  Attaching to alpine-secret_secrettest_1
  secrettest_1  | very secret :-)
  alpine-secret_secrettest_1 exited with code 0
```

5.6.1   Sharing MariaDB/MySQL Passwords between Two Containers

The following example is somewhat more sophisticated. Here, you first create the two text files *mysql-user-pw.txt* and *mysql-root-pw.txt* in the same directory where *docker-compose.yml* is located. These files contain two passwords.

In each of the wordpress and mariadb services, you can use secrets to specify which of the secrets files you want to use. You can initialize the environment variables WORD-PRESS_DB_PASSWORD_FILE, MYSQL_ROOT_PASSWORD_FILE, and MYSQL_PASSWORD_FILE provided in the WordPress or MariaDB image with the corresponding paths to */run/secrets/<name>*. (The rest of the listing structure is the same as the *docker-compose.yml* file from Section 5.4).

```
# File test/docker-compose.yml (listing shortened)
version: '3.1'
services:
  db:
    image: mariadb:latest
```

```
    secrets:
      - mysql_root
      - mysql_user
    environment:
      MYSQL_ROOT_PASSWORD_FILE: /run/secrets/mysql_root
      MYSQL_PASSWORD_FILE: /run/secrets/mysql_user
      ...

  wordpress:
    image: wordpress:latest
    secrets:
      - mysql_user
    environment:
      WORDPRESS_DB_PASSWORD_FILE: /run/secrets/mysql_user
      ...

secrets:
  mysql_root:
    file: ./mysql-root-pw.txt
  mysql_user:
    file: ./mysql-user-pw.txt
```

5.6.2   Secure Exchange of Secrets

Behind the scenes, secrets are transported in different ways:

- When you use docker compose, the local secret file gets mapped to the container's file system via mount --bind or using gRPC (a protocol for calling functions in distributed systems). Current Docker versions use gRPC and its file system driver grpcfuse to exchange directories between a host and a container.

- If, on the other hand, you use docker stack deploy, the command will first create the required secrets with docker secret create. These are made available to the service and thus ultimately to the container as a temporary file system (tmpfs).

  If you use docker stack deploy, you also specify external: true instead of file: <name> in the top-level secrets section.

  ```
  secrets:
    secret_name:
      external: true
  ```

  This means that docker stack deploy is supposed to use a secret that already exists (from another service, or because you previously defined it via docker secrets).

Both variants prevent the secret from ending up in the container's file system and thus being stored permanently.

Chapter 6
Tips, Tricks, and Internal Details

This chapter contains tips, tricks, and technical details for using Docker on a broad list of topics:

- **Docker with Visual Studio Code and Portainer**
  In this book, we assume that you use Docker functions at the command level. Sometimes, however, graphical user interfaces (GUIs) can make Docker easier to use. Two examples are the *VS Code* editor and the web interface, *Portainer*.

- **Pull limit**
  Since the end of 2020, Docker allows only 100 anonymous pull requests within a period of six hours. We'll explain why this limit was established and what you can do if it restricts your Docker application.

- **Different CPU architectures**
  The dominance of the x86-64 architecture is on the wane. We'll describe what you need to consider when working on computers with a different CPU architecture. In this context, we'll specifically refer to ARM and Apple computers with M1 CPUs.

- **Automatic container start**
  Depending on the application, it may be desirable for Docker to start certain containers automatically, either as soon as you log in, or without logging in for server operations. In the first case, it's sufficient to run the container with the `--restart` option. We'll cover the second case for Linux only and show you how to set up an appropriate service file for systemd.

- **Internal details**
  In the final section of this chapter, we'll take a look behind the scenes of Docker. Among others, we'll answer the following questions: Where and how are containers and images stored? What are namespaces? How does Docker work on macOS and Windows? How do you limit the main memory used by Docker on Windows?

6.1 Visual Studio Code

There are two extensions for the popular VS Code editor that simplify working with Docker: *Docker Extension* and *Remote Containers*. In this section, we'll briefly introduce both extensions.

> **VS Code on Linux**
>
> On Linux, the Docker extensions for VS Code only work satisfactorily if the docker command can be executed without sudo. For this purpose, you must either use rootless Docker or connect your account to the docker group (sudo usermod -aG docker <username>). Keep in mind that this group assignment indirectly gives the respective user root privileges (see Section 6.6).

6.1.1   Docker Extension

Microsoft's official *Docker Extension* provides a whole host of features (see Figure 6.1).

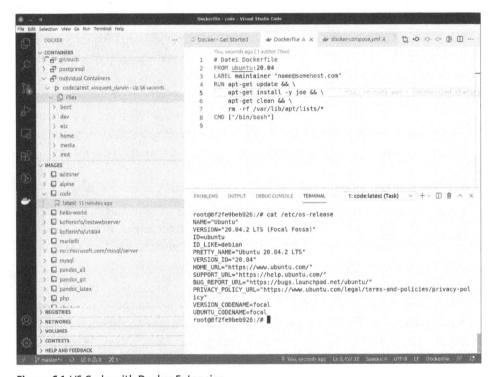

Figure 6.1 VS Code with Docker Extension

By clicking on the **Docker** icon, you can scroll through all containers, images, volumes, and networks in the sidebar (in the Explorer). You can start and stop containers, update images (pull), create new containers from images, delete unused volumes, and so on, by a click of the mouse.

For running containers, you can even look into the container's file system, open individual files, and modify them directly in VS Code.

VS Code helps you write *Dockerfiles* and Docker Compose files with syntax highlighting and keyword auto-completion.

Using the context menu (or pressing `F1`) and selecting **Docker images: Build image** allows you to create an image for a *Dockerfile*. Similarly, when editing a Docker Compose file, context menu commands such as **Compose up** are available for selection in the sidebar.

6.1.2   Remote Containers

The *Remote Containers* extension has also been developed by Microsoft. Strictly speaking, it's a variant of the much better known *Remote SSH* extension, which allows you to use VS Code to edit files located on an external computer that's accessible via SSH.

The *Remote Containers* extension works in a similar way by allowing you to edit files that are located in a (currently running) container. What's new, however, is the associated concept of *Development Containers*: This concept involves adding the *.devcontainer* directory to a software development project. This directory, in turn, contains a *Dockerfile* and the *devcontainer.json* file. These two files describe the image required for the development and its application.

To familiarize yourself with Remote Containers, you should install the sample project provided by Microsoft on your computer:

```
git clone https://github.com/Microsoft/vscode-remote-try-node
```

In VS Code, open the project directory via `F1`, and select **Remote-Containers: Open Folder in Container**. VS Code then automatically creates the image described by the *Dockerfile* and starts a container derived from it. After that, you can edit the project files in VS Code. A green section at the bottom left of the VS Code status bar indicates that you aren't currently working locally but in a development container (see Figure 6.2).

We haven't tested Development Container comprehensively. However, the concept definitely seems to be pretty useful as it enables you to quickly and easily get a development project managed with `git` up and running on different development machines. That doesn't necessarily mean the idea will gain widespread acceptance, however.

In a way, the Development Container extension seems to reflect the different worlds of thinking of Microsoft versus Unix/Linux. Microsoft usually tries to create *one* user interface (UI) or program that covers all needs. For developers, this product used to be Visual Studio, and now VS Code is evolving in this direction. On Linux, on the other hand, the goal is usually to develop many small, independent tools that are functional in themselves and can be combined in any way. Both approaches are very successful, but they probably appeal to different target groups.

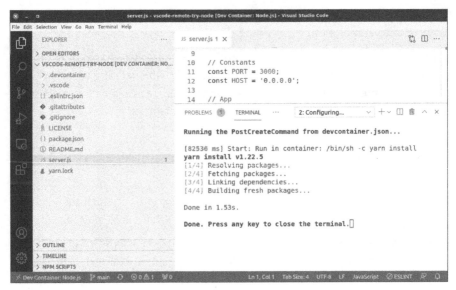

Figure 6.2 A Development Container Opened in VS Code

If you want to read more about Development Container, the best place to start is the Remote Container plug-in page and the syntax description for the *devcontainer.json* file:

- *https://marketplace.visualstudio.com/items?itemName=ms-vscode-remote.remote-containers*
- *https://code.visualstudio.com/docs/remote/devcontainerjson-reference*

Development Container versus Developer Environment

Interestingly, the current version of Docker Desktop advertises a very similar, but not yet finished, feature called *Developer Environments*. On the GitHub roadmap page, the idea is promoted separately from VS Code as a future feature of Docker, which Docker is actively working on right now. Possibly a new feature of Docker will grow out of this idea by the time this book is published:

https://github.com/docker/roadmap/issues/201

6.2 Portainer

If you're looking for a UI to administrate Docker and related products, you should take a look at the *Portainer* program (see Section 6.3). It helps you manage Docker, Docker Swarm, Kubernetes, and Azure Container Instances (ACI). The open-source program can be used either as a free Community Edition or as a Business Edition with additional functions (*https://portainer.io*).

Portainer currently only supports Ubuntu and Windows. It should also work on other distributions, but we've carried out our tests only with the Community Edition on Ubuntu 21.04.

Figure 6.3 Portainer Web UI

Significantly, Portainer is installed as a Docker container. Basically, only the first two commands are required to set up Portainer as a web application that can be used through port 9000.

```
docker volume create portainer_data
```

```
docker run -d -p 8000:8000 -p 9000:9000 --name=portainer \
  --restart=always \
  -v /var/run/docker.sock:/var/run/docker.sock \
  -v portainer_data:/data \
  portainer/portainer-ce
```

Tip

Instead of manually typing the preceding commands, which is rather error-prone, you can copy them from the following page:

https://documentation.portainer.io/v2.0/deploy/ceinstalldocker

---

After starting the Portainer container, you must open the *localhost:9000* page in the web browser and set a password for the admin user. The next step is to log in and specify that you want to administrate Docker (not Docker Swarm or Kubernetes). This will take you to the web interface where you can administrate containers, stacks (usually container groups created by docker compose), images, volumes, and so on.

In our tests, Portainer made an exceptionally good impression. While the features of Docker Desktop seem very half-hearted, Portainer actually simplifies the administration of a large number of containers and images. Of course, the docker command ultimately provides the same functions, but Portainer can be used intuitively and efficiently even if you haven't memorized all the docker commands and options. Portainer is the editor's choice!

6.2.1   Tidying Up

If Portainer doesn't convince you, you can uninstall it as follows:

```
docker stop portainer
docker rm portainer
docker volume rm portainer_data
```

6.3   Pull Limit in Docker Hub

In mid-2020, Docker whipped its fan community into a frenzy with the following announcement: "Free access for pull requests in Docker Hub has been limited." After it turned out that many Docker users weren't affected at all by that or could work around the limit with a *free* account, it has become a bit quieter again around this topic.

This section describes why Docker has decided to impose a pull limit, which exceptions apply, and how you can increase or work around the limit if necessary.

Restrictions also for Docker Desktop

Note that apart from the pull limit, there are also restrictions on the commercial use of Docker Desktop, which is the GUI for Docker. Free use is only permitted for home users and small businesses:

www.docker.com/pricing/faq

6.3.1   Lots of Activity in Docker Hub

During the *DockerCon Live* event in spring 2021, Docker published the following figures, not without pride:

- There are currently more than 7 million applications (images) in Docker Hub.
- There are more than 11 million developers using Docker Hub every month.
- More than 13 billion images are downloaded per month (about 18 million images every hour!).

This makes Docker Hub by far the largest public marketplace for images. Not explicitly stated was the fact that Docker Hub is of course also available to alternative container systems such as Podman. In other words, any container software compatible with Docker (and thus any competing product) may also use Docker Hub. When you install Podman (see Appendix A), Docker Hub gets set up as an image repository by default.

It's obvious that running the infrastructure for Docker Hub is expensive. At the same time, however, Docker finds it difficult to make money from its offerings. That situation led to the sale of Docker's enterprise division in 2019. The revenue generated in this way went into the further development of Docker products and infrastructure. Docker's purpose with regard to the pull limit is twofold: (1) to encourage companies to purchase paid Docker accounts; and (2) to motivate larger Docker users to set up or use their own repositories. In fact, various alternative image repositories have been announced recently.

6.3.2   No Unlimited Access to Images

Thus, since the end of 2020, pull access to Docker Hub has been limited (see Table 6.1). If you exceed the limit that applies to you when running docker pull or docker run, the following error will occur:

```
docker pull <imagename>
  You have reached your pull rate limit. You may increase the
  limit by authenticating and upgrading:
  https://www.docker.com/increase-rate-limits
```

Account	Quantity
Anonymous access without login	100/6 hours
Personal (free of charge, but with login)	200/6 hours
With Pro or Team account	5,000/24 hours

Table 6.1 Number of Pull Requests Permitted (as of September 2022)

You probably won't reach these limits in your normal everyday development work. (During the rather intensive work on this book, we didn't even come close to the limits.) But the limit can very likely apply if you download images and launch containers in an automated manner across several hosts—that is, if you use Docker, possibly in combination with Kubernetes—in production operation on a group of servers. The same applies to automated build systems with continuous integration and continuous delivery (CI/CD).

Limits Apply per User, Not per Image!

The pull limits are calculated on a user-specific basis and aren't assigned to individual images. So, for example, 10,000 different anonymous users can download the same

> image within six hours. However, *one* user can download no more than 100 images per six hours.
>
> But there's a serious problem with anonymous access to Docker: For requests without login, Docker uses the IP addresses for counting purposes. For companies or cloud systems whose private network uses only *one* IPv4 address externally (Network Address Translation [NAT]), all pull requests are added up. This means that when several developers or build tools work in parallel, they'll exceed the limit very quickly.

You can use the following commands on macOS or Linux to determine the total number of permitted downloads (pull requests) within six hours when accessing Docker Hub anonymously (ratelimit-limit). The ratelimit-remaining line indicates how many accesses are still available. Here, w reveals the time period in seconds that applies to the limit.

```
TOKEN=$(curl "https://auth.docker.io/token?service=registry.\
  docker.io&scope=repository:ratelimitpreview/test:pull" \
  | jq -r .token)

curl --head -H "Authorization: Bearer $TOKEN" \
  https://registry-1.docker.io/v2/ratelimitpreview/test/\
  manifests/latest

  HTTP/1.1 200 OK
  content-length: 2782
  ...
  ratelimit-limit:      100;w=21600
  ratelimit-remaining:  99;w=21600
```

Instead of typing the preceding commands, it's better to copy them from the following Docker documentation page. There you'll also find commands that apply to pull requests with login, that is, for a Free, Pro, or Team account:

https://docs.docker.com/docker-hub/download-rate-limit

The command to determine a token uses jq. This tool helps to process JavaScript Object Notation (JSON) strings. It may need to be installed separately:

```
apt/dnf install jq        (Linux)
brew install jq           (macOS)
```

6.3.3   Bypassing the Limit

If you're affected by the pull limit, there are a number of ways to raise the limit or work around it:

■ **Using Docker with login**
As a first step, you should set up a Personal account on the Docker website. If you use macOS or Windows, you should log in to Docker Desktop afterwards. On Linux, you need to run `docker login` once instead (see Chapter 4, Section 4.3). This doesn't cost anything and at least doubles the pull limit.

If multiple developers work on a shared company network with NAT, using Personal accounts is mostly unavoidable. As mentioned earlier, Docker maps the anonymous pull requests to the externally visible IP address and therefore adds the anonymous requests of all coworkers.

■ **Pro or Team account**
Docker would of course be delighted if you or your company purchased a Pro or Team account.

■ **Exceptions for open-source projects**
Established open-source organizations can apply with Docker to be included in an open-source program. Not only does the somewhat vague description of this program promise unlimited and free use by project participants, but also the resulting images will be exempt from the download limit for *all* Docker users: "For the approved ... projects, we ... will suspend data pull rate restrictions, where no egress restrictions will apply to any Docker users pulling images from the approved OSS namespaces."

www.docker.com/blog/expanded-support-for-open-source-software-projects

We haven't found any further information on this topic. Because most of the images provided in Docker Hub are based on open-source software, we're quite skeptical about whether or how this program will be implemented in practice.

■ **Mirror registry**
For larger enterprises, it may be appropriate to set up a separate image registry that acts as a cache for Docker Hub. The first pull request is then redirected to Docker Hub, but on the second request, the mirror can respond to the request. This leads to a significant reduction in the number of pull requests to Docker Hub. You can find corresponding instructions here:

– *https://docs.docker.com/registry*

– *https://docs.docker.com/registry/recipes/mirror*

– *https://circleci.com/docs/2.0/docker-hub-pull-through-mirror*

– *https://goharbor.io/docs/2.1.0/administration/configure-proxy-cache*

Subsequently, you must enter the address of your mirror in the local */etc/docker/daemon.json* file using the `registry-mirror` keyword:

```
{
  "registry-mirrors": ["https://<my-local-registry-mirror>"]
}
```

- **Using another registry**

  No one forces you to use Docker Hub as an image repository. Of course, Docker Hub is the first and most convenient choice, but since Docker introduced the pull limit, more and more large IT companies (including Amazon) have announced that they are setting up their own registries (see the following section).

6.3.4   Using Alternative Registries

Quite a few companies—Amazon, Google, IBM/Red Hat, Microsoft—provide image registries:

- Amazon: *https://aws.amazon.com/de/ecr*
- Google: *https://cloud.google.com/container-registry*
- IBM/Red Hat: *https://catalog.redhat.com/software/containers/explore*
- Microsoft: *https://docs.microsoft.com/en-us/azure/container-registry*

The registries work in a very similar way to Docker Hub, but they are mostly reserved for paying customers. The use of such registries is a good idea if you or your company already use cloud or container services with one of the companies in question. Then the registry usage may already be included in the price.

In the simplest case, you need to prepend the desired registry to the image name when running docker pull or docker run. The following two commands download the amazon-linux image (a variant to CentOS Linux 7) from the public Amazon Web Services (AWS) registry and execute it. (If you've already downloaded the latest version, you only need to execute the second command.)

```
docker pull public.ecr.aws/amazonlinux/amazonlinux
  latest: Pulling from amazonlinux/amazonlinux
  b703fcc79e4a: Pull complete
  ...
  public.ecr.aws/amazonlinux/amazonlinux:latest

docker run -it --rm public.ecr.aws/amazonlinux/amazonlinux
```

Quality and Timeliness Vary Greatly Depending on the Registry

If you've only worked with Docker Hub so far, you can assume that the most important images provided there (at least all official images as well as all images from verified providers) are always up to date. Unfortunately, if you switch to other public registries, this assumption is far from always true. You should use only well-maintained images from trusted sources. This basic rule also applies to Docker Hub, of course; but it applies even more to registries that aren't as established yet.

Surprisingly, Docker doesn't provide a way to set up another registry as the default source for images instead of Docker Hub:

- *https://stackoverflow.com/questions/33054369*
- *https://github.com/moby/moby/issues/11815*

For this reason, you must always prefix the registry name with the docker pull or docker run commands. Things are much easier when you use Podman. In this case, the registries to be used can be defined in */etc/containers/registries.conf* (see also Appendix A).

6.4   Using Different CPU Architectures

Until recently, one thing was clear to most development teams: new code is to be programmed on computers with x86-compatible CPUs from Intel or AMD. Servers with x86 CPUs are also used in production operation. However, this view of the world is currently being severely shaken: from Raspberry Pi to the new Macs with ARM ("Apple Silicon") to new types of servers with countless cores (*Ampere Altra*, *NEOVERSE*, etc.), computers with ARM CPUs are on the rise. The main arguments for the ARM architecture are lower prices and higher performance per watt.

Basically, Docker has been supporting machines with different architectures for years. However, in this section, we'll focus specifically on using Docker on ARM systems due to the lack of testing capabilities on other architectures.

Running Docker requires more than ARM-compatible binaries of docker, dockerd, and so on. All images also need to be compiled for the ARM architecture. For example, if you run a container with Alpine Linux on an Apple machine with an M1 CPU, it will use a completely different image than on a Windows or Linux notebook with an Intel or AMD CPU.

Each image must therefore explicitly support the architecture in question and be compiled accordingly. Because almost all Docker images are based on open-source software, that isn't a fundamental problem. Nevertheless, porting software, including all the necessary libraries, to other architectures often isn't a trivial matter.

A prominent example of this problem was the MySQL database server. In 2021, there was no official MySQL image for ARM. Docker recommended switching to MariaDB until an ARM-compatible version of MySQL became available, which happened only a few months later.

We took a look at Docker Hub in 2021, where you can filter very well for images based on architecture (see Figure 6.4). Even though the range of offerings for ARM is considerable, it can't keep up with the abundance of images for x86 architectures by far (see Table 6.2). Of course, numbers can be deceptive, as there are countless images in Docker Hub that were created as part of a test or a small project, but haven't been maintained in a long time. Figuratively speaking, there's lots of chaff, but little wheat. Ultimately, the only thing that matters is that you find the images that are important to you.

The greater the number of Docker users who work on ARM architectures in their day-to-day development, the larger the range of images provided will naturally be. In this respect, we expect the figures presented here to change significantly in favor of ARM in the coming months.

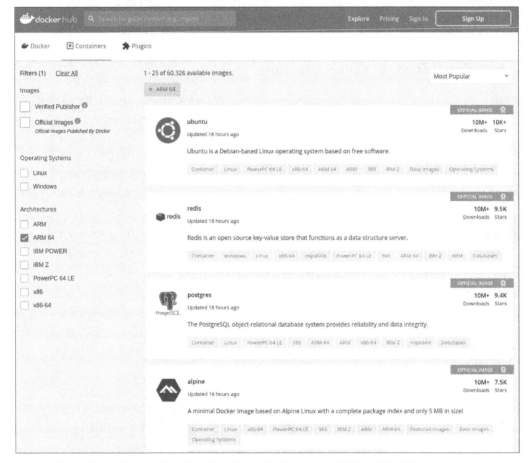

Figure 6.4 In Docker Hub, You Can Search For Images in Different Architectures

CPU Architecture	Total Number of Images	Official/Verified Images
x86-64	Approx. 6,200,000	Approx. 8,200
ARM 64	Approx. 200,000	Approx. 2,500
ARM	Approx. 80,000	Approx. 1,700

Table 6.2 Images Provided in Docker Hub for Selected CPU Architectures (as of Sept. 2022)

6.4.1   Working on ARM Computers

If you're unsure as to which architecture the Docker installation on your machine uses, you can simply run `docker version`:

```
docker version | grep Arch
  OS/Arch:  darwin/arm64
  OS/Arch:  linux/arm64
```

Basically, you don't need to follow any special rules when working on a computer with ARM architecture. When you use `docker run` to download an image and launch the corresponding container, Docker automatically considers only images that are available for your architecture. If necessary, you'll receive an error message that the desired image doesn't support the CPU architecture of your computer:

```
docker pull mysql
  latest: Pulling from library/mysql
  no matching manifest for linux/arm64/v8 in the manifest
  list entries
```

In Docker repositories, an image can have variants for multiple architectures. An enumeration of the architectures available for selection is provided by `docker manifest inspect <imagename>`:

```
docker manifest inspect alpine | grep architecture
  "architecture": "amd64",
  "architecture": "arm",
  "architecture": "arm",
  "architecture": "arm64",
  "architecture": "386",
  "architecture": "ppc64le",
  "architecture": "s390x",

docker manifest inspect mysql | grep architecture
  "architecture": "amd64",
```

Practical Experience

We tested many examples (but admittedly not all) on a Mac mini with M1 CPU while working on this book. Our experience with it has been predominantly good. In many cases, Docker behaves absolutely identically regardless of the architecture used. The biggest hurdle is currently the still comparatively small range of ARM-compatible images.

6.4.2   Running Containers of a Different Architecture

You can run images of a different architecture using an emulator (predominantly qemu or Rosetta). However, the use of an emulator is associated with noticeable performance drawbacks and is rarely recommended. The following command, which we tested on an Apple machine with an M1 CPU, runs the x86-64 image of Alpine Linux there:

```
armhost$ docker run -it --rm --platform linux/amd64 alpine
```

Note, however, that conversely it isn't straightforward to run a container based on an ARM image on an x86 machine:

```
x86host$ docker run -it --rm --platform arm64 alpine

  standard_init_linux.go:219: exec user process caused:
  exec format error
```

What you can do in those cases is install qemu and binfmt-support. This will allow Docker to run containers from other architectures through qemu. You can find concrete instructions on this process here:

- *www.stereolabs.com/docs/docker/building-arm-container-on-x86*
- *https://docs.nvidia.com/datacenter/cloud-native/playground/x-arch.html*

To determine which architecture a downloaded image uses, you need to run docker image inspect. Instead of the image name, you can also specify the image ID. This is useful if you've downloaded versions for different architectures from one image. Unfortunately, the docker images command doesn't give any indication of the architecture in such cases.

```
docker images

  REPOSITORY  ...  IMAGE ID      CREATED       SIZE
  alpine           6dbb9cc54074  6 weeks ago   5.61MB
  alpine           3fcaaf3dc95c  6 weeks ago   5.35MB
  ...
docker image inspect 6dbb9cc54074 | grep Arch
      "Architecture": "amd64",

docker image inspect 3fcaaf3dc95c | grep Arch
      "Architecture": "arm64",
```

Creating Your Own Multiplatform Images
The currently still experimental buildx command makes it relatively easy to create images that support multiple CPU platforms. buildx is basically compatible with

docker build, **but it works with additional keywords. You can find more information on it here:**

- *https://github.com/docker/buildx*
- *https://docker.events.cube365.net/dockercon-live/2021/content/Videos/6ee6H7Jm-LKqAv8C3Y*
- *www.docker.com/blog/multi-arch-build-and-images-the-simple-way*
- *https://docs.docker.com/desktop/multi-arch*

6.5   Starting Containers Automatically

Especially for testing server functions, it's often required that a container should be running permanently. So, when you log in and start working, the container should start immediately. This request can be easily fulfilled by passing the --restart always option when you start the container for the first time with docker run:

```
docker run -p 8080:80 --name apache \
  -v "${PWD}":/usr/local/apache2/htdocs \
  -d --restart always httpd
```

For the sake of completeness, we want to briefly repeat the meaning of the remaining options (see also Chapter 3):

- -p connects port 80 of the container to port 8080 of the host computer.

- --name assigns a name to the container.

- -v connects the current directory (the contents of the PWD environment variable) to the */usr/local/apache2/htdocs* directory of the container. This allows the web server to serve all files in the current directory via HTTP. (If you use Fedora, RHEL, and Co, you must additionally pass the SELinux flag :z with this option.)

- -d starts the web server as a background service. More information about using the httpd image will follow in Chapter 9, Section 9.1.

What's relevant for this section is the --restart option. There are four possible settings available:

- --restart no is applied by default. When the container ends, for whatever reason, it won't be restarted.

- --restart always causes the container to restart automatically when it ends. This restart rule also applies to a reboot of the computer! This starts the Docker service as part of the init process, which in turn starts all containers that were last running with the --restart always option.

  But be careful—--restart always also applies to a program termination caused by an error. If the container contains an error, the container may get started again and again. The only exception is a manual stop (`docker stop`) in which the container won't be restarted immediately. However, if you shut down your computer, the container will be started again on the next Docker restart.

- `--restart unless-stopped` works quite similar to `--restart always`. The difference is that a container terminated with `docker stop` won't be started automatically on the next Docker restart.

- `--restart on-failure` results in an automatic restart after a failure in the container, but no auto start when the Docker system is restarted.

You can determine the restart behavior set for a container with `docker inspect`:

```
docker inspect <containername>
  ...
  "RestartPolicy": {
      "Name": "always",
      "MaximumRetryCount": 0
  },
  ...
```

Using `docker update` you can change the update behavior of a container while it's running:

```
docker update --restart on-failure <containername>
```

6.5.1   Restart Behavior with docker compose

You can also specify an automatic restart in the *docker-compose.yml* file, using the `restart` keyword:

```
services:
  db:
    image: mariadb:latest
    restart: always
```

The four permitted settings are `no` (default), `always`, `unless-stopped`, and `on-failure`. The meaning of the keywords is similar to that for the `--restart` option of `docker run` described previously. The `restart: always` setting is valid until the services described by the *docker-compose.yml* file are explicitly stopped and deleted by `compose down`.

Make sure that you specify the `restart` keyword in the correct level, that is, directly in the settings of the respective container (`db` in the previous example)! One of the authors of this book has wondered for weeks why the restart behavior didn't work for the following *docker-compose.yml* file:

```
# Caution, the restart setting is incorrect here!
services:
  db:
    image: mariadb:latest
    volumes:
      - vol-db:/var/lib/mysql
    environment:
      MYSQL_USER: wpuser
      MYSQL_PASSWORD: secret
      restart: always
```

The cause of the error should be clear: the `restart` option is indented too far and doesn't reference the `db` container but instead references the `environment` settings, where `restart` is simply ignored. However, the incorrectly placed option doesn't result in a warning or even an error message.

6.5.2   Automatically Starting Docker Containers on a Linux Server with systemd

Instead of controlling the launch of containers through Docker, it's also possible to do this through operating system functions. This procedure is relatively cumbersome and is therefore rarely chosen in practice. However, it has the advantage that a container can be treated like a service of the operating system and controlled with the same commands. Furthermore, this startup variant also works in combination with rootless Docker and with Podman.

In this section, we'll focus on *systemd*, the dominant init system of Linux. Once the configuration is working, commands such as `systemctl restart` and `systemctl enable --now` can be applied to the container in question.

The starting point of the following example is a MySQL container that was first set up as a test and is now supposed to be started permanently. The volume with the databases is located in */home/kofler/docker-mysql-volume*. When the container was set up for the first time, the MySQL root password was set as well. It's stored in a database in the volume directory and therefore doesn't need to be passed with -e `MYSQL_ROOT_PASS-WORD=....`.

6.5.3   A Separate Service File

For systemd to take care of the startup on its own, a **.service* file must be set up in the */etc/systemd/system* directory. In our example, the file looks as follows:

```
# File /etc/systemd/system/docker-mysql.service
[Unit]
Description=starts MySQL server as Docker container
```

```
After=docker.service
Requires=docker.service

[Service]
RemainAfterExit=true
ExecStartPre=-/usr/bin/docker stop mysql-db-buch
ExecStartPre=-/usr/bin/docker rm mysql-db-buch
ExecStartPre=-/usr/bin/docker pull mysql
ExecStart=/usr/bin/docker run -d --restart unless-stopped \
  -v /home/kofler/docker-mysql-volume:/var/lib/mysql \
  -p 13306:3306 --name mysql-db-buch mysql
ExecStop=/usr/bin/docker stop mysql-db-buch

[Install]
WantedBy=multi-user.target
```

The Unit section describes the service. The Requires and After keywords ensure that the service won't get started before Docker.

The service section specifies the actions required to start or stop the service. The three ExecStartPre statements ensure that the container named mysql-db-book gets stopped and deleted and that the latest version of the MySQL image is downloaded. The minus sign in front of the stop and rm commands means that when these commands are executed, an error will simply be ignored. (If the image has already been stopped and/or deleted before, then this isn't a cause for concern.)

The ExecStart statement that runs across several lines finally starts the container using the volume directory /home/kofler/docker-mysql-volume and the host port 13306.

ExecStop specifies what needs to be done to stop the service.

RemainAfterExit=true means that systemd memorizes the currently activated state. Without this option, systemd would assume that the service has already ended after the successful execution of docker run, although the container continues to run in the background.

WantedBy in the Install section specifies that the service should be part of the multiuser target, which describes the normal operating state of a Linux server.

Of course, you can also call docker compose in the service file instead of docker. This is convenient if the desired service consists of a whole group of containers instead of just one container. You should keep in mind that when you call docker compose, you must explicitly specify the full location of the *docker-compose.yml* file via the -f option.

6.5.4   Starting and Ending the Service

For systemd to take the new service file into account, you must run the following command once:

```
systemctl daemon-reload
```

> **Note**
>
> If you've included an error in the service file and correct it later, don't forget to reexecute the preceding command!

The following commands enable you to test whether manually starting and stopping the Docker container works:

```
systemctl start docker-mysql
```

```
systemctl status docker-mysql
  docker-mysql.service - starts MySQL server as Docker container
    Loaded: loaded (/etc/systemd/system/docker-mysql.service;
                    disabled; vendor preset: enabled)
    Active: active (exited) since 19:28:20 CEST; 3min 41s ago
    ...
```

```
systemctl stop docker-mysql
```

If everything works out, you now need to permanently activate the automatic start of the service:

```
systemctl enable --now docker-mysql
```

If you don't need the service later on, you can terminate it permanently as follows:

```
systemctl disable --now docker-mysql
```

> **Comprehensive systemd Documentation**
>
> We can't go more into detail here about the basics of the systemd init system, but systemd is more than comprehensively documented:
>
> *www.freedesktop.org/wiki/Software/systemd*
>
> The problem is rather to find a reasonable starting point without being overwhelmed by details. A good introduction for readers with an affinity for Linux is the ArchLinux Wiki:
>
> *https://wiki.archlinux.org/title/Systemd*

6.6   A Look Behind the Scenes

If you merely want to use Docker, you can safely skip this section. But if you want to know how the processes of a Docker container work, where image files are stored, how the file system of a container is composed, and so on, then you'll find first answers in this section.

We're going to start with the Linux Docker Engine, that is, when a Linux machine is used as the Docker host. At the end of the section, you'll then see that this information is basically also valid for Windows and macOS. The key difference is that the file system and process execution are natively integrated on Linux, whereas on Windows and macOS, the Docker engine runs as a tiny Linux system in a virtual environment (WSL2 or macOS Hypervisor Framework).

6.6.1   docker, dockerd, and containerd

In addition to the docker command you're already familiar with, a Docker system runs two background services: dockerd and containerd. Strictly speaking, it's these background services that do all the work, such as downloading and saving images, creating and running containers, and so on. The primary purpose of the docker command is to pass commands to the Docker daemon and return its responses to the user.

In detail, docker communicates with dockerd, which in turn communicates with containerd. dockerd is responsible for the high-level tasks, while containerd communicates with the kernel, uses SELinux and control groups (cgroups) functions, and so on.

6.6.2   The Overlay File System

A central function of Docker is the handling of images and the file systems for the containers that are built on top of them. The basic approach is simple: multiple images are layered on top of each other as read-only file systems (see Figure 6.5). The foundation is the infrastructure provided by the Docker host, which consists of the kernel, device mapper, cgroups, and so on.

The starting point for a container is usually a base image, that is, an image that contains a minimal Linux system (e.g., Alpine Linux or Debian). Further images can then add applications to this system, such as a web server and a web application. In fact, in practice, there are usually many more layers than are shown here. The many layers are created in the build process, when an existing image is extended by additional components in the course of several steps.

At the top of this construction is the *container layer*. All changes to the file system composed by multiple images are physically stored in the container layer.

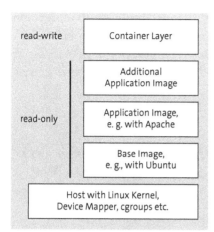

Figure 6.5 The Container's File System is Composed of Read-Only Images and a Mutable Container Layer

For the actual implementation of the overlay file system, Linux provides several variants to choose from. On most Linux distributions, Docker uses the overlay2 driver. If the host system uses btrfs, this file system can also perform the layering functions. Obsolete alternatives include aufs (refers to advanced multi-layered unification filesystem) and the vfs driver, which is primarily intended for testing purposes. On Windows and macOS, Docker uses the overlay2 driver, just like on Linux. Podman, on the other hand, is based on fuse-overlayfs.

You can determine which driver for the overlay file system you're using via docker info:

```
docker info | grep Storage
  Storage Driver: overlay2
```

6.6.3   The /var/lib/docker Directory

Now the question remains where the Docker images and container layers are actually stored in the host file system. Basically, all Docker data ends up in the */var/lib/docker* directory. However, this is again divided into numerous subdirectories, of which two are described here:

- */var/lib/docker/image* contains metadata about the images.

- */var/lib/docker/<overlay-driver>* contains the unpacked images, each optimized for the overlay file system in use (aufs, overlay2, btrfs, etc.). The diffs and merged subdirectories contain the changed and new files of the container layer, respectively, for each container.

The architecture of the overlay file system is very complex, which is also reflected in the mount statements that extend across multiple lines. (You should run mount | grep docker while a container is running!) Many files and directories use user identifiers

(UIDs) as names and are accordingly difficult to read. In general, it's best to consider the entire contents of */var/lib/docker* as a black box and not touch it. If you want to clean up, you can delete containers and images that are no longer needed using the docker rm or docker rmi commands mentioned earlier. In addition, a great help in tidying up is docker system prune.

> **Rootless Docker and Podman**
>
> If you run the docker command without root privileges, the Docker files end up in the *.local/share/docker* directory inside the *home* directory. Podman uses the *.local/share/container* subdirectory instead.

6.6.4   Process Management

There are two elementary differences in process management between virtual machines and containers: (1) the number of active processes, and (2) the direct control of these processes by the host process management.

In ordinary Linux installations on physical hardware or in virtual machines, dozens of processes typically run concurrently. Although that isn't forbidden in Docker containers, it's uncommon. Many containers are designed to run exactly one process at startup—for example, bash, a web server, or a database server.

Although there's no strict one process per container rule, according to best practices for the *Dockerfile* (*https://docs.docker.com/develop/develop-images/dockerfile_best-practices*), each container should only perform exactly one manageable task, which then almost automatically results in a very small number of processes.

Docker processes don't run in their own virtual environment on Linux but are managed by the host system's process management. When you run ps ax on the host system, the process list also includes all Docker processes. You can see this especially clearly when you run pstree or ps axf.

The following heavily abbreviated output was created while Docker was running a container. Within this container, the Nginx web server was executed (process numbers 2680, 2742, and 2743) and a shell session (docker exec -it sh, process number 3056).

```
hostcomputer$ ps axf

   838 /usr/bin/dockerd -H fd:// --containerd=/run/...
  2638    /usr/bin/docker-proxy -proto tcp -host-port 80 ...
  2644    /usr/bin/docker-proxy -proto tcp -host-port 80 ...
  2660 /usr/bin/containerd-shim-runc-v2 -namespace moby ...
  2680    nginx: master process nginx -g daemon off;
  2742       nginx: worker process
```

```
2743          nginx: worker process
3056     sh
```

6.6.5   Resource Management through Control Groups

Basically, Docker processes can consume the entire CPU power or memory of the host. You can prevent this by specifying limits on memory, number of CPU cores, and so on when `docker run` creates a container.

The two most important options are `-m 256m` (the container may use a maximum of 256 MiB of memory) and `--cpus="2.5"` (the container may utilize an average of 2.5 CPU cores). There are countless other options for granular control, which are documented here:

https://docs.docker.com/config/containers/resource_constraints

Behind the scenes, Docker uses the Linux-specific control mechanism, *control groups* (`cgroups`), as mentioned earlier, in versions 1 and 2 (as of Docker Engine 20.10) to ensure compliance with these limits.

On Windows and macOS, the overall performance of all Docker containers is also limited by the configuration of the Docker Engine, which sets the maximum number of CPU cores and available RAM for all containers combined.

6.6.6   Container Isolation through Namespaces

Docker containers are less isolated from each other and from the host than virtual machines, but that doesn't mean there's no separation at all:

- Docker uses *namespaces* to ensure that each container has its own UIDs, GIDs, and PIDs (i.e., its own user, group, and process numbers) and thus can't see the processes of the host or other containers.

- Mount namespaces give each container its own view of the file system. The container can't access any other directories of the host file system except for its overlay file system described earlier and any shared volumes. Mount namespaces are implemented at the kernel level and are more secure than a `chroot` environment. (`chroot` is a relatively simple Linux command that denies a process access to directories outside a startup directory.)

- Finally, each container gets its own network stack.

Docker Security Risk

Despite a variety of container isolation measures, you need to be aware that Docker can't keep up with virtual machine security models (and even there, we've seen recurring problems in the past). As long as Docker is only used for development and testing tasks, this plays a minor role. However, if Docker is used for server services in production use, you should execute extreme caution!

What's particularly problematic is the fact that Docker processes are often executed with root privileges. This isn't always mandatory, but it's the easiest and most convenient solution from a developer's point of view. Unfortunately, not all *Dockerfile* authors currently make the effort to optimize their images from a security perspective. (Most official images are a laudable exception.)

These security concerns are why the Docker alternative Podman has focused on working without root privileges as much as possible from the start. Docker has followed this trend with *rootless Docker*. Unfortunately, running containers without root privileges comes with limitations, which is why not every application scenario can be mapped by rootless Docker or Podman.

Further details on container isolation and other safety topics can be found in Chapter 18 and the following:

- *https://docs.docker.com/engine/security*
- *https://docs.docker.com/engine/security/rootless*
- *https://security.stackexchange.com/questions/107850*
- *https://blog.aquasec.com/rootless-containers-boosting-container-security*

Evidence that security risks posed by Docker are by no means just abstract came in the form of a bug related to the processing of links discovered in May 2019. Under certain circumstances, this bug gives containers read and write access to the file system of the host:

https://nvd.nist.gov/vuln/detail/CVE-2018-15664

Of course, the bug has long been fixed, but it can't be ruled out that other security problems will follow.

6.6.7   Why the docker Command Usually Requires Root Privileges

Unless you use rootless Docker, the docker command to control containers on Linux must be run with root privileges or with sudo. dockerd and docker communicate with each other through the */var/run/docker.sock* socket file. This file can only be read and written to by root and by members of the docker group:

```
ls -l /var/run/docker.sock
  srw-rw----. 1 root docker ... /var/run/docker.sock
```

To make the docker command accessible to more users, the obvious solution is to simply add these users to the docker group, for example like this:

```
usermod -aG docker kofler   (Caution, security problem!)
```

This will allow `kofler` to execute all `docker` commands without `sudo` or `su` after a new login. Unfortunately, this convenience comes with a huge security problem, as the following box explains.

Caution, Security Problem!

An assignment to the `docker` group is convenient, but it indirectly gives the user in question `root` privileges! The user can set up a container that has access to the root directory / of the host and can thus bypass all security mechanisms of the Linux host. Be sure to read the following web page and specifically the "Docker daemon attack surface" section:

https://docs.docker.com/engine/security/security

On a development machine, adding a user to the `docker` group may still be appropriate; otherwise, there's a risk that all work (not just running `docker` commands) will be done as `root`, which is never a good idea.

6.6.8   More "sudo" Convenience

If you don't want to add your account to the `docker` group but still want to avoid typing `sudo` all the time, you can define the following alias in *.bashrc* for yourself:

```
# in file /home/<accountname>/.bashrc
...
alias docker='sudo docker'
```

This setting becomes active as soon as you start a new terminal window. Now, every time you run `docker`, `sudo docker` will be executed automatically. However, `sudo` will annoy you by continuing to ask for your password. You can prevent the password prompt by adding a rule to `/etc/sudoers` that allows you to run the `docker` command without a password. Of course, you must replace `accountname` with the name of your Linux account.

```
# in file /etc/sudoers
...
accountname  ALL=(ALL:ALL) NOPASSWD: /usr/bin/docker
```

6.6.9   Network Management

By default, Docker containers run on a private network whose management is taken care of by Docker itself. You can get an overview of the current network configuration via the `docker network ls` and `docker network inspect` commands:

```
docker network ls
  NETWORK ID      NAME        DRIVER      SCOPE
  3646ca641eed    bridge      bridge      local
```

```
  812c2a539b16         host           host        local
  9ea2794fb2df         none           null        local
  f216244842c2         testnet        bridge      local
docker network inspect testnet    (output heavily shortened)
  "Subnet": "172.18.0.0/16",
  "Gateway": "172.18.0.1"
  ...
  "Containers":
      "Name": "mariadb-test",
      "IPv4Address": "172.18.0.2/16",
      ...
      "Name": "pma",
      "IPv4Address": "172.18.0.3/16",
      ...
```

On Windows and macOS, you can change some network configuration parameters in Docker settings. If you want to adapt the Docker network beyond that, you can find detailed background information starting from the following web page:

https://docs.docker.com/network

6.6.10   Windows (WSL2)

While Docker on Linux simply uses the existing Linux kernel and the file system of the Linux distribution, running Docker containers on Windows requires a virtual machine running either through Hyper-V (deprecated) or through the *Windows Subsystem for Linux* (WSL2).

Here, we'll focus on the WSL2 variant. Docker startup involves setting up two WSL virtual machines, docker-desktop and docker-desktop-data. You can check this using the wsl command:

```
wsl -l -v
    NAME                    STATE          VERSION
  * Ubuntu                  Stopped        2
    docker-desktop-data     Running        2
    docker-desktop          Running        2
```

docker-desktop-data is responsible for storing the images, and docker-desktop handles running the containers. With wsl, you can even take a look inside the Linux system, docker-desktop:

```
wsl -d docker-desktop -u root
```

```
ls /
```

```
bin                           lib            run
dev                           lost+found     sbin
docker-desktop-deploy-version media          srv
docker-desktop-proxy          mnt            sys
etc                           opt            tmp
home                          proc           usr
init                          root           var

uname -a
 Linux win10 5.4.72-microsoft-standard-WSL2 ... x86_64 Linux

ps
 PID   USER   COMMAND
   1   root   /init
  16   root   wsl-bootstrap run --base-image /mnt/host/c/...
 ...
1190   root   /usr/bin/containerd-shim-runc-v2 -namespace ...
1210   root   /bin/sh
```

Background information on the implementation details of the WSL2 backend for Docker can be found here:

- *https://docs.docker.com/docker-for-windows/wsl*
- *www.docker.com/blog/new-docker-desktop-wsl2-backend*

6.6.11   Limiting RAM Utilization through Docker and WSL2

Microsoft has been pushing WSL heavily in recent years, and Docker makes excellent use of these features. That's why the integration of Docker with Windows seems almost as seamless as it does on Linux. For example, WSL doesn't have a rigidly predefined RAM quota like a virtual machine but instead shares memory dynamically with Windows.

However, this advantage can become a disadvantage if you run containers that use a lot of RAM. For such cases, WSL provides the option to limit the storage requirements of WSL. For this purpose, you can use an editor to set up the *.wslconfig* file in your user directory (typically *C:\Users\<name>*). The following two settings cause WSL to use a maximum of 5 GB of RAM and a maximum of three CPU cores:

```
# File C:\Users\<name>\.wslconfig
[wsl2]
memory=5GB
processors=3
```

149

Note that these settings don't become valid until after a restart of WSL (wsl --shutdown), and they not only apply to Docker but to all Linux distributions run by WSL. Additional WSL configuration options are documented here:

https://docs.microsoft.com/en-us/windows/wsl/wsl-config

6.6.12 macOS (Hypervisor and Virtualization Framework)

By design, the Docker Engine on macOS has many similarities to that of Windows. Once again, the Docker Engine runs as a virtual machine, this time either based on the *hypervisor framework* or the new *virtualization framework* of macOS. (The latter option was still considered experimental in September 2022.)

- *https://developer.apple.com/documentation/hypervisor*
- *https://developer.apple.com/documentation/virtualization*

The image file and various other virtual machine files are saved in the following directory: */Users/<accountname>/Library/Containers/com.docker.docker/Data.*

You can change the location of the image file in the **Preferences • Resources** dialog. At this point, you can also enlarge the image file (see Figure 6.6).

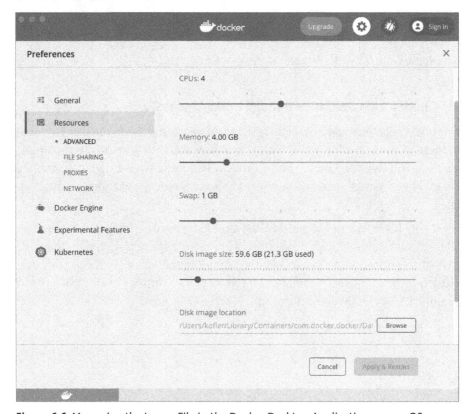

Figure 6.6 Managing the Image File in the Docker Desktop Application on macOS

Previously, it was possible to use the screen command to open a TTY file of the virtual machine and explore the inner workings of the Docker host environment. However, this no longer works with current Docker versions (see also *https://github.com/docker/for-mac/issues/4822*). An alternate way is to use docker run to start Debian or another base image and run the nsenter command there. nsenter runs a process (e.g., bash) in a foreign namespace (see nsenter --help).

```
docker run -it --rm --privileged --pid=host debian \
  nsenter -t 1 -m -u -n -i bash
```

The preceding command creates a container of the Debian image, runs it interactively (-it), and deletes it as soon as you leave the container (--rm). The --privileged option gives the Docker container root privileges to access all resources on the host system. The option should therefore be used with great caution.

The bash shell is executed in the container via nsenter. The nsenter options have the following meaning:

- -t 1 specifies the target process whose namespace is to be used.
- -m uses the mount namespace.
- -u uses the Unix Timesharing System (UTS) namespace and gives access to the host name and other information.
- -n activates the network namespace.
- -i uses the System V Interprocess Communication (System V IPC) namespace.

As a result, you can execute commands that apply directly to the virtual machine where the Docker processes are running. In particular, you can determine the running Linux kernel, take a look at the */var/lib/docker* directory, and so on:

```
uname -a
  Linux docker-desktop 5.10.25-linuxkit ... aarch64 Linux


du -h -d 1 /var/lib/docker
  4.0K    /var/lib/docker/runtimes
  28.0K   /var/lib/docker/volumes
  52.0K   /var/lib/docker/network
  4.0K    /var/lib/docker/swarm
  2.0M    /var/lib/docker/containers
  16.0K   /var/lib/docker/plugins
  644.0K  /var/lib/docker/buildkit
  14.1M   /var/lib/docker/image
  10.9G   /var/lib/docker/overlay2
  4.0K    /var/lib/docker/tmp
  4.0K    /var/lib/docker/trust
  10.9G   /var/lib/docker
```

```
cat /etc/os-release
  PRETTY_NAME="Docker Desktop"
ps -a
  PID   USER     TIME    COMMAND
    1   root     0:01    /sbin/init
    2   root     0:00    [kthreadd]
    3   root     0:00    [rcu_gp]
    4   root     0:00    [rcu_par_gp]
  ...
```

Background information about the nsenter command and the namespace functions of the Linux kernel can be found here:

- *https://en.wikipedia.org/wiki/Linux_namespaces*
- *https://man7.org/linux/man-pages/man1/nsenter.1.html*

High RAM Requirement

Unlike Linux, where Docker containers share memory with the operating system, Docker on macOS uses a traditional Linux virtual machine. This immediately reserves all the memory specified in the settings dialogs of the Docker Desktop upon startup. This memory can't be used for any other tasks on macOS, even if Docker isn't currently running a single container. For this reason, it's recommended that you don't skimp on memory when purchasing a Mac to run Docker on.

Chapter 7
docker Command Reference

This chapter provides a reference of the main commands you can run with docker. The commands are described in Table 7.1 in alphabetical order.

Command	Function
docker attach	Connect the input and output of a container with a terminal
docker build	Create a new image according to *Dockerfile*
docker commit	Create a new image from a container
docker compose	Create and run multiple containers
docker container	Manage containers
docker create	Create a new container, but don't start it
docker diff	Show changed files of the container
docker events	Show actions of the Docker system
docker exec	Run the command in a running container
docker export	Save a container to the file archive
docker image	Manage images
docker images	List images
docker import	Create a container from file archive
docker info	View the status of the Docker system
docker inspect	Display the configuration and status of a container
docker kill	End container execution immediately
docker login|logout	Log in/out of a Docker account
docker logs	Show logging output of a container
docker network	Manage network configuration
docker node	Manage nodes of a Docker swarm
docker pause|unpause	Stop/continue container execution

Table 7.1 "docker" Commands Presented in This Chapter

Command	Function
docker port	List port assignments of a container
docker ps	List containers
docker pull	Download or update image
docker push	Upload your own image to a Docker repository
docker rename	Rename container
docker restart	End container and restart
docker rm|rmi	Delete container or image
docker run	Create and start a new container
docker secret	Manage secrets for services
docker service	Manage services
docker stack	Create a group (stack) of services
docker start	Restart existing container
docker stats	Show CPU and memory requirement regularly
docker stop	End (in the background) running container
docker swarm	Set up or manage a Docker swarm
docker system	View information about the Docker system
docker tag	Change image name or tag
docker top	Display processes of a container
docker update	Change options of a container
docker volume	Manage volumes
docker wait	Wait for the end of a container

Table 7.1 "docker" Commands Presented in This Chapter (Cont.)

The command reference presented in this chapter focuses on the most important commands and the most frequently needed options. For a complete description of all commands, visit the following Docker website:

https://docs.docker.com/engine/reference/commandline/docker

> **Subcommand Required**
>
> Some Docker commands expect subcommands that specify what to do. For example, docker container can't run on its own but must be supplemented by a subcommand (docker container rm or docker container stop). In this chapter, such commands are indicated by an asterisk in the heading, such as "docker container *", for example.

7.1   docker attach

docker attach <cname/cid> connects the standard input and output of a container to the current terminal. This is only useful for containers where it's not the case anyway, that is, which weren't started via docker run -it or docker start -a -i.

For Docker containers of server services running in the background, docker attach often allows you to read logging messages on the fly.

7.2   docker build

docker build [options] <directory/url> reads the *Dockerfile* file from the specified location and creates a corresponding image (see also Chapter 4, Section 4.1 and Section 4.3).

The -t name:tag option can be used to mark the image with a *tag*. In addition, various options identical to those of the docker run command can be used to specify defaults for containers that will be created from the image at a later point (see Table 7.2 later in this chapter).

7.3   docker commit

docker commit <cname/id> [<[accountname/]imagename[:tag]>] creates a new image from a container with the specified name. If the second parameter is missing, the image won't get a name, just a random ID number. Any volumes won't be integrated into the image.

If the container is currently running, it will be temporarily halted while docker commit is running. Although you can prevent this using --pause false, you'll then risk an inconsistent image that can result if the container's file system changes during the commit.

If you want to set up new images yourself, it's usually more appropriate to write a *Dockerfile* and then run docker build. While docker commit is often easier and more convenient to use, the process isn't reproducible later. In this respect, docker commit is more of a debugging aid to store a container in a certain state and create new, identical containers from it again later if needed.

7.4   docker compose *

docker compose starts or manages a group of containers. The setup of the group must be described in the *docker-compose.yml* file (see also Chapter 5). Alternatively, the file name can be specified via the -f option. For older installations or on Linux, the command must be executed as docker-compose.

The following sections describe the main subcommands of docker compose. As usual, we'll limit ourselves to the most important variants and options for practical use. You can find the complete documentation here:

https://docs.docker.com/compose/reference

7.5   docker-compose config

docker-compose config checks if *docker-compose.yml* is free of syntax errors and displays the file. Of course, the file doesn't get output unchanged by cat or less, but as it's interpreted by docker compose. Among other things, relative paths are replaced by absolute ones.

Unfortunately, the order of the settings won't be preserved. Rather, all keywords in each hierarchy level are ordered alphabetically. That being said, docker-compose config can help you understand how docker compose processes individual settings internally.

7.6   docker-compose down

docker-compose down stops all containers, networks, and so on described by *docker-compose.yml* and deletes them.

7.7   docker-compose events

docker-compose events displays the events of all running containers of the project until the command gets terminated via ⌨Ctrl+⌨C.

7.8   docker-compose kill

docker-compose kill terminates all containers immediately. This command is only a stopgap if docker-compose stop or down doesn't work.

7.9   docker-compose logs

docker-compose logs [<servicename>] displays the logging output of all containers or the specified container. Note that the command works only for running containers. If the startup of a container fails, docker-compose logs isn't a troubleshooting tool. It's better to run docker-compose up without the -d option so that you see any error messages immediately.

Typically, docker-compose logs ends with the output of the logging lines. If you want to follow the logging output *live*, you need to run the command with the -f (*follow*) option. You must press Ctrl+C if you want to end the command.

7.10   docker-compose pause and docker compose unpause

docker-compose pause pauses the execution of all containers described in the compose file. docker-compose unpause resumes the execution.

7.11   docker-compose ps

docker-compose ps lists all containers in the project:

```
docker-compose ps
    Name                Command                         State
    test_db_1           docker-entrypoint.sh mysqld     Up
    test_wordpress_1    docker-entrypoint.sh apach ...  Up
```

7.12   docker-compose rm

docker-compose rm deletes all stopped containers after a query. With -f, the command waives the security prompt; with -v, it also deletes the associated anonymous volumes (i.e., volumes whose location you haven't explicitly specified yourself).

7.13   docker-compose run

docker-compose run <servicename> [<command>] starts the container selected via <servicename> and runs either the specified command (e.g., /bin/sh) or the default command of the images in the foreground. When a shell is started with run, it can be operated interactively.

docker-compose run starts all dependent containers in addition to the container selected in the first parameter. Such dependencies must be formulated using the depends_on keyword in *docker-compose.yml*. You can prevent this behavior with the --no-deps option.

To specify volumes, ports, and environment variables, you can use the -v <volume>, -p <port>, and -e VAR=value options, respectively. The additional --rm option causes the container to be deleted immediately after it has been used. With -d, the command can be executed in the background.

7.14   docker-compose start, docker-compose stop, and docker compose restart

docker-compose stop stops the execution of the containers; docker-compose start restarts the containers; and docker-compose restart corresponds to the combination of stop and start.

7.15   docker-compose top

docker-compose top displays the processes of all containers (some columns are missing in the following listing due to space limitations):

docker-compose top

```
test_db_1
UID    PID    C   STIME   TIME       CMD
-------------------------------------------
999    27869  3   12:51   00:00:00   mysqld


test_wordpress_1
UID       PID    C   STIME   TIME      CMD
----------------------------------------------------------
root      27979  1   12:51   00:00:00  apache2 -DFOREGROUND
www-data  28159  0   12:51   00:00:00  apache2 -DFOREGROUND
www-data  28160  0   12:51   00:00:00  apache2 -DFOREGROUND
www-data  28161  0   12:51   00:00:00  apache2 -DFOREGROUND
www-data  28162  0   12:51   00:00:00  apache2 -DFOREGROUND
www-data  28163  0   12:51   00:00:00  apache2 -DFOREGROUND
```

7.16   docker-compose up

docker-compose up creates and starts the containers listed in *docker-compose.yml* in the services section. At the same time, a network is set up for the container group, in which the containers communicate with each other.

The names of all containers, networks, volumes, and so on are prefixed with the name of the current directory. So, for example, if the service mydb is described in the *docker-compose.yml* file, and that file is located in the *nctest* directory, then the container name nctest_mydb_1 results from that. If you want a different project name, you can specify it with the -p option.

With the commonly used -d option, docker compose runs the containers in the background. If this option is missing, on the other hand, docker compose will continue to run until all containers end—with server services, this is usually infinite. This has the advantage that the collected logging and error messages of all containers will be displayed.

For debugging purposes, it can be quite useful to deliberately omit the -d option. To end the command, you must then press ⌈Ctrl⌉+⌈C⌉. Then, the containers will be stopped but not deleted. The execution of the containers can be continued using docker-compose start.

7.17   docker container *

docker container is the starting point of more than two dozen commands for managing containers. In many cases, however, there are equivalent shorter commands that are more widely used and are given preference in this book. So instead of docker container rm <name/id>, you can just run docker rm <name/id>; instead of docker container stop <name>, you can just run docker stop <name>; and so on.

7.18   docker create

docker create [options] <imagename> [<command> [arguments]] creates a container derived from the specified image, similar to docker run. Unlike docker run, however, the container won't be started. To start it, you need to run docker start <containername> at a later time. For an overview of the many options you can pass to docker create, see the description of docker run later in this section.

7.19   docker diff

docker diff <cname/cid> returns a list of all files that have changed in the container compared to the image. The files or directories are marked with three letters: A (added), D (deleted), or C (changed).

```
docker diff apache
  C /usr/local/apache2/logs
  A /usr/local/apache2/logs/httpd.pid
```

7.20   docker events

docker events continuously displays the actions the Docker system is performing. This includes, for example, starting and stopping containers, establishing network connections, connecting containers to volumes (*mount*), and so on. The command intended for debugging purposes runs until it gets terminated via `Ctrl`+`C`.

7.21   docker exec

docker exec [options] <containername> command [arguments] executes another command in an already running container. As with docker run, the -i -t options enable an interactive operation. With the -d option, the command can be executed in the background (detached).

```
docker exec -it mariadb_container /bin/sh
```

7.22   docker export

docker export <cname/cid> > file.tar writes all files of a container into a TAR archive. On Linux and macOS, the resulting file can then be viewed with tar tf file.tar or unpacked with tar xf file.tar. On Windows, ZIP UIs take over these functions. You can use docker import to create a new image from the TAR file.

If you want to compress the archive right away, you need to execute the command on Linux or macOS as follows:

```
docker export <cname> | gzip -c > export.tar.gz
```

docker export processes *all* files in the container, not just those that have changed in comparison to the underlying image. Files located in volumes, on the other hand, aren't taken into account.

7.23   docker image *

docker image is the starting point for various subcommands for managing images. Some commands are also available in shorter forms. For example, docker image rm is equivalent to the docker rmi command. The subcommands include the following:

- docker image build <path/url> processes the Dockerfile in the specified directory or address and generates a new image from it (see Section 7.2).
- docker image prune deletes all images that aren't needed by other images after a query. If the command is executed with the -a option, it also deletes all images from which no containers were derived.

- docker image pull/push downloads an image from Docker Hub or uploads a custom-built image (see Section 7.36 and Section 7.37).

- docker image rm <name/id> deletes an image (see Section 7.40).

Caution

Be careful not to accidentally run docker images ls or any other subcommand. docker images with plural "s" is a separate command (see the next section). For docker images xy, xy isn't interpreted as a subcommand but as an image name. Typically, there are no images called ls, prune, and so on; consequently, docker images doesn't lead to any result, but it doesn't cause any error message either. It then looks as if the command wouldn't work at all.

7.24   docker images

docker images [<reponame:tag>] lists all locally available images. If the name of a repository gets passed to the command, then only images from that source will be displayed.

The following options can be passed to the command:

- With -a, the command also shows interim images that are created when you build custom images with docker build.

- With -f "key=value", the command displays only images that meet a certain criteria (filter). Valid filters are dangling, before, since, and reference. For example, the command with -f "dangling=true" returns images that aren't currently used by any container.

- With -q, the command only returns a list of image IDs, but no further information (quiet). The option is recommended if the IDs are to be passed to another command.

7.25   docker import

docker import <file.tar> <imagename> creates a new image from a TAR archive previously created with docker export. If you want to read the TAR archive from standard input, you need to specify the - character instead of the file name:

```
gunzip -c datei.tar.gz | docker import - newimagename
```

7.26   docker info

docker info as well as the equivalent docker system info command display comprehensive information about the Docker installation:

```
docker info
  Containers: 37
    Running: 5
    Paused: 0
    Stopped: 32
  Images: 83
  Server Version: 20.10.6
  Storage Driver: overlay2
    Backing Filesystem: extfs
    Supports d_type: true
    Native Overlay Diff: true
  ...
```

> **Even More Information**
>
> More detailed information about the installed Docker version is provided by `docker version`. On the other hand, if you want information about a specific container, `docker inspect` can help you. `docker system df` finally reveals information about Docker's space utilization.
>
> The `docker events` and `docker stats` commands continuously display information about the running Docker system. `docker stats` corresponds to the `top` command known on Linux and macOS.

7.27   docker inspect

`docker inspect <containername>` provides comprehensive information about the specified container. From the data represented in JSON syntax, which is usually more than 200 lines long, the following pieces of information emerge, among others: the underlying image, the locations for the container and its volumes, the current status, and various configuration and network parameters. Instead of the name, you can of course also pass the ID number of the container to the command.

```
docker inspect -s apache-test

[
  {
    "Id": "e53b...",
    "Created": "2021-05-28T12:03:44.9498538012",
    "Path": "httpd-foreground",
    "Args": [ ],
    "State": {
        "Status": "exited",
```

```
    "Running": false,
  ...
```

If you want to filter out only a certain element from the data, you can select this element using -f (format). The following two examples show how you can view the status of the container and all volumes:

```
docker inspect -s -f "{{.State.Status}}" apache-test
  exited

docker inspect -s -f "{{.Mounts}}" mariadb-test1
  [{volume 0fbd.... /var/lib/docker/volumes/0fbd.../_data
    /var/lib/mysql local  true }]
```

7.28   docker kill

docker kill <cname/id> sends the KILL signal to the container by default. As a rule, this signal immediately terminates the execution of the container. The process has no way to close files or terminate transactions. The -s option can also be used to send other signals, such as -s TERM.

As a rule, you should prefer docker stop if you want to stop the execution of a container. docker stop first sends a TERM signal to the main container process, giving the container a chance to shut down properly. Only if the process doesn't react after a certain time will a KILL signal follow.

7.29   docker login and docker logout

docker login connects to a Docker account and stores the authentication token permanently. For example, a login is required before you upload a custom-built image to Docker Hub via docker push.

docker logout deletes an authentication token that has been set up with docker login.

7.30   docker logs

docker logs <containername/id> displays the logged messages of the container. This access to the logging data only works if the underlying image has been set up accordingly. This is already the case with many popular images. Depending on the configuration, the logging messages are written to a ring buffer. Once this buffer fills up, new logging messages will overwrite old ones.

If docker logs doesn't return any results, you can search for logging files in the container. To do this, you need to start a shell in parallel with the container (e.g., with docker exec <cname> /bin/bash) and take a look at the */var/log* directory.

Configuring Logging for Custom Images

If you compile Docker images yourself, you can find detailed information about Docker's logging mechanisms and how to use and configure them on the following web page:

https://docs.docker.com/config/containers/logging/configure

7.31   docker network *

docker network is the starting point to several subcommands for the administration of Docker network functions. The commands don't affect individual containers or images but the Docker system in its entirety.

By default, Docker provides a private network with web access to its containers via a preconfigured network called bridge. IP addresses in the range 172.17.0.0/16 are assigned to the containers.

For the execution of individual containers, the default configuration is usually sufficient. To separate groups of containers from other containers, on the other hand, a separate network is often set up for them in which the containers communicate with each other. Basically, this can be done manually, but it's easier to automate the process (see Chapter 5).

- docker network create/rm creates or deletes an additional network for Docker.

- docker network connect <nwid> <cname/cid> connects a network to a container.

- docker network inspect <nwname/nwid> provides details about a specific network:

```
docker network inspect bridge
  [
    {
      "Name": "bridge",
      "Id": "91ad2ea2...",
      "Created": "2021-06-01T07:25:42.526455289+02:00",
      "Scope": "local",
      "Driver": "bridge",
      "EnableIPv6": false,
      "IPAM": {
        "Driver": "default",
        "Options": null,
        "Config": [
```

```
      {
        "Subnet": "172.17.0.0/16",
        "Gateway": "172.17.0.1"
      }
    ]
  },
...
```

- `docker network ls` lists which (virtual) networks are known to Docker:

```
docker network ls
  NETWORK ID     NAME    DRIVER  SCOPE
  91ad2ea2bccf   bridge  bridge  local
  416eaaaac506   host    host    local
  0f0d89d189f8   none    null    local
```

- `docker network prune` deletes all networks that aren't currently being used. The command is useful for eliminating orphaned networks after experimenting with docker-compose or docker stack deploy.

Background information on Docker network configuration can be found here:

https://docs.docker.com/network

7.32   docker node *

If you configure multiple Docker instances as a swarm (Section 7.47), docker node helps you administrate the nodes of the swarm. docker node is the starting point for various subcommands:

- `docker node ls` lists all nodes and shows their ID strings, host names, and statuses.
- `docker node inspect <nodeid/hostname>` returns detailed information about a node. The --pretty option formats the output to make it more readable as text.
- `docker node rm <nodeid/hostname>` removes a node from the swarm.

7.33   "docker pause" and "docker unpause"

docker pause <cname/cid> pauses the execution of a container; docker unpause <cname/cid> resumes the execution of a paused container.

7.34   "docker port"

docker port <cname/cid> lists all port mappings of a container:

```
docker port apache
  80/tcp -> 0.0.0.0:8080
```

If you specify a port of the container as the second parameter, `docker port` simply returns the corresponding port on the host system:

```
docker port apache 80/tcp
  0.0.0.0:8080
```

7.35   docker ps

Without any further options, `docker ps` returns a list of all running containers. With the `-a` option, the list contains all the containers that have been set up, regardless of whether they're currently running or not.

If you add the `-s` option, you'll also get to know the container size. The size is specified in two numbers. The first number also indicates the space required by the images. However, it's possible for multiple containers to share an image. That's why the virtual size is also provided in parentheses. This is the size of the mutable overlay file, that is, the data that differentiates the container from its base image. (Both values don't take into account the size of the volumes. The easiest way to find out the total size of all volumes is to use `docker system df`).

You can specify a filter criterion via the `-f <criterion=value>` option. The following keywords can be used, among others:

- `id/name/label=...`
  Returns containers with a given ID number, name, or label.

- `status=created|restarting|running|removing|paused|exited|dead`
  Returns containers in the specified state.

- `ancestor=<imagename/id>`
  Returns containers derived from the specified image.

- `before=<cname/id>` and `since=<cname/id>`
  Returns containers created before or after a reference container.

7.36   docker pull

`docker pull <image[:tag]>` downloads the latest version of an image. Because this process is performed automatically anyway as part of the first execution of `docker create` or `docker run` for a given image, it isn't necessary to explicitly run `docker pull` before setting up a new container.

As a result, `docker create` or `docker run` continues to use images once downloaded, even if newer versions have already become available in the meantime. With `docker pull`, you can force an update of an image. However, when doing that, it's important that you understand the internal mechanisms of Docker:

- Existing containers based on an old version of an image remain unchanged, so they won't get updated. Such container updates aren't even foreseen in Docker.

- `docker ps` then displays the ID number of the old image instead of the image name in the `IMAGE` column for such containers, so it looks like the old image doesn't even exist anymore. In fact, however, all layer files of the old image will be preserved as long as there are containers built on top of them.

- Only new containers set up using `docker create` or `docker run` will from then on use the latest image version downloaded with `docker pull`.

7.37   docker push

`docker push <accountname/imagename[:tag]>` uploads a custom-built image to your Docker account. A prerequisite for this is that you've previously logged in with `docker login` and that you've created your own image with `docker build` or `docker commit`.

7.38   docker rename

`docker rename <oldname/id> <newname>` gives a container a new name.

7.39   docker restart

`docker restart <cname/id>` stops a container and then starts it again. The command corresponds to the combination of `docker stop` and `docker start`.

7.40   docker rm and docker rmi

`docker rm <containername/id>` deletes the specified container. With the `-f` (*force*) option, the command can be executed even if the container is still running. Volumes are preserved by default. They can either be deleted immediately with the additional `-v` option or at a later time via `docker volume rm <volid>`.

`docker rmi <imagename/id>` deletes an image in a similar way. If there are multiple images of the same name with different tags, you must specify the tag as well, for example, `docker rmi ubuntu:18.04`.

By default, you can delete only images that aren't used by a container. The `-f` option enables you to bypass this protection mechanism. However, the image won't be completely deleted. Rather, the layer files of the image are preserved so that the container can continue to run. However, you can't derive new containers from this image. In addition, docker ps no longer displays the image name in the IMAGE column, just an ID number.

7.41   docker run

The command creates a new container and then executes it immediately. Subsequently, however, you need to use the docker start command to re-execute the already existing container. The options passed to docker run permanently determine the properties of the new container (see Table 7.2).

Option	Meaning
--cpus="1.25"	Allows the container to use a maximum of 1.25 CPU cores
-d	Runs the container as daemon
-e VAR=value	Sets the environment variable for the container
-h hostname	Sets the host name for the container
-i	Runs the container interactively this time
-m 512m	Limits the container RAM to 512 MiB
--name cname	Assigns a name to the container
--network nname	Uses the specified network
-p localport:cport	Connects ports of the container with ports of the host
-P	Connects all ports of the container with random host ports
--rm	Deletes a container as soon as an execution ends
--restart xxx	Defines the restart behavior (see Chapter 6, Section 6.5)
-t	Connects pseudo-terminal with standard input
-u uid:gid	Runs the container with these permissions (instead of as root)
-v cdir	Sets up a container directory as a volume
-v vname:cdir	Creates a named volume
-v /localdir:cdir	Connects the host directory with the container directory
--volumes-from cn	Uses volumes of another container

Table 7.2 Important Options of the docker-run Command

We're going to focus here on the most important options. The manual text of man docker-run would span across 15 pages in the layout of this book! The general syntax for docker run looks as follows:

```
docker run [options] <imagename> [<command> [<arguments>]]
```

If you don't specify a command after the image name, the default command specified for the image will be executed (see also the description of the CMD and ENTRYPOINT keywords in Chapter 4, Section 4.1). For base images for Linux distributions, the default command is often bash, permitting the interactive use of the container.

Note that when you create a new container, you commit yourself not only with the options but also with the command to execute! If you later run the container created with docker run again with docker start, the same command will be executed in the container as the first time it was started. There is the option to execute another command in parallel with a running container using docker exec, but this option is primarily intended for debugging purposes.

You can then change the individual options of a container later with docker update.

7.42   docker secret *

Secrets provide a way to transfer passwords, keys, certificates, and other sensitive data into a service in such a way that it never persistently ends up in the file system of the container. Secrets require that you set up a Docker swarm and use services (see Section 7.47 and Section 7.43).

The docker secret command is the starting point to several subcommands:

- docker secret create <secretname> <filename> creates a secret, optionally taking the data from either a file or standard input (filename -):

  ```
  echo "secret" | docker secret create mysecret -
  ```

- docker secret inspect <sid/sname> displays details about the secret, such as when the secret was set up. The content won't be displayed.
- docker secret ls lists the names of all secrets.
- docker secret rm <sid/sname> deletes a secret.

In practice, secrets are rarely managed manually. Far more often, references to confidential files are specified in *docker-compose.yml* (see Chapter 5). docker stack deploy then automatically runs docker secret and passes the confidential data to the services.

7.43   docker service *

docker service is the starting point for various commands to manage services. In Docker, *services* help you administrate Docker services in a cluster or swarm. The service commands are as follows:

- docker service create creates a new service. Similar to docker run or docker create, a large number of parameters need to be passed. It's more efficient to describe the services in a *docker-compose.yml* file and deploy them with docker stack deploy.

- docker service inspect <sname/sid> returns detailed information about a service. The --pretty option formats the output to make it more readable as text.

- docker service logs <name/sid> displays logging information about a service.

- docker service ls lists all running services.

- docker service ps <sname/sid> lists the tasks (processes) of a service.

- docker service remove <name/sid> deletes a service.

- docker service update <name/sid> changes the parameters of a service.

7.44   docker stack *

docker stack is the starting point for various commands to manage stacks. A *stack* is a group of services that can run in a Docker cluster (swarm). The command therefore assumes that the current machine is part of a Docker swarm (see also the description of docker swarm init in Section 7.47). The various commands for managing stacks follow:

- docker stack deploy -c <file> <stackname> creates a group of multiple services, evaluating the *docker-compose.yml* file specified by <file>. <stackname> assigns a name to the new stack. The command must be executed on a manager node.

  For the syntax of *docker-compose.yml* and an example of how to use docker stack deploy, see Chapter 5.

- docker stack ls lists all stacks along with the number of services they consist of.

- docker stack ps <stackname> lists all tasks in a stack. The command must be executed on a manager node.

- docker stack rm <stackname> deletes the specified stack with all its services, networks, and so on. This command must also be executed on a manager node.

- docker stack services <stackname> returns a list of all services that make up the specified stack. This command also works only on a manager node.

7.45   docker start and docker stop

docker start [options] <containername> starts a container that has already been set up but isn't currently running. With the -a option (attach), standard output and error messages are forwarded. The -i option (interactive) applies in a similar way to standard input as it does with docker run.

docker stop [-t <n>] <containername> terminates a container that's running in the background. The main process is requested to shut down with the TERM signal. If the container is still running after 10 seconds, the main process gets terminated immediately with the KILL signal. The time period for the reaction to TERM can be set with the -t option.

7.46   docker stats

docker stats [options] [cname/cid] continuously shows which container is using how much CPU power, memory, network, and I/O resources. The output is updated regularly until you stop executing the command with [Ctrl]+[C]. The command thus has a similar function as the top command on Linux or macOS.

docker stats takes into account all running containers by default. With the -a option, the command also lists all currently stopped containers. Conversely, docker stats only displays information about one or more containers if their names or IDs are passed as parameters.

The following listing is heavily shortened due to space limitations:

```
docker stats
  ID        NAME     CPU %   MEM        NET I/O   BLOCK I/O   PIDS
  b1d9...   dock...  1.81%   49.05MiB   1.07kB    94.2kB      21
  4cf3...   u180...  0.00%   1.008MiB   578B      0B          1
  e53b...   mari...  0.00%   92.53MiB   1.11kB    14.2MB      30
```

---

docker top and docker system df

If you want to know which processes are running *inside* a container, you need to use docker top. If you're interested in how much space images, containers, and so on take up on your Docker machine, you should use docker system df.

7.47   docker swarm *

A *Docker swarm* is a network of multiple computers, each of which is running *Docker*. Such a network is often referred to as a *cluster*. It provides various options for making large Docker installations fail-safe and scalable.

docker swarm is the starting point for various commands to manage a Docker swarm:

- docker swarm init initializes the swarm functions in the current Docker instance. Executing this command is already sufficient for you to subsequently run docker stack. However, the swarm then consists of only one computer for the time being.

  Even in swarm mode, the Docker instance can of course continue to run "ordinary" containers.

- docker swarm join adds the current computer as a node or manager to a swarm. To manage the nodes, you can use the docker node command. Each node can operate as a worker, a manager, or both, depending on its configuration.

- docker swarm leave removes the current computer from a Docker swarm.

Network and Firewall

When the swarm functions are used, Docker sets up new networks. These are used for the communication between the nodes and to establish a connection to the physical network. In the listing via docker network ls, these networks have the names docker_gwbridge and ingress.

Ports 7946 (TCP/UDP) and 4789 (UDP only) are used for the communication between nodes. Port 2377 (TCP) is also required to perform cluster administration. These ports must be enabled in the firewall. You can find more information about swarm-specific network details here:

https://docs.docker.com/network/overlay

7.48   docker system *

docker system is the starting point for various commands that provide information about the current state of the Docker system:

- docker system df lists the space requirements of images, containers, and volumes:

```
docker system df
   TYPE            TOTAL  ACTIVE  SIZE     RECLAIMABLE
   Images          6      5       3.206GB  85.07MB (2%)
   Containers      7      0       3.537MB  3.537MB (100%)
   Local Volumes   3      1       371.2MB  239MB (64%)
   Build Cache                    0B       0B
```

If you also pass the -v option, the command lists all images, containers, and so on in detail, including their sizes.

- docker system info displays comprehensive information about the Docker installation. The command returns the same result as docker info.

- docker system prune deletes all currently unused data. Caution! The term "unused" here refers to containers that aren't running and images that aren't needed by other images (i.e., *dangling images*).

  If you pass the --volumes option, all volumes that aren't used by any container will also be deleted. Before executing this major cleanup, you must confirm a query with y.

  Note that the command doesn't delete images that you've downloaded for creating images. If you want to delete those as well, you need to run docker image prune -a.

7.49   docker tag

docker tag <iname/id> <[repository/]newname[:tag]> identifies the specified image with a name or *tag*. The following command assigns the image with the ID 8d..., the name ubuntu, and the tag 1804beta:

```
docker tag 8dcaef637b41 ubuntu:1804beta
```

7.50   docker top

docker top <cname/cid> returns a list of all processes running inside a container. For many simple containers, this is just a process. Unlike the top command known from Linux, the output occurs only once, which means the process list doesn't get updated on a regular basis.

```
docker top docker_reload_1
  PID     USER    TIME    COMMAND
  8275    0       0:00    npm
  8404    0       0:00    sh -c gulp
  8405    0       0:04    gulp
```

7.51   docker update

docker update [options] <cname/id> modifies container options that have been set with docker run or docker create. In particular, you can use it to limit the maximum CPU, memory, and I/O usage of the container (--cpus, -m, and --blkio-weight options, respectively). You can also change the restart behavior:

```
docker update --restart always <containername>
```

docker update can also be run while a container is running. However, the command doesn't work with Windows containers.

7.52 docker volume *

docker volume is the starting point to several subcommands:

- docker volume ls lists all known volumes of all containers.
- docker volume inspect <volname> returns detailed information about a volume, including the mount point within the container. However, the command doesn't reveal to which container a volume belongs.
- docker volume prune deletes all volumes that aren't associated with any container.
- docker volume rm <volname> deletes the specified volume.

7.53 docker wait

docker wait <cname/cid> waits until the execution of the specified container ends, and then outputs the exit code.

PART II

Toolbox

Chapter 8
Alpine Linux

All kinds of Linux distributions are used as the basis for Docker containers: Debian, Oracle Linux, Ubuntu, and so on. However, this chapter focuses on a Linux distribution—*Alpine Linux*—that's largely unknown outside of the Docker world (and possibly in the *Embedded Linux* environment). Alpine Linux is optimized in terms of security and the economical use of resources and differs in many technical details from other Linux distributions. The most important distinguishing feature, however, can be seen in Table 8.1: the space requirement of the image is vanishingly small compared to that of other distributions.

Distribution	Docker Image Size
Alpine Linux	Approx. 6 MB
Debian 10	Approx. 115 MB
Debian 11	Approx. 125 MB
Ubuntu 20.04	Approx. 70 MB
Ubuntu 22.04	Approx. 80 MB
AlmaLinux 9 (compatible to Red Hat Enterprise Linux [RHEL] 9)	Approx. 190 MB

Table 8.1 Docker Image Size of Major Linux Distributions

In general, we assume in this book that you know the basic features of Linux and are familiar with its most important functions and commands.

But even many Linux professionals have never heard of Alpine Linux. For this reason, this chapter provides a brief summary of the details in which Alpine Linux differs from other distributions and how you can use it. One of our main focuses in this context will be package management, which is important when you compile your own images.

8.1 Characteristics

To keep Alpine Linux as lean as possible, its developers have chosen different components from those that are commonly used in "big" Linux libraries. For example, Alpine Linux uses the standard C library `musl` instead of `glibc` or the init system OpenRC instead of systemd. Even the basic Linux commands aren't available in their full versions but come in a trimmed-down version from the BusyBox package.

Alpine Linux therefore provides comparatively little comfort when working interactively. But Alpine Linux is sufficient to run a server service such as Apache or Nginx with minimum overhead—and that's what matters in the Docker environment. You can find more information on this here:

- *https://alpinelinux.org/about*
- *https://en.wikipedia.org/wiki/Alpine_Linux*

8.1.1   Trying Out Alpine Linux

Even though Alpine Linux isn't intended for interactive use, you should create a container to try out its basic functions. The quickest way to do this is using the following command:

```
docker run -it --rm -h alpine --name alpine alpine
```

This will take you to an interactive root shell where you can determine the version number of Alpine Linux:

```
cat /etc/os-release
  NAME="Alpine Linux"
  ID=alpine
  VERSION_ID=3.16.2
  PRETTY_NAME="Alpine Linux v3.16"
  HOME_URL="https://alpinelinux.org"
  BUG_REPORT_URL="https://gitlab.alpinelinux.org/alpine/aports/-/issues"
```

8.1.2   Shell

In Alpine Linux, the /bin/sh shell is executed by default, which is part of BusyBox (see the following section). This shell can't keep up with the comfort of bash (i.e., use of cursor keys to reference/change commands, use of [Tab] key for command and file name completion), which is used with other Linux distributions. For this reason, it may be worth installing the much larger bash to explore Alpine Linux. Details about the apk command will follow in Section 8.2.

```
apk add --update bash bash-completion
```

```
/bin/bash
  bash-5.1#
```

If you then run docker ps -s in a second terminal, you'll see that the container size has grown from a few bytes to approximately 5 MB. In other words, bash alone takes up almost as much space as the entire Alpine image!

8.1.3 BusyBox

BusyBox is a relatively large program by Alpine standards (0.8 MB), but it contains implementations of about 140 standard commands such as cat, echo, grep, gzip, hostname, ip, ls, mount, ping, rm, route, and su. These commands are available as symbolic links on busybox:

```
ls /bin /sbin -l
  /bin
  ...         12  ash -> /bin/busybox
              12  base64 -> /bin/busybox
              12  bbconfig -> /bin/busybox
          824904  busybox
              12  cat -> /bin/busybox
                  ...

  /sbin
              12  acpid -> /bin/busybox
              12  adjtimex -> /bin/busybox
           69704  apk
              12  arp -> /bin/busybox
                  ...
```

The obvious advantage of BusyBox is that the space required for these standard commands is small. The disadvantage of BusyBox is that the commands are partly implemented in a simplified form with various options missing that are common on Linux. An overview of all commands and options that can be used with BusyBox can be found here:

https://busybox.net/downloads/BusyBox.html

8.1.4 Init System and Logging

On Linux, the init system is responsible for starting background and network services when the computer is booted. However, there's no need for this when using it in Docker (also true for other Linux images for Docker).

The situation is similar for logging: by default, logging isn't provided in the Alpine image. If needed, you can install the rsyslog package and take care of its startup.

8.1.5 The "musl" Library

The musl library used in Alpine Linux is a leaner libc implementation than the widely used glibc. However, this library sometimes leads to problems. One is that the evaluation of /etc/resolv.conf has been simplified. Thus, musl ignores the domain and search keywords. If you have trouble resolving domain names, you should take a look at the following web page:

https://github.com/gliderlabs/docker-alpine/blob/master/docs/caveats.md

Binary files that haven't been compiled for Alpine Linux also cause difficulties. They sometimes use symbols that exist in glibc but not in musl. The ldd <binary> command helps you troubleshoot that.

Another problem is the lack of support for localization files (*locales*). One possible way around this is to install a variant of glibc optimized for Alpine Linux. You can find more details on this topic here:

- *https://github.com/gliderlabs/docker-alpine/issues/144#issuecomment-339906345*
- *https://github.com/sgerrand/alpine-pkg-glibc*

8.1.6   Documentation

In Alpine Linux, neither the man command nor the associated help texts are installed by default. The following commands help you solve this issue; they also activate less at the same time, so you can comfortably navigate through the help texts:

```
apk add --update mandoc mandoc-apropos man-pages less less-doc
export PAGER=less
```

Note that this will return the man pages for various standard commands but not those for specifically installed packages. On Alpine Linux, it's common for documentation files to be in a separate package named <packagename>-doc. So, if you want to read the man pages for the bash shell, you must also install the bash-doc package:

```
apk add --update bash-doc
```

You can also find useful Alpine-specific documentation in the wiki of the project site. A good place to start is here:

https://wiki.alpinelinux.org/wiki/Tutorials_and_Howtos

8.1.7   Missing "root" Password

In May 2019, it was revealed that Docker images of Alpine Linux were shipped without a root password. Fortunately, this sounds more dramatic than it actually is. In the Docker environment, it's rather unusual for user management to be active within a container. By default, this isn't the case in Alpine Linux nor in countless images built on it. Conversely, however, it can't be ruled out that individual Docker users install additional packages for user management via apk. Then the option of a root login without a password really becomes a security risk.

The problem has, of course, long since been fixed. `cat /etc/shadow` shows that an exclamation mark in the sense of "invalid password" is stored in the hash code column for the `root` password:

```
cat /etc/shadow
  root:!::0:::::
  bin:!::0:::::
  daemon:!::0:::::
  ...
```

8.2   Package Management with "apk"

On Debian and Ubuntu, you can use `apt` to install packages; on Fedora, it's `dnf`; and on RHEL, it's `yum`. The equivalent command on Alpine Linux is called `apk`. In the previous section, you've already gotten to know the two most important commands: `apk update` for reading the package sources and `apk add <name>` for installing a package. Some other commands are summarized in Table 8.2. More details and options can be found here:

https://wiki.alpinelinux.org/wiki/Alpine_Linux_package_management

By default, only the following packages are installed in the Docker image of Alpine Linux:

```
apk info | sort
  alpine-baselayout
  alpine-keys
  apk-tools
  busybox
  ca-certificates-bundle
  libc-utils
  libcrypto1.1
  libssl1.1
  libtls-standalone
  musl
  musl-utils
  scanelf
  ssl_client
  zlib
```

Command	Function
apk add <name>	Installs the specified package
apk del <name>	Removes the specified package

Table 8.2 The Most Important Commands for Package Management

Command	Function
apk info	Lists the installed packages
apk search <name>	Searches for packages in the package sources
apk stats	Shows how many packages are installed
apk update	Determines which packages are currently available
apk upgrade	Displays all installed packages

Table 8.2 The Most Important Commands for Package Management (Cont.)

8.2.1   Package Sources

The package sources for Alpine Linux are defined in the */etc/apk/repositories* file:

```
cat /etc/apk/repositories
  https://dl-cdn.alpinelinux.org/alpine/v3.13/main
  https://dl-cdn.alpinelinux.org/alpine/v3.13/community
```

The offer of packages isn't quite as huge as on Debian or Ubuntu, but with almost 14,000 packages, it's still more than respectable:

```
apk update
  ...
  OK: 13888 distinct packages available
```

The package source index files are stored in */var/cache/apk* and take up about 1 MB of space. To save disk space, you can delete the files located there once the installation work has been completed.

With apk search, you can search for packages in the package sources:

```
apk search php7 | sort
  cacti-php7-1.2.17-r0
  php7-7.4.19-r0
  php7-apache2-7.4.19-r0
  php7-bcmath-7.4.19-r0
  ...
```

Alternatively, you can take a look at the following web page for package search:

https://pkgs.alpinelinux.org/packages

Don't Forget "apk update"!

Before you can install the first package, you must use apk update to create a local index that contains all packages currently available in the package sources. Alternatively, you

---

can call apk add with the --update option; then apk update will be executed automatically.

If you use apk in a *Dockerfile* to create a new image that uses additional packages, you should use the --no-cache option instead of the --update option just mentioned. This option also causes an apk update, but the downloaded package index will immediately be deleted from the cache after installation. This prevents the image from being inflated by unnecessary data.

It's also advisable to immediately delete packages that are only needed temporarily, as shown in the following example:

```
# File Dockerfile
...
RUN apk add --no-cache \
    build-base \
    python3-dev \
    py3-pip \
    jpeg-dev \
    zlib-dev \
    ffmpeg \
    && pip3 install sigal \
    && pip3 install cssmin \
    && apk del build-base python3-dev jpeg-dev zlib-dev
```

8.2.2 Packages and Their Files

apk info <name> summarizes the most important details about a package:

```
apk info musl
  musl-1.2.2-r0 description:
  the musl c library (libc) implementation
  musl-1.2.2-r0 webpage: https://musl.libc.org
  musl-1.2.2-r0 installed size: 608 KiB
```

With apk info -L <name>, the command returns a list of all files belonging to a package:

```
apk info -L musl
  musl-1.2.2-r0 contains:
  lib/ld-musl-x86_64.so.1
  lib/libc.musl-x86_64.so.1
```

Conversely, you can use apk info --who-owns <file> to determine which package the specified file belongs to:

```
apk info --who-owns /bin/ls
  /bin/ls symlink target is owned by busybox-1.32.1-r6
```

Chapter 9
Web Servers and Company

This chapter describes how you can run common web servers in a Docker container. Although Docker isn't limited to server services, in practice, these are the services that Docker is often used for. Here, we'll focus on the following programs:

- Apache
- Nginx (with Secure Sockets Layer [SSL] certificates from Let's Encrypt)
- Node.js with Express
- HAProxy
- Traefik

Predefined Images versus Custom Images

For all programs presented here, there are already ready-to-use Docker images available for download from Docker Hub. Whether you want to use them or prefer to create your own images is entirely up to you and depends on the specific requirement. But for a quick start, the prebuilt images are very suitable.

To implement a specific project, it's usually useful to develop your own image based on a Linux distribution and then install and adapt the desired program there. This is especially useful if you want to use special modules in addition to the standard components.

9.1   Apache HTTP Server

The "grande dame" in the circle of web server software is the *Apache HTTP Server*. First released in April 1995, it consisted of many extensions (*patches*) to the then-common NCSA HTTPd server. Even though *Nginx* is gaining popularity (details will follow in Section 9.2), the Apache web server still has the widest distribution.

9.1.1   Using an Official Docker Image

Of course, there's an official Docker image available for Apache, which we want to use for the first test. You can find the description and links to the *Dockerfiles* at *https:// hub.docker.com/_/httpd*. You can use the image directly without your own *Dockerfile*, for example, to put HTML files from the current directory online:

```
docker run -p 8080:80 --rm --name apache \
  -v "${PWD}":/usr/local/apache2/htdocs/ httpd:2.4
```

The parameters of the preceding command perform the following functions:

- -p 8080:80 connects port 8080 on your host to port 80 of the container, so you can access the content via *http://localhost:8080*.

- --rm immediately deletes the container after execution.

- --name apache causes the container to be addressable by the name apache in addition to the container ID.

- -v "${PWD}":/usr/local/apache2/htdocs/ integrates the current directory on the host (which you specify in the PWD variable) into the container at the location, /usr/local/apache2/htdocs.

- httpd:2.4 specifies the desired image. The official Apache web server image is called httpd. From this image, you start version 2.4.

After that, the web server runs in the foreground; thus, it blocks your current terminal. For this, you can then open the address *http://localhost:8080* in your browser. You'll see either the list of files in the current directory or, if the *index.html* file is in the directory, you'll see the contents of that file.

To stop the web server, you can press [Ctrl]+[C] in the blocked console. Alternatively, you can open a second terminal window and terminate the running container using docker stop apache.

9.1.2   Using a Custom Dockerfile

For a serious project, you may want to create your own *Dockerfile*. The integration of local directories from the host makes the Docker image inflexible. So, it would probably make sense to copy the web content to the image or use a volume for it. You may also want to change a couple of settings in the web server (e.g., load an additional module).

Which base image you use for the project depends heavily on what additional features you want to have in your target image. The official image of Apache just used is built on Debian and consumes about 200 MB of disk space, which isn't excessively much. However, you can have it take up even less space by using the Apache web server as a package in the slim Alpine Linux distribution:

```
# File: webserver/apache/alpine/Dockerfile
FROM alpine:3.14
RUN apk --no-cache add apache2 apache2-utils
RUN mkdir -p /run/apache2
EXPOSE 80
CMD ["/usr/sbin/httpd", "-DFOREGROUND"]
```

The resulting image, which also starts the Apache web server, is impressively small at just 9.5 MB. Of course, the package selection of Alpine Linux can't keep up with Debian. So, if you need some more components for your project, you have to decide on which base image you want to use.

We'll mainly use the Debian base image and packages from the Debian community in the remaining parts of this book. To create a Docker image yourself with the current Debian base image, the following *Dockerfile* is suitable:

```
# File: webserver/apache/debian/Dockerfile (docbuc/apache)
FROM debian:buster
RUN apt-get update && apt-get install -y \
  apache2 \
  && rm -rf /var/lib/apt/lists/*
RUN a2enmod rewrite headers
COPY default.conf /etc/apache2/sites-enabled/
COPY html /var/www/html
EXPOSE 80
CMD [ "/usr/sbin/apache2ctl", "-DFOREGROUND" ]
```

This will first update the local cache of packages in the current base image debian:buster (apt-get update) and then install the *apache2* package with apt-get install -y. The -y is crucial here, as otherwise the package manager will get stuck asking if you really want to install the package and other packages needed for it.

In the same RUN call, the just-updated package cache gets cleared again. The Docker documentation suggests this approach because each command in the *Dockerfile* creates a "layer" in the Docker image. If the package cache, which is a few megabytes in size, is deleted in the same step, it won't be reflected in the size of the Docker layer and doesn't unnecessarily increase the size of the final Docker image.

The Docker documentation also recommends that when installing packages, each package is written on its own line with the trailing backslash \. This seems to be unnecessary in the present example. However, if you use multiple packages when compiling your *Dockerfile*, this approach will result in a much better readability of the file. Often, you'll need to add or remove a package. Deleting or inserting a line is then much easier than searching for the name in a long line.

The next RUN statement activates the rewrite and headers modules, which are two frequently used extensions for Apache. After that, a configuration file is copied to the image. In it, you specify the settings for your virtual host. COPY enables you to copy the html folder in the current directory to the image. Here, you should store the HTML files delivered by the web server. The folder */var/www/html* is defined as DocumentRoot in the *default.conf* file.

EXPOSE 80 is used in the *Dockerfile* to document that the image uses port 80. It doesn't change anything about the actual function of the container, but it does indicate to the user that the port is being used by the container. To illustrate this, you can start an Apache container and see from the output of docker ps that port 80 is open in the container:

```
docker run -d --rm httpd:2.4
  085e9ac80f304b3e46dcdd618eab8eb2de1664cd698cef7aadde56d9fcdb491

docker ps --format "table {{.ID}}\t{{.Names}}\t{{.Ports}}"
  CONTAINER ID    NAMES                  PORTS
  085e9ac80f30    nervous_pike           80/tcp

docker stop nervous_pike
  nervous_pike
```

In addition, EXPOSE enables the -P parameter on the docker run command to connect port 80 to a free port on your host. To find out which port the command has chosen, you can use the docker port <container name> command. If the port used by the container is connected to a port on the host, this will be indicated as in the following listing:

```
docker run -d -P --name apachePortTest --rm httpd:2.4
  659754e22aa11bb5b537ef2351a047f4755f599b9c196b2de12c3a106443a19

docker port apachePortTest
  80/tcp -> 0.0.0.0:49153
  80/tcp -> :::49153
docker stop apachePortTest
  apachePortTest
```

One advantage of this approach is that the Docker daemon takes care of finding a free port on the host system. Especially when multiple containers are started, this can be very useful.

As a command to be executed when a container is started, the apache2ctl program is specified with the -DFOREGROUND parameter. This option causes the Apache web server to run as a foreground process rather than in the background, which is usually the case. According to the Docker philosophy, a container should only be responsible for one task, and this task is also directly linked to the container. If the task "dies," the container should also be terminated.

Now you can create the Apache image—the output of the build process will look similar to the following listing:

```
docker build -t docbuc/apache .
  Sending build context to Docker daemon  5.632kB
  Step 1/7 : FROM debian:buster
   ---> 85c4fd36a543
  Step 2/7 : RUN apt-get update && apt-get install -y   apache2
&& rm -rf /var/lib/apt/lists/*
  ...
  Successfully built 8b1cada79633
  Successfully tagged docbuc/apache:latest
```

Docker works through the layers in the *Dockerfile* and finally gives the image the name docbuc/apache:latest. The latest extension is used because we didn't specify a specific version for the tag in the build command.

You can now start the new Apache container with the following command:

```
docker run --rm -p 8080:80 docbuc/apache
```

Open the browser using the address *http://localhost:8080*, and the Apache web server will deliver your HTML file.

9.1.3   Using the Official Docker Image

The method described in the previous section is very simple for skilled Linux administrators: Those who have already dealt with the Debian Linux distribution know where the configuration files are located and to which position the HTML contents have to be copied. If you prefer to use the official Docker image from Apache Software Foundation, you usually can't avoid looking at the documentation for this image in a bit more detail.

We now want to create a Docker image based on the official httpd image with the server state module enabled. By default, very few Apache modules are enabled, which makes the image less vulnerable. To change the configuration, we could copy a modified version of the configuration file to the new image, as in the previous example. Here, however, we'll take a different approach and modify the existing configuration file. The noninteractive editor sed can perform this task:

```
RUN sed -i \
  -e 's/^#\(LoadModule info_module modules\/mod_info.so\)/\1/' \
  -e 's/^#\(Include conf\/extra\/httpd-info.conf\)/\1/' \
  conf/httpd.conf
```

In this process, the *conf/httpd.conf* file is opened, then the line containing #LoadModule info_module modules/mod_info.so is searched for, and, finally, the comment character (#) gets removed. The -i parameter (in place) causes the editor to modify the file directly (usually the file isn't modified, but the result is written to the console), and -e executes the *find-replace* command as a regular expression. We'll apply the same technique for another line in the configuration file, where additional settings are loaded from the *conf/extra/httpd-info.conf* file.

Using the *search-replace* process in *Dockerfiles* is a common practice. If you aren't that familiar with regular expressions, a short crash course on one of the many websites on the subject can be very helpful. For example, *https://regexr.com* has a very interesting, interactive user interface that invites you to try out regular expressions.

The *Dockerfile* for the official Apache image sets the WORKDIR to the folder that stores all resources for the web server. For this reason, we can use the relative path conf/httpd.conf in the sed statement. However, this setting doesn't need to be done for every image, so a look at the documentation for the image is usually essential.

By default, the server status module is accessible only from the local IP address, which doesn't allow us to access it from outside the container. For testing purposes, we'll disable this restriction again using the sed command. In production operation, you would definitely have to set up another kind of access restriction (e.g., user name and password). Here's the entire *Dockerfile*, where we also copy the HTML file again:

```
# Dockerfile for docbuc/apache-httpd-status (docbuc/httpd-status)
FROM httpd:2.4
RUN sed -i \
  -e 's/^#\(LoadModule info_module modules\/mod_info.so\)/\1/' \
  -e 's/^#\(Include conf\/extra\/httpd-info.conf\)/\1/' \
  conf/httpd.conf
RUN sed -i \
  -e 's/^ *Require host/## Require host/' \
  -e 's/^ *Require ip/## Require ip/' ,\
  conf/extra/httpd-info.conf
COPY ./html/ /usr/local/apache2/htdocs/
```

Note that we don't need a final CMD in the *Dockerfile* here to start the web server; the base image httpd:2.4 does that for us. Using the familiar Docker commands build and run, we first want to create the image and then start the container:

```
docker build -t docbuc/apache-httpd-status .
docker run -d -p 8080:80 --name apache-httpd-status \
  docbuc/apache-httpd-status
```

Calling the web page *http://localhost:8080/server-status* then shows us the current state of the newly started web server, and via *http://localhost:8080/server-info*, we can find numerous internal details about the server, such as all loaded modules and their configuration.

The main difference with the *Dockerfile* presented in the previous section, where we installed the web server from Debian's package sources, is that you can always stay up to date with the official Apache image. When using the package sources, you automatically put in the version the Debian developers think is appropriate for their distribution.

9.2   Nginx

Nginx entered the stage of the internet 10 years after Apache. The objective was to develop a high-performance web server that's easy to configure and at the same time has a low resource consumption. Nginx was and is successful, which is reflected in the constantly increasing user numbers. Thanks to its sophisticated ability to redirect requests (proxy function), Nginx is popularly used as a *load balancer* or *SSL termination proxy*.

There's also an official Docker image for Nginx in the store and on Docker Hub. A closer look at the *Dockerfile* for this image reveals that the base image used is `debian:buster-slim`; that is, the current Debian version is a reduced version that's currently still marked as *experimental*. For common processor architectures, the Nginx package and the four Nginx modules `xslt`, `geoip`, `image-filter`, and `njs` are then installed from the *nginx.org* package sources.

9.2.1   Usage with a Custom Dockerfile

We want to use Nginx with the classic Debian base image, and, as with the Apache example, we'll copy the HTML files into the image. The required *Dockerfile* looks like this:

```
# File: webserver/nginx/debian/Dockerfile (docbuc/nginx)
FROM debian:buster
RUN apt-get update && apt-get install -y \
  nginx \
  && rm -rf /var/lib/apt/lists/*
COPY default /etc/nginx/sites-available/
COPY html/ /var/www/html/
EXPOSE 80
CMD ["nginx", "-g", "daemon off;"]
```

To customize the configuration of Nginx, the `default` file must be copied to the appropriate location in the file system. If you want to have a template for this file, you can simply copy it from a "fresh" Debian container. For this purpose, you want to run the following commands:

```
docker run -it --name nginxTemplate debian:buster
  root@2129f9fb9021:/# apt-get update && apt-get install -y nginx
    Get:1 http://security.debian.org/debian-security
      buster/updates InRelease [65.4 kB]
    ...
    Setting up nginx-full (1.14.2-2+deb10u4) ...
    Processing triggers for libc-bin (2.28-10) ...
  root@2129f9fb9021:/# exit

docker cp nginxTemplate:/etc/nginx/sites-available/default .
docker rm nginxTemplate
```

Using the first command, docker run, you create a new container from the current Debian image and name it nginxTemplate. In addition, you start the container as an interactive session (-it). You then install Nginx at the root prompt in the container (outputs are shown here in an abbreviated version). After that, you exit the container and copy the default configuration file from the container to the local file system (docker cp). Then you can delete this container again (docker rm).

Now you can change the configuration according to your needs (for this example, it's sufficient to leave the default settings unchanged). You also create the *html* folder. In this folder, you save the following file:

```
<!-- File: html/index.html -->
<!DOCTYPE html>
<html>
  <head>
    <meta charset="utf-8">
    <title>nginx</title>
  </head>
  <body>
    <h1>Nginx web server in Debian container</h1>
  </body>
</html>
```

Now you can create the image:

```
docker build -t docbuc/nginx .
```

To try out the new Nginx image, you need to start the container:

```
docker run --rm -p 8080:80 docbuc/nginx
```

Again, we use port 8080 on the local computer and connect it to port 80 on the container where Nginx is responding (refer to Figure 9.1).

Figure 9.1 Nginx Web Server in the Docker Container

9.3   Nginx as Reverse Proxy with SSL Certificates from Let's Encrypt

A common setup with Docker web applications is to use a web server as a *reverse proxy* on the physical host. This server then redirects all accesses on ports 80 and 443 to the corresponding Docker container. The configuration options here are diverse because you can address different containers not only via the host name but also on the basis of the URL path. For example, your application programming interface (API) can be accessible under the same host name as static content and only access a different container based on the URL (e.g., /api/...).

Another advantage of such a setup is that encrypted connections are managed in one place and don't need to be considered at all in the various containers. In this technique, also referred to as a *TLS/SSL termination proxy*, encrypted traffic over the insecure internet is decrypted by the proxy server and then redirected unencrypted through the private, secure Docker network to the respective containers.

The various services running in individual Docker containers behind the proxy are securely accessible via the internet, but they don't manage SSL certificates themselves.

> **Traefik**
>
> Very convenient and meanwhile widely used for the setup described here is the specially developed proxy server called *Traefik*. You can find a detailed description in Section 9.6, at the end of this chapter.

For the following example, we want to use the free certificates from Let's Encrypt to secure the upstream proxy server. With Let's Encrypt, it has been possible for several years to have a certificate for one's own domain created automatically and free of charge.

The organization behind Let's Encrypt, Internet Security Research Group, operates on a nonprofit basis and provides the infrastructure for managing the certificates. If you've ever applied for a certificate yourself from an official certification authority or created a self-signed certificate, you're probably familiar with the process of creating a *Certificate Signing Request* (CSR), which must be signed with a private key, and then receiving the certificate.

Fortunately, with Let's Encrypt, this process is somewhat simplified. Ideally, all that's needed is to call the command-line program `certbot` with the corresponding domain name, and the configuration is adjusted as if by magic. To make it work in the Docker environment, we need to make a few adjustments.

> **Domain Name and Public IP Address Required**
>
> To successfully run the following example, you must have a valid domain name and run the example on the server to which the domain name is assigned according to the Domain Name System (DNS) configuration. Let's Encrypt checks whether the certificate request is initiated from the corresponding server.

9.3.1   Nginx Reverse Proxy

We'll start with configuring the reverse proxy server. For this process, it's important which name you assign to the directory where you save the *docker-compose.yml* file of the reverse proxy. `docker compose` names both containers and volumes based on this directory. We'll use *nginxterminator* as the directory name and store the following *docker-compose.yml* file there:

```
# File: webserver/nginx/nginxterminator/docker-compose.yml
version: '3'
services:
  proxy:
    image: nginx:1
    restart: always
    ports:
      - "80:80"
      - "443:443"
    volumes:
      - ./conf.d:/etc/nginx/conf.d
      - certs:/etc/letsencrypt
      - certs-data:/data/letsencrypt
```

```
volumes:
  certs:
  certs-data:
```

We define only one service that uses the default Nginx image in the current version 1.x of Docker Hub. Both port 80 and port 443 are redirected to the physical host. The volumes section in this example is more interesting. First, a local *./conf.d* folder gets included in the container under */etc/nginx/conf.d*. The Nginx image is configured to automatically process files that end in *.conf* and are located in this directory, so it's very easy to add a new service: just copy a new file with the appropriate settings into this directory and restart the server.

The following two volumes are specific to Let's Encrypt:

- The certs volume, which is mounted in the container under /etc/letsencrypt, stores the issued certificates and some settings for Let's Encrypt.
- The certs-data volume is used by Let's Encrypt to ensure that the domain name for which the request for a certificate is executed will be assigned to the server that runs the certbot program. Technically, this is done using a temporary file, which is created by certbot in this volume and is provided by the Nginx server. Only if the Let's Encrypt validation server can successfully retrieve the file will the certificate be issued and certbot delete the temporary file again.

You should now save a minimum Nginx configuration in the *conf.d/* folder. The location entry provides the temporary file to validate the domain.

```
# File: webserver/nginx/nginxterminator/conf.d/default.conf
server {
    listen        80;
    server_name   localhost;

    location ^~ /.well-known {
      allow all;
      root  /data/letsencrypt/;
    }
}
```

Now you need to start the docker compose setup so that Nginx makes your server reachable on port 80.

9.3.2   Creating the First Certificate

Under the domain name api.dockerbuch.info, a REST API is supposed to be accessible, which runs as a container behind the Nginx proxy and is accessible over the internet via HTTPS. As a first step, we'll apply and download the certificate for the domain. As mentioned earlier, this step is handled by the certbot command, which we also run from a container:

```
docker run -it --rm \
      -v nginxterminator_certs:/etc/letsencrypt \
      -v nginxterminator_certs-data:/data/letsencrypt \
      certbot/certbot \
      certonly \
      --webroot --webroot-path=/data/letsencrypt \
      -d api.dockerbuch.info

  Unable to find image 'certbot/certbot:latest' locally
  latest: Pulling from certbot/certbot
  339de151aab4: Pull complete
  ...
  Saving debug log to /var/log/letsencrypt/letsencrypt.log
  Enter email address (used for urgent renewal and security no...
   (Enter 'c' to cancel): info@dockerbuch.info
  Please read the Terms of Service at
  https://letsencrypt.org/documents/LE-SA-v1.2-November-15-201...
  agree in order to register with the ACME server. Do you agree?
  ...
  Account registered.
  Requesting a certificate for api.dockerbuch.info
  Successfully received certificate.
  Certificate is saved at: /etc/letsencrypt/live/api.dockerbuc...
  Key is saved at:        /etc/letsencrypt/live/api.dockerbuc...
  This certificate expires on 2021-09-28.
```

The first time you use certbot, you'll be prompted for an email address to which security alerts can be sent. You also need to accept the terms and conditions of the Let's Encrypt service. If the docker run command was successful, the new certificate will be stored in the certs volume at /etc/letsencrypt/live/<domainname>/fullchain.pem.

In the background, the certbot program saved the temporary file mentioned above to the shared Docker volume nginxterminator_certs-data, and the Let's Encrypt servers confirmed the domain.

You can then store a configuration file for the service in the *conf.d* directory:

```
# File: webserver/nginx/nginxterminator/conf.d/api.conf
server {
  listen        80;
  server_name   api.dockerbuch.info;
```

```
  location / {
    proxy_set_header    Host $host;
    proxy_set_header    X-Real-IP $remote_addr;
    proxy_set_header
      X-Forwarded-For $proxy_add_x_forwarded_for;
    proxy_set_header    X-Forwarded-Proto $scheme;
    proxy_pass
      http://dockerbuch_api_1.nginxterminator_default:80;
    proxy_read_timeout  90;
  }

  location ^~ /.well-known {
    allow all;
    root  /data/letsencrypt/;
  }
listen 443 ssl;
  ssl_certificate
    /etc/letsencrypt/live/api.dockerbuch.info/fullchain.pem;
  ssl_certificate_key
    /etc/letsencrypt/live/api.dockerbuch.info/privkey.pem;
  include /etc/letsencrypt/options-ssl-nginx.conf;
  if ($scheme != "https") {
    return 301 https://$host$request_uri;
  }
}
```

The Nginx web server processes requests for the host name, api.dockerbuch.info. It's started unencrypted on port 80 and encrypted on port 443. The location sections define what happens with accesses to the server. If the URL starts with /.well-known, the directory for HTML documents is set to */data/letsencrypt*, which is the area the certbot program can also access via the shared Docker volume. This configuration must be entered for each web server after the proxy so that the certificate can be renewed via this server before it expires.

All other accesses to the web server are processed in the location / section. Once the proxy headers have been added, the crucial proxy_pass line follows. This line specifies the Docker container that provides the corresponding service, in this case, access to a REST API.

The interesting thing here is the host name to which the request will be redirected. In the docker compose environments we've seen so far, you could simply use the names of the respective services in use as the host name. However, the container in which the API service runs is not entered in the docker compose configuration of the Nginx proxy server, which is absolutely correct. The services behind the proxy should work completely independently of the proxy configuration. The solution to the problem is an external type Docker network, which we'll describe later in Section 9.3.3. The connection is unencrypted on port 80, since we're in a secure network here.

In the other lines of the Nginx configuration, you specify the location for the Let's Encrypt certificates (in the shared nginxterminator_certs volume) and include the SSL settings of Let's Encrypt. Among other things, this is where you specify which SSL version and which encryption key collection is activated. Finally, unencrypted accesses will get redirected to the secure HTTPS protocol.

The SSL settings of Let's Encrypt aren't yet located in the designated volume. You can download them with a simple wget call from the certbot GitHub page:

```
docker run -it --rm -v nginxterminator_certs:/etc/letsencrypt \
  alpine wget -O /etc/letsencrypt/options-ssl-nginx.conf \
  https://raw.githubusercontent.com/certbot/certbot/master/\
    certbot-nginx/certbot_nginx/_internal/tls_configs/\
    options-ssl-nginx.conf
```

This very clear configuration can serve as a template for different services behind the proxy. You just need to adjust the host name, proxy_pass line, and the location of the certificates accordingly.

9.3.3   Application Programming Interface Server

As mentioned in the previous section, one advantage of the solution presented here is that the containers behind the proxy don't require any configuration adjustments for the encryption. The services run on the standard ports within the container. However, a small extension is still necessary: you must connect the containers to the proxy server's network in addition to your own network (default).

This can be done by adding the external: true entry for the nginxterminator_default network in the networks section of the *docker-compose.yml* file:

```
# File: webserver/nginx/dockerbuch/docker-compose.yml
version: '3'
services:
  api:
    image: nginx
    restart: always
    networks:
      - nginxterminator_default
      - default
networks:
  nginxterminator_default:
    external: true
```

You can easily determine that your container now manages two network interfaces by using Linux command ip addr show in the container (the output has been slightly shortened):

```
docker exec dockerbuch_api_1 ip -4 -o addr show
```

```
1:  lo    inet 127.0.0.1/8 scope host lo [...]
90: eth0   inet 172.19.0.2/16 brd 172.19.255.255
           scope global eth0
92: eth1   inet 172.18.0.2/16 brd 172.18.255.255
           scope global eth1
```

The -4 parameter instructs the ip command to display only IPv4-relevant information, while -o (one line) stands for single-line output. Both eth0 and eth1 have been given a network address in the 172.x.y.z network segment. To find out more precisely which network interface belongs to which network, you can use the docker inspect command. This will give you a lot of information about the corresponding container. For us, only the Networks section is relevant:

```
docker inspect dockerbuch_api_1
  ...
"Networks": {
   "dockerbuch_default": {
       "IPAMConfig": null,
       "Links": null,
       "Aliases": [
          "api",
          "262638be9926"
       ],
       "NetworkID":          "295f448b...",
       "EndpointID":         "402588be...",
       "Gateway":            "172.19.0.1",
       "IPAddress":          "172.19.0.2",
       "IPPrefixLen":        16,
       ...
       "MacAddress":         "02:42:ac:13:00:02",
       "DriverOpts":         null
   },
   "nginxterminator_default": {
       "IPAMConfig": null,
       "Links": null,
       "Aliases": [
          "api",
          "262638be9926"
       ],
```

```
      "NetworkID":        "3093b7db...",
      "EndpointID":       "11d59ab3...",
      "Gateway":          "172.18.0.1",
      "IPAddress":        "172.18.0.2",
      "IPPrefixLen":      16,
      ...
      "MacAddress":       "02:42:ac:12:00:02",
      "DriverOpts":       null
   }
}
```

9.3.4   Renewing Certificates

If you've successfully configured the setup so far, your various services are now running securely over the internet behind the proxy server. The Let's Encrypt certificates are currently only valid for 90 days, which is why an automated certificate renewal makes sense. Fortunately, the certificate renewal is also a one-liner.

Like you did when creating the certificate, you must use the two Docker volumes, nginxterminator_certs and nginxterminator_certs-data, and run the certbot program with the renew parameter:

```
docker run -t --rm \
  -v nginxterminator_certs:/etc/letsencrypt \
  -v nginxterminator_certs-data:/data/letsencrypt \
  certbot/certbot \
  renew \
  --webroot --webroot-path=/data/letsencrypt
```

This will check all your active certificates for a possible renewal. If a renewal is necessary, it will also be performed completely automatically. To avoid forgetting about renewing the certificates, it's useful to set up a cron job on the host that runs the check periodically. A cron entry for a weekly check on Sunday at five minutes past four in the morning might look like the following (the docker run command has been shortened here):

```
5 4 * * 0   docker run -t --rm -v nginxterminator_certs:/et[...]
```

> **Note**
>
> You should check your certificates regularly with a service such as SSL Labs. The online service (*www.ssllabs.com/ssltest*) alerts you to new security vulnerabilities or configuration errors on your server. There are ready-made plug-ins for monitoring services such as Nagios or Icinga.

9.4   Node.js with Express

Node.js is not a web server but an interpreter for JavaScript. The reason we've included it in this chapter is because Node.js is so popular with web applications and, therefore, also readily extended to include the web server component. To learn how to use Node.js without a server component and get a few technical details about the runtime, see Chapter 11, Section 11.1.

9.4.1   Express Framework

The Node.js web server in Chapter 1, Section 1.3, is already a de facto web server, but it isn't very suitable for practical use because it always responds with the same page, no matter what the request. To cover the various demands on a web server as well as possible, it's best to use a Node.js module, with the *Express framework* being the most popular module here. To install it, you should use the npm command-line utility, which is the Node.js package manager:

```
npm i express
```

As some additional libraries are installed during this call, it may take some time depending on your internet connection. Finally, you need to program the server. This sounds more complicated than it is because the following short JavaScript file is sufficient to deliver static files from the *files* folder via HTTP to port 8080:

```
// File node-express-test/index.js
const express = require('express');
const app = express();
app.use(express.static('files'));
app.listen(8080);
```

A big advantage of using Node.js as a web server is that you don't need to install an additional programming language as JavaScript is provided out of the box. In the rest of this section, we'll create a development and a production environment for an Express web server in Docker.

9.4.2   Docker Development Environment for Express

Again, you need to create a custom directory for this example; let's call it *node-express*. Node.js uses a configuration file called *package.json* for managing projects. All metadata items relevant to the application, such as the application name, version, required Node.js packages, and more, are stored there. You can create this file with a text editor, but it's easier to call npm init and answer some questions.

If you want to create a serious project with Express, the express-generator module is even better for getting started. It creates a file structure and includes modules for a HTML template system and a stylesheet compiler.

You don't need a Node.js runtime on your computer for the following example; we'll handle all the requirements inside Docker containers. First, you want to create a *Dockerfile* that will serve as the base for your development environment:

```
# File: webserver/node-express/Dockerfile-dev (docbuc/node-ex...
FROM node:16
WORKDIR /src
RUN npm i -g express-generator nodemon
USER node
```

Its image is derived from the official Node.js image. Then, two Node.js modules must be installed in it: express-generator and nodemon. The -g parameter (global) in the npm command makes sure that the modules will be installed in a directory in the search path rather than in the current directory. Finally, you need to switch to the unprivileged user, node.

Now create a *docker-compose.yml* file so that you don't have to enter the parameters for the docker run command every time:

```
# File: webserver/node-express/docker-compose.yml
version: '3'
services:
  dev:
    build:
      context: .
      dockerfile: Dockerfile-dev
    volumes:
      - ./src:/src
      - node_exp_modules:/src/node_modules
    ports:
      - 8080:3000
    environment:
      DEBUG: "src"
    command: [ "nodemon", "bin/www" ]
volumes:
  node_exp_modules:
```

The dev service uses the *Dockerfile-dev* file described earlier as a starting point and mounts two volumes. A directory named *src/* in the current directory is mounted under /src in the container. Both static and dynamic content for the web server is stored there. A Docker-managed volume named node_exp_modules serves as storage location for the various Node.js modules. The command that's executed when the container is started is `nodemon bin/www`. We'll get to that momentarily.

First, you want to create the project structure with the Express generator and overwrite the start command with `express --view hbs`. In this example, you use the templating system. The `express -h` call enables you to display other variants as well. Before that, you should create the *./src* directory for your source code:

```
mkdir src

docker compose run -u $UID dev express --view hbs

  destination is not empty, continue? [y/N] y

   create : public/
   create : public/javascripts/
   create : public/images/
   create : public/stylesheets/
   create : routes/
   create : routes/index.js
   ...

   install dependencies:
     $ npm install

   run the app:
     $ DEBUG=src:* npm start
```

You can answer the question as to whether a nonempty directory should be used for the project with yes (y); here, the already mounted mountpoint of `node_modules` is recognized. In the output, you can already see which files have been created and what the next steps are. Next, you need to install the necessary modules:

```
docker compose run -u root dev chown -R $UID /src/node_modules/
docker compose run -u $UID dev npm i
```

The `chown` command is necessary because `docker compose` uses `root` as the owner when mounting new directories; however, you want these directories to be installed under your user ID. `npm i` makes sure that the Node.js modules listed in the *package.json* file will be installed, including their dependencies.

Now your development environment is ready, and you can start the server via `docker-compose up dev`. This command starts the previously installed `nodemon` program, which checks the files for changes and reloads the web server if necessary. This ensures that you can always control the current version of your work. Open *http://localhost:8080* in your browser to see the welcome screen.

203

9.4.3 Docker Production Environment for Express

When your application is ready to go live, you need to package the source code and runtime into a Docker image:

```
# File: webserver/node-express/Dockerfile (docbuc/node-express)
FROM node:16
WORKDIR /src
COPY ./src/package.json /src/
RUN npm i --production
COPY /src/ /src/
EXPOSE 3000
USER node
CMD [ "node", "/src/bin/www" ]
```

Create the image with `docker build -t docbuc/node-express .`, and then run it using `docker run -p 8080:3000 docbuc/node-express`. Your web application is now running in production mode at *http://localhost:8080*. If you run this image on a server, you may want to use a reverse proxy solution (Section 9.3).

9.4.4 Debugging the Applications

You may have noticed the `DEBUG` environment variable in the *docker-compose.yml* file. The Express framework also automatically installs a Node.js module for debugging your application.

Using it in the code is very simple: For example, if you want to examine the request headers, you can simply call `debug('headers: ', req.headers);` in the JavaScript code. The advantage over the `console.log` command is that the output only occurs if the `DEBUG` variable has been set. Here you can see the listing with the debug lines that processes the request to the home page:

```
// File: node-express/src/routes/index.js
var express = require('express');
var router = express.Router();
const debug = require('debug')('src');
/* GET home page. */
router.get('/', function(req, res, next) {
  debug('Headers: ', req.headers);
  res.render('index', { title: 'Express' });
});
module.exports = router;
```

With this technique, you can very easily add debug entries to your code without having to exclude them for production use. If you want to enable debugging temporarily in production mode as well, it's sufficient to start the container via the following command: `docker run -p 8080:3000 -e "DEBUG=src" docbuc/node-express`.

9.5   HAProxy

HAProxy is a very efficient proxy server and load balancer for HTTP and TCP connections in general. The software is currently used by some very prominent and popular websites, such as GitHub, Stack Overflow, Reddit, and Twitter. You can find even more references here:

www.haproxy.org/they-use-it.html

In the Docker environment, a load balancer solution is particularly exciting because containers can be duplicated very easily and a load balancer can distribute requests accordingly to less utilized containers.

9.5.1   Hello World!

For the first attempt with HAProxy, we'll use the official Docker Hub image. A load balancer alone makes little sense, but because we've already implemented one web server as a Docker image in each of the first two sections, we'll put the load balancer in front of these two running containers here. To avoid making the network setup too complex for this example, we'll use `docker compose` (see Chapter 5).

But first, you need to create the `Dockerfile` for the HAProxy image:

```
# File: webserver/haproxy/manual/Dockerfile (docbuc/haproxy)
FROM haproxy:2.4.1
COPY haproxy.cfg /usr/local/etc/haproxy/haproxy.cfg
```

The proxy configuration file *haproxy.cfg* must have the following content:

```
# File: webserver/haproxy/manual/haproxy.cfg
defaults
    mode http
    timeout connect 5000ms
    timeout client 50000ms
    timeout server 50000ms

frontend http-in
    bind *:80
    default_backend servers

backend servers
    server apache apache:80 maxconn 32
    server nginx nginx:80 maxconn 32
```

We don't want to get too much into the configuration options of HAProxy here, so our proxy starts with a minimal variant. In the `defaults` section, the mode is set to `http`, and then some timeout settings are made.

The more exciting part is in the `frontend` and `backend` sections: the frontend connects to port 80 of all network interfaces and points to `servers` at `default_backend`. In the corresponding section, two servers are defined: the first is named *apache* and has the host name `apache:80`, while the second is named *nginx* and has the host name `nginx:80`. The naming of the servers in the HAProxy configuration is arbitrary; the host names of the two servers originate from the network created by `docker compose`.

```
# File: webserver/haproxy/manual/docker-compose.yml
version: "3"
services:
  haproxy:
    image: docbuc/haproxy
    build: .
    ports:
      - 8080:80
  nginx:
    image: docbuc/nginx
  apache:
    image: docbuc/apache
```

`docker compose` assigns host names on the local network according to the service names in the *docker-compose.yml* file. You can also use the names in the HAProxy configuration. HAProxy thus finds the way to its backend servers.

Now, as soon as you start `docker compose up` in the current directory, Docker will create three containers and start them. When you then call the page *http://localhost:8080* in your browser, you should get the response from one of the two web servers. When reloading the page several times, you'll see that the proxy accesses the two servers alternately.

It's fascinating that it takes so little configuration work to create a working setup for a load-balancing web server.

HAProxy Documentation

Before using HAProxy in production operation, you should read the detailed documentation on the possible proxy settings:

https://cbonte.github.io/haproxy-dconv/2.4/configuration.html

9.6   Traefik Proxy

Traefik is a reverse proxy *and* load balancer, so it's very popular software in the environment of containers and microservices. Unlike the solutions discussed so far with Nginx or HAProxy, which existed before Docker, Traefik was developed specifically to meet the modern requirements of container infrastructures. Accordingly, its use in combination with Docker is more convenient.

In the best case, a few lines in your project's *docker-compose.yml* file will suffice, and an upstream Traefik proxy server will take care of creating the Let's Encrypt certificates and redirect all requests to the correct service. You'll also get a modern dashboard that informs you of the current status of the proxy server (see Figure 9.2). We'll show you how to create containers that are managed automatically by Traefik in this section.

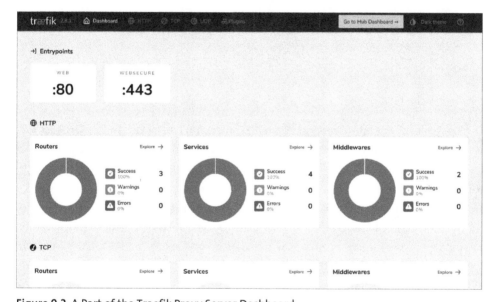

Figure 9.2 A Part of the Traefik Proxy Server Dashboard

To fully test this example, you need a server with a public IP address and at least two DNS entries which reference that server. We rented a virtual server for this, installed Docker on it, and put the DNS records for demo.dockerbuch.info and me.dockerbuch.info on it.

9.6.1   Installing and Configuring Traefik

The Traefik proxy is available for download on GitHub under the free MIT license. There you can download compiled binary packages, or you can launch Traefik as a Docker container. Of course, we chose the second option and will use the following *docker-compose.yml* file:

```
# File: webserver/traefik/docker-compose.yml
version: '3'
services:
  traefik:
    restart: unless-stopped
    image: traefik:v2.4
    networks:
      - web
    ports:
      - "80:80"
      - "443:443"
    volumes:
      - /var/run/docker.sock:/var/run/docker.sock:ro
      - ./acme.json:/acme.json
      - ./traefik.yml:/traefik.yml
      - ./traefik_api.yml:/traefik_api.yml
networks:
  web:
    external: true
```

The service uses the latest version v2.4 of Traefik's official Docker image. We start the service on the web network, which is defined as an external network at the end of the file. All applications that Traefik is supposed to manage are also connected to this network.

The ports for HTTP (80) and secure HTTPS (443) are redirected from the server to the container. Four local files are also included. The Docker socket is needed so that Traefik can detect if there's a new service or if an existing service has changed. The *acme.json* file is used to store the SSL certificates. We store them outside the container so that we don't lose the certificates even if we update the Traefik version.

Finally, we use two configuration files for the Traefik proxy: in *traefik.yml*, we define which ports are served, if and how SSL certificates are managed, and which *providers* are available.

```
# File: webserver/traefik/traefik.yml
entryPoints:
  web:
    address: ':80'
    http:
      redirections:
        entryPoint:
          to: websecure
          scheme: https
  websecure:
    address: ':443'
```

```
api:
  dashboard: true
certificatesResolvers:
  lets-encrypt:
    acme:
      email: info@dockerbuch.info
      storage: acme.json
      tlsChallenge: {}
providers:
  docker:
    watch: true
    network: web
    exposedByDefault: false
  file:
    filename: traefik_api.yml
```

In the entryPoints section, the redirection of the insecure web port 80 to the encrypted port 443 is specified. The next section, api, activates the internal API service of Traefik. The dashboard integrated there displays a graphical overview of the services managed by Traefik (refer to Figure 9.2).

The certificatesResolvers section contains the settings for creating the Let's Encrypt certificates. The last section is once again more exciting: Traefik can manage different configurations via *providers*. In addition to the *file* and *Docker* providers used here, Traefik can handle Kubernetes or Amazon ECS, for example.

We enable the Docker provider and configure it with the web network defined in the *docker-compose.yml* file. watch ensures that changes to a Docker service running behind the proxy will automatically be integrated. The exposedByDefault setting defaults to true, which would cause Traefik to expose any service that exports a port. We want to have a bit more control here and explicitly enable the services with the label traefik.enable=true (see the following code). The file provider references the *traefik_api.yml* file where the settings for the dashboard are configured:

```
# File: webserver/traefik/traefik_api.yml
http:
  middlewares:
    simpleAuth:
      basicAuth:
        users:
          - 'admin:$apr1$BljPhhOR$G5q4JAD2r11vw3VFfO4Bm/'
  routers:
    api:
      rule: Host(`demo.dockerbuch.info`)
      entrypoints:
```

```
    - websecure
middlewares:
  - simpleAuth
service: api@internal
tls:
  certResolver: lets-encrypt
```

The first part of the file defines *middleware* that requires the admin user with the password secret. *HTTP Basic Authentication* is used here, which leads to the familiar dialog box when called in the browser (see Figure 9.3).

Figure 9.3 HTTP Basic Authentication for Access to the Traefik Dashboard

To generate the hash value for the password, you can simply call the htpasswd program from the Apache Docker image:

```
docker run --rm httpd htpasswd -nb admin geheim
  admin:$apr1$BljPhhOR$G5q4JAD2r11vw3VFfO4Bm/
```

To make the dashboard accessible over the internet, we define the appropriate host name for it in the routers section (demo.dockerbuch.info). In addition, the middleware just mentioned is activated, and a Let's Encrypt certificate is requested. The service name api@internal is preset by Traefik.

We start this configuration with docker compose up -d, and after a short time, we can access the dashboard at *https://demo.dockerbuch.info* (refer to Figure 9.2). Make sure you create the *acme.json* file before starting docker compose and set permissions to read/write for the root user only.

9.6.2   Connecting Docker Services with Traefik

For the purpose of simplicity, the docker compose application, which is launched behind the Traefik proxy, consists of only one Nginx service. This service runs on port 80 and displays the default Nginx start page. If you want to use a different compose configuration, you just need to add the appropriate labels in your *docker-compose.yml file*.

```
# File: webserver/traefik/me/docker-compose.yml
version: '3'
services:
  book:
    image: nginx:1
    networks:
      - default
      - web
    labels:
      - traefik.enable=true
      - traefik.http.routers.buch.rule=Host(`me.dockerbuch.info`)
      - traefik.http.routers.buch.tls=true
      - traefik.http.routers.buch.tls.certresolver=lets-encrypt
      - traefik.http.services.buch.loadbalancer.server.port=80
networks:
  web:
    external: true
```

In the docker compose configuration, Docker labels (see Chapter 4, Section 4.1) are used to pass necessary settings to the Traefik proxy server. By taking a closer look, you'll probably notice the similarities to the *traefik_api.yml* file. However, the entries are used here in a short notation where dots are used.

Because we've disabled automatic enabling of all services in the Traefik configuration (exposedByDefault: false, in the *traefik.yml* file), we need to enable the proxy for this service first (traefik.enable=true).

As with the dashboard configuration, we set the host name (me.dockerbuch.info) and request the Let's Encrypt certificates. The last entry (loadbalancer.server.port) tells Traefik to which port of this service the requests should be redirected. In our example, we could even have omitted this line because the Nginx Docker image explicitly specifies port 80 with the EXPOSE keyword, and Traefik evaluates this setting. However, if an image releases multiple ports or the EXPOSE keyword is missing, it's necessary to configure the redirection process manually.

After calling docker compose up -d again, the Traefik proxy generates the SSL certificates within a few seconds and sets up the redirection (see Figure 9.4). You don't have to take care of the first issuance of the certificate nor the regular renewal, as Traefik will do that for you.

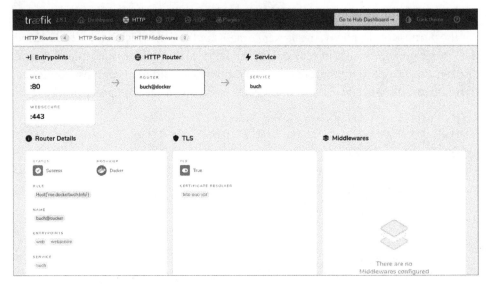

Figure 9.4 Traefik Dashboard with the New Router Details

Chapter 10
Database Systems

Most application programs need to store data in some way. In some cases, simple files are sufficient for this purpose. However, for more complex apps that need to be network-enabled, multiuser and transaction capable, there's no way around a "real" database management system (DBMS).

Thanks to Docker, you can avoid the tedious configuration of a database server, at least for test and development operations, and instead get the desired database system up and running with just a few commands or a few lines in *docker-compose.yml*.

In this chapter, we'll take a look at the following database systems:

- MySQL/MariaDB
- PostgreSQL
- MongoDB
- Redis

Examples of the actual use of these database systems follow in Chapter 12 and in Part III of this book.

10.1   MySQL and MariaDB

MySQL is one of the most popular open-source database systems for developing web applications. Websites such as Facebook and Wikipedia have grown with MySQL as a DBMS. MySQL is a "classic" relational DBMS with SQL as the primary language.

MySQL versus MariaDB

MySQL was originally developed by MySQL AB, a Swedish company. Later, Oracle became the owner of MySQL. Some of the original MySQL founders then initiated a new project, the result of which is a largely MySQL-compatible database server called MariaDB.

So now you have the choice between MySQL and MariaDB. In the Docker application, you'll notice few differences between the two systems. The configuration is exactly the same; even the documentation on Docker Hub is identical over long passages of text:

- *https://hub.docker.com/_/mysql*
- *https://hub.docker.com/_/mariadb*

In this section, we'll focus on MariaDB. In general, we give preference to MariaDB in this book because this system is more widely used in the Linux environment. To switch between MariaDB and MySQL, it's sufficient to use the image name `mysql` instead of `mariadb`. It should be noted, however, that such a change is only successful as long as no data has been saved. This is because the database files of MariaDB and MySQL aren't compatible with each other. (However, manual porting of the data using the `mysqldump` and `mysql` commands is usually possible.)

Despite their popularity, neither MySQL nor MariaDB is an ideal DBMS candidate for Docker deployment! Two reasons speak against MySQL and MariaDB:

- **Concept**
  MySQL and MariaDB are optimized for server use and can handle countless databases and client connections when properly configured. In the Docker environment, however, often there's not just one but several database containers set up side by side. This requires a lot of space and speed.

- **Space requirements**
  The paradigm of Docker is that images, containers, and volumes should be as lean as possible. However, MySQL and MariaDB are comparatively huge systems (see Table 10.1). The volume is required for the */var/lib/mysql* directory, which contains database, logging, and transaction files. As soon as databases are created, the space requirement there naturally increases.

DBMS	Image Size	Initial Volume Size
MariaDB 10.5	410 MB	130 MB
MySQL 8	560 MB	200 MB

Table 10.1 MySQL and MariaDB: Docker Heavyweights

In practice, however, there's often no way around MariaDB or MySQL. Many web applications require these programs or are at least optimized for them. In production operations, you should try to avoid running multiple containers or services with MySQL or MariaDB at the same time. For performance reasons, it's better if there's *one* dedicated MySQL or MariaDB container with sufficient resources allocated to it. If you're dealing with really large databases, you may want to consider a native MySQL or MariaDB installation, even if that means losing the flexibility you're used to with Docker.

10.1.1   Setting Up and Using MariaDB Containers Manually

In Chapter 3, we already showed you how to set up MariaDB as a container and try it out. We pointed out that it's usually appropriate to name the volume for the container directory */var/lib/mysql* or to associate it with a local directory in the first place. If you forgo this step, Docker itself will set up a volume and store the database file there. This complicates further administration because the volume is identified only by a long universally unique identifier (UUID).

The following command creates a container to run MariaDB, names it mariadb, uses secret as the MariaDB root password, and stores all database files in the *./dbvolume* directory:

```
mkdir dbvolume
docker run -d --name mariadb -e MYSQL_ROOT_PASSWORD=secret \
  -v $(pwd)/dbvolume:/var/lib/mysql mariadb
```

The container will then run in the background. You can read logging messages with docker logs mariadb and test client connections through docker exec:

```
docker exec -it mariadb mysql -u root -p
  Enter password: ******** (root password for MariaDB)
```

For instructions on how to administrate the MariaDB instance with phpMyAdmin, see Chapter 3, Section 3.8.

If there are already database files in the volume for the */var/lib/mysql* directory, docker run uses them when setting up a new container, rather than overwriting them. If you explicitly require a restart, you need to delete the files yourself. For the preceding example, that would look like the following:

```
rm -rf ./dbvolume/*
```

10.1.2 Setting Up a MariaDB Service with "docker-compose"

Setting up MariaDB manually is certainly an exception. Typically, you'll set up MariaDB as part of a whole group of Docker services using docker-compose.

In the simplest case, the MariaDB-specific lines in *docker-compose.yml* looks like the following:

```
# File: docker-compose.yml
version: '3'
services:
  mariadb:
    image: mariadb
    restart: always
    environment:
      MYSQL_ROOT_PASSWORD: secret
    volumes:
      - ./db:/var/lib/mysql
```

To start the database in the background, you need to run the following command, specifying `docker compose` without the hyphen for current versions:

```
docker-compose up -d
```

During the initialization of the container, the following environment variables are evaluated:

- **MYSQL_ROOT_PASSWORD**

  This variable determines the `root` password for the database server.

  Note that this variable (as well as the other variables) remains permanently set in the container. Any user who is allowed to run `docker exec -it <mariadbcontainer> bash` can read this variable. The variable is also stored in the container properties and can thus be determined by `docker inspect <mariadbcontainer>`.

- **MYSQL_DATABASE**

  If this variable is set, a database with the specified name will be created during initialization.

- **MYSQL_USER and MYSQL_PASSWORD**

  If these two variables are set, the initialization script sets up a corresponding user. The user is granted unrestricted access rights to the database specified by `MYSQL_DATABASE` (GRANT ALL).

- **MYSQL_ALLOW_EMPTY_PASSWORD**

  If this variable is set to `yes`, the initialization script accepts an empty `root` password. For safety reasons, of course, this isn't recommended.

- **MYSQL_RANDOM_ROOT_PASSWORD**

  If this variable is set to `yes`, the initialization script generates a random `root` password and outputs it in the terminal.

The variables just listed can also be used in the form `<NAME>_FILE=filename`, for example, `MYSQL_ROOT_PASSWORD_FILE=./pw.txt`. In this case, the initialization script reads the content of the variable from the specified file. This avoids the need to specify the password in plain text in *docker-compose.yml*.

The `_FILE` environment variables can also be combined with the secrets mechanism (see Chapter 5, Section 5.6).

Instead of the `MYSQL_xxx` variables, you can also use the equivalent variables with the `MARIADB_` prefix. We'll stick to the `MYSQL_xxx` variants in this book because they work equally well for MariaDB and MySQL.

Additional Examples

A lot of concrete examples of *docker-compose.yml* files will follow in Chapter 12. There, MariaDB is used as a database backend for WordPress, Nextcloud, and Joomla. The

---

WordPress example also shows how you can use secrets to set the MySQL root password.

10.1.3 Setting Up the Database during Initialization

The initialization script evaluates the directory */docker-entrypoint-initdb.d*. All scripts found there (*.sh* files) will be executed; all SQL files found there (*.sql* as well as *. sql.gz* files) will be imported into the database designated by MYSQL_DATABASE.

The following example shows how you can use this mechanism. For this purpose, you need to create the *init* directory and store an SQL file there, which may be the result of a previous backup:

```
mkdir init
cp /my-backups/db.sql init
```

In docker-compose, you use this directory as the volume for the *entrypoint* directory mentioned earlier:

```
# File: wordpress/docker-compose.yml
version: '3'
services:
  mariadb:
    image: mariadb
    restart: always
    environment:
      MYSQL_ROOT_PASSWORD: secret
      MYSQL_DATABASE: db1
    volumes:
      - ./db:/var/lib/mysql
      - ./init:/docker-entrypoint-initdb.d
```

In the example, it's assumed that docker-compose up is executed for the first time. If the volume directory *./db* already contains database files, no more initialization work will take place. So, if necessary, you should delete the contents of the *db* directory upfront.

10.1.4 Backups

The simplest type of backup consists of backing up the entire volume directory. During this process, the container or the service mustn't be in operation!

Often, a backup in SQL format is more desirable instead. Especially for small databases, the space requirement is much smaller because the volume for /var/lib/mysql contains not only the databases but also various other files.

You can create a backup of a database in SQL format using the `mysqldump` command. In the first variant, the `root` password is passed in plain text. The following example is based on the assumption that the container is named `mariadb` and the database is named `db1`. Note that the password immediately follows the `-p` option and isn't separated by a space.

```
docker exec -it mariadb mysqldump -u root -psecret db1 > db1.sql
```

The second variant is more elegant but requires more typing. Here, `docker exec` executes a shell to which the `mysqldump` command is passed as a string. The advantage here is that the shell can evaluate environment variable `MYSQL_ROOT_PASSWORD`. This avoids passing the password in plain text.

```
docker exec mariadb sh -c \
  'exec mysqldump -u root -p"$MYSQL_ROOT_PASSWORD" db1' > db1.sql
```

10.1.5   Using a Custom Configuration File (my.cnf)

The MariaDB server is configured via the */etc/mysql/my.cnf* file. In addition, various other *.cnf* files in the */etc/mysql* directory and its subdirectories are evaluated as well.

Any settings that differ from these should be written in a separate configuration file that you include as a volume file. For example, in the container you can use the path */etc/mysql/conf.d/myown.cnf*.

Thus, if you require a particularly fast (but not compliant with atomicity, consistency, isolation, and durability [ACID]) transaction logging, you should set up the following *myown.cnf* file:

```
# File myown.cnf
[mysqld]
innodb_flush_log_at_trx_commit=0
```

When listing the volumes in *docker-compose.yml*, you can now add a corresponding entry:

```
# File: docker-compose.yml
version: '3'
services:
  mariadb:
    volumes:
      - ./myown.cnf:/etc/mysql/conf.d/myown.cnf
      ...
```

10.2 PostgreSQL

PostgreSQL has been holding its own in the open-source database market for many years. With features that usually only very expensive *enterprise database systems* have, PostgreSQL has proven itself to be the database of choice for many large projects.

In contrast to MySQL/MariaDB, PostgreSQL not only provides the classic relational database model but also an object-oriented approach that enables the inheritance of tables, for example.

What's been said before for Docker and MariaDB also applies to PostgreSQL: running many PostgreSQL containers in parallel contradicts the concept of this database. For production environments with many database accesses, a highly available, dedicated database environment is the tool of choice.

However, PostgreSQL in a Docker container is definitely suitable for development purposes or smaller projects. You'll even benefit from being able to determine exactly which version of PostgreSQL you want to use and that the files aren't distributed in the operating system of your developer machine during installation but can be deleted completely with a single command.

The Docker images of PostgreSQL on Docker Hub are very well maintained and are available in the past five versions, one each based on Debian and Alpine Linux, although the difference in size for this image is significant (see Table 10.2).

Image Variant	Image Size	Base Image
postgres:13	315 MB	Debian Buster Slim (10)
postgres:13-alpine	160 MB	Alpine Linux 3.14

Table 10.2 Size Differences between PostgreSQL 13 Docker Images

Like MariaDB/MySQL, PostgreSQL also takes into account shell scripts (*.sh) or SQL files (*.sql, *.sql.gz) in the /docker-entrypoint-initdb.d directory, which are executed or imported into the database, respectively, when the container is started. In conjunction with docker compose or docker stack deploy, this allows you to create database users or stored procedures without having to build your own Docker image.

10.2.1 PostgreSQL and pgAdmin with "docker compose"

For many database professionals, the command line is the tool of choice for performing work on the database. For a quick overview, however, a graphical user interface (GUI) can be very helpful. For PostgreSQL, there has been a tool called *pgAdmin* available for quite some time. What used to be a desktop application has become a very modern and easy-to-use web interface since version 4.

pgAdmin 4 provides many things that make the day of a database administrator: work-load graphs, a query tool, and, of course, an overview of all elements of the database.

Sample Data

We've put a small sample data set as a PostgreSQL dump for you on GitHub. Just clone the Git repository from *https://github.com/docbuc/postgresql* or download the com-pressed dump from the *init* folder. The database contains more than 190,000 geo-graphically referenced objects in Germany from the free data set of *www.geonames. org* (and 2.2 million in the US).

The following *docker-compse.yml* file starts a container with the current PostgreSQL version and another container with the pgAdmin web frontend (in this case, on local port 5050):

```
# File: db/postgres/docker-compose.yml
version: '3'
services:
  db:
    image: postgres:13
    environment:
      POSTGRES_PASSWORD: secret
      POSTGRES_DB: geonames
    volumes:
      - ./init:/docker-entrypoint-initdb.d
      - pgdata:/var/lib/postgresql/data
pgadmin:
    image: fenglc/pgadmin4
    ports:
      - 5050:80
    volumes:
      - pgadmindata:/var/lib/pgadmin
    environment:
      DEFAULT_USER: info@dockerbuch.info
      DEFAULT_PASSWORD: secret
volumes:
  pgdata:
  pgadmindata:
```

As mentioned previously, PostgreSQL supports the database initialization during startup in the */docker-entrypoint-initdb.d* folder. If you saved the sample file from GitHub in the *init* directory or placed another PostgreSQL dump there, you'll see an output similar to this (shortened here) when you start the containers:

```
[...]
db_1 | server started
db_1 | CREATE DATABASE
db_1 | /usr/local/bin/docker-entrypoint.sh: running /docker-e...
db_1 | SET
[...]
db_1 | CREATE TABLE
db_1 | ALTER TABLE
```

Once the database server has been started, PostgreSQL will create the database you defined as the POSTGRES_DB environment variable in the *docker-compose.yml* file. Then, the *docker-entrypoint.sh* script imports the database dump. With or without demo data, you can now reach pgAdmin at *http://localhost:5050*. At the first login, you must enter the user name and password from the environment variables of the pgadmin container, and then add a server using the **Add New Server** link in the dashboard. In the dialog that opens, you need to enter the **Host** name ("db"), **Username** ("postgres"), and **Password** ("secret") for the database (see Figure 10.1).

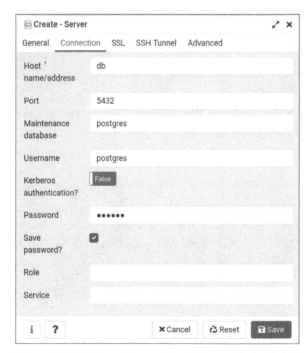

Figure 10.1 Database Connection in the pgAdmin Web Frontend

If you've imported the demo data, you can now navigate to the geonames database in the left area of the user interface. You'll find the imported data under **Schemas • public • Tables** (see Figure 10.2).

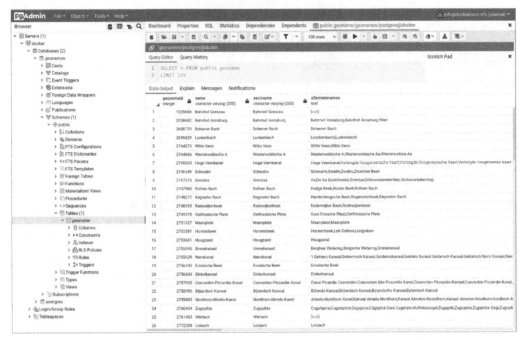

Figure 10.2 pgAdmin 4 Web Frontend with the geonames Demo Database

10.2.2   Backups with "docker compose"

Regarding backups, the same applies to PostgreSQL as to MariaDB: the easiest way without turning off the database is via docker exec:

```
docker exec postgres_db_1 pg_dump --username=postgres \
  geonames > geonames_backup.sql
```

Here we want to show you yet another way to conveniently create backups with docker compose. For this purpose, you should create another configuration file in addition to the existing *docker-compose.yml*. We'll name it *docker-compose.backup.yml*.

```
# File: db/postgresql/docker-compose.backup.yml
version: '3'
services:
  backup:
    image: postgres:13-alpine
    depends_on:
      - db
    volumes:
      - backup_vol:/backup
    command: >
      pg_dump --host db -F c -f /backup/geonames.dump
      --username=postgres geonames
```

```
    environment:
      PGPASSWORD: secret
volumes:
  backup_vol:
```

This file contains only the backup service. This service uses the current PostgreSQL image and uses the depends_on statement to indicate that the database server must also be started. As a command for the backup service, it's not the PostgreSQL database that should be started but pg_dump (here, in the multiline YAML Ain't Markup Language [YAML] notation).

The backup file is stored in /backup/geonames.dump. In this case, it's a volume managed by Docker, but you can of course mount a local directory of your computer here. The pg_dump command reads from the environment variable PGPASSWORD, which is the database password defined in the environment section.

The trick with this setup is that docker compose is called with both configuration files and the run statement for the backup service:

```
docker compose -f docker-compose.yml \
  -f docker-compose.backup.yml run --rm backup
```

This starts a container that runs the backup service and uses the pg_dump command to save the backup to /backup. After that, the container gets deleted again (--rm), and the volume remains with the backup.

10.3 MongoDB

With MongoDB, we want to introduce just one of the many NoSQL databases. Unlike relational database systems (RDBMS), NoSQL databases don't use tables and fixed structures. Data is stored in *documents* whose structures aren't bound to a strict schema. On one hand, this is very convenient because it saves complicated database schema adjustments, but on the other hand, it can also lead to confusion if each document has a different structure.

Especially in the environment of modern web applications, NoSQL databases are very popular. The JavaScript Object Notation (JSON) format, which is widely used as an exchange format between the frontend and backend, can be stored or updated very conveniently in NoSQL databases, often without modifying it. MongoDB also has the reputation of scaling well with very large data volumes (keyword *Big Data*), even where relational databases reach their limits. However, there are trade-offs in terms of transaction security and possible data duplication.

10.3.1   Simple "docker compose" Setup with MongoDB

For the first example, as in the previous section on PostgreSQL, we'll again import the Germany data set from Geonames. MongoDB already has some very handy spatial query features in the default installation. Because the sample data set contains georeferenced points, you can easily create queries with MongoDB, such as *Give me all hotels within one kilometer of Cologne Cathedral*. This is exactly what we want to achieve in the following example.

The official image on Docker Hub is built on Debian and, like PostgreSQL and MariaDB, enables you to set up a database during initialization. Unsurprisingly, the folder in which the data must be present is again called *docker-entrypoint-initdb.d*. However, MongoDB doesn't accept database dumps here but requires either shell scripts or Java-Script files to be applied directly to whichever database is specified in the MONGO_INITDB_DATABASE environment variable.

Download the comma-separated values (CSV) file from *http://download.geonames. org/export/dump/DE.zip*, and unpack it in a directory named *init*. You now have a *DE.txt* file there, which contains more than 190,000 points in Germany in CSV format (separated by tabs). Using the small shell script *01_seed.sh*, you'll "feed" this data into the database:

```
# File: db/mongo/init/01_seed.sh
mongoimport --db geonames --collection geoname \
  --type tsv \
  --fields=geonameid,\
name,\
asciiname,\
alternatenames,\
latitude,\
longitude,\
feature_class,\
feature_code,\
country_code,\
cc2,\
admin1_code,\
admin2_code,\
admin3_code,\
admin4_code,\
```

```
population,\
elevation,\
dem,\
timezone,\
modification_date\
 /docker-entrypoint-initdb.d/DE.txt
```

The list of all fields in the CSV file must be passed to the mongoimport command because the data record doesn't contain its own header line with this information (otherwise, you could transfer it using the --headerline option). The name of the database is geonames, and the *collection* is called geoname (a collection is roughly comparable to a folder for documents). MongoDB is very forgiving here: if the database or collection doesn't exist, it will be created. The tsv type tells the importer that the fields are separated by tabs and not by other separators (e.g., commas or semicolons).

To create spatial queries, you need a special index in the collection. An index of type 2d can calculate distances on a flat surface; type 2dsphere can be used to calculate distances on an earthlike sphere. The following script enables you to create the necessary structure and index:

```
// File: db/mongo/init/02_createindex.js
print("Create GeoJson points...");
let i = 0;
db.geoname.find().forEach(data => {
  i++;
  db.geoname.update( { _id: data._id }, {
    $set: { location: { type: "Point",
      coordinates: [parseFloat(data.longitude),
                    parseFloat(data.latitude)] } }
  })
});
print(i + " Points created, create 2d index...")
db.geoname.createIndex( { location: "2dsphere" } );
```

The forEach loop runs across all documents in the collection (find() without restriction returns all documents) and adds a location entry to each document. Here, longitude and latitude information is stored in the standardized *GeoJSON* format. The final line creates the index of type 2dsphere in the location field.

All that's missing now is the *docker-compose.yml* file to complete the MongoDB setup:

```
# File: db/mongo/docker-compose.yml
version: '3'
services:
  db:
    image: mongo:4
```

```
    volumes:
      - mongo:/data/db
      - ./init:/docker-entrypoint-initdb.d
      - ./queries:/queries
    environment:
      MONGO_INITDB_DATABASE: geonames
volumes:
  mongo:
```

Now you should start the setup using docker compose up. The output should look like the following:

```
db_1  | /usr/local/bin/docker-entrypoint.sh: running
  /docker-entrypoint-initdb.d/01_seed.sh
db_1  | {"t":{"$date":"2021-06-24T06:59:28.574+00:00"},"s":"I"...
[...]
db_1  | 2021-06-24T06:59:28.575+0000     connected to:
  mongodb://localhost/
db_1  | {"t":{"$date":"2021-06-24T06:59:28.601+00:00"},"s":"I",
  "c":"INDEX",     "id":20345,    "ctx":"conn4","msg":"Index build:
  done building","attr":{"buildUUID":null,"namespace":"geoname...
db_1  | 2021-06-24T06:59:31.575+0000     [#####################..]
  geonames.geoname    22.4MB/23.6MB (94.8%)
db_1  | 2021-06-24T06:59:31.701+0000     [######################]
  geonames.geoname 23.6MB/23.6MB (100.0%)
db_1  | 2021-06-24T06:59:31.701+0000     198305 document(s)
  imported successfully. 0 document(s) failed to import.
[...]
db_1  | /usr/local/bin/docker-entrypoint.sh:
  running /docker-entrypoint-initdb.d/02_createindex.js
db_1  | Create GeoJson points...
db_1 | 198305 points created, create 2d index...
db_1  | {"t":{"$date":"2021-06-24T07:00:57.047+00:00"},"s":"I",
  "c":"STORAGE",   "id":20663,    "ctx":"IndexBuildsCoordinatorMong
  od-0","msg":"Index build: completed successfully","attr":{"buil
  dUUID":{"uuid":{"$uuid":"927476e9-e82c-4d51-a884-6b9a5f6a9ef...
```

The *docker-entrypoint.sh* script executes the files in the *init* directory in alphabetical order, which makes naming the files *01_seed.sh* and *02_createindex.js* useful. As you can see, the shell script that imports the 198,305 data records is executed first, followed by the JavaScript file that generates the GeoJSON points and creates the index.

10.3.2   Database Access

Typically, you'll access the database via a programming language. In this example, however, we don't want to write a program but execute queries via the supplied command-line program, mongo. mongo can be called with a JavaScript file as a parameter, similar to what we've already seen with the 02_createindex script. Save the following script in a *queries* folder; in the docker compose configuration, we've already included the folder in the container:

```
// File: db/mongo/queries/cologne.js
let cath = db.geoname.findOne({
  { alternatenames: /Catedral.*Colonia/ }
});
const query = [
  {
    $geoNear: {
      near: cath.location,
      spherical: true,
      distanceField: 'dis',
      query: { feature_code: 'HTL' }
    }
  }, {
    $limit: 10
  }
];
let res = db.geoname.aggregate(query);
res.forEach(data => {
  print(Math.round(data.dis)+ "m: " + data.name);
});
```

Two queries are executed in this script: First, we look for exactly one document (find-One) in which the alternatenames field contains the regular expression Cathedral.*Colonia/. The result remains stored in the variable cath. The second query uses this result and uses it in the aggregate query at near. In addition, in the process, we narrow down the documents we're looking for using the feature_code field. Finally, a forEach loop runs across all found results and returns the distance as well as the name of the hotel. You can now execute the script in the container using the mongo command:

```
docker compose exec db mongo geonames /queries/cologne.js
```

```
MongoDB shell version v4.4.6
connecting to: mongodb://127.0.0.1:27017/geonames?compressor...
Implicit session: session { "id" : UUID("c3edf8b2-da57-479b-...
MongoDB server version: 4.4.6
90m: Dom Hotel Le Meridien
```

```
121m: Dom Hotel - A Meridien Hotel
126m: Althoff Dom Hotel Koln
147m: Sofitel Cologne Mondial Am Dom
156m: City Class Hotel Europa Am Dom
166m: Sofitel am Dom
168m: Eden Früh Am Dom
185m: Gir Keller Gästehaus
185m: Altstadthotel Und Apartments Hayk
185m: Hotel Römerhafen
```

To all those who have now acquired a taste for MongoDB and want to get to grips with this database a little more intensively, we recommend the very useful *Compass* tool (see Figure 10.3):

www.mongodb.com/products/compass

In the free GUI, you can manage your Mongo databases clearly, and it helps especially in creating and analyzing *aggregation pipelines*, a very powerful query facility that was used in this example ($geoNear).

Figure 10.3 The MongoDB Compass Program When Creating an Aggregate Query

10.3.3 MongoDB with Authentication

By default, access to MongoDB doesn't require any authentication. This sounds a bit scary at first, but it can be sufficient for a compartmentalized setup or a pure development environment. However, for a production system, it's not a bad idea to require a user name and password for MongoDB as well.

To enable authentication, it's sufficient to set the two environment variables, MONGO_INITDB_ROOT_USERNAME and MONGO_INITDB_ROOT_PASSWORD. When the container gets started, the `--auth` parameter will be passed automatically to the database server; the service can then only be accessed with the appropriate authentication.

The startup script can also handle the more modern variant of *Docker secrets* (see Chapter 5, Section 5.6). For this purpose, you can simply use the MONGO_INITDB_ROOT_PASSWORD_FILE variable instead of MONGO_INITDB_ROOT_PASSWORD, then add the necessary secrets section to the *docker-compose.yml* file, and save the *mongo_root.txt* file with the password in the current directory:

```
# File: db/mongo-auth/docker-compose.yml
version: '3.5'
services:
  db:
    image: mongo:4
    volumes:
      - mongo:/data/db
      - ./init:/docker-entrypoint-initdb.d
    environment:
      MONGO_INITDB_DATABASE: geonames
      MONGO_INITDB_ROOT_USERNAME: dockerbuch
      MONGO_INITDB_ROOT_PASSWORD_FILE: /run/secrets/mongo_root
    secrets:
      - mongo_root
volumes:
  mongo:
secrets:
  mongo_root:
    file: ./mongo_root.txt
```

The superuser created in this way is usually used to manage the rights for the users of the databases but not to create and populate databases itself. So, if you enable authentication for the database, it's also useful to add a user with write permissions to a database when you start the container. We'll now set up a geonames user that will have write access to the geonames database. When you execute the JavaScript files in the *docker-entrypoint-initdb.d* directory, authentication isn't yet required, so the following short script suffices to create the user:

```
// File: db/mongo-auth/init/adduser.js
db.createUser({user: 'geonames', pwd: 'secret',
    roles: [{role: 'readWrite', db: 'geonames'}]});
```

If you connect to the database in this setup without specifying a user name and password, you'll no longer be able to run any queries:

```
$ docker compose exec db mongo geonames
  MongoDB shell version v4.4.6
  connecting to: mongodb://127.0.0.1:27017/geonames?compressors=disabled&
gssapiServiceName=mongodb
  Implicit session: session { "id" : UUID("c4c4f5e4-3e56-4c3b-95f9-
79facfd0eef0") }
  MongoDB server version: 4.4.6
  Welcome to the MongoDB shell.
> db.getCollectionNames()
  uncaught exception: Error: listCollections failed: {
    "ok" : 0,
    "errmsg" : "command listCollections requires authentication",
    "code" : 13,
    "codeName" : "Unauthorized"
  } :
...
```

If you start the command by specifying the user name, you can use the mongo shell as usual after entering the password.

```
$ docker compose exec db mongo -u geonames geonames
  MongoDB shell version v4.4.6
  Enter password:
  [...]
> db.getCollectionNames()
  [ "geoname" ]
```

10.4   Redis

Redis is a lightweight database server that manages a *key-value* storage in volatile memory. Because of the high speed of read and write accesses, Redis is often used for session data in web applications. In addition, Redis is often used in the function of a *full-page cache*, which noticeably accelerates the speed of applications with a high database load. Because Redis supports data types such as lists, sets, and hash tables, it's also popular in the context of queues or ranked lists.

In our first attempt, we want to launch the official Redis image of Docker Hub:

```
docker run -d --name rd redis
```

The container named rd runs in the background. Now you should start the command-line program redis-cli in the Redis container to query the database:

```
docker exec -it rd redis-cli
```

```
127.0.0.1:6379> get myKey
(nil)

127.0.0.1:6379> set myKey "Hello world"
OK

127.0.0.1:6379> get myKey
"Hello world"
```

You can use get and set to query and store data in Redis, respectively. Our first request for the value for the myKey key is answered with (nil). This isn't surprising because no value has been assigned to this key yet. Once we've saved the *Hello world* value with set, we can also query it successfully.

Redis Volumes

Redis is an in-memory database, but the contents can still be swapped out to the hard drive so that they're available even after a server restart. To do this, you want to mount a volume under /data; Redis will take care of saving it on shutdown.

10.4.1 Redis Replication with "docker compose"

The term *database replication* is often associated with a complex installation or configuration. However, Redis and Docker show us that it doesn't have to be that way. The setup to install a master-slave replication couldn't be easier:

```
# Fie: db/redis/docker-compose.yml
version: '3'
services:
  rd-master:
    image: redis:6
  rd-slave:
    image: redis:6
    command: redis-server --slaveof rd-master 6379
```

Two services are defined in the *docker-compose.yml* file: `rd-master` and `rd-slave`. Both use the latest `redis:5` image from Docker Hub.

The difference between the two services is only in the start command of the container. While the master starts the database regularly, the slave passes the parameter `--slaveof rd-master 6379`. Of course, you recognized right away that this is the host name (in the `docker compose` network) and the port of the master.

Now you should open two terminal windows side by side. In one window, you connect to the master and in the second to the slave. Then you want to run the SUBSCRIBE function of Redis on the slave, which waits for messages on a specific topic:

```
docker compose exec rd-slave redis-cli

  127.0.0.1:6379> SUBSCRIBE myChannel
  Reading messages... (press Ctrl-C to quit)
  1) "subscribe"
  2) "myChannel"
  3) (integer) 1
```

On the master, you need to execute the PUBLISH command with the parameters myChannel (the *channel* for this message) and a string as the message:

```
docker compose exec rd-master redis-cli

  127.0.0.1:6379> PUBLISH myChannel "Test message from master"
  (integer) 0
```

You should now see the message in the terminal window with the slave connection.

Chapter 11
Programming Languages

This chapter describes some current programming languages and provides examples of how you can use them in combination with Docker. There's a very short sample program that runs through the entire chapter: it loads the news page of the popular Slashdot news (*https://slashdot.org*), extracts the news headlines, and outputs them to the console. The example can be implemented in any programming language with very little code, and we always use external libraries to illustrate the installation in a *Dockerfile* for you. For the example to work, you'll of course need an internet connection.

We'll deal with the following languages in this chapter:

- JavaScript (Node.js)
- Java
- PHP
- Ruby
- Python

You may wonder why programming languages such as C or Go are missing here. This is due to the fact that these languages aren't so well suited for Docker deployment. Typically, in such cases, it's convenient to install the respective compiler locally. The code developed in C, C++, or Go will be compiled with it. The compilation can then be distributed independently (i.e., without a runtime environment). This process isn't made any easier by Docker.

11.1 JavaScript (Node.js)

JavaScript, an interpreted *high-level* programming language, achieved widespread use through its use in web browsers. Once used only for relatively small interactive elements in web pages, JavaScript has now become a popular language in both client and server programming. The ability to develop both backend and frontend in one programming language using the same libraries is very attractive.

If you want to use JavaScript without a browser, you need a standalone interpreter. With Node.js, there's open-source software available that's published under the MIT license and enjoys great popularity.

In the Node.js release schedule, Long-Term Support (LTS) versions are marked with an even version number (10.x, 12.x, 14.x, 16.x); the current LTS branch is version 16, which receives security updates until the end of April 2024.

Because the core of Node.js is deliberately kept very lean, small libraries are used for common operations such as data transfer via HTTP or reading and writing files. To avoid losing the overview here, Node.js provides the package manager npm, which manages these libraries and their dependencies among each other.

With the widespread use of Node.js in modern applications, it almost goes without saying that ready-made images are available on Docker Hub. The default image is built on Debian Linux (although different Debian versions are also offered here for all supported Node.js versions), but there are also very lean versions available for Alpine Linux.

11.1.1 Trying Out Node.js

If you want to quickly try out the Node.js interpreter with a one-liner, you can issue the following command:

```
docker run --rm node:16 node -e \
  'console.log(Math.max(2, 4, 6, 1, 0));'
```

The docker run command loads version 12 of the Node.js image from Docker Hub and starts a container in which node gets called. Then, the string of JavaScript statements passed with -e gets executed by the interpreter. In this example, the highest number of a list is determined with the integrated function Math.max and output to the screen via console.log.

11.1.2 "printheadlines": Packaging Node.js Script as a Docker Image

The following example shows how you can package a Node.js script as a Docker image. The very small test program outputs the headlines of the Slashdot news ticker as text in the console.

You should now create a new directory and save the *printheadlines.js* file there with the following content:

```
// File: prog/nodejs/printheadlines.js
const Parser = require('rss-parser')
  parser = new Parser()
  moment = require('moment');

parser.parseURL('https://rss.slashdot.org/Slashdot/slashdotMain')
  .then(feed => {
    feed.items.forEach(entry => {
      console.log("* [%s]: %s",
        moment(entry.pubDate).format("Y-MM-DD HH:mm:ss"),
        entry.title);
    })
  });
```

The source code isn't very complicated. At the beginning, the rss-parser library gets loaded, which in turn loads the newsfeed of the Slashdot news ticker (parseURL()). If the request is successful, the feed variable provides access to the XML document.

The individual news items are stored in the feed.items variable. The forEach loop runs across all entries and outputs the title (entry.title) and a formatted date with the console.log function. Because the standard JavaScript library doesn't contain very flexible methods for date formatting, we use the widely used moment library here.

Node.js projects use a configuration file called *package.json* that you can create manually. However, this is much easier using the package manager npm:. To do this, you need to start an interactive shell in a container with node:12 and mount the current directory in this container under the */src* directory. Specifying -u $UID:$GID makes the container run under your user identifiers (UIDs) and group identifiers (GIDs), which makes the generated files yours:

```
docker run -it --rm -w /src -v ${PWD}:/src -u $UID:$GID \
  node:16 bash
```

Now you can create the *package.json* file in this container using the command npm init -y. -y causes the default settings to be saved in the file without prompting. Then you should install the required libraries rss-parser and moment using command npm i --save rss-parser moment. Specifying --save causes a line to be added to the *package.json* file indicating the dependency of our program on this library. If the installation was successful, you can try out the node printheadlines.js program.

To create your own Docker image that contains the Node.js runtime, all libraries, and your custom script, you can now create a *Dockerfile*:

```
# File: prog/nodejs/Dockerfile (docbuc/printheadlines:node)
FROM node:16
WORKDIR /src
RUN chown node:node /src
USER node
COPY --chown=node:node package.json package-lock.json /src/
RUN npm i
COPY printheadlines.js /src/
CMD [ "node", "printheadlines.js" ]
```

The command docker build -t docbuc/printheadlines:node . enables you to create the image, while docker run docbuc/printheadlines:node starts a container from the image that outputs the messages of the Slashdot news ticker onto the console. Here you can see a shortened view:

```
* [2022-11-12 16:24:54]: Reuters Reports $1B of Client Funds Missing at FTX
* [2022-11-12 16:24:54]: Crypto.com Preliminary Audit Shows 20% of Its Assets
Are In Shiba Inu Coin
```

```
* [2022-11-12 16:24:54]: Kevin Conroy, Iconic Batman Voice Actor, Dies At 66
* [2022-11-12 16:24:54]: Volkswagen Builds Star Trek Captain's Chair That Goes
12 MPH
* [2022-11-12 16:24:54]: FTX Crypto Wallets See Mysterious Late-Night Outflows
Totalling More than $380M
* [2022-11-12 16:24:54]: Microsoft To Spend $1 Billion On Datacenters In North
Carolina
[...]
```

In the very short *Dockerfile*, we first change the owner of the */src* directory to the node user and switch to this user ID. We then copy the *package** files (again including a change of the owner), install the Node.js modules, and then copy the actual program to */src*.

This approach pays off especially when you modify the JavaScript code and re-create the image. This is because Docker will then use the cache function and won't reinstall the Node.js modules with every docker build call. On the other hand, if you copy your source code already prior to installing the modules, the cache will be invalidated, and npm i will be run again every time you modify your program.

More Examples
More examples of much more complex Node.js projects will follow in Chapter 13 and in Chapter 15.

11.2   Java

For many years, Java has been the number one in the *TIOBE index* of the most commonly used programming languages. Java is an object-oriented language that was developed with great attention to portability. Today, Java code runs virtually everywhere: on mainframes as well as on smartphones. Java is well suited for programming novices but lacks a more elegant notation in many areas. In that context, modern programming languages such as Ruby or current JavaScript versions are more convenient to use.

Java, as a compiled language with huge libraries, is actually not predestined for Docker use. But since Oracle had the glorious idea to drive developers and Linux distributors crazy with semiannual major releases, Docker is a good way to run or further develop individual projects independently in suitable Java releases.

The official Java images on Docker Hub include the OpenJDK implementation of the Java Developer Kit (*https://hub.docker.com/_/eclipse-temurin*). In July 2021, the major versions 8, 11, 16, 17, and 18 were available for selection there, with 16 marked as the *latest* as it was considered to be the most stable version at that time. The number of different build variants for the five versions is so large that it's no longer even displayed on the Docker Hub website. Among them are builds based on different versions of WindowsServerCore and various Linux distributions (Debian and Oracle Linux).

The decision as to whether you want the entire development environment or just the runtime has at least been taken away from you by the developers in the more recent versions: current Docker images of OpenJDK are only available complete with the compiler.

The space requirements of the OpenJDK images are considerable (see Table 11.1).

Image Variant	Image Size	Base Image
openjdk:18	472 MB	OracleLinux 8-slim
openjdk:16	467 MB	OracleLinux 8-slim
openjdk:16-alpine	324 MB	Alpine Linux 3.13

Table 11.1 Image Sizes of Some OpenJDK Image Variants

11.2.1   "printheadlines" Example

Unfortunately, we couldn't find an easy-to-install and up-to-date RSS library for Java. For this reason, we'll extract the news directly from the Slashdot news ticker website in the following example. We'll do this by using an add-on library, *jsoup*, which allows you to search the Document Object Model (DOM) tree of an HTML document using tags and Cascading Style Sheet (CSS) classes. The drawback of this approach is that this program stops working as soon as the website owner changes the design, that is, renames the CSS classes. Here you can see the Java class for extracting the message list:

```
// File: prog/java/printheadlines.java
import org.jsoup.Jsoup;
import org.jsoup.nodes.Document;
import org.jsoup.nodes.Element;
import org.jsoup.select.Elements;
import java.io.IOException;

public class printheadlines {
  private static String url = "https://slashdot.org/";

  public static void main(String[] args) throws IOException {
    Document doc = Jsoup.connect(url).get();
    Elements news = doc.select("article h2.story>span.story-title>a");

    for (Element item : news) {
      System.out.println("* "+ item.text());
```

```
        }
      }
   }
```

In the main function of our small Java program, we first load the HTML page with the jsoup function connect(url).get(). The following doc.select call creates a list of HTML elements that match the CSS statement. In the for loop, the elements are output to the screen, with the text() function of jsoup removing spaces and other HTML tags within the element.

In Java, it's common for external libraries to be downloaded as jar files and specified in the classpath both at compile time and at execution time. In our *Dockerfile*, we'll download the library in the currently current version 1.11.3 from the project's website and store it in the Docker image. In addition, when creating the Docker image, we'll translate the source code so that a derived container has access to the final compiled program.

```
# File: prog/java/Dockerfile (docbuc/printheadlines:java)
FROM openjdk:16
RUN adduser -r java
WORKDIR /src
RUN chown java /src
USER java
ENV JSOUP_VER 1.13.1
RUN curl -SL https://jsoup.org/packages/jsoup-$JSOUP_VER.jar \
   -o jsoup-$JSOUP_VER.jar
COPY printheadlines.java /src/
RUN javac -verbose -cp /src/jsoup-$JSOUP_VER.jar:. \
   printheadlines.java
CMD java -cp jsoup-$JSOUP_VER.jar:. printheadlines
```

For security reasons, we don't want to run the container as root user. Because there's no suitable unprivileged user in the Oracle Linux system, we'll create the user via the adduser command, where the -r parameter specifies that the user becomes a system user and thus won't get a normal login.

Specifying an environment variable, in this case, JSOUP_VER, is handy if you want to update the library at a later time. As long as the structure of the download links remains the same, it's then sufficient to adjust the version number.

For the first attempt, we use version 16 of the Java Developer Kit (JDK), which is currently (as of July 2021) marked as latest. By the time you hold this book in your hands, however, that will probably have changed: Oracle has significantly accelerated the development cycle and releases new major versions once every six months.

No matter how this evolution continues, Docker gives you the ideal tool to test and deliver your software with different Java versions. You just need to change the version number of the official Docker image in your *Dockerfile* from 16 to 17, and you'll be testing with the latest developer version. Parallel installations of different versions of the JDK in one operating system are basically possible, but, in practice, they always cause difficulties. Docker is made to save you trouble in the process.

What you should do here is build the Docker image using `docker build -t docbuc/print-headlines:java .`, and then run it via `docker run docbuc/printheadlines:java`. Here you can see the slightly shortened output of the build process:

```
Sending build context to Docker daemon  3.584kB
Step 1/10 : FROM openjdk:16
 ---> f4f1dadedfab
Step 2/10 : RUN adduser -r java
 ---> Running in ac0ca27aee3c
Removing intermediate container ac0ca27aee3c
 ---> 0cef2ee2d7f2
[...]
Step 9/10 : RUN javac -cp /src/jsoup-$JSOUP_VER.jar:.   printh...
 ---> Running in 232ab7613846
Removing intermediate container 232ab7613846
 ---> d6bc5ff51cba
Step 10/10 : CMD java -cp jsoup-$JSOUP_VER.jar:. printheadlines
 ---> Running in ee090202f84b
Removing intermediate container ee090202f84b
 ---> 5cafad4b0f90
Successfully tagged docbuc/printheadlines:java
```

Try changing the Java version in your *Dockerfile*. Our tests with the experimental version 18 were successful.

11.2.2 Resource Management

Older Java versions were known to be too wasteful with RAM and CPU power. This blog post describes the problem and some suggested solutions:

https://developers.redhat.com/blog/2017/03/14/java-inside-docker

If you use Linux as a Docker host, the Java Virtual Machine (JVM) of OpenJDK 8 and 9 can detect the limits provided in Docker for the container when you invoke the Java interpreter with the following options:

```
java -XX:+UnlockExperimentalVMOptions -XX:+UseCGroupMemoryLimitForHeap
```

Starting with OpenJDK 11, you can save yourself the trouble. As of this version, Java itself recognizes the restrictions that apply to containers on Linux.

The situation is different if you use Windows as a Docker host. In that case, you can use the `start` command in Windows to control which resources `java` is allowed to use via options:

- *https://hub.docker.com/_/eclipse-temurin*
- *https://ss64.com/nt/start.html*

11.3   PHP: Hypertext Preprocessor

Although a bit outdated, PHP is still widely used and has held its own as a programming language for web applications for an astonishingly long time. In the current version 8, even the possibility to strictly type variables has found its way into the language.

Most often, PHP is used in conjunction with a web server, either as an integrated module (Apache) or as an external process with the *FastCGI Process Manager* (FPM). Basically, however, PHP can also be used as a programming language on the command line. We'll describe both variants here.

11.3.1   Official PHP Docker Images

The selection of variants of the official Docker image of PHP is impressively long. Some of those variants are listed here:

- **8-cli**
  The current version with the command-line interpreter.
- **8-apache**
  The Apache web server with the PHP-8 module (HTTP on port 80).
- **8-fpm**
  The FPM with PHP 8 (on port 9000).
- **8-zts**
  The command-line interpreter with the new *Zend Thread Safety* (ZTS).
- **8-alpine**
  The command-line interpreter in slim Alpine Linux.
- **8-fpm-alpine**
  The FPM in Alpine Linux.

The first four images are based on Debian Buster, while the alpine variants were created with Alpine Linux as the base image.

11.3.2   PHP as a Command-Line Program

With the following example, as in the previous Node.js example, you can load the RSS feed of the news page of *https://rss.slashdot.org/Slashdot/slashdotMain* and extract the text of the headlines. Just as with Node.js, we use an external library to process the XML code, in this case, zend-feed and zend-http from the Zend framework.

For the installation of PHP packages and their dependencies, a tool called composer has been widely used for some time. Unfortunately, it isn't included in the standard PHP package, so we'll create our own Docker image based on Debian Buster. Debian's default package sources include both PHP 7 and the composer tool, so all you need to do is launch the package manager and install the necessary packages:

```
# File: prog/php/Dockerfile (docbuc/printheadlines:php)
FROM debian:buster-slim
RUN apt-get update && apt-get install -y --no-install-recommends\
  composer \
  php7.3 \
  php7.3-dom \
  php7.3-zip \
  unzip \
  && rm -rf /var/lib/apt/lists/*
RUN useradd -ms /bin/bash php7
WORKDIR /home/php7
USER php7
RUN composer require zendframework/zend-feed \
  zendframework/zend-http
COPY printheadlines.php ./
CMD ["php", "printheadlines.php"]
```

Start the example with the debian:buster-slim base image; it contains all the libraries you need and results in a smaller image. *Slim builds* try to remove as many files as possible from the system that aren't necessarily needed in Docker images (e.g., help texts). This makes the slim variant almost half the size (approx. 55 MB) of the original image (approx. 100 MB).

When installing Debian packages with the already known apt-get command, this time you should also use the --no-install-recommends switch. Usually, apt-get also installs the packages that aren't strictly necessary for the execution but are also recommended by package maintainers. In this example, that would be the Apache web server, among others, which you don't need here.

The composer program strongly warns against running it with root privileges. For this reason, you should add a new user in the container via useradd. After setting the WORKDIR to the new user's home directory, you must switch to the new user ID in the

Dockerfile and use the `composer` to install the desired modules (`zendframework/zend-feed` and `zendframework/zend-http`).

Finally, you need to copy the short *printheadlines.php* script to */home/php7* and run it along with the container:

```php
<?php
// File: php/printheadlines.php
use Zend\Feed\Reader\Reader;
require 'vendor/autoload.php';
$feed = Reader::import('https://rss.slashdot.org/Slashdot/slashdotMain');
foreach($feed as $entry) {
  printf("* [%s]: %s\n",
    $entry->getDateModified()->format("Y-m-d H:i:s"),
    $entry->getTitle());
}
```

The reader module from the Zend framework reads the XML document from the Slashdot web server and provides an array of entries. In the `foreach` loop, as in the previous examples, the formatted date and title of the entry are output.

To create and then launch the Docker image for the PHP variant, you should use the following commands:

```
docker build -t docbuc/printheadlines:php .
docker run docbuc/printheadlines:php
```

11.3.3 PHP with Web Servers (EXIF Example)

As already mentioned at the beginning of this section, PHP plays an important role mainly in connection with web servers. There are ready-made Docker images for both the popular combination of Apache and PHP and for the not as common but increasingly used setup of Nginx and PHP with FPM.

In the Docker environment, the FPM variant is very popular because the PHP process is decoupled from the web server, following the concept of microservices. This means that the process runs in its own container and can thus be scaled independently.

The following example using the Nginx/PHP-FPM combination reads and displays the meta information of a digital photo (see Figure 11.1). This requires installing the Exchangeable Image File Format (EXIF) module in PHP, which is a simple exercise using prebuilt script `docker-php-ext-install`.

Exif information:

- Camera: Fairphone/FP3
- Date: 2021:06:09 13:09:17
- Exposure time: 469483/1000000000
- f-stop: 180/100
- ISO: 101

Figure 11.1 Display of the EXIF Data of a Digital Photo in the Browser

If you want to avoid the hassle of writing HTML code yourself, you can use an external PHP library that converts the simple Markdown syntax into HTML. The PHP script for generating the HTML page then looks like the following:

```php
<?php
// File: prog/php-fpm/www/index.php
require 'vendor/autoload.php';
$Parsedown = new Parsedown();
$img = 'erto.jpg';
$exif = exif_read_data($img);

// Read Markdown code
$md =  <<<EOD
![pic]($img)
```

```
# Exif Info:

* Camera: {$exif['Make']}/{$exif['Model']}
* Recording date: {$exif['DateTimeOriginal']}
* Exposure time: {$exif['ExposureTime']}
* Aperture: {$exif['FNumber']}
* ISO: {$exif['ISOSpeedRatings']}
EOD;

// Convert Markdown code to HTML and output it
echo $Parsedown->text($md);
```

11.3.4   Dockerfile for the EXIF Example

In the Docker image, you need to install both the composer extension and the EXIF module:

```
# File: prog/php-fpm/Dockerfile (docbuc/php-fpm:alpine-exif)
FROM php:8-fpm-alpine
RUN curl -sS https://getcomposer.org/installer \
  | php -- --install-dir=/usr/bin --filename=composer
RUN docker-php-ext-install exif
WORKDIR /var/www/html
COPY www/ /var/www/html/
RUN chown -R www-data /var/www/html
USER www-data
RUN composer require erusev/parsedown
VOLUME [ "/var/www/html", "/var/www/html/vendor" ]
```

The example uses the official PHP 7 image in the FPM variant based on Alpine Linux. The reduced Alpine Linux is completely sufficient for the task at hand here. With about 79 MB, the PHP image is very compact.

As a first step, you want to install the package manager composer using the installation script from its home page at *https://getcomposer.org*. This is especially easy because the installation script is executed in PHP and doesn't contain any other dependencies.

Next, the EXIF module for PHP must be installed. The docker-php-ext-install script takes care of the module's dependencies, compiles and installs the necessary C library, and then removes the packages that are no longer needed from the Docker image. This makes the derived image only slightly larger than the base image.

The following listing shows an abbreviated version of the screen output during the build process for the image:

```
docker build .
  ...
  Step 3/9 : RUN docker-php-ext-install exif
 ---> Running in 33f7d0fb42fe
  fetch https://dl-cdn.alpinelinux.org/alpine/v3.13/main/\
          x86_64/APKINDEX.tar.gz
  fetch https://dl-cdn.alpinelinux.org/alpine/v3.13/community/\
          x86_64/APKINDEX.tar.gz
  (1/27) Upgrading musl (1.2.2-r0 -> 1.2.2-r1)
  (2/27) Installing m4 (1.4.18-r2)
  (3/27) Installing libbz2 (1.0.8-r1)
  (4/27) Installing perl (5.32.0-r0)
  (5/27) Installing autoconf (2.69-r3)
  (6/27) Installing pkgconf (1.7.3-r0)
...
  (27/27) Installing .phpize-deps (20210701.102334)
  Executing busybox-1.32.1-r6.trigger
  OK: 245 MiB in 58 packages
  Configuring for:
  PHP Api Version:        20200930
  Zend Module Api No:     20200930
  Zend Extension Api No:  420200930
  ...
  /bin/sh /usr/src/php/ext/exif/libtool --mode=install
  cp ./exif.la /usr/src/php/ext/exif/modules
  cp ./.libs/exif.so /usr/src/php/ext/exif/modules/exif.so
  cp ./.libs/exif.lai /usr/src/php/ext/exif/modules/exif.la
  PATH="$PATH:/sbin" ldconfig -n /usr/src/php/ext/exif/modules
  ...
  Build complete.
  ...
  (1/26) Purging .phpize-deps (20210701.102334)
  (2/26) Purging autoconf (2.69-r3)
  ...
```

After the EXIF installation, you must use the directory where the web server finds the documents as the working directory (*WORKDIR*) in the *Dockerfile*. docker build then copies the contents of the local *www* directory to the working directory and installs the composer module erusev/parsedown at this location.

Before you do this, you need to change the access rights for the files below /var/www/ html so that the user www-data has write permission here, and you must change to this user ID.

As mentioned previously, *Parsedown* allows the conversion of Markdown syntax into HTML. Finally, the two volumes /var/www/html and /var/www/html/vendor are created, and the latter is the installation location for composer modules.

11.3.5 docker-compose.yml for the EXIF Example

The separation of the two directories into two different volumes becomes clear when we look at the following *docker-compose.yml* files:

```
# File: prog/php-fpm/docker-compose.yml
version: '3'
services:
  php:
    build: .
    image: docbuc/php-fpm:alpine-exif
    volumes:
      - www:/var/www/html
      - vendor:/var/www/html/vendor
  nginx:
    image: nginx:1
    volumes:
      - ./default.conf:/etc/nginx/conf.d/default.conf
      - www:/var/www/html
      - vendor:/var/www/html/vendor
    ports:
      - 8080:80
volumes:
  vendor:
  www:
```

The preceding *docker-compose.yml* file could represent a production system. All files are located in Docker-managed volumes. Thus, the server runs independently of the local file system. For application development, the setup is a bit tedious: To get an update from your changes, you need to rebuild the image (docker-compose build php), stop and delete the existing service (docker-compose stop && docker-compose rm), and then restart the service (docker-compose up).

Docker also provides the option to extend or overwrite the existing configuration with another *docker-compose* file. To do that, you should create another file named *docker-compose.override.yml* in the project directory:

```
# File: prog/php-fpm/docker-compose.override.yml
version: '3'
services:
  php:
```

```
    volumes:
      - ./www:/var/www/html
  nginx:
    volumes:
      - ./www:/var/www/html
```

When `docker-compose` is called, the *docker-compose.override.yml* file gets detected and included in the configuration. In this case, this overwrites the Docker-managed volume www with a `bind` `mount` to the local *./www* directory (note the leading *./*). Any changes you'll now make to files in the *www* directory can be immediately tried out by a browser reload, just as you would imagine in a development environment. The libraries installed by the `composer` don't have to be copied to the *www/* directory because this is a separate Docker volume.

11.4   Ruby

The development of Ruby as an object-oriented programming language began as early as 1993, but the language didn't become widely known until around 2005, when *Ruby on Rails* saw the light of day on the internet. The framework for web applications based on the Model View Controller (MVC) paradigm was enthusiastically received, and even today you can find many major web applications developed on this basis, such as Airbnb, GitHub, Hulu, and Kickstarter.

11.4.1   "printheadlines" Example

As with the previous programming languages, we'll use an example to show you how to use Ruby. To process the already known RSS feed from the Slashdot news ticker, we'll use the RSS library in Ruby.

Libraries are referred to as *gems* in Ruby. The name of the package manager is also derived from this. Usually you'd install the RSS library by calling `gem install rss`, but the official Docker image of Ruby already includes this gem. The *Dockerfile* for this example is therefore particularly short:

```
# File: prog/ruby/Dockerfile (docbuc/printheadlines:ruby)
FROM ruby:3
WORKDIR /src
COPY printheadlines.rb /src/
USER www-data
CMD [ "ruby", "printheadlines.rb" ]
```

The Ruby program for processing the messages also requires only a few lines (note that the line breaks at the backslash here are due to the text layout, but the code is executable even as is):

```
require 'rss'
require 'time'

feed = RSS::Parser.parse("https://rss.slashdot.org/Slashdot/slashdotMain")
feed.items.each do |item|
    d = Time.parse(item.updated.content.to_s)
    puts "* [#{d.strftime('%Y-%m-%d %H:%M:%S')}]:"\
    "#{item.title.content}"
end
```

With `docker build -t docbuc/printheadlines:ruby .`, you now create the image and start it with `docker run docbuc/printheadlines:ruby`. As output, you should see the list of current messages in the console window.

11.5 Python

Python has become a very popular programming language over the course of many years. Linux distributions use the language for developing important tools, in operation, and maintenance. Python is also popular as a teaching language for beginning programmers, as the strict indentation requirements make it easy to read, and the interpreted language quickly leads to a sense of accomplishment.

11.5.1 "printheadlines" Example

To get started, let's take a look at the example now familiar from the previous sections in a Python variant: The script should extract the news from the RSS feed of the Slashdot news ticker and output it as a list in the console window. The script uses the feedparser module, which is installed in the *Dockerfile*:

```
# File: prog/python/Dockerfile (docbuc/printheadlines:python)
FROM python:3
WORKDIR /src
RUN pip install --no-cache-dir feedparser
COPY printheadlines.py /src/
USER www-data
CMD [ "python", "/src/printheadlines.py" ]
```

The example uses the latest version 3 of Python and builds on the official Docker Hub image. This in turn is based on Debian Buster.

The working directory is */src*. The `feedparser` module installed with `pip` parses the XML document and converts it to Python variables. The `--no-cache-dir` option causes no cache files to be permanently stored during installation, thus minimizing the image size. (The cache would only be beneficial if `pip` was used multiple times.) COPY copies the

Python script to the working directory. CMD specifies that the Python interpreter will be executed with the script as parameter upon container startup.

The Python script itself imports the module, loads the news ticker URL from *slashdot.org*, and then executes the loop across all news elements in a lambda function:

```
#!/usr/bin/env python3
# File: python/printheadlines.py
import feedparser
import time
feed = feedparser.parse(
  "https://rss.slashdot.org/Slashdot/slashdotMain")
[ print("* [%s]: %s" %
    (time.strftime("%Y-%m-%d %H:%M:%S", entry.published_parsed),
     entry.title))
    for entry in feed.entries ]
```

Now you should call docker build -t printheadlines:python . to build the image and then run it via docker run printheadlines:python. The output should be the familiar list of current headlines.

11.5.2 Packaging an Existing Python Application as a Docker Image

Trying to get an existing Python application to work on the newly installed server or laptop can quickly become a kind of nightmare: the special library A depends on library B, but unfortunately B can no longer be compiled on the new system.

One of the great advantages of Docker is that software can run in a precisely defined environment. You determine which libraries are available in which versions when you create the Docker image.

The idea for the following example came from a Docker workshop with the local weather service office. Here Python scripts are used to display the air pressure distribution across Europe in graphs. Reading the binary data and calculating the isobars is a laborious process; unfortunately, the development of the *basemap* library, which had previously been used for output purposes, has been discontinued. The installation on a new server is therefore a difficult task.

The following *Dockerfile* shows the installation of the Python library matplotlib with the basemap extension:

```
# File: prog/python-legacy/Dockerfile (docbuc/python-legacy)
FROM python:2.7
RUN pip install --no-cache-dir matplotlib
WORKDIR /tmp
RUN curl -L http://download.osgeo.org/geos/geos-3.6.1.tar.bz2 \
    > geos.tar.bz2 \
```

```
    && tar xf geos.tar.bz2 && cd geos-3.6.1/ \
    && export GEOS_DIR=/usr/local \
    && ./configure --prefix=$GEOS_DIR \
    && make && make install \
    && rm -rf /tmp/geos-3.6.1/ /tmp/geos.tar.bz2
RUN curl -L https://downloads.sourceforge.net/project/matplotlib\
    /matplotlib-toolkits/basemap-1.0.7/basemap-1.0.7.tar.gz > \
    basemap.tar.gz \
    && cd /tmp && tar zxf basemap.tar.gz \
    && cd basemap-1.0.7 && python setup.py install \
    && rm -rf /tmp/basemap-1.0.7 /tmp/basemap.tar.gz
WORKDIR /src
COPY *.py /src/
USER www-data
CMD [ "python", "main.py" ]
```

The interesting aspects of this *Dockerfile* are both the installation of the geos library, which is a prerequisite for the basemap, and the basemap itself. You have to compile both libraries yourself, and they are loaded beforehand as compressed archive files from the internet. With geos, this is done with the classic three-step configure && make & & make install. Basemap has a Python setup script that carries out the installation.

For installations of this type, administrators preferred to log the commands to a text file so that they can repeat the setup on another server. As you can see, the *Dockerfile* is actually this very file.

When this example was developed in February 2018, the *Dockerfile* worked exactly with these instructions. During the proofreading phase in June 2018, docker build aborted with an error message. Somewhat horrified, we realized that this section suddenly had lost its validity. After all, we wanted to demonstrate here that *Dockerfiles* also work at a later point in time. The problem was quickly found: For *matplotlib*, there was an update from version 2.1.2 to version 2.2.2 that contained an incompatibility with the basemap library. As a solution, a fixed version number must be specified when installing matplotlib:

```
# File: prog/python-legacy/Dockerfile (excerpt)
FROM python:2.7
RUN pip install --no-cache-dir matplotlib==2.1.2
```

11.5.3   Sample Code

To demonstrate how the matplotlib library works, we want to develop a short Python program that plots the current day-night situation on a world map. This is a slight modification of an example of the basemap web page (*https://matplotlib.org/basemap/ users/examples.html*). In our case, the graphic gets saved to a file:

```
import matplotlib
matplotlib.use('Agg')
import numpy as np
from mpl_toolkits.basemap import Basemap
import matplotlib.pyplot as plt
from datetime import datetime
plt.figure(figsize=(10.24, 7.68), dpi=100)
mp = Basemap(projection='merc', llcrnrlat=-80, urcrnrlat=80,\
    llcrnrlon=-180, urcrnrlon=180, lat_ts=20, resolution='c')
mp.drawcoastlines()
mp.drawparallels(np.arange(-90,90,30), labels=[1,0,0,0])
mp.drawmapboundary(fill_color='aqua')
mp.fillcontinents(color='coral', lake_color='aqua')
date = datetime.utcnow()
CS = mp.nightshade(date)
plt.title('Day and night on %s (UTC)' %
        date.strftime("%d %b %Y %H:%M:%S"))
plt.savefig('/src/out/day_night.png')
```

Usually, `matplotlib` issues the output on a screen. But because there's no display available in the Docker container, we initialize the `Agg` backend in the second line of the listing, which allows for computation even without a screen output.

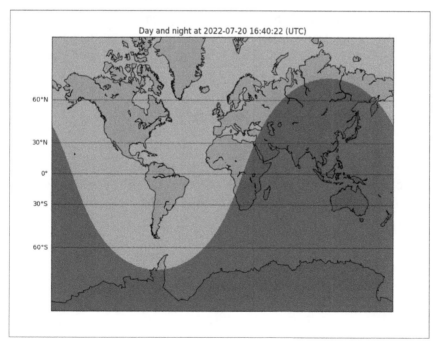

Figure 11.2 Output of the Python Sample Program Displaying the Day-Night Illumination of the Earth

After the `import` statements, the plot size is set to 1024 × 768 pixels (10.24 inches at 100 pixels per inch). The basemap maps the world from 80 degrees north to 80 degrees south in the Mercator projection. After drawing the continents and the latitudes, the script determines the current time and date and calls the `nightshade` method of the basemap. Finally, we save the map to the file *day_night.png* file (see Figure 11.2).

Create the Docker image using the following:

```
docker build -t docbuc/python-legacy .
```

Next, run it via the following:

```
docker run -v ${PWD}:/src/out -u $UID:$GID docbuc/python-legacy
```

By including the current directory in the container under `/src/out`, the PNG graphic gets saved in the current folder. Specifying `-u $UID:$GID` will cause the container to run with your user and group ID rather than `www-data`, as specified in the *Dockerfile*. This allows the file to be created in the current directory (provided you have write permissions here).

11.5.4   Localization and Character Sets in Python Programs

If you use non-ASCII characters (e.g., umlauts) in the source code, you must pay special attention in Python. In Python 2, under certain circumstances, an umlaut in a comment is enough for Python to abort the execution of the program. If you use the official Docker images for Python from Docker Hub, you need to note that they don't have *locales* support built in yet. Therefore, if you're located in Europe, for example, you may have a problem, as the following illustrates:

```
docker run --rm python:3 python -c \
    'import time, locale; print(time.strftime("%c"))'
  Thu Jul  1 13:50:09 2021
```

The Python function `time.strftime("%c")` outputs the current time in the usual format for the region. Because Python doesn't know which region it's in, American date formatting is used here. To output the time in the German locale, for example, you must first set this in Python via `locale.setlocale`:

```
docker run --rm python:3 python -c \
    'import time, locale;
    locale.setlocale(locale.LC_ALL, "de_DE.UTF-8");
    print(time.strftime("%c"))'
```

```
Traceback (most recent call last):
  File "<string>", line 2, in <module>
  File "/usr/local/lib/python3.9/locale.py", line 610,
      in setlocale
    return _setlocale(category, locale)
locale.Error: unsupported locale setting
```

But here, Python aborts with an error message because the desired locale setting isn't available. To use the correct locale in the official Python images, you subsequently need to install the locales package and activate the desired language. A corresponding *Dockerfile* looks like the following:

```
# File: prog/python-locale/Dockerfile (docbuc/python-locale)
FROM python:3
WORKDIR /src
RUN apt-get update \
  && apt-get install -y locales \
  && rm -rf /var/lib/apt/lists/*
RUN sed -i -e 's/# de_DE.UTF-8 UTF-8/de_DE.UTF-8 UTF-8/' \
        /etc/locale.gen \
  && locale-gen
COPY umlaut.py /src/
USER www-data
CMD [ "python", "umlaut.py" ]
```

The locales package gets installed with apt-get. To minimize the image size, rm -rf clears the cache for the package sources.

The next step is to remove the comment character (#) before the corresponding language in the */etc/locale.gen* file. The Unix tool sed is the tool of choice here. The regular expression for searching and replacing is specified with the parameter -e (execute), while -i stands for changing the file directly (in place).

After this change, the locale-gen program generates the enabled locales, and then your Python image can not only output umlauts correctly but also display the date and time in German format. The following script serves as proof:

```
# -*- coding: utf-8 -*-
# File: prog/python-locale/umlaut.py
import time, locale
locale.setlocale(locale.LC_TIME, 'de_DE.UTF-8')
print("Fix Schwyz! quäkt Jürgen blöd vom Paß")
print(time.strftime("%c"))
```

The program uses the `time` and `locale` libraries to display the time in German format:

```
docker build -t docbuc/python-locale .
```

```
  Sending build context to Docker daemon  3.072kB
  Step 1/7 : FROM python:3
    ---> a2aeea3dfc32
```

```
...
  Successfully tagged docbuc/python-locale:latest
```

```
docker run docbuc/python-locale
```

```
  Fix Schwyz! quäkt Jürgen blöd vom Paß
  Do 01 Jul 2021 13:39:28 UTC
```

Chapter 12
Web Applications and Content Management Systems

In this chapter, we'll launch some common web applications in containers. Software products based on PHP and MySQL/MariaDB still have a large user community: The entry barrier for developers is low because PHP isn't a very complex language, and yet most programs show a good performance.

With WordPress and Joomla, we'll present two widely used content management systems (CMSs). Nextcloud is a very popular *private cloud* solution that provides universal access to your files.

12.1 WordPress

WordPress started in 2003 as a fork of the blogging software, *b2*. As a technological basis, the developers have relied on PHP and MySQL from the beginning, which keeps the entry barrier low for potential employees. According to recent statistics (see *https://trends.builtwith.com/cms/WordPress*), WordPress is currently actively used by about 20 million websites. It's the most successful blogging and content management software.

For WordPress, you can find many different variants of the official image on Docker Hub:

https://hub.docker.com/_/wordpress

Whether you want to use the classic Apache PHP MySQL image, a lean image based on Alpine Linux or an image with FPM (the FastCGI Process Manager [FPM] that lets PHP run independently of the web server)—there's a ready-made image for every taste.

In a classic *microservice architecture*, the image doesn't contain a database; MySQL or MariaDB must be started as a separate service and *linked* to the WordPress container. When you use an FPM image, you also need a web server service. If you plan a more elaborate WordPress website that you want to extend with complex WordPress plugins, you'll run into the problem of PHP extensions being required.

12.1.1 Custom Docker Images

At that point at the least, you'll need to create your own Docker image, and it's a good idea to build on the prebuilt images by starting your *Dockerfile* with the following line, for example:

```
FROM wordpress:fpm
```

This builds on the current WordPress image for FastCGI, which in turn builds on the php:fpm image. To install PHP extensions in this case, you must use the docker-php-ext-install and docker-php-ext-enable scripts from this base image.

For the WordPress example, we want to use the default combination of apache and MariaDB. To connect the two services as easily as possible, you want to use docker compose:

```
# File: wordpress/docker-compose.yml
version: '3'
services:
  web:
    image: wordpress:apache
    restart: always
    volumes:
      - webdata:/var/www/html
    ports:
      - 8080:80
    environment:
      WORDPRESS_DB_HOST: mariadb
      WORDPRESS_DB_NAME: dockerbuch
      WORDPRESS_DB_USER: dockerbuch
      WORDPRESS_DB_PASSWORD: johroo2zaeQu

  mariadb:
    image: mariadb:10
    restart: always
    environment:
      MYSQL_ROOT_PASSWORD: eengi7suXeut
      MYSQL_DATABASE: dockerbuch
      MYSQL_USER: dockerbuch
      MYSQL_PASSWORD: johroo2zaeQu

volumes:
  webdata:
```

The web service uses the apache variant of the WordPress image and mounts the webdata volume. This is defined at the end of the *docker-compose.yml* file as a volume managed by Docker. If this volume doesn't exist yet, the PHP files, stylesheets, and other assets of the WordPress installation will be copied here when the WordPress container gets created.

With the port mapping of 8080:80, the host port 8080 is connected to the container port 80, which allows you to reach the WordPress site at the *http://localhost:8080* address on the host.

In the configuration file of the WordPress container, four environment variables are defined in addition to the settings already mentioned:

- WORDPRESS_DB_HOST references the host name of the database container on the internal Docker network, in this case, mariadb.
- Furthermore, the name of the database (WORDPRESS_DB_NAME), a user name for logging in to the database server (WORDPRESS_DB_USER), and the corresponding password for the user (WORDPRESS_DB_PASSWORD) are specified as well. As you've probably already noticed, these values correspond to the environment variables used when defining the mariadb service. The service also requires a root password (MYSQL_ROOT_PASSWORD).

Now you can start the WordPress installation using docker compose up -d. Once the images have been downloaded and the containers created, you can start the WordPress setup process at *http://localhost:8080* (see Figure 12.1).

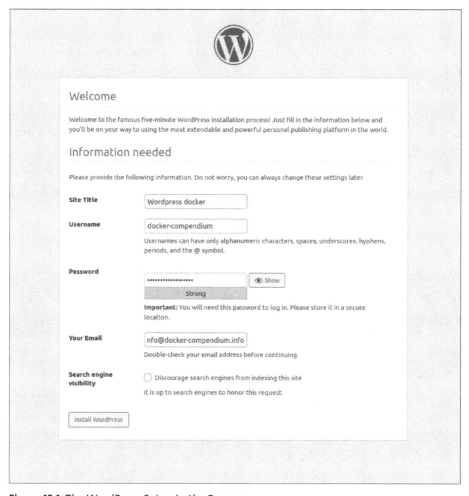

Figure 12.1 The WordPress Setup in the Browser

12.1.2   The "wp-cli" Command

Among the official Docker images for WordPress on Docker Hub, you can find, besides the server variants, images for the WordPress wp-cli command-line tool. Using this powerful tool, you can administrate WordPress without the web interface. For example, you can use commands such as plugin update --all to automatically update all installed plug-ins to the latest version.

To use the Docker image for calling the command-line interface (CLI), you need to both mount the volume with the WordPress installation and join the network where Docker is running. If you used the wordpress directory for your Dockerfile as we did, your network will be named wordpress_default. In that case, the call for the WordPress CLI looks like the following:

```
docker run --rm -t \
  --volumes-from wordpress_web_1 --network wordpress_default \
  wordpress:cli plugin update --all
```

The container created by the docker run command is to be deleted again immediately after execution (--rm); furthermore, it's specified with -t that the output is to be sent to a terminal. You'll then get nicer formatted tables and colored status texts.

--volumes-from wordpress_web_1 mounts the shared volume webdata under /var/www/html. The --network parameter connects the container to the wordpress_default network, which is created by docker compose during startup.

As the image from which the container is to be derived, you can use wordpress:cli. The command to execute is plugin update --all. For a new installation, the output should read Success: Plugin already updated.

You can use the user list command to output a list of registered users.

CLI Commands

An overview of all commands for the WordPress CLI can be found here:

https://developer.wordpress.org/cli/commands

12.1.3   Dealing with Passwords

Storing passwords in plain text in a configuration file or setting them in an environment variable always triggers some discomfort. Even if the passwords are automatically generated, as is the case here, one still gets the feeling that there should be a more elegant solution to the problem.

The Docker developers probably thought the same and presented us with a way to write passwords to a transient file when the container gets created, which is never stored on the hard drive. However, the database server and WordPress configuration can read the secrets from these files, which still allows for an automatic configuration.

The official images of WordPress and MariaDB have already implemented this new mechanism. The *docker-compose.yml* file thus changes as follows:

```
# File: webapps/wordpress-secrets/docker-compose.yml
version: '3.5'
services:
  wordpress:
    image: wordpress:apache
    restart: always
    ports:
      - 8080:80
    volumes:
      - webdata:/var/www/html
    environment:
      WORDPRESS_DB_HOST: mariadb
      WORDPRESS_DB_NAME: dockerbuch
      WORDPRESS_DB_USER: dockerbuch
      WORDPRESS_DB_PASSWORD_FILE: /run/secrets/mysql_user
    secrets:
      - mysql_user

  mariadb:
    image: mariadb:10
    restart: always
    secrets:
      - mysql_root
      - mysql_user
    environment:
      MYSQL_ROOT_PASSWORD_FILE: /run/secrets/mysql_root
      MYSQL_PASSWORD_FILE:      /run/secrets/mysql_user
      MYSQL_DATABASE:           dockerbuch
      MYSQL_USER:               dockerbuch
volumes:
  webdata:
secrets:
  mysql_root:
    file: ./mysql_root.txt
  mysql_user:
    file: ./mysql_user.txt
```

The changes affect the lines MYSQL_PASSWORD, MYSQL_ROOT_PASSWORD, and WORDPRESS_DB_
PASSWORD, respectively. The _FILE appended to the variables references the files containing the passwords.

The global secrets section defines the passwords to be used, in this case, mysql_root and
mysql_user. Here, the values for the passwords are read from files in the current directory. Instead of the file: assignment, external: true could also be specified. Then the
password would have to have been previously created with docker secret create (this
only works in Docker Swarm mode; see Chapter 19).

"pwgen" Command

If you work on Linux, you can generate passwords very comfortably using the pwgen
command. For example, to create the file *mysql_user.txt* with a random password of 14
characters, the command pwgen 14 1 > mysql_user.txt is sufficient, where 14 is the
number of characters and 1 is the number of passwords. You can use pwgen --help to
get more information about the command.

12.1.4   Update

Updates are an indispensable part of software on the web. WordPress has its own
update mechanism, which independently makes sure that the latest version is
installed. For this purpose, the account of the web server needs to have write permissions in the directory of the WordPress installation (and in all subdirectories).

These requirements are met in the Docker image for WordPress, so the updates work
by default (see Figure 12.2). However, this only affects the source code of WordPress, not
the versions of Apache and PHP. As usual with Docker images, you're responsible for
applying the updates yourself.

The setup shown here uses the named volume webdata for /var/www/html. Both Word-
Press source code and uploaded content (e.g., images and PDFs) are located there.

When the Docker images are updated (docker compose pull) and the configuration is
restarted (docker compose up -d), a new container gets created with the updated Word-
Press source code. However, the webdata volume gets mounted *via* the source code and
thus isn't affected by the update. This may seem confusing at first, but it works very
well in practice. The big danger of a security gap in the WordPress code should be ban-
ished by the automatic update, while the administrator needs to take care of security
gaps on the underlying software layers.

Because tags are used for the configuration of the Docker image (wordpress:php7.2-
apache in this example), it's very likely that there are incompatibilities with an updated
image, and an automatic update via cron on the host can be performed safely. For this,

it's sufficient to execute the two commands docker compose pull and docker compose up
-d in the corresponding directory one after the other.

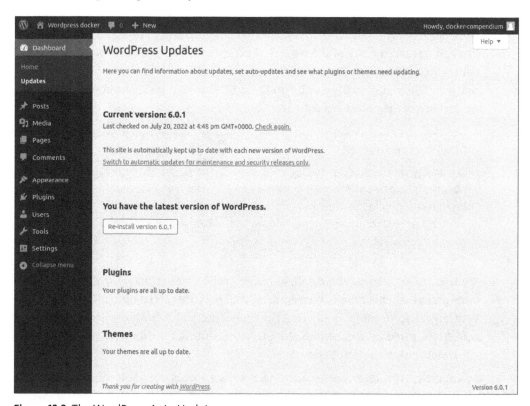

Figure 12.2 The WordPress Auto Update

12.1.5   Backup

Even though Docker allows you to configure the setup in a redundant and distributed
manner, you still shouldn't do entirely without a classic backup. For a complete backup
of the WordPress containers presented here, you need a dump of the database as well
as a backup of the files under */var/www/html*.

Because the files are organized in a volume, they can be easily used and backed up in
another Docker container using --volumes-from. To create a compressed *tar* file, the following command is sufficient:

```
docker run --rm -v /var/backups/wordpress:/backup \
  --volumes-from=wordpress_web_1 \
  alpine tar zcvf /backup/wordpress.tar.gz /var/www/html
```

For this purpose, you should use the Docker image from Alpine Linux and run the tar
command from it. -v /var/backups/wordpress:/backup allows you to mount the local

directory /var/backups/wordpress under /backup in the container. The crucial parameter is --volumes-from, which embeds the PHP source code and uploaded files, just like the WordPress CLI.

If you want to run this call by cron script every night and save multiple versions of the file, you can add the day of the week to the file name. On Linux, this works with a file name extension such as /backup/wordpress-$(date +%w).tar.gz, where date +%w outputs the day of the week (starting with Sunday as 0). This way, you'll always have a backup file for each of the past seven days.

> ### Other Backup Strategies
>
> Explaining various backup strategies is beyond the scope of this book. However, a backup of the past seven days is certainly better than no backup, and this simple strategy can be extended to other days if needed (e.g., date +%j returns the day of the year, from 001 to 365/366). Incremental backups also allow you to optimize backup storage space requirements.

We want to implement the database backup with a classic database dump. For very large databases, this type of backup isn't ideal because the resulting file can become very large despite compression, and the time required for the dump can be considerable. In the worst case, the tables also get locked during the dump, so your WordPress site won't work for a short period.

Fortunately, WordPress uses the transaction-safe InnoDB table format in current versions, which provides a big advantage when dumping: the --single-transaction parameter in combination with --skip-lock-tables ensures that the state of the tables at the time of the command call is *frozen* and the database accepts changes in the background. The backup file stores a state that's consistent across all tables.

Unlike the file backup, we don't start a separate container here but call the mysqldump command in the running MariaDB container. To get access to the container, we use docker compose exec mariadb in the appropriate directory. If you've saved the passwords as environment variables in the *docker compose* file, you can run the backup via the following command:

```
docker compose exec mariadb sh -c 'mysqldump \
    --password=$MYSQL_ROOT_PASSWORD --single-transaction \
    --skip-lock-tables dockerbuch' > \
    /var/backups/dockerbuch-wordpress.sql
```

Here, we use a little trick to obtain the environment variable from the *docker compose* file. Actually, you could call docker compose exec mariadb mysqldump ..., but then you wouldn't have access to the $MYSQL_ROOT_PASSWORD variable. On the other hand, if you start a shell with a command (sh -c), then you can use the variables when executing the command.

The mysqldump command returns the output directly to the terminal, which is redirected to a file (*/var/backups/duckerbuch-wordpress.sql*) in our example. This file isn't located inside the container, but, like the docker compose exec call, it's on the host. (Make sure that you have write permissions in the directory!)

Of course, as with backing up files, you can add a date value to the backup file names.

12.2 Nextcloud

Cloud storage now has a permanent place in everyday computing. Whether it's Google, Apple, Amazon, or Dropbox, somewhere we all have more or less data stored because it's very convenient and works well. If you don't like to store your private data with one of the big IT service providers and have sufficient access rights to a server, then you can install your own cloud.

A widely used and mature private cloud solution, which is open source, is *Nextcloud* (*https://nextcloud.com*), a fork of the popular ownCloud project. Not only can you manage your files with Nextcloud as you know it from Dropbox, but you can also use *apps* to extend Nextcloud with many useful functions. Popular apps include the calendar, an address book, or a web mail extension.

12.2.1 Installation via "docker compose"

In this section, we'll install Nextcloud in a microservice architecture using docker compose. The first version contains three services: database, PHP, and a web server. In the nextcloud directory, we'll create the following *docker-compose.yml* file:

```
# File: webapps/nextcloud/docker-compose.yml
version: '3'
services:
  db:
    image: mariadb:10.5
    restart: unless-stopped
    volumes:
      - db:/var/lib/mysql
    environment:
      - MYSQL_ROOT_PASSWORD=ciel5eeNgeez
      - MYSQL_PASSWORD=IeMaovahM2ba
      - MYSQL_DATABASE=nextcloud
      - MYSQL_USER=nextcloud
```

```
app:
  image: nextcloud:fpm
  volumes:
    - nextcloud:/var/www/html
    - nextcloud_data:/var/www/html/data
  restart: unless-stopped
  environment:
    - MYSQL_PASSWORD=IeMaovahM2ba
    - MYSQL_DATABASE=nextcloud
    - MYSQL_USER=nextcloud
    - MYSQL_HOST=db
web:
  image: nginx:1
  ports:
    - 8080:80
  volumes:
    - ./nginx.conf:/etc/nginx/nginx.conf:ro
    - nextcloud:/var/www/html
    - nextcloud_data:/var/www/html/data
  restart: unless-stopped

volumes:
  db:
  nextcloud:
  nextcloud_data:
```

The database service uses the official MariaDB image in version 10.x and stores the data in a volume called db. The environment variables define the necessary database settings (see Chapter 10).

To make the microservice architecture as flexible as possible, we use the FPM image of Nextcloud (in the app service) and Nginx as web server (in the web service). Due to the specification of the MYSQL_ variable in the environment section of the app service, Nextcloud automatically configures database access.

To make backing up data easier, we use two volumes in the Nextcloud container: (1) the nextcloud volume containing the PHP application data, and (2) the nextcloud_data volume, which stores the data we upload. With a backup of the second volume and a database backup, the system can be restored after a crash.

Start the configuration via docker compose up now. After a few seconds, you can access the web address *http://localhost:8080* (see Figure 12.3).

Figure 12.3 Installation Screen When Nextcloud Is Started for the First Time

12.2.2   Creating Backups

Regularly backing up data should be a matter of course. The `nextcloud_data` volume enables you to start a simple backup of the data:

```
docker run --rm \
  -v nextcloud_nextcloud_data:/data:ro \
  -v $(pwd):/backup alpine \
  tar cjvf /backup/data.tar.bz2 -C /data ./
```

The `docker run` command creates an archive of the Nextcloud data that's packed with `tar` and compressed with `bzip2`. Because both `tar` and `bzip2` are included in the lightweight Alpine Linux distribution, we derive a container from this image and mount the Nextcloud volume (`nextcloud_nextcloud_data`) in read-only mode in this container.

The `tar` command creates the backup file *data.tar.bz2* in the */backup* directory, which is connected to the current directory via another volume.

12.3   Joomla

Joomla was launched in 2005 as a fork of the open-source CMS called Mambo. Like WordPress, it's based on PHP and MySQL/MariaDB and enjoys great popularity.

The official image on Docker Hub is well maintained and available in two different variants:

- PHP 7 and Apache, the current default image
- PHP 7 FPM

While the Apache variants are based on the PHP module integrated in the web server, the FPM variants use a standalone server—the FastCGI Process Manager. This server processes PHP files similar to the Apache module without starting a separate process for each call, not within the web server, and as an independent server.

All images are based on the official images of PHP and don't provide a database yet; the FPM variants also require a web server. In our example, we want to use the current PHP 7 version with the Apache web server and MariaDB database.

To launch the services together, we'll use docker compose as in the previous examples. The corresponding file looks like the following:

```
# File: webapps/joomla/docker-compose.yml
version: '3.1'
services:
  joomla:
    image: joomla:apache
    ports:
      - 8080:80
    volumes:
      - webdata:/var/www/html
    environment:
      JOOMLA_DB_HOST: mariadb
      JOOMLA_DB_NAME: dockerbuch
      JOOMLA_DB_USER: dockerbuch
      JOOMLA_DB_PASSWORD: johroo2zaeQu
  mariadb:
    image: mariadb:10
    environment:
      MYSQL_ROOT_PASSWORD: eengi7suXeut
      MYSQL_DATABASE: dockerbuch
      MYSQL_USER: dockerbuch
      MYSQL_PASSWORD: johroo2zaeQu
volumes:
  webdata:
```

The `joomla` and `mariadb` services are configured in the `services` section. 8080 is used as the local port for the web server. The named volume `webdata` contains the entire installation of Joomla.

As with WordPress, the database access data can be specified as an environment variable, but in the initial configuration dialog, these values weren't taken over in our tests.

When you start this configuration via `docker compose up` and navigate to the address *http://localhost:8080* in your browser, you'll see the three-step installation wizard of Joomla. After specifying the page title, an admin user, and database access data, the program will indicate that all requirements for operation have been met (see Figure 12.4).

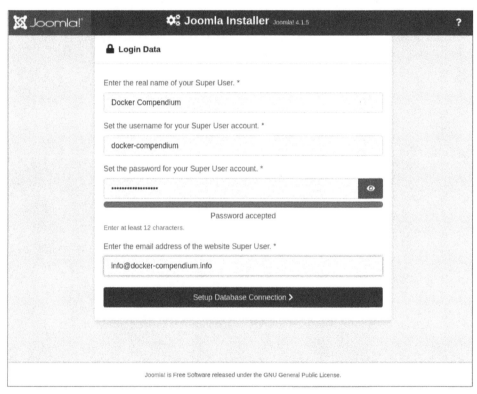

Figure 12.4 Installation Check at the First Start of Joomla

PART III

Exercises

Chapter 13
A Modern Web Application

In this chapter, we want to introduce the interaction of Docker with a modern web application framework. The setup contains the following components:

- A web frontend with *Vue.js* (as a *single-page application*)
- An application programming interface (API) backend server based on Node.js (Express)
- A database backend (MongoDB)
- A session backend (Redis)

The application should be easily scalable. Docker helps us do that:

- The web frontend, a single-page application, runs in a container with Nginx as the web server.
- The REST API runs in a container with Node.js.
- The MongoDB database runs in three containers configured as a replicated setup with automatic *failover*.
- The Redis database provides transient session storage in a container (see Figure 13.1).

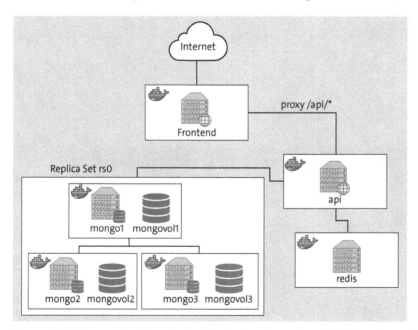

Figure 13.1 Microservice Setup for the Production Operation of the Sample Application

The entire application is programmed in a modern version of JavaScript. Some of the Docker tricks we'll describe in this chapter are specific to tools from the JavaScript and Node.js environments. Good knowledge of this programming language is therefore advantageous.

13.1   The Application

The simple sample application will be used to write a diary. Each entry will be accompanied by a photo, but the text has priority. A new diary entry starts with the upload of an image. The resolution of the images will be downsampled prior to the upload. The text for an entry will be written in Markdown format and displayed in HTML format.

You'll be able to navigate to older entries via a calendar module. All entries will be displayed in the bottom area of the page (see Figure 13.2).

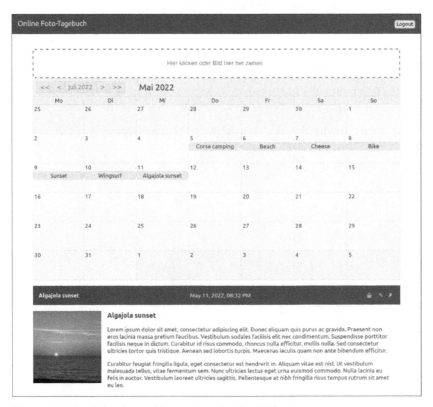

Figure 13.2 The Calendar and Some Diary Entries in the App

Individual entries can be released publicly and, of course, can also be changed and deleted (see Figure 13.3).

In addition, a *lightbox* module will be integrated that can display individual images enlarged (see Figure 13.4).

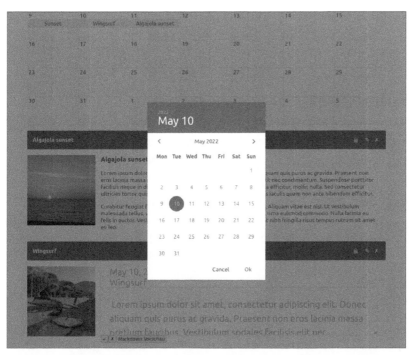

Figure 13.3 Editing a Diary Entry with the "vue-simple-calendar" Module

Figure 13.4 Enlarged Image View

The user administration is located in the Mongo database. Passwords will be hashed using the `bcrypt` algorithm, which is currently considered secure, and will be stored in the `users` collection.

13.1.1   Technical Background

For this chapter, we set ourselves the following goal: the computer used for application development shouldn't require any special software, apart from the version management system Git (for managing the source code) and, of course, Docker.

In practice, especially in application development, locally installed software is often used to control the build process. For Vue.js, this includes several tools from the Node.js environment (e.g., webpack, `eslint`, and `babel`). In our example, however, such tools are integrated directly in the Docker setup. This setup provides the following advantages:

- Can be used right away
- Can be ported to another development machine at any time
- Uses a stable version of the Node.js runtime
- Doesn't depend on the operating system

Editors in the Container

Regarding the Docker integration, we drew the line at the editor. While it would be conceivable to also launch an editor in the Docker container and thus make the setup even more independent of the operating system used, we didn't want to overdo it here and decided to let you work with the editor of your choice.

If you're interested in fancy Docker techniques, we recommend the *Dockerfiles* by Jessie Frazelle:

https://github.com/jessfraz/dockerfiles

The former Docker employee has used various tricks to wrap desktop editors such as Visual Studio Code (VS Code), Atom, or Sublime Text in *Dockerfiles*. A running X server is required for execution because the X11 socket is included in the container.

13.2   The Frontend: Vue.js

Vue.js is a very lightweight JavaScript framework for building web applications. The compressed file for productive use is just 30 KB in size and can be integrated directly into a HTML page. However, here we want to show you a way to use Vue.js with some practical tools in a local development environment. The Vue.js library gets compiled with all its components and other Node.js modules into an optimized JavaScript bundle. All of these tools, of course, run in a Docker container.

13.2.1   Vue.js Setup

When you start a new project, Vue.js allows you to use a command-line utility to automatically generate the initial project structure. This step will save you a lot of typing and headache with configuration settings for tools such as webpack, eslint, and babel.

Because we assume there's no Node.js runtime installed on your computer and you don't want to install it, you can simply use a Docker image to run the Vue.js command-line program:

```
# File: mwa/frontend/setup/Dockerfile (docbuc/mwafe-setup:2)
FROM node:16-alpine
RUN apk add --no-cache git
RUN npm i -g --save @vue/cli
WORKDIR /src
CMD ["vue", "create", "vue"]
```

We created the image using the following commands and deposited it in our Docker Hub account:

```
docker build -t docbuc/mwafe-setup:2 .
docker push docbuc/mwafe-setup:2
```

You can start the initialization using the following Docker command, preferably in the *frontend* directory of the current project:

```
docker run -it --rm -u $UID:$GID \
  -v ${PWD}:/src docbuc/mwafe-setup:2
```

The -it parameter is needed to make an interactive input in the terminal. Using --rm, you can delete the container immediately after execution; it won't be needed afterwards. The initialization program creates files in a subfolder of the current folder that you'll later edit in an editor of your choice.

If you use Linux, you can start the container under your user and group identifiers with the parameter -u $UID:$GID. $UID and $GID are environment variables that contain the numeric identifier of your user account and primary group, respectively. That isn't necessary on Windows or Mac.

Use the following settings in the installation wizard:

- **preset:** default ([Vue 2] babel, eslint)
- **package manager:** Use NPM

The command creates the *vue* subfolder, which contains all files needed for the frontend. The *src* folder contains the source code for the application. You can place your Vue.js components in the *components* subfolder.

13.2.2   Development and Production Image (Multistage Builds)

Especially when developing the frontend, that is, the component that runs in the browser, the problem arises that the requirements for development and for productive operation are very different. Although you could work with two different *Dockerfiles*, Docker provides a different, more elegant option to deal with the problem: *multistage builds*.

To use a multistage build, you simply need to add another FROM statement in your *Dockerfile*. The advantage over separate *Dockerfiles* is that you can access the layers of the first in the second *Dockerfile*.

The Vue.js framework in our example is based on the Node.js runtime for development. For this reason, you want to derive the *Dockerfile* from the official node:16 image. In the first part of the statements, you'll install the necessary Node.js modules, copy the source code to the */src/vue* directory, and start the Vue.js build process (npm run-script build). The result is the finished web app in the */src/vue/dist* folder. The app consists of HTML, JavaScript, and stylesheet files. We'll go into more detail about how the ENTRY-POINT script works a little later.

```
# File: mwa/frontend/Dockerfile (docbuc/mwafe:2)
FROM node:16 as builder
RUN npm i -g --save @vue/cli
WORKDIR /src/vue
COPY vue/package* /src/vue/
RUN chown -R node:node /src
USER node
RUN npm install
COPY vue/ /src/vue/
RUN npm run-script build
COPY dev-entrypoint.sh /src/
ENTRYPOINT [ "/src/dev-entrypoint.sh" ]
CMD [ "npm", "run-script", "serve" ]
FROM nginx:alpine
WORKDIR /usr/share/nginx/html
COPY --from=builder /src/vue/dist/ .
COPY default.conf /etc/nginx/conf.d/
RUN touch /var/run/nginx.pid && \
  chown -R nginx:nginx /var/run/nginx.pid
USER nginx
HEALTHCHECK --interval=10s --timeout=3s CMD wget -O - \
  http://localhost:8080/ || exit 1
```

The Docker image is more than 1 GB in size at this point, which is unnecessarily large for the purpose of providing a few HTML pages. In addition, the image doesn't contain a web server yet. That's where the multistage build comes into play: you should use the additional FROM statement to derive a new Docker image from nginx:alpine, the light-weight variant of Nginx.

The COPY --from=builder statement accesses the layer you created in the first part of the *Dockerfile*, which contains the finished web application. The files are then copied to WORKDIR from where Nginx provides them by default. The finished Docker image is now only 18 MB in size and still has the full functionality the application needs.

Now, you could quite rightly say that a few megabytes more or less don't matter in this day and age. But what comes with the smaller image sizes are lightning-fast updates and a reduction in attack opportunities: if an image only has the absolutely necessary libraries, an attacker can only attack these. Thanks to multistage builds, these benefits can be implemented with almost no additional effort.

13.2.3   Implementation via docker-compose.override.yml

To use multistage builds with docker compose (we again use the extended configuration with *docker-compose.override.yml* here, see Chapter 11, Section 11.3), we've added the target entry to the build context. You must specify at least 3.4 as the version number in your configuration file:

```
# File: mwa/docker-compose.override.yml (excerpt)
version: '3.4'
services:
[...]
  frontend:
    build:
      context: frontend
      target: builder
    image: docbuc/mwafe-build:latest
    environment:
      - HEALTH_URL=http://localhost/
      - API_BASE=/api
    volumes:
      - ./frontend/vue:/src/vue
    ports:
      - 8080:8080
```

The call of docker compose build frontend stops after the first part of the *Dockerfile* file because we specified builder as the target here. The Docker image gets the docbuc/mwafe-build:latest name (actually the *tag* in Docker terminology). The entry for the frontend in the *docker-compose.yml* file, on the other hand, doesn't use a target, which means that the entire *Dockerfile* (with all stages) gets processed. You "tag" the Docker image created via the command docker compose -f docker-compose.yml build frontend with docbuc/mwafe:2:

```
# File: mwa/docker-compose.yml (excerpt)
version: '3.4'
services:
[...]
  frontend:
    restart: always
    build: frontend
    image: docbuc/mwafe:2
    depends_on:
      - api
    ports:
      - 80:8080
```

You should also note the other differences in the configurations: In the development environment, you include the local */frontend/vue* directory in the container and connect port 8080, where the webpack DevServer (see the next section) is running, to the host. For production operation, port 80 is connected to the Nginx server running on unprivileged port 8080 in the container.

13.2.4   Bundling JavaScript Code with Webpack

If you develop using Vue.js, you can easily include external libraries as Node.js modules. These libraries can be general JavaScript libraries, such as the useful moment.js library, or specific Vue.js libraries that represent a Vue.js component.

In the background, *webpack* is responsible for integrating the modules. This program collects all the necessary libraries and can then make certain changes to your source code. This way all console.log messages can be removed for production use.

During the development of the application, you'll need additional external libraries, which are usually simply imported via npm i --save-dev <lib>. However, in our case, there's no npm command on the developer computer. For this reason, you must use the following command:

```
docker compose exec frontend npm i --save-dev vue2-dropzone
```

This installs the vue2-dropzone module in the frontend container, filling the locally included *package.json* file with the installation statement. This makes the module immediately available in the development environment; for the production environment, the next Docker build process loads and installs the files from the *package.json* file. You often need to try out modules during development but then find that a module doesn't provide the desired effect. To remove such modules, you can also use the docker compose command:

```
docker compose exec frontend npm rm --save-dev exif-reader
```

The configuration file we present here uses the webpack DevServer, mentioned earlier, which is a module of webpack that provides quite a lot of convenience during development. The server monitors the source code and automatically performs a new build with webpack when files are changed. It also automatically reloads the browser that opened the web page through the development server. The immediate feedback when saving a file makes development very dynamic and encourages trial and error.

The server is started with the entry CMD ["npm", "run-script", "serve"] at the end of the first part of the *Dockerfile*. Configuration settings for the webpack DevServer can also be found in Section 13.3, in the "Accessing the Application Programming Interface" section.

13.2.5   Docker "ENTRYPOINT" Script for Node.js Modules

The ENTRYPOINT script performs two tasks for the developer image: (1) all necessary Node.js modules get installed, and (2) the value from the API_BASE environment variable gets entered in the configuration file:

```
#!/bin/bash
# File: mwa/frontend/dev-entrypoint.sh

# install all npm packages to be on the safe side
npm i

# Caution: changes the config/index.js file
API_BASE=${API_BASE:-https://api.dockerbuch.info}
sed -i "s|^const apiBase = .*$|const apiBase = '$API_BASE'|" \
    /src/vue/config/index.js
exec "$@"
```

Installing the Node.js modules is especially useful when you use them for the first time. Although the modules are present in the image, if you include the local directory in the *docker-compose.override.yml* file, they'll be missing. Calling npm i makes sure that the required modules will be present in any case prior to the container start command.

The replacement of the JavaScript constant apiBase is done via the sed command from Unix. The regular expression looks for the string const apiBase = at the beginning of the line in config/index.js and replaces this line with the assignment of the environment variable API_BASE or, if that hasn't been set, with the set default value, https://api.dockerbuch.info. Note, however, that the shell substitution outputs the value of $API_BASE, not the name of the variable.

> **Caution: Version Conflicts**
>
> Replacing the `apiBase` constant in the JavaScript file is a mixed blessing. While it's an uncomplicated way to change the setup from proxy through the frontend to stand-alone API server, the changes will rewrite the versioned source code. And that doesn't happen until you start a container in the development environment! Therefore, it may be better for your use case to make changes to this setting manually in the file.

The last line in the `ENTRYPOINT` script (`exec "$@"`) passes the execution to the command defined as `CMD`. The result of this notation is that the command is assigned process ID 1, and thus it responds correctly to signals for the container (see Chapter 7).

13.2.6   Source Code

We can't go into the entire source code of the sample app in this section as that would take us too far away from Docker. However, to give you an idea of how Vue.js works, we want to present here at least the initial script and one component.

As mentioned earlier, webpack compiles the JavaScript code in the background and also provides you with a server component during development. The configuration of webpack expects an entry point; in our case, that's the *main.js* file:

```
// File: mwa/frontend/vue/src/main.js
import Vue from 'vue'
import App from './App'
import router from './router'
import store from './store'
import DateFilter from './filters/date'

Vue.filter('dateFormat', DateFilter)

/* eslint-disable no-new */
new Vue({
  el: '#app',
  router,
  store,
  template: '<app/>',
  components: { App }
})
```

After the `import` statements for the required JavaScript libraries, you create a global filter that can later be used in all of your HTML templates. The subsequent `new Vue` call instantiates the application with the most important parameters: The value of the `el` key denotes the HTML element (here the Cascading Style Sheets [CSS] selector `#app`) into which the Vue.js app will be integrated. The *index.html* file used for this purpose contains only this Div tag in the HTML body element. The router module takes care of the correct handling of URL paths, while the store module provides a data store that can be used by the entire application.

Vue.js components insert their contents via a *template*. In our example, only the next component App gets loaded in the template. This component is implemented as a *single-file component*. All parts belonging to the component are located in a file with the extension .*vue*. This file is divided into three sections:

- `<template>`
  The template is a mixture of HTML and the template syntax in the familiar *mustache* format ({{ variable }}).

- `<script>`
  JavaScript code controls the operation of the component.

- `<style>`
  CSS statements affect this component.

Thanks to the flexible build system with webpack, the individual parts can also be edited by other tools. Due to the `<style lang="scss">` specification, the CSS statements will be converted with the Sass compiler.

13.2.7   The Main Vue.js Component

In the first part of the app component, you create the header area of the app, which will be displayed on all pages. It consists of a link to the home page in the left-hand pane and—depending on whether the user is logged in or not—a link to the login page or the logout component:

```
<!-- File: mwa/frontend/vue/src/App.vue (excerpt) -->
<template>
  <div id="app">
    <header>
      <span>
        <router-link to="/">Online photo diary</router-link>
      </span>
      <logout v-if="loggedIn"></logout>
      <span v-else>
        <router-link to="/login">Login</router-link>
      </span>
    </header>
    <main>
      <router-view></router-view>
```

```
    </main>
  </div>
</template>
```

Whether or not the logout component will be displayed depends on the content of the loggedIn variable. You can check that using the Vue.js syntax v-if. This doesn't simply hide the HTML part with the CSS statement display: none, but the elements will only be included in the document if the variable is true. Instead of the router-link component, you could simply use HTML element <a href=...>. However, the component has the advantage that it suppresses page reloads in interaction with the HTML5 History API. CSS classes are also inserted to indicate whether the link points to the current page. After the <header>, you load the <router-view> component, which displays the appropriate content depending on the URL path.

In the JavaScript code for this component, you first import the Logout module and the helper module, request, which handles requests to the backend server:

```
<!-- File: mwa/frontend/vue/src/App.vue (excerpt) -->
<script>
import Logout from './components/Logout'
import request from './util/request'
export default {
  name: 'app',
  created () {
    request.get('/session')
      .then(resp => {
        if (resp.user) {
          this.$store.commit('login', resp.user)
        }
      })
  },
  computed: {
    loggedIn () { return this.$store.state.loggedIn },
    user () { return this.$store.state.user }
  },
  components: { Logout }
}
</script>
```

The name key is used to give your component a name. This key also serves as a reference for the HTML element to include the component in other components (in this case, in <app></app>).

The created function gets called as soon as the component has been created (at this point, it isn't yet visible in the browser). Now you should start a request to the API server to check if there's an active session for this browser (more on this in the next section). If the server responds with a user name (resp.user), the login function will be executed in the global store module. More information on the features available for all Vue.js components can be found in this excellent Vue.js documentation:

https://vuejs.org/v2/guide/instance.html

Dynamic variables within a component are stored in the computed object. Accessing this.loggedIn executes the corresponding function and, in this case, returns the status from the store module.

Finally, here's an excerpt from the stylesheet statements of the app component. You can format the header using display: flex and justify-content: space-between. This will keep the two span elements on the left and right of the page margin.

```scss
<!-- File: mwa/frontend/vue/src/App.vue (excerpt) -->
<style lang="scss">
header {
  margin: 0;
  height: 56px;
  padding: 0 16px;
  background-color: #35495E;
  color: #ffffff;
  display: flex;
  justify-content: space-between;
  span {
    font-size: 20px;
    font-weight: 400;
    padding-top: 16px;
  }
}
```

Due to the use of Sassy CSS (SCSS), the span area can be indented below the header area.

The preset configuration for programming style (eslint) has strict defaults. Even the output of a console.log message leads to an error message. Earlier versions of Vue.js used to override the output in the browser with the error message, making the application unusable. As you probably know, such measures are open to considerable debate. If you find this is too much paternalism in programming, you can simply adjust the rules or completely disable the tool during setup.

For example, to enable console.log messages to be output without error messages, you can create an *.eslintrc.js* file with the following contents in the *mwa/frontend/vue* folder:

```js
// File: mwa/frontend/vue/.eslintrc.js
module.exports = {
  root: true,
```

13

```
  env: {
    node: true
  },
  'extends': [
    'plugin:vue/essential',
    '@vue/standard'
  ],
  rules: {
    'no-console': 'off'
  },
  parserOptions: {
    parser: 'babel-eslint'
  }
}
```

The `eslint` configuration extends the defaults of `@vue/standard`, a Node.js module that you still need to install:

```
docker compose exec frontend npm i --save-dev \
  @vue/eslint-config-standard
```

Vue.js Documentation and Sample Project Code

If your interest in Vue.js is piqued, we'd like to recommend this very good documentation to you:

https://vuejs.org/v2/guide

The source code for the entire sample project can be found on our GitHub page:

https://github.com/docbuc/mwa

13.3   The API Server: Node.js Express

The backend server, which receives requests from the web frontend and communicates with the database, has also been implemented in JavaScript. Especially if you program the frontend and backend yourself, it's very convenient not to have to switch between different programming languages.

We also use a multistage Docker image for the backend. In this case, however, it isn't a matter of copying compiled files from one layer to another, but solely a matter of keeping the size of the production images small.

```
# File: mwa/api/Dockerfile (docbuc/mwaapi:2)
FROM node:16 as dev
WORKDIR /src
```

```
RUN chown node:node /src
USER node
COPY package.json /src/
RUN npm i
COPY server.js routes.js dev-entrypoint.sh /src/
ENV TZ="Europe/Amsterdam"
ENTRYPOINT [ "/src/dev-entrypoint.sh" ]
CMD [ "npx", "nodemon", "server.js" ]
FROM node:16-alpine
WORKDIR /src
RUN chown node:node /src
USER node
COPY package.json /src/
RUN npm i --production
COPY server.js routes.js health.js /src/
HEALTHCHECK --interval=10s --timeout=3s CMD node /src/health.js \
  || exit 1
EXPOSE 3000
ENV TZ="Europe/Amsterdam"
CMD [ "npm", "start" ]
```

While the first part of the Docker image is based on the standard version of the Node.js image, we use the Alpine Linux variant again in the production image. We also add the --production parameter to the npm call, which installs only those Node.js packages that were saved with --save, not the --save-dev packages. As with the frontend image, the difference in size is considerable: the developer image is 1.06 GB, while the production image is 195 MB.

For the dev image, you need to first install the required Node.js modules under the node user ID in the */src* folder. Then you want to copy the two files that contain the source code for the server (*server.js* and *routes.js*) and the ENTRYPOINT script (*dev-entrypoint.sh*) to this folder as well.

The ENTRYPOINT script again has the task of installing missing Node.js modules. The functionality is the same as that of the script we described in the previous section, except that no further variable substitution takes place here.

You should use nodemon.server.js instead of node server.js as the startup command for the dev image. Similar to the webpack DevServer, the nodemon module monitors your source code and restarts the server if necessary. The preceding npx command ensures the correct execution of nodemon.

The HEALTHCHECK quickly provides information about the status of the container. You could use curl or wget here to check the specially created route on the API server. But because it's easy in Node.js to write your own client with a few lines of code, and it also makes you independent of the packages installed on the system, you can use the following script:

```
// File: mwa/api/health.js
const http = require('http');
const url = process.env.HEALTH_URL ||
  'http://localhost:3000/health';
http.get(url, res => {
  console.log("status: ", res.statusCode);
  if (res.statusCode === 200) {
    process.exit(0);
  } else {
    process.exit(1);
  }
});
```

In the JavaScript program, you must first check the contents of the HEALTH_URL environment variable, and, if it doesn't contain a value, set the default value to http://localhost:3000/health. This makes the script flexible, as you can check a different route by setting a variable in the *docker-compose.yml* file. Then you need to load the URL with the http module and check the status of the response. If you have code 200, the process will be terminated without an error (return value 0); if you have another response code with 1 as a return value, an error will be displayed.

13.3.1   Stateless or Stateful?

A common pattern in single-page applications is a backend server that issues a token when a user logs in and expects it in a header for each subsequent request. In this context, *JSON Web Tokens* (JWT) are frequently used. This is a standardized format (*https://www.rfc-editor.org/rfc/rfc7519*) that stores JavaScript Object Notation (JSON) objects in a URL-safe string. The string can be signed and encrypted. As a rule, tokens have a validity period that can be chosen between a few minutes, days, or months, depending on the use case.

The advantage for the server with such a setup is that no information about currently logged-in users needs to be stored on the server. The server runs *stateless* because each request sends along the authorization token, which can be readily checked for validity by the server. This is just about the ideal state for a microservice setup where you want to scale containers at will: no matter which of the multiple launched containers the client connects to, each one can verify the validity of the token.

Unfortunately, this advantage also entails a few drawbacks, especially if the client is a web browser. The frontend application in the browser must cache the token somewhere. Because the encrypted tokens are usually larger than the 4 KB allowed for cookies, most applications make use of the browser memory localStorage here. But that's precisely where a security problem arises: while HttpOnly cookies are prevented from being accessed by the browser for JavaScript, any JavaScript running on the web page can access the localStorage. This is also true for JavaScript files that are provided via a content delivery network or that are integrated into the application as a Node.js module. This results in a large gateway for attackers trying to scam a token.

Another problem with tokens is that there's no inherent way to mark them as invalid. Thus, there's also no way to perform a correct logout. Although the token can be deleted in the frontend, the server continues to accept the token as valid until its expiration date.

With sessions, the situation is quite different. After the user logs in, a cookie with an ID is returned to the browser. The server stores data for this ID somewhere, which, in this case, keeps the *state* on the server. Accordingly, the server can also end a running session simply by deleting the data for it; the cookie is thus worthless. Attacking the cookie, which is just as much a *key* as the token, is much more difficult because HttpOnly cookies can't be read by JavaScript.

One disadvantage of sessions is that a client must always communicate with the same server after logging in. This limitation arises because web application servers usually keep session information locally (in the memory or in local files). This complicates scalability because a new server can't simply be added when the load increases.

To get around this limitation, we use the common technique of swapping out session data to a database that the application servers have access to. For this purpose, Redis is well suited as a database because it works at a high performance and requires little to no configuration work. This is the variant we ultimately implemented in our example.

13.3.2 Node.js Modules in the Development Environment

Because the core of the Node.js runtime is kept very lean, the use of modules is a matter of course. Node.js modules are installed using the npm program in the *node_modules/* directory in the root directory of a project. In the *package.json* file, all modules are referenced with their version numbers, which facilitates the installation on another system.

A common pattern when developing with Node.js and Docker is to store the modules in their own Docker volume (see Chapter 9, Section 9.4). This way, you can make sure that your source directory won't get loaded with hundreds of megabytes of modules, and there won't be any issues related to file permissions when Docker installs new modules.

Modern editors such as VS Code or Vim can make suggestions for code completion by analyzing the modules (see Figure 13.5). The prerequisite for this is that the *node_modules* folder can be read. In this example, we therefore decided against mounting the folder as a separate Docker volume, and we let Docker install the modules in the local folder instead.

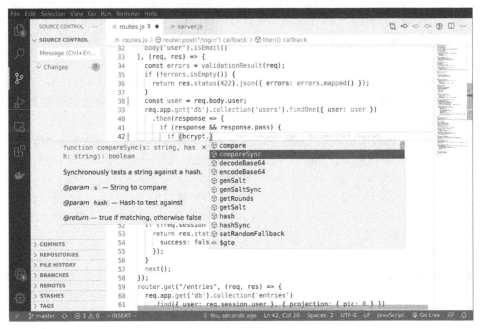

Figure 13.5 Code Completion for the Node.js Module "bcrypt" in the VS Code Editor

Local Node.js Installation versus Docker Installation

If you choose the setup suggested here, where all components except the editor run in Docker containers, then you shouldn't use a locally installed Node.js runtime in parallel. If you do, you'll run into problems with the modules in most cases.

This is partly because some modules download or compile binary packages that are compatible with your container but not necessarily with your operating system. Secondly, problems can also arise because the Node.js and node package manager (npm) versions in the container and on the host are usually not identical.

To install new modules, you need to call the `npm` command in the appropriate container:

```
docker compose exec api npm i --save express-validator
```

13.3.3   Accessing the Application Programming Interface

The API server can be accessed via a proxy statement in the frontend server. Technically, this is a simple solution of adding a section to the Nginx configuration file for production use:

```
# File: mwa/frontend/default.conf (excerpt)
location /api {
  proxy_set_header    Host $host;
  proxy_set_header    X-Real-IP $remote_addr;
  proxy_set_header    X-Forwarded-For $proxy_add_x_forwarded_for;
  proxy_set_header    X-Forwarded-Proto $scheme;
  rewrite     /api/(.+)$ /$1 break;
  proxy_pass  http://api:3000;
  proxy_read_timeout  90;
}
```

All accesses to the URL path /api will be redirected to the api host on port 3000. Prior to that, the first part of the path, /api, will be removed from the address via the rewrite statement. The API server doesn't have this namespace, but expects requests such as /entries or /viewimage.

To achieve the same effect in the development environment (after all, it's not Nginx running here, but the webpack DevServer), you need to adjust the Vue.js configuration file in the frontend. You should create the *vue.config.js* file with the following content:

```
// File: mwa/frontend/vue/vue.config.js
module.exports = {
  devServer: {
    proxy: {
      '^/api': {
        target: 'http://api:3000',
        changeOrigin: true,
        pathRewrite: {
          '^/api': ''
        }
      }
    }
  }
}
```

However, the API doesn't need to be accessed via the proxy. If for some reason, it's desirable not to redirect the API calls through the frontend server, the API server can work without a proxy at all. The prerequisite for this is that the server sends along the corresponding *Cross-Origin Resource Sharing* (CORS) headers. Assuming that the front-end web server can be reached via the *https://diary.dockerbuch.info* URL, and the API server can be reached at *https://api.dockerbuch.info*, the API server must send the following headers:

```
access-control-allow-origin: https://diary.dockerbuch.info
access-control-allow-credentials: true
```

You may be familiar with the specification of `allow-origin` with the wildcard *: in this case, you must explicitly specify the domain from which the script is loaded, because you also want to transfer cookies for authentication. The second header, `allow-credentials`, allows this usage.

13.3.4   Source Code (server.js)

Here are some of the important sections from the API server source code. The code has been divided across two files—*server.js* and *routes.js*:

- `server.js` contains the general server logic (session initialization, database connection, general headers).
- `routes.js` handles the requests (HTTP requests) according to the path. Details will follow in the next section.

```
// File: mwa/api/server.js (excerpt)
const express = require("express"),
  cors = require("cors"),
  MongoClient = require('mongodb').MongoClient,
  session = require('express-session'),
  redis = require('redis'),
  RedisStore = require('connect-redis')(session),
  routes = require('./routes'),
  app = express();

const port = process.env.PORT || 3000;
const mongourl = process.env.MONGO_URL || 'mongodb://mongo:27017'
const secretsalt = process.env.SECRETSALT || 'waitieOrah5ie[...]'
const redisClient = redis.createClient({
  host: 'redis',
});
```

First of all, the used libraries get loaded. Here, in addition to the modules for MongoDB and Redis, you'll also find the `cors` module, which inserts the headers described in the previous section. In addition, the default settings for the port on which the server will run, the connection settings for the Mongo database (`mongourl`), and an initialization value for signing sessions (`secretsalt`) can be overridden with environment variables.

```
app.use(cors({
  origin: 'https://diary.dockerbuch.info',
  credentials: true
}));

app.use(express.json());
app.use(session({
```

```
  store: new RedisStore({
    client: redisClient,
  }),
  saveUninitialized: false,
  secret: secretsalt,
  resave: false
}));

app.use('/', routes);
app.get("/health", (req, res) => {
  debug("health-check von ", req.ip);
  res.json({ healthy: true });
});
app.listen(port, () => {
  console.log("API-Server auf Port ", port);
});
```

The express-session module can access different backends; we want to store the session data in a Redis database. When the session is initialized, a new RedisStore is created for this purpose, which in turn includes the previously created RedisClient. This client contains the Redis database server specification, which, in this case, is the entry for the Redis server in the *docker-compose.yml* file.

The specification of the secret option is mandatory. secret contains the previously mentioned initialization value for signing the session cookie. The app.use statement that follows sets your routes module (see the next section) for all accesses to the server. Next, you need to define the first /health route to be used by Docker HEALTHCHECK to verify that the Node.js server is running. This will send the JSON object { healthy: true } with the HTTP status code 200. The app.listen call finally starts the server on the port defined at the beginning.

Once the database connection has been established successfully, the db variable is set with the database reference (diary) to the Express application. Your routes module accesses the database via this variable.

```
function connect() {
  console.log('Connect to MongoDB: ', mongourl);
  MongoClient.connect(mongourl, { useNewUrlParser: true,
      useUnifiedTopology: true },
    (err, client) => {
    if (err) {
      throw err;
    }
    const diary = client.db('diary')
    app.set('db', diary);
```

```
  });
}
setTimeout(connect, 20000);    // gives some time to the replica set
```

The `setTimeout` function delays the database connection by 20 seconds. This is a work-around to give the MongoDB replica set some time to get started.

13.3.5 Source Code (routes.js)

The `routes` module defines the paths that the API makes available. For this purpose, the `router` function from the `express` module is used, which provides HTTP functions such as `.get()`, `.post()`, or `.patch( )`. When these functions are called, a callback function is used, which is passed the request parameters (`req`) and the response functions (`res`). The `req.app` parameter provides access to the Express application where you previously stored the database reference with `app.set()`.

```
// File: mwa/api/routes.js (excerpt)
const Jimp = require('jimp'),
[...]
  express = require('express'),
  router = express.Router(),
  debug = require("debug")("api"),
  bcrypt = require('bcryptjs');

router.get("/openblogs", (req, res) => {
  req.app.get('db').collection('entries')
    .find({ publicEntry: true })
    .project({ pic: 0 })
    .sort({ date: -1 })
    .limit(5).toArray((err, blogs) => {
      res.json(blogs);
    });
});
```

The call of `/openblogs` results in a database query, where the `entries` collection is searched for all entries with the property `publicEntry: true`. The search is limited to five results, sorted by date, and the `pic` entry is removed from the result (only the `thumbnail` entry is used for the preview).

The login is mapped with the following route:

```
// File: mwa/api/routes.js (excerpt)
router.post("/login", [
  body('password').not().isEmpty(),
  body('user').isEmail()
```

```
], (req, res) => {
  const errors = validationResult(req);

  if (!errors.isEmpty()) {
    return res.status(422).json({ errors: errors.mapped() });
  }
  const user = req.body.user,
    pass = req.body.password;

  req.app.get('db').collection('users').findOne({ user: user })
    .then(response => {
      if (response && response.pass) {  // user found
        if (bcrypt.compareSync(pass, response.pass)) {
          req.session.user = user;
          res.json({ success: true });
        } else {  // wrong password
          return res.status(401).send({
            success: false, message: 'login failed'
          });
        }
      } else {  // user not in database
        return res.status(401).send({
          success: false, message: 'login failed'
        });
```

At the start, you check the user and password parameters with the body function from the express-validator module, which is used as middleware. If errors already occur during this process, an HTTP status of 422 will be sent to the browser. If the user name and password match the defaults, you should look for the entry in the users collection of MongoDB.

The password from the input form gets passed with the hash value from the database to the bcrypt.compareSync function, which checks the password. After the verification, the status 200 is submitted with the JSON object { success: true }. In addition, a user entry is made in the req.session object, starting the session. If the password isn't correct or the user doesn't exist in the database, the status 401 (**Unauthorized**) will be sent.

To check if the user has an active session, you can add a simple /session route:

```
// File: mwa/api/routes.js (excerpt)
router.get("/session", (req, res) => {
  res.json({
    user: req.session.user || ''
  });
});
```

In the client, you can then simply check the value of user to determine if a session is active.

A final excerpt from the server source code shows you a technique for using the Express framework to restrict paths so that they can be accessed only by logged-in users:

```
// File: mwa/api/routes.js (excerpt)
router.use((req, res, next) => {
  if (!req.session || !req.session.user) {
    return res.status(403).send({
      success: false, message: 'login required'
    });
  }
  next();
});
```

All entries listed after this middleware function can only be called if there's an active session for the client.

13.4   The Mongo Database

If you aren't interested in NoSQL databases, you can skip this section. For this example, you can simply use the official MongoDB Docker image, and the application will work beautifully. However, we'll go a step further in this section and describe a replicated setup of MongoDB that supports automatic *failover* when a node fails.

If data is the gold of the 21st century, the storage space for it should be very reliable. MongoDB was developed with Big Data in mind and promises horizontal scalability. With *sharding* and *replica sets*, very sophisticated techniques are available to cope with rapidly growing data volumes and access numbers.

These techniques are independent of Docker and its ability to scale containers. As a result, high-availability databases are still installed on dedicated hardware or virtual machines by cloud providers and run independently of microservices provided by different applications.

In this respect, you should view the following section primarily as a proof of concept that shows how you can use MongoDB in a replica set. If you use it on a host with docker compose, you'll gain neither data security nor any speed in the process. However, things get exciting when you roll out this configuration in the cloud, which we'll demonstrate later in Chapter 19.

For the purpose of database replication, we use three database instances, mongo1, mongo2, and mongo3:

```
# File mwa/docker-compose.yml (excerpt)
version: '3.4'
services:
  mongo1:
    image: mongo:4
    command: --replSet "rs0"
    volumes:
      - mongovol1:/data/db
  mongo2:
    image: mongo:4
    command: --replSet "rs0"
    volumes:
      - mongovol2:/data/db
  mongo3:
    image: mongo:4
    command: --replSet "rs0"
    volumes:
      - mongovol3:/data/db
[...]
volumes:
  mongovol1:
  mongovol2:
  mongovol3:
```

All instances use the current mongo:4 image and start the container with the --replSet
"rs0" addition. This parameter tells the database server that it belongs to replica set rs0,
where the string rs0 is of course freely selectable. Each container writes the database
data to its own Docker-managed volume. After starting the three databases, you need
to initialize the replication once via the following command:

```
docker compose exec mongo1 mongo --eval '
rs.initiate( {
   _id : "rs0",
   members: [
      { _id: 0, host: "mongo1:27017" },
      { _id: 1, host: "mongo2:27017" },
      { _id: 2, host: "mongo3:27017" }
   ]
})
'
```

You connect to the first node from the replica set and execute the mongo --eval ... command there. Without specifying the --host parameter, the mongo program connects to
localhost, that is, the container itself, on the MongoDB default port 27017. Provided the

three database servers are active, the command should return a response in JSON format:

```
MongoDB shell version v4.2.8
  connecting to: mongodb://127.0.0.1:27017/?compressors=disab...
  Implicit session: session { "id" : UUID("3ebde6a4-2f3c-4e21...
  MongoDB server version: 4.2.8
  {
      "operationTime" : Timestamp(1624446340, 1),
      "ok" : 1,
  [...]
```

In our attempts, we didn't succeed in running the command in any form as ENTRYPOINT or as an automatically executed script in the */docker-entrypoint-initdb.d* directory. However, you only need to enter the command the first time you start the configuration as MongoDB stores these settings internally.

To check the status of your replication, you should run the following command:

```
docker compose exec mongo1 mongo --eval 'rs.status()'
```

```
  ...
  MongoDB server version: 4.2.8
  {
    "set" : "rs0",
    "date" : ISODate("2021-06-23T11:10:00.865Z"),
    "myState" : 2,
    "term" : NumberLong(13),
    "syncingTo" : "mongo3:27017",
    "syncSourceHost" : "mongo3:27017",
    "syncSourceId" : 2,
    "heartbeatIntervalMillis" : NumberLong(2000),
    ...

    "members" : [
        {
            "_id" : 0,
            "name" : "mongo1:27017",
            "health" : 1,
            "state" : 1,
            "stateStr" : "PRIMARY",
        ...
```

Under the members key, you can see the individual nodes with their statuses. In this case, the mongo1 node has been chosen as PRIMARY and the other two are SECONDARY.

First, we want to create a user in the database who'll get access to the diary application. For this purpose, you should use the mongo program from one of the database containers, and set the --host parameter to the connection of the rs0/mongo1,mongo2,mongo3 replica set. MongoDB itself finds the *primary* node and inserts the record there.

```
docker compose exec mongo1 mongo \
  --host 'rs0/mongo1,mongo2,mongo3' diary --eval '

db.users.insert({
  "user":"info@dockerbuch.info",
  "pass":"$2b$10$PY3p2eGZ2TrOEoD4dvNRhOIbKV2xjabSq.8TUxcU0a[...]"
})'
```

Passwords in the Database

The user tables in the database always represent a sensitive security issue. If passwords are stored there with a weak hash procedure or even in plain text, that's just what intruders are waiting for. Currently, the *bcrypt* algorithm is considered relatively secure, which is what we also use in our example.

To try it out, you can create and check such a hash on the following website: *https://bcrypt-generator.com*. Alternatively, you can use the htpasswd program of the Apache web server, which also supports the bcrypt algorithm:

```
$ docker run --rm httpd htpasswd -nbBC 10 info secret
  info:$2y$10$56jvsy/s7wOKbZN6DuxMJeCrKAG65wzC6OGvyfZfzkcUBFoMtXeq6
```

To check if the replication works, you should simply start mongo on one of the SECONDARY database servers and display the content of the users collection:

```
docker compose exec mongo3 mongo diary
  MongoDB shell version v4.2.8
  [...]
  rs0:SECONDARY> rs.slaveOk()
  rs0:SECONDARY> db.users.find().pretty()
  {
    "_id" : ObjectId("5cc1a68421c1f2cf2d8c3544"),
    "user" : "info@dockerbuch.info",
    "public" : false,
    "pass" : "$2b$10$PY3p2eGZ2TrOEoD4dvNRhOIbKV2xjabSq.8TUx[...]"
  }
```

The rs.slaveOK() function is necessary because MongoDB doesn't read from replicas by default. In this case, however, we want to do just that.

Finally, you can try out what happens when you turn off the current PRIMARY node. In our case, that's mongo1:

```
docker compose stop mongo1
  [+] Running 1/1
     Container mwa_mongo1_1  Stopped                    2.3s
```

Then reconnect to the replica set and check the status:

```
docker compose exec mongo2 mongo \
    --host 'rs0/mongo1,mongo2,mongo3' diary --eval 'rs.status()'

  [...] CONNPOOL [ReplicaSetMonitor-TaskExecutor] Connecting to
  [...] NETWORK  [ReplicaSetMonitor-TaskExecutor] Confirmed ...
  Implicit session: session { "id" : UUID("07e40a68-b807-4eb6-...
  MongoDB server version: 4.2.8
  {
    "set" : "rs0",
    "date" : ISODate("2021-06-23T11:22:45.489Z"),
    "myState" : 1,
    ...
    members" : [
      {
        "_id" : 0,
        "name" : "mongo1:27017",
        "stateStr" : "(not reachable/healthy)",
        "lastHeartbeatMessage" : "Error connecting to
mongo1:27017 :: caused by :: Could not find address for
mongo1:27017:SocketException: Host not found (authoritative)",
```

Although the database server mongo1 isn't accessible, the replica set is fully functional.

13.5   The Session Storage: Redis

As described in Section 13.3, the decision between sessions or tokens on the backend was in favor of sessions. Nevertheless, to make the system flexible and scalable, we store the session data in a database that can be accessed from all backend servers.

You should use Redis 4 (the current version) but not persistent data. Although this means that when Redis gets restarted, all current sessions will disappear and users will have to log in again, for this example, this limitation isn't a problem. The configuration effort can thus be kept to a minimum; two lines in the *docker-compose.yml* file are sufficient, in which we include the Alpine Linux variant of the Redis image:

```
# File: mwa/docker-compose.yml (excerpt)
version: '3.4'
services:
```

```
[...]
  redis:
    image: redis:6-alpine
```

If your application becomes extremely popular, and the session storage of Redis becomes a bottleneck (which seems rather unlikely), you can add a master-slave replication to the configuration. We've already described the required procedure in Part II of the book (see Chapter 10, Section 10.4).

Chapter 14
Grafana

In the IT environment, there are myriads of data that need to be analyzed. Most people—statisticians aside—have a hard time making sense of numbers in tables at a glance. We prefer using graphics for this, and if those graphics look good too, then all the better.

It's true that there's a large number of libraries for all kinds of programming languages that can be used to draw graphics. However, they usually require some programming effort, which doesn't allow the end user to significantly influence the output.

Grafana has been developed to manage graphically beautiful dashboards whose content is flexible. This should also be possible for nonprogrammers, namely via a web interface.

Why do we present Grafana in this book? If you want to try Grafana once, the packages provided for all platforms will help you only to a limited extent. What you need is a service that collects data and another service that stores data in a compatible format to visualize it with Grafana. You've probably noticed already that a single Windows EXE file isn't enough here, and on Linux you'll also need to install various packages with several dependencies to get to a runnable Grafana system.

With Docker, you can accomplish this task in the twinkling of an eye, as it were—you'll need three different Docker images for the three services addressed in a docker compose setup, as well as minimal configuration work to launch a test system. We're talking about a few minutes of work here, and if you aren't satisfied after your tests, you can delete containers, images, and volumes from your computer (docker compose down --rmi all -v), and your system will remain *clean*.

14.1 Grafana-Docker Setup

In this section, we'll describe a Docker setup in which Grafana works with a database and a collector. The setup reads performance data from your computer and generates graphs from it (see Figure 14.1).

> **Sample Code on GitHub**
>
> As with most of the examples in this book, you can find the full source code for this chapter on GitHub:
>
> *https://github.com/docbuc/grafana*

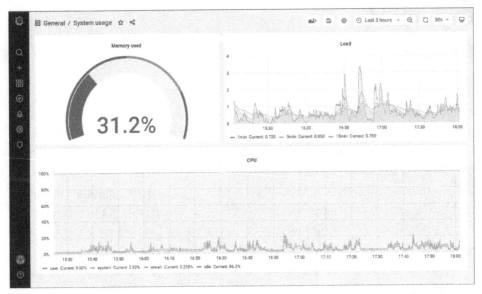

Figure 14.1 Information about the System Load in Grafana (Here with the Light Theme)

14.1.1 Generating Data with Collectors (Telegraf)

We'll generate the data we want to visualize by fetching it from the running computer. Performance data on the utilization of your computer is excellently suited for a display using Grafana.

In a classic microservices architecture, we'll use a Docker container for each service. For data collection purposes, we'll use Telegraf, which is a service written in the Go programming language that uses plug-ins to collect a wide variety of data. The list of *input plug-ins* is pretty long. Here's just a brief excerpt of some of the better known services:

- Apache
- Amazon CloudWatch
- Docker
- Dovecot
- iptables
- Kubernetes
- MongoDB
- MySQL
- ping

Once we've collected the data, we can transform and aggregate it before passing it to an *output plug-in*. For the output, a time series–optimized database is usually used, such as InfluxDB, which originated from the same software project. You can find more details on this topic in the next section.

In our setup, we want to visualize statistics on system utilization (CPU and memory), network availability (ping), and Docker itself. The corresponding excerpt from the *docker-compose.yml* file looks like the following:

```
telegraf:
  image: telegraf:1.19
  hostname: telegraf
  volumes:
    - ./telegraf.conf:/etc/telegraf/telegraf.conf:ro
    - /var/run/docker.sock:/var/run/docker.sock:ro
  restart: always
```

We use the official Docker image for Telegraf in the current version 1.19 and mount two volumes: the *telegraf.conf* configuration file from the current directory and the Docker socket. Both will be integrated in read-only mode, which you can recognize by the terminating string :ro. While statistics on the host computer's CPU and memory can also be queried within the container, we need the included socket for Docker statistics. Because Telegraf doesn't store any data itself, we don't use a separate Docker volume here.

Docker on Windows

The Docker socket /var/run/docker.sock isn't available on Windows. If you want to run the configuration presented here with the current version of Docker on Windows, the easiest way is to comment out this line. Of course, then you won't receive any statistics about the Docker daemon.

The Telegraf configuration file (slightly shortened here) isn't complicated at all:

```
[agent]
  interval = "10s"
[[outputs.influxdb]]
  urls = ["http://influx:8086"]
  database = "telegraf"
  timeout = "5s"
[[inputs.cpu]]
  percpu = true
  totalcpu = true
[[inputs.mem]]
[[inputs.system]]
[[inputs.ping]]
  urls = ["www.google.com"]
  count = 1
[[inputs.docker]]
  endpoint = "unix:///var/run/docker.sock"
...
```

As you can see, there's a *global* section [agent] where you set the query interval. The other sections define input and output plug-ins, respectively. The Docker input plug-in requires the specification of an endpoint; in our case, that's the included Unix socket. The plug-in could also monitor a Docker daemon on a remote system when it can be accessed through the network. The line should then contain the IP address accordingly, for example, endpoint = "tcp://1.2.3.4:2375".

If you're interested in more input plug-ins, it's best to copy the original configuration file from the Telegraf container. The file contains very detailed comments and explains numerous settings. For example, you can use the following command for copying:

```
docker run --rm -v ${PWD}:/src telegraf:1.19 \
  cp /etc/telegraf/telegraf.conf /src/example.conf
```

For this purpose, you need to include the local directory in the container under the */src* folder and copy the default configuration file there. The container will then be terminated and deleted (--rm).

Telegraf also has an option that prints the current configuration on the command line. You can start a container and redirect the output to a file on your computer using the default configuration file:

```
docker run --rm telegraf:1.19 telegraf config > telegraf.conf
```

Configuration without Comments

If you want to see only the active configuration settings without comments or empty lines, you must execute the following command on Linux:

```
docker run -t telegraf:1.19 telegraf config | egrep -v '(^ *^M$|^ *#)'
```

In the regular expression after egrep, you need to type the ^M as Ctrl+V followed by Ctrl+M on the keyboard. (This is the different end of line on Windows.)

Another way to formulate the regular expression is to look for any control character instead of the Windows line end. In this case, the syntax looks like the following:

```
egrep -v '(^ *[[:cntrl:]]$|^ *#)'
```

14.1.2   Storing Data with InfluxDB

As already seen in the Telegraf configuration file, we use InfluxDB to store the data. This *time series database*, which is a special type of database that specializes in time-related content. In particular, queries that have been aggregated over a longer period of time can be answered efficiently with such databases.

> **More Information about InfluxDB**
>
> For more information and statistics on the current use of time series databases, refer to the following web page:
>
> *www.influxdata.com/time-series-database*

You can use InfluxDB on the basis of the free MIT license. InfluxDB works perfectly straightforward as a container in the docker compose setup. For a start, the image doesn't require any further configuration settings. In order not to lose the collected data even if containers get restarted, we use a named volume:

```
# File: grafana-manual/docker-compose.yml (excerpt)
...
influx:
  image: influxdb
  restart: unless-stopped
  volumes:
    - influx:/var/lib/influxdb

volumes:
  influx:
...
```

The influx volume gets associated with the */var/lib/influxdb* folder, which is the default folder for the database data. We don't want to say much more about InfluxDB in this context except that it simply works.

14.1.3 Visualizing Data with Grafana

Now that the data is available in the dedicated database, we still need to visualize it. This is where Grafana comes into play. In the Grafana image on Docker Hub, a configuration file is used whose values can be overridden with environment variables, which is ideal for our Docker setup.

If you prefer to work with a configuration file, you can also copy it from a running container, modify it accordingly, and bind it to your container using a bind mount. To copy the standard configuration file with a command from the image, you want to overwrite the entrypoint in Grafana, for example, by using the following command:

```
docker run --rm -v ${PWD}:/src -u $UID:$GID --entrypoint=cp \
  grafana/grafana /etc/grafana/grafana.ini /src/
```

The trick is that the entrypoint for the container is the cp command and that the parameters for the command (source file and destination directory) are listed after the name of the image. Because we mount ${PWD} in the container under /src, the configuration file ends up in the current directory.

For the first version, however, we won't make many settings in the configuration file at all; it's sufficient to set a password for the web interface using variable GF_SECURITY_ ADMIN_PASSWORD. We also want to set up a volume for the mutable data in Grafana and connect port 3000 of the container to the host. Here you can see the full *docker-compose.yml* file that we'll use to launch the first version of Grafana:

```
# File: grafana-manual/docker-compose.yml
version: '3'
services:
  grafana:
    image: grafana/grafana:latest
    restart: unless-stopped
    ports:
      - 3000:3000
    environment:
      - GF_SECURITY_ADMIN_PASSWORD=secret
    volumes:
      - grafana:/var/lib/grafana
  telegraf:
    image: telegraf:1.19
    hostname: telegraf
    volumes:
      - ./telegraf.conf:/etc/telegraf/telegraf.conf:ro
      - /var/run/docker.sock:/var/run/docker.sock:ro
    restart: unless-stopped
  influx:
    image: influxdb
    restart: unless-stopped
    volumes:
      - influx:/var/lib/influxdb
volumes:
  influx:
  grafana:
```

Now you can launch the setup using docker compose up -d. After that, you can log in with the user name admin and the password secret at the following address: *http://localhost:3000* (see Figure 14.2).

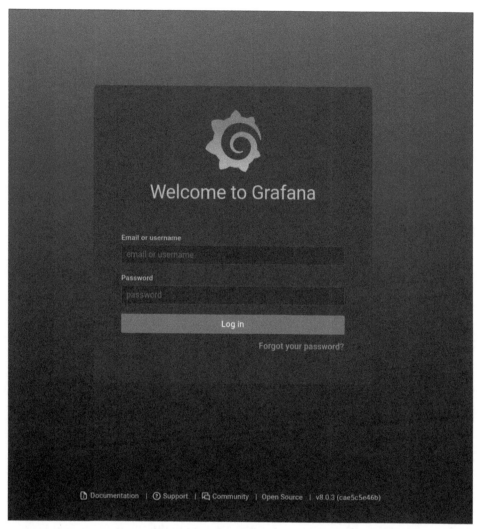

Figure 14.2 Grafana Login Screen

Creating a Data Source and Dashboard

After successful login, the first thing you need to do is add a data source. Select **InfluxDB** from the dropdown list under **Name**, and enter a descriptive **Name** (we used "InfluxDB"). Under **HTTP**, enter "http://influx:8086" in the **URL** field, and select **Server (default)** in the **Access** dropdown field (see Figure 14.3).

The Grafana container accesses the Influx container via the URL *http://influx:8086*. Because this URL isn't accessible outside the Docker network, the Grafana container must use a proxy to hide this address from the web browser.

Figure 14.3 Settings for the InfluxDB Data Source

As another entry on this page, you have to set the name of the database in the **Database** field. You should use the name you've set as database in the [[outputs.telegraf]] section of the *telegraf.conf* file (so here, enter "telegraf"). Finally, you should set the minimum time interval to 10 seconds (>10s). Because you started Telegraf with a 10-second interval, it makes no sense for InfluxDB to answer queries that come in at intervals shorter than 10 seconds.

Grafana manages the graphical output in *dashboards* that are easy to create (via the web interface) and even easier to distribute (as JSON strings). This will be important for our plan to develop a flexible, ready-to-run Docker setup.

Once the data source is working, you can create your first dashboard (see Figure 14.4). In the new *panel*, click **Add Query** to create the query that will fetch the data from the database.

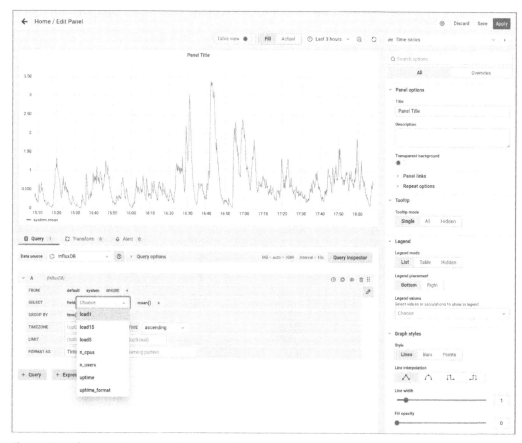

Figure 14.4 The First Diagram with Data on the System Load in Grafana

The suggested query already helps a lot in generating the first graph. The syntax is as follows:

```
SELECT mean("value")
FROM "measurement"
WHERE $timeFilter
GROUP BY time($__interval) fill(null)
```

If you're familiar with the SQL database language, you'll know your way around here right away. But even if you aren't familiar with SQL, it's easy to adjust the syntax with the graphical editor. Simply select **System** under **Select Measurement**, and then select **load1** in the **field (value)** field (see Figure 14.4). This will make the first line graphic appear in the display.

But you don't need to start from scratch when you create a dashboard. On the Grafana website, you'll find a large number of dashboards created by the community that you can import very easily into your own Grafana installation.

Now you should filter the list of available dashboards at *https://grafana.com/dash-boards* by InfluxDB and Telegraf, and pick an appealing dashboard. To import it, you can simply copy the ID of the dashboard from the **+ Create · Import** menu into the empty text line. In the subsequent step, you'll be asked for the data source. Here you want to select the previously configured InfluxDB (see Figure 14.5).

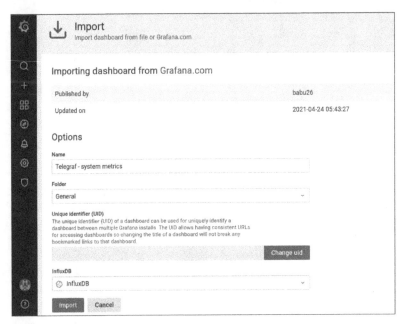

Figure 14.5 Importing a Dashboard from the Grafana Website

After a successful import, you can modify and save the graphics in the new dashboard per your requirements. In some dashboards, you'll find a variable called **Host** or **Server**. The setup presented so far uses only one collector; for more information on a distributed setup, refer to Section 14.3.

Grafana Dashboards

We don't want to dive too much into the configuration of Grafana dashboards here. There are numerous design options available, and, once you understand the concept, you can set them up very easily via the web interface. There's more useful information about Grafana available on its well-documented website:

https://grafana.com/docs/grafana/latest/dashboards

14.2   Provisioning

The default installation of Grafana doesn't include any preconfigured data sources or dashboards, so you usually have to set them up via the web interface first. Since the release of Grafana 5, however, you have the option to provide dashboards and data sources for an installation in advance (*provisioning*), which we'll do in the following sections. The advantage of this is that we can provide a working Grafana instance without doing any configuration in the web interface.

In the current version, Grafana can preconfigure both dashboards and data sources. The specifications for this are expected as YAML Ain't Markup Language (YAML) files in the */etc/grafana/provisioning* folder. The default for the InfluxDB database in our case looks like this:

```
# File: grafana/provisioning/datasources/influx.yml
apiVersion: 1
datasources:
- name: InfluxDB
  type: influxdb
  access: proxy
  orgId: 1
  url: http://influx:8086
  database: telegraf
  isDefault: true
  version: 1
  jsonData:
    timeInterval: ">10s"
  editable: true
```

The `access: proxy` entry is important so that queries which Grafana redirects to the database will be hidden from the browser. You can see the minimum time interval for queries to the database in the `jsonData - timeInterval` structure. The final `editable` setting allows you to set whether the data source can be edited in the web interface or is read-only.

The defaults for dashboards look a little different. Again, YAML files are evaluated in the */etc/grafana/provisioning/dashboards/* folder. However, these only contain the path to the folder where the dashboards are stored as JSON files (you can also specify multiple folders). For example, you can save a *default.yml* file to this folder as follows:

```
# File: grafana/provisioning/dashboards/default.yml
apiVersion: 1
providers:
- name: 'default'
  orgId: 1
  folder: ''
  type: file
  disableDeletion: false
  editable: false
```

```
    options:
      path: /var/lib/grafana/dashboards
```

Grafana now looks for dashboards in the */var/lib/grafana/dashboards* folder. For your Docker setup to work correctly, you now need to include the appropriate folders in the *docker-compose.yml* file:

```
# File: grafana/docker-compose.yml (excerpt)
grafana:
  image: grafana/grafana:latest
  [...]
  volumes:
    - ./dashboards:/var/lib/grafana/dashboards
    - ./provisioning:/etc/grafana/provisioning
[...]
```

For the setup to work automatically, you need to include a trick in the dashboard configuration. Grafana stores the data source in the dashboard definition as a variable. For the dashboard to automatically link to the data source, you must correctly define the variable in the dashboard.

The naming of the variables is based on the name you assigned to the data source. If, as in our case, the data source is called InfluxDB, the name of the variable is DS_INFLUXDB. You can define this variable in the dashboard settings (**Variables · New · General · Type · Datasource**), and feel free to hide it (**Variables · Edit · General · Hide-Variable**); otherwise, it will be displayed at the top of the dashboard (see Figure 14.6).

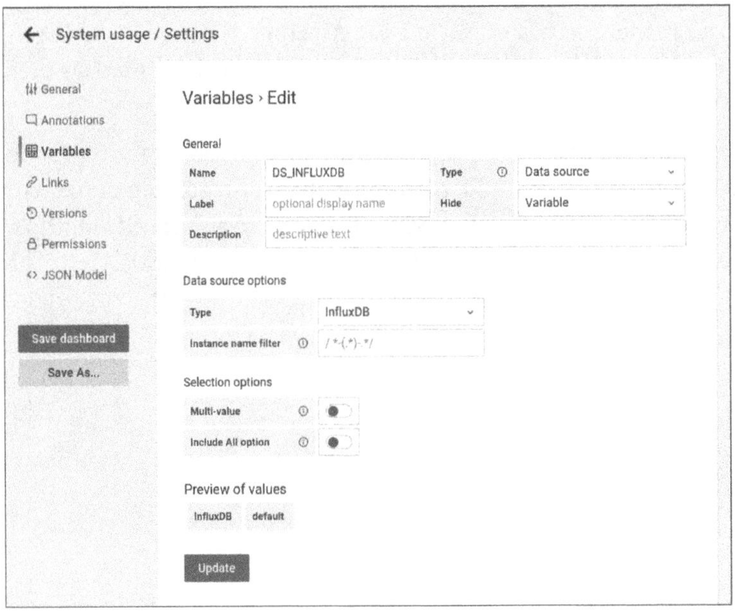

Figure 14.6 Variable Definition in Grafana

Now you can export your dashboard using **Share Dashboard • Export**, and then place the JSON file in the *dashboards* folder. The file system tree in your project directory should look similar to the following:

```
.
|-- dashboards
|    `-- System usage-1624617338414.json
|-- docker-compose.yml
|-- provisioning
|    |-- dashboards
|    |    `-- default.yml
|    `-- datasources
|         `-- influx.yml
`-- telegraf.conf
```

It's best to put this setup in a Git repository as well, like we did on GitHub:

https://github.com/docbuc/grafana

14.3   A Customized Telegraf Image

The setup with Grafana, InfluxDB, and Telegraf is now running on a computer and diligently collecting data. In the next step, we want to create a Docker image based on Telegraf that can be launched on another machine and send performance data to the running InfluxDB.

The image should work without any additional files. So it should be possible to start it with the following call:

```
docker run -d docbuc/telegraf
```

At this point, the service sends data directly to InfluxDB. This is a simple exercise if you enter the data in the *telegraf.conf* file and copy the file to the image:

```
# File: grafana/telegraf/Dockerfile (docbuc/telegraf)
FROM telegraf
COPY telegraf.conf /etc/telegraf
```

However, the solution is a bit inflexible because you can use the image only with exactly this InfluxDB server. A better way is to set the server address, server port, and user name/password for the database as environment variables at startup. In the container, we then need a way to replace these variables in the configuration file.

Because the variables aren't available in the container until runtime, you can't make this substitution in the *Dockerfile*. Instead, you need to create an ENTRYPOINT script that will perform this task. Basically, any executable program that's present in the image can be used as ENTRYPOINT. For our purpose, we'll use a short *Bash script*:

```
#!/bin/bash
# File: grafana/telegraf/entrypoint.sh
set -e

INFLUXDB_HOST=${INFLUXDB_HOST:-influx}
INFLUXDB_PORT=${INFLUXDB_PORT:-8086}
INFLUXDB_USER=${INFLUXDB_USER:-telegraf}
INFLUXDB_PASS=${INFLUXDB_PASS:-secret}

sed -i "s/influx:8086/$INFLUXDB_HOST:$INFLUXDB_PORT/g;
  s/username = \"telegraf\"/username = \"$INFLUXDB_USER\"/g;
  s/password = \"secret\"/password = \"$INFLUXDB_PASS\"/g" \
    /etc/telegraf/telegraf.conf

if [ "${1:0:1}" = '-' ]; then
    set -- telegraf "$@"
fi

exec "$@"
```

There are some interesting Bash tricks hidden in this script that are very useful in the Docker environment:

- **Script termination settings**
  set -e terminates the script with an error status as soon as a step in the script fails. Because the ENTRYPOINT is the process associated with the container status, the container will also be terminated if the script fails.

- **Variable definition**
  The subsequent lines define the variables INFLUXDB_*. The contents of the passed variables with the same name are evaluated, and if they haven't been set, a default value is set (after the - character).

- **Variable substitution**
  The sed command replaces certain strings in the configuration file, */etc/telegraf/telegraf.conf*. The -i parameter (in place) causes the replacement without creating a copy of the file. During the replacement, the content of the variable and not the name of the variable is stored in the file.

- **Check of CMD**
  We've taken the following if structure directly from the original *Dockerfile* of the telegraf image. It checks whether the command passed at container startup begins with the - character. This process uses the extended Bash variable functions to extract the first character of the $1 variable (${1:0:1}). $1 in Bash scripts corresponds

to the first parameter passed to the script. If the condition is true, the `telegraf` string will be set before all other passed parameters (`set -- telegraf "$@"`).

- **Execution of CMD**
  Finally, all script parameters are executed via the `exec` command. This causes the shell script to relinquish control to the program, which is listed as `$1` in the list of parameters. That program will receive process ID 1, and signals to the container will be redirected to it.

In the *Dockerfile*, you now have to copy the script and set the `ENTRYPOINT`:

```
# File: grafana/telegraf/Dockerfile (docbuc/telegraf)
FROM telegraf
COPY telegraf.conf /etc/telegraf
COPY entrypoint.sh /
ENTRYPOINT ["/bin/bash", "/entrypoint.sh"]
CMD ["telegraf"]
```

With the described `ENTRYPOINT` script in combination with `CMD`, your Docker image has become very flexible. You can start a container that runs Telegraf with the given configuration:

```
docker run -d -v /var/run/docker.sock:/var/run/docker.sock:ro \
  docbuc/telegraf
```

The container starts with the settings from the *telegraf.conf* file, with the substitutions in the *entrypoint.sh* script using the default values. The password remains empty. Because you didn't pass a command with the `docker run` command, the `CMD` from the *Dockerfile* will be used, which will start `telegraf`. If you include the Docker socket, as indicated previously, Docker statistics will also be logged.

You can also simply display the help page for `telegraf`:

```
docker run --rm docbuc/telegraf --help

  Telegraf, The plugin-driven server agent for collecting and
  reporting metrics.

  Usage:
  telegraf [commands|flags]
  ...
```

This is where the `if` query comes into play: the passed command starts with the `-` character, so the parameter list will be reassembled. After that it will consist of `telegraf --help`.

In addition, variable substitution works in the configuration file in the container, as the following example shows:

315

```
docker run --rm -e INFLUXDB_HOST=influx.dockerbuch.info \
  -e INFLUXDB_PORT=8086 -e INFLUXDB_PASS=iijineeZ9iet \
  docbuc/telegraf cat /etc/telegraf/telegraf.conf


...
[[outputs.influxdb]]
  urls = ["http://influx.dockerbuch.info:8086"] # required
  database = "telegraf" # required
  username = "telegraf"
  password = "iijineeZ9iet"
...
```

As another benefit of this variant, you can launch any other program installed in the image:

```
docker run --rm -it docbuc/telegraf bash
```

Unsurprisingly, a shell is started, and you can look around the container. If you display all running processes in the container (ps xa), you'll notice that your shell has process ID 1:

```
root@9f7c30fca7df:/# ps xa
  PID TTY       STAT   TIME COMMAND
    1 pts/0     Ss     0:00 bash
   13 pts/0     R+     0:00 ps xa
```

GitHub and Docker Hub

The source code for the Docker image is located on GitHub. On Docker Hub, we linked to the GitHub account under our account and set up an *automated build*. As soon as we change something in the image and put a new version on GitHub (git push), a build will start automatically on Docker Hub.

- GitHub: *https://github.com/docbuc/telegraf*
- Docker Hub: *https://hub.docker.com/r/docbuc/telegraf*

You can now launch the Docker image on a few different computers and let it send the data to InfluxDB:

```
docker run -v /var/run/docker.sock:/var/run/docker.sock:ro \
  --name telegraf -d -e INFLUXDB_HOST=influxdb.dockerbuch.info \
  -e INFLUXDB_PORT=80 -e INFLUXDB_PASS=iijineeZ9iet \
  --hostname laptop@home docbuc/telegraf
```

For this purpose, we started an InfluxDB container on the host INFLUXDB_HOST= influxdb.dockerbuch.info, which accepts requests from the internet on port 80. The explicit specification of the `--hostname` parameter is useful because Telegraf also sends the host name of the computer on which the program is executed when sending the metrics. Within a Docker container, the host name would be an automatically generated identifier, such as `eeafca0dc73c`. In the dashboard, it's more convenient to see a meaningful name for your computers.

14.3.1 Dashboard Customizations

Now that you've launched the Telegraf image on different computers, and your performance data is being sent to a central Influx database, you need to customize the dashboard a bit.

You should add a variable named *server* to the dashboard. You can access the menu via **Settings · Variables · New** in the **Dashboard** view. The variable must be of type **Query**, and the corresponding query for InfluxDB is as follows:

```
SHOW TAG VALUES WITH KEY = "host"
```

If you've set everything correctly, you'll already get a preview of the available hosts (see Figure 14.7).

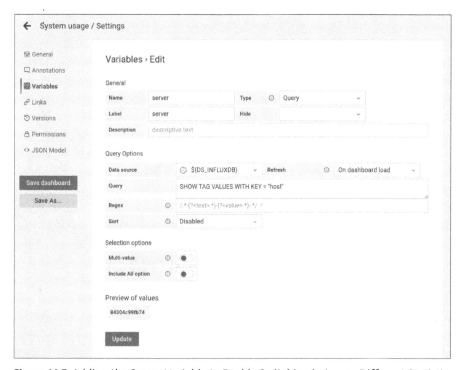

Figure 14.7 Adding the Server Variable to Enable Switching between Different Statistics

Back in the dashboard, you can already see the new dropdown menu. Unfortunately, the values don't change accordingly yet. For the individual graphs to be displayed with the correct values for the host, you must edit the individual *panels*. For each query in the **Metrics** tab, you need to add the following statement:

```
WHERE ("host" =~ /^$server$/)
```

The useful *query builder* in the web interface helps enormously here and immediately suggests the correct values.

Chapter 15
Modernizing a Traditional Application

One of the use cases where container technology plays an important role is the modernization of traditional applications. In this context, you may consider the term *traditional* as a synonym for *legacy*.

In this chapter, we want to present a real-life example from our own practice: a web application that has undergone several enhancements over the years (see Figure 15.1). The development of the application started from a content management system (CMS) we had implemented with WordPress. In the subsequent years, we kept adding components: first customizations to the WordPress theme, and then a WordPress extension in PHP. Later, it turned out that the required functionality would actually justify an application that runs independently of WordPress.

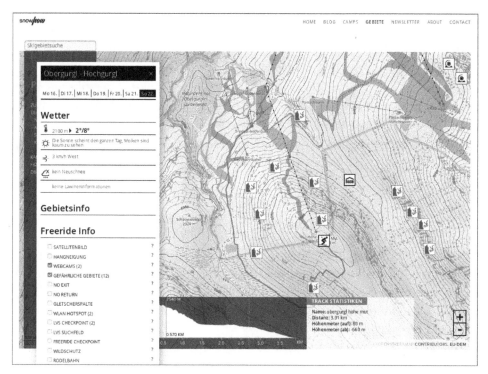

Figure 15.1 The Existing Application: Maps and Weather Information Integrated into WordPress

The new component was implemented in Node.js with MongoDB as the database backend. Because many user accounts had already been created, the authentication process should still be handled by WordPress. At the time, the WordPress REST application programming interface (API) wasn't yet part of the system, so we chose a different way to connect the authentication of the two applications. We used a Memcached server as the storage location for the session cookies, to which both applications had access. Because the two applications ran under the same domain, both endpoints received the cookie from the browser and were able to check it for validity in the database.

The setup worked without any problem. However, the server update from Ubuntu 14.04 to the next long-term support (LTS) version 16.04 became a nail-biter: Would the updated versions of PHP, Node.js, and MongoDB still work with the existing code? Unfortunately, there were no unit tests, integration tests, or even end-to-end tests.

It was Docker that rescued our application, and we want to present the transformation to Docker in the following sections. Unlike the previous chapters, you won't find any instructions to follow here, but a documentation of the relatively smooth conversion of the application.

Update 2021

The migration presented here took place in 2018. In the meantime, the application has changed even further, and you'll no longer find the application as shown in the screenshots on the internet. The CMS has been swapped out, and weather information is now only available in the mobile app.

However, you can transfer the mechanisms shown in this conversion process one-to-one to any other project. This is only to explain that you shouldn't wonder about outdated version numbers in the software you're using.

Please also note that *https://snowhow.info* website is presented in German, which should not impact the lessons in this chapter.

15.1   The Existing Application

As mentioned at the beginning, the project started as a simple WordPress site. Its functionality was initially limited to the registration for avalanche courses in the Austrian Alps. The CMS was running on a dedicated Ubuntu root server that also hosted other web projects. The project got off to a good start, so the digital offering was soon expanded.

The first stage of expansion was a digital map based on OpenStreetMap with additional information for winter sports enthusiasts. The map included a separate layer for slope gradient, points for danger spots in alpine terrain, and points of tourist interest such as ski resorts and inns. As with Google Maps and OpenStreetMap, the map was calculated in different zoom levels and stored as *map tiles* on the server.

To further improve the tour planning options for winter sports enthusiasts, current weather data and information from the avalanche warning services were integrated on a daily basis. The extension was technically based on PHP and MongoDB (see Figure 15.2).

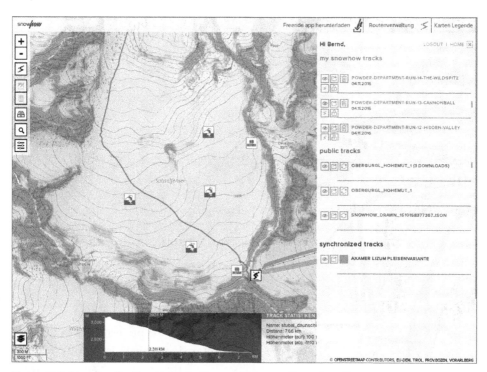

Figure 15.2 Map Application Helps to Plan and Manage Your Own Tours

As a further step, an app for mobile devices was created that stores the map material and safety information offline. Individual tours can be recorded and synchronized with the portal if desired. Meanwhile, the combination of MongoDB and Node.js proved to be a very efficient working environment for other projects, so Node.js was used for the API. The fact that the smartphone app also worked with JavaScript under the hood made development even more enjoyable.

While the web app still used a mix of PHP files accessing the database directly and API calls, there was inevitably a clear separation in the mobile app. The calls for loading the updated avalanche situation reports or saving the recorded tours are made exclusively via the API. Tour management, which is used to rename or publish a tour, is done in the app or via the web interface.

In summary, the following technologies were used:

- WordPress as CMS with user management (PHP and MariaDB)
- Map application with PHP and MongoDB

- Node.js Express server that provides the API
- Memcached as session storage

All access was encrypted under the domain *https://snowhow.info*, with the various services divided into three namespaces:

- `/cms`
  The entire WordPress content.
- `/map`
  The map application.
- `/api`
  The younger API for accessing the geodata.

These links should of course continue to exist in this way.

15.2 Planning and Preparation

There were two main motivations that made the modernization necessary:

- We wanted to create a setup that runs largely independent of the underlying server.
- We wanted to use a development environment that could be run with one command if possible.

The latter, in particular, became a major concern: Because the project wasn't subject to continuous development, even small bug fixes mutated into a half-day job. By the time the necessary package dependencies were installed on the new laptop and the current database extracts were made and imported, several hours had passed.

It was clear that the final setup would run on a Linux server, and therefore shell scripts could be used. While it would also be possible to implement these helpers in their own Docker containers, we didn't want to be more Catholic than the Pope here either. Basically, it's the backup script and a script for preparing the migration.

If we first consider the individual server components in the setup, we can already schedule some Docker images (see Figure 15.3):

- Nginx (as web server frontend)
- MariaDB (as WordPress database)
- Node.js Express (API)
- Memcached (as session storage)
- MongoDB (as geodata storage)

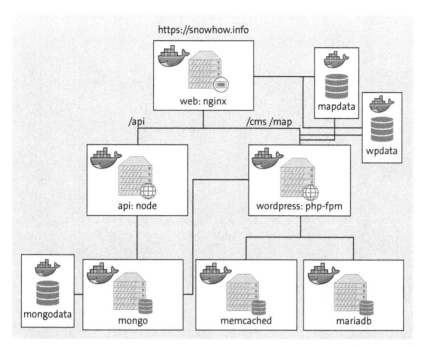

Figure 15.3 Docker Setup for the Conversion of the Web Application

The following is an overview of the most important files and directories of the Docker project:

```
|-- api
|   |-- README.md
|   |-- server.js
|   |-- [...]
|-- docker-compose.override.yml
|-- docker-compose.yml
|-- backup.sh
|-- devupdate.sh
|-- .git
|   |-- [...]
|-- .gitignore
|-- mongo
|    `-- dump
|        |-- [...]
|-- prod.sh
|-- web
|   |-- Dockerfile
|   |-- htpasswd
|    `-- nginx.conf
```

```
`-- wordpress
    |-- cms
    |   |-- wp-config.php
    |   `-- wp-content
    |       |-- plugins
    |       |-- themes
    |       `-- uploads
    |-- dev_error_reporting.ini
    |-- Dockerfile
    |-- .dockerignore
    |-- error_reporting.ini
    |-- map
    |   |-- index.php
    |   |-- [...]
    |-- memcached.ini
    `-- sql
        `-- snowhowinfo-migrate-20190510103700.sql.gz
```

15.2.1   The Web Server

When we implemented the microservices architecture, we decided to use Nginx with PHP-FastCGI Process Manager (FPM), that is, to run the web server and PHP in their own containers. Although we made minimal changes to the official Docker image for Nginx, we didn't use a bind mount here but created our own image. In production operation, all images used were to be deployed without dependence on the local file system.

```
# File: snowhow/web/Dockerfile
FROM nginx:1
COPY nginx.conf /etc/nginx/conf.d/default.conf
COPY htpasswd /etc/nginx/
```

The corresponding excerpt from the *docker-compose.yml* file looks like the following:

```
# File: snowhow/docker-compose.yml (excerpt)
  web:
    restart: always
    image: gitlab.snowhow.info/snowhow/webapp/web:latest
    build: web/
    depends_on:
      - "wordpress"
    ports:
      - 8080:80
    volumes:
      - wpdata:/var/www/html/cms
```

```
  - mapdata:/var/www/html/map
  - wpuploads:/var/www/html/cms/wp-content/uploads
```

The completed Docker setup is operated behind a *Secure Sockets Layer (SSL) termination proxy*. However, because the proxy server doesn't run as a Docker container, in contrast to what we described in Chapter 9, Section 9.2, we need to redirect a port (8080) to the host where the proxy server sends the requests. The depends_on statement prevents an error from being thrown when Nginx starts up if the PHP container can't be reached yet. Slightly shortened, the main entries in the Nginx configuration file look as follows:

```
# File: snowhow/web/nginx.conf
server {
  listen      80;
  server_name  _;
  root    /var/www/html;
  [...]
  fastcgi_buffers          16 16k;
  fastcgi_buffer_size      32k;
  client_body_buffer_size  10M;
  client_max_body_size     10M;
  location ~ \.php$ {
    try_files $uri =404;
    fastcgi_pass    wordpress:9000;
    fastcgi_param   SCRIPT_FILENAME
        $document_root$fastcgi_script_name;
    include         fastcgi_params;
  }
  location /api/ {
      rewrite     /api/(.+)$ /$1 break;
      proxy_pass http://api:3000;
  }
  location /map/admin/ {
    auth_basic "admin area";
    auth_basic_user_file /etc/nginx/htpasswd;
  }
  [...]
```

Because the application also sends larger amounts of data than JavaScript Object Notation (JSON) strings, the buffer sizes and the client_max_body_size parameter must be adjusted. The ~ \.php$ expression represents all PHP scripts and redirects the requests to the WordPress container on port 9000 with the fastcgi_pass statement. All requests where the path starts with /api/ will be redirected to the API container. This removes the api/ string from the request before redirecting (rewrite), which means that the

Express server doesn't need its own /api namespace. Thus the request *https://snow-how.info/api/bulletins* arrives at the API container as /bulletins.

A part of the website is secured with HTTP basic authentication in addition to the WordPress user login. The password file required for this is copied to the Docker image, just like the Nginx configuration file.

15.2.2   WordPress

As another container we need the PHP FPM. As mentioned at the beginning, we use Memcached for storing the session data. Unfortunately, the matching PHP module isn't available in the official WordPress Docker image nor in the official PHP image.

But Docker wouldn't be Docker if there wasn't a simple solution for this as well: we can create our own image derived from the official PHP image. In the *Dockerfile*, we first install the necessary plug-ins and then the current WordPress version:

```
# File: snowhow/wordpress/Dockerfile
FROM php:7-fpm

ENV WORDPRESS_VER=5.3
ENV MEMCACHED_VER=3.1.3

RUN apt-get update && apt-get -y install \
  curl \
  libjpeg-dev \
  libpng-dev \
  libmemcached-dev \
  && rm -rf /var/lib/apt/lists/* \
  && docker-php-ext-configure gd --with-png-dir=/usr \
    --with-jpeg-dir=/usr \
  && docker-php-ext-install gd mysqli
RUN mkdir -p /usr/src/php/ext/memcached \
  && curl -SL "https://github.com/php-memcached-dev/php-memcached
/archive/v{$MEMCACHED_VER}.tar.gz" \
  | tar xzC /usr/src/php/ext/memcached --strip 1 \
  && docker-php-ext-configure memcached \
  && docker-php-ext-install memcached

WORKDIR /var/www/html

RUN curl \
  -SL "https://wordpress.org/wordpress-${WORDPRESS_VER}.tar.gz" \
  | tar xzC /var/www/html \
  && mv wordpress/ cms/ \
  && chown -R www-data:www-data cms/
```

```
COPY cms/ cms/
COPY map/ /var/www/html/map/
RUN chown -R www-data:www-data cms/
COPY memcached.ini error_reporting.ini /usr/local/etc/php/conf.d/
VOLUME ["/var/www/html/cms"]
```

You already learned about the `docker-php-ext-install` scripts in Chapter 12, Section 12.1. These scripts help you install common PHP extensions in an uncomplicated way. For Memcached, we still need to reach into the bag of tricks and download the corresponding tar file from GitHub, unzip it, and then configure and install it using the `docker-php-ext-*` scripts.

In the second step, we download and unzip the current version of WordPress. The local `cms` directory contains the customized WordPress theme and also the WordPress plugins that were created during the project. In addition, the WordPress configuration file *wp-config.php* is also located there.

After that, we entered the user name and password for the MariaDB server (you shouldn't do that with an image you share with other people!) and also enabled the *reverse proxy* setup setting:

```
if (isset($_SERVER['HTTP_X_FORWARDED_PROTO'])
    && $_SERVER['HTTP_X_FORWARDED_PROTO'] === 'https') {
    $_SERVER['HTTPS'] = 'on';
}
```

The extension in the configuration file is necessary because the server running WordPress is unencrypted on port 80 and knows nothing about the upstream SSL proxy.

The next line copies the map application (in the `map` directory). There won't be any changes to these files in the container. When a bug fix or new feature is added, a new Docker image will be created.

The two files *memcached.ini* and *error_reporting.ini* are copied to the PHP configuration directory. There, the session files are redirected to the Memcached server, and error messages are suppressed for productive operation.

```
# File snowhow/wordpress/memcached.ini
session.save_handler = memcached
session.save_path='memcached:11211'
```

The PHP error display gets completely disabled in production mode:

```
# File snowhow/wordpress/error_reporting.ini
display_errors = Off
error_reporting = E_ALL & ~E_DEPRECATED
```

For the development environment, however, the error messages are useful. To enable the error display, we use the function to extend and override the compose configuration with the *docker-compose.override.yml* file. The following excerpt also shows that both the part relevant for the map application and the WordPress uploads are overwritten with local folders:

```
# File: snowhow/docker-compose.override.yml (excerpt)
  wordpress:
    volumes:
      - ./wordpress/map:/var/www/html/map
      - ./wordpress/cms/wp-content/uploads:\
        /var/www/html/cms/wp-content/uploads
      - ./wordpress/dev_error_reporting.ini:\
        /usr/local/etc/php/conf.d/error_reporting.ini
```

The *dev_error_reporting.ini* file contains the appropriate PHP statements to report the errors:

```
# File: snowhow/wordpress/dev_error_reporting.ini
display_errors = On
error_reporting = E_ALL & ~E_NOTICE
log_errors = On
```

When the Docker image gets created, Docker sends the contents of the current directory to the daemon, which then processes the instructions. For the setup described in Section 15.3, images and other media files are stored in the *uploads/* subfolder, which are unnecessarily sent to the Docker daemon whenever an image is created. The solution to this problem is the *.dockerignore* file, which specifies files or directories that have nothing to do with the image build process:

```
# File: snowhow/wordpress/.dockerignore
cms/wp-content/uploads/*
```

Depending on how many files are in the folder, the Ignore statement can significantly speed up the build.

15.2.3   WordPress Database Migration

WordPress stores internal links with the complete URL, including the host name. When you develop on the local computer, you need to replace these strings with the link to localhost. Replacing the occurrences in the SQL dump file wouldn't be complicated, but unfortunately some links are stored in serialized PHP objects where strings are given a length specification.

```
php > echo serialize("https://snowhow.info/cms");
s:24:"https://snowhow.info/cms";
```

Because the length of the host names snowhow.info and localhost aren't the same, the PHP objects are invalid after replacing the string with sed. The WordPress plug-in MigrateDB provides a remedy for this (see Figure 15.4) and also rewrites the lengths of the string.

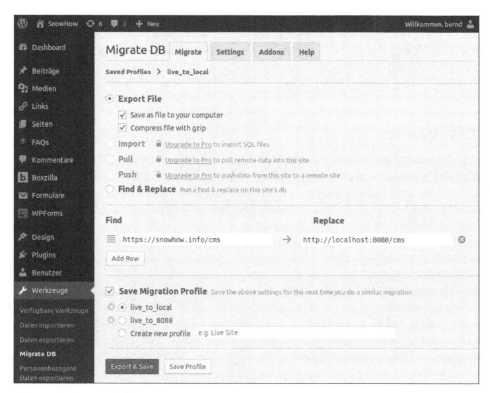

Figure 15.4 Export of the Database for the Development Environment

In addition, the plug-in can also be used to replace paths if the location of the Word-Press installation has changed. Multiple profiles with different replacements can be saved in the web interface.

The installation is done in the administration area of the WordPress interface under **Plugins · Add New**. Using the integrated search functions, you can find the MigrateDB plug-in and install it with a click of a button. The free version is sufficient; however, as you'll see in Section 15.3, the Pro version makes this considerably easier and can be an interesting option.

15.2.4   Automatic Updates in WordPress

WordPress has had a very handy automatic update system built in for quite some time. As long as no *breaking changes* occur, the version gets updated in the background when the page is called. This has always worked without a problem on the previous server; however, it's actually unsuitable for the Docker setup. It would be desirable to have a state where the functionality of the applications in the Docker image (in this case, in the WordPress application) can be tested and run stably. When the application updates itself in the container, this is no longer guaranteed.

Due to the constant updates in the container, the state between the Docker image and the running container instance drifts apart. The solution for our system is that we install the WordPress source code in the image, but overwrite it with a volume during operation. Because the volume is empty during the first installation, only the updated files take effect when they are overwritten.

15.2.5   MariaDB

The database configuration for WordPress contains few surprises. We use the official MariaDB image and pass the credentials as environment variables:

```
# File: snowhow/docker-compose.yml (excerpt)
  mariadb:
    restart: always
    image: mariadb:10
    volumes:
      - wpdb:/var/lib/mysql
    environment:
      - MYSQL_ROOT_PASSWORD=topsecret
      - MYSQL_USER=snowhow
      - MYSQL_PASSWORD=secret
      - MYSQL_DATABASE=snowhow
```

The database configuration still provides a named volume for the database files. Even if the container gets deleted, these files will remain and be mounted again when a new container is started.

It's very useful for the development environment if an updated database dump can be imported. The MariaDB image provides the */docker-entrypoint-initdb.d/* directory for this purpose, which we'll connect to the local *wordpress/sql/* directory in the *docker-compose.override.yml* file:

```
# File: snowhow/docker-compose.override.yml (excerpt)
  mariadb:
    volumes:
      - ./wordpress/sql:/docker-entrypoint-initdb.d
```

The zipped SQL file from the export of MigrateDB is stored in the *wordpress/sql* directory, which causes the dump to be imported when a container that doesn't yet contain a database gets started.

15.2.6 Node.js Server

For the Node.js server, we create a separate image that contains all the files for production operation. The entry in the *docker-compose.yml* file looks like the following:

```
# File: snowhow/docker-compose.yml (excerpt)
  api:
    restart: always
    build: api/
    image: gitlab.snowhow.info/snowhow/webapp/api:latest
    environment:
      - MONGODB_HOST=mongo
      - MEMCACHED_DB_HOST=memcached
```

The host name of the MongoDB database and the host name of the Memcached server are passed as environment variables. The *api/* directory contains the very clearly structured *Dockerfile* file:

```
# File: snowhow/api/Dockerfile
FROM node:12
WORKDIR /src
RUN chown -R node:node /src
USER node
COPY package*.json /src/
RUN npm install
COPY . /src/
EXPOSE 3000
CMD ["node", "/src/server.js"]
```

The file shows the classic installation flow of a Node.js application: We use the official Node.js image in version 12, create the working directory, and set the permissions for the node user. All further installation tasks will be performed as this unprivileged user. The information about the software packages used gets copied and installed. Not until the step after that will the actual software be copied into the */src* folder. The intermediate step allows for a better caching of Docker layers because changes to the code that don't require new software packages preserve the layers that have already been installed.

To meet the requirement of also being able to run a development system with the Docker setup, it should be possible to edit the files locally. It would also be convenient if the server could reload changed files on its own. This is where the *docker-compose.override.yml* file comes into play again.

As we've already shown in Chapter 11, Section 11.3, it's very easy to save a slightly modified setup using the *override* file. In this case, we want the local *api/* folder, which contains the JavaScript source code, to be included using the files present in the image:

```
# File: snowhow/docker-compose.override.yml (excerpt)
version: '3'
services:
  api:
    volumes:
      - ./api:/src
      - apimodules:/src/node_modules
    environment:
      - DEBUG=server
      - LOG_LEVEL=debug
      - NODE_ENV=development
    command: [ "/src/node_modules/.bin/nodemon", "--inspect",
      "/src/server.js" ]
```

For the local directory, we use a bind mount volume. The *node_modules* directory is mounted as a named Docker volume. This way the modules don't end up in the folder that contains the source code and is copied to the image. Because no Node.js runtime needs to be installed on the developer machine, new modules will be installed directly in the container:

```
docker-compose exec -u root api npm install --save moment
```

In the API source code, the debug module is used, which can be activated by environment variable DEBUG. For the development environment we also set the variables NODE_ENV and LOG_LEVEL, which are also evaluated in parts of the API. Finally, the start command for the container gets overwritten. The nodemon server automatically restarts whenever files are modified, which is extremely convenient during development.

This part of the application can be updated very well in a Docker workflow: after the local development and testing, a new image gets created and uploaded to the private Docker registry. This works with docker-compose build and docker-compose push. To apply the update to the production system, it's sufficient to download the image with docker-compose pull (even after the download, the *old* container is still running with the *old* image) and start it with docker-compose -f docker-compose.yml up -d.

15.2.7   The Map Application

The development of the map application started with PHP, but over time, more and more pure frontend code was added. Stylesheets were compiled with Less.js and JavaScript code was reduced using UglifyJS. As the development of the API progressed in parallel, we increasingly abandoned PHP. To facilitate the development of the map application, we used the Grunt software and created tasks with it to automatically transform stylesheets and JavaScript code.

The result—that is, the mix of PHP, HTML, JavaScript, and stylesheets—was copied to a separate volume and had to be mounted in both the PHP and Nginx containers:

```
# File: snowhow/docker-compose.yml (excerpt)
version: '3'
services:
  wordpress:
    restart: always
    image: gitlab.snowhow.info/snowhow/webapp/wordpress:latest
    build: wordpress/
    volumes:
      - wpdata:/var/www/html/cms
      - mapdata:/var/www/html/map
      - wpuploads:/var/www/html/cms/wp-content/uploads
  [...]
  web:
    restart: always
    image: gitlab.snowhow.info/snowhow/webapp/web:latest
    build: web/
    depends_on:
      - "wordpress"
    ports:
      - 8080:80
    volumes:
      - wpdata:/var/www/html/cms
      - mapdata:/var/www/html/map
      - wpuploads:/var/www/html/cms/wp-content/uploads
```

This works very well for a production system, but we had to make some adjustments for the development environment. As in the previous section on the API container, the Docker override configuration is used here as well. The named volume mapdata gets overwritten with the local directory *wordpress/map*. This directory contains the source code for the map application, and this is where all changes should take place. For the changes to become visible, the aforementioned Grunt tasks must be processed. For the development environment, we use a custom Docker image that occurs only in the *docker-compose.override.yml* file:

```
# File: snowhow/docker-compose.override.yml (excerpt)
  mapdev:
    image: gitlab.snowhow.info/snowhow/webapp/mapdev:latest
    build: wordpress/map/
    volumes:
      - ./wordpress/map:/src
      - mapmodules:/src/node_modules
```

Grunt and its associated modules for transforming JavaScript and Less.js stylesheets require Node.js as a runtime. Again, we use a named volume (mapmodules) to store the Node.js modules. The source code is mounted under */src* in the container where grunt will eventually do its job. In the *Dockerfile* for the Grunt task runner, the necessary packages are installed (defined in *package.json*), and the watch task is started through Grunt:

```
# File: snowhow/wordpress/map/Dockerfile
FROM node:12
WORKDIR /src
RUN chown -R node:node /src
USER node
COPY package.json /src
RUN npm i
COPY . .
CMD ["node_modules/.bin/grunt", "watch"]
```

15.2.8 Cron Jobs

The daily updated data the system processes is fetched by the business partners via cron jobs and stored in the Mongo database. The scripts that do this work are written for the Node.js runtime and reside in the API part. The adjustments we need to make to the host so that the calls are executed inside the Docker containers are minimal:

```
# File: /etc/cron.d/snowhow-bulletins
# old system:
# 11,28,39 * * * * root /home/snowhow/api/updateBulletins.js
# Docker:
11,28,39 * * * * root cd /var/docker/snowhow && \
  /usr/local/bin/docker-compose exec -T api \
  /src/updateBulletins.js
```

With docker-compose exec, the job to update the avalanche situation reports is started within the running api service. There, the settings of the docker-compose environment apply, ensuring access to MongoDB. The -T parameter is necessary because docker-compose wants to emulate a terminal, but a crontab job runs without a terminal.

15.2.9 Backups

The previous system already created regular backups of the databases and stored them in a folder on the host. This folder is copied to an external backup system every night. The same should happen for the databases running in Docker, which is what a small Bash script can be used for:

```
# File: snowhow/backup.sh
# MongoDB
docker run --rm --network snowhow_default \
    --volume /var/backups/snowhow/mongodump:/backup \
    mongo:3.6 bash -c 'mongodump --quiet -h mongo -o /backup'
# MariaDB
docker run --rm --network snowhow_default \
    --volume /var/backups/snowhow/:/backup \
    mariadb:10 bash -c 'mysqldump \
    --all-databases -h mariadb --password=topsecret \
    | gzip -c > /backup/wordpress.sql.gz'

# Docker volumes
docker run --rm --network snowhow_default \
    --volume /var/backups/snowhow/:/backup \
    --volumes-from snowhow_wordpress_1 \
    alpine tar zcf /backup/wordpress_volumes.tar.gz \
    -C /var/www/html ./
```

The two database backup calls connect to the Docker network of the snowhow_default project and start the respective dump program. The host mounts a volume in which the data is finally stored. The MariaDB SQL dump is additionally compressed by a gzip pipe.

For the files in the file system, we launch a Docker container from the lightweight Alpine Linux image. The tar command is sufficient to back up the Docker volume files to the host. The --volumes-from call mounts the named volumes from the WordPress container, keeping the paths the same as in the original container (which in this case is */var/www/html/*). The archive is reduced in size using efficient gzip compression, with the -C parameter first changing to the specified directory before the archive is created there. This eliminates the */var/www/html* path in the archive.

15.3   The Development Environment

The move to Docker is a big win for our new development environment: With a flick of the wrist, the entire setup is ready to use on the local laptop, and it isn't dependent on a locally installed database or programming language. It's enough to clone the Git repository and use docker-compose up to launch the containers.

Because the application displays new data from the avalanche warning services and weather services on a daily basis, it's useful to update the data before working in the development environment. The same applies to changed content in the WordPress CMS. Three steps are necessary to mirror the current state of the production system locally:

15

1. Import the WordPress database.
2. Copy the WordPress assets (images, PDFs, and everything in the *wp-uploads* folder).
3. Import the Mongo database.

Because the host name changes in the local development environment (access occurs via `localhost`, not `snowhow.info`), the MigrateDB plug-in is used again for the WordPress database. As we've already described, the export is done via the web interface using a saved profile. Here the Pro version of the plug-in has a decisive advantage because it can start the process via an API. This allows all work steps to be mapped in a shell script. With the free version, however, the database export remains a manual intermediate step. But no matter how the dump is created, it will be stored in the *wordpress/sql* folder.

The second step consists of copying the WordPress assets. For example, the `rsync` program is suitable for transferring the *uploads* folder from the production system to the local developer machine.

To update MongoDB, we copy a dump of the production data back to the *mongo/dump* folder using the `rsync` command. The dump gets imported using `docker-compose exec mongo mongorestore` while the system is running.

The following shell script performs these tasks and brings the development environment up to date:

```
#!/bin/bash
# File: snowhow/devupdate.sh
echo "1. Export WordPress and copy to wordpress/sql"
ls -l wordpress/sql
read
echo "2. Synchronize WordPress assets"
rsync -rv snowhow.info:/var/snowhow/cms/wp-content/uploads/ \
    wordpress/cms/wp-content/uploads/
echo " Press <Enter> to start docker-compose"
read

echo "3. Start docker-compose"
docker-compose pull
docker-compose up -d

echo "4. Synchronize MongoDB dump (<Ctrl-C> to abort)"
read
rsync -rv snowhow.info:/var/backups/mongodump/ mongo/dump/
echo "Restore Mongo dump"
docker-compose exec mongo mongorestore
```

> **Clean Up Compose Volumes**
>
> In case of multiple attempts with the `docker-compose` setup, the best way to delete containers and volumes is to use the following command:
>
> `docker-compose down -v`
>
> However, you should use this command with great caution! Even on a production system, all container data (including the databases) will be deleted without prompting.

15.4   Production Environment and Migration

All that's really needed on the production system is the *docker-compose.yml* file. This file contains all the information that's required to start the containers. On our system, we've nevertheless checked out the Git repository and run the `compose` setup from it. This way, we can also track any changes to the `compose` file itself. In any case, the containers don't need access to the local folders, only the named Docker volumes are important.

A downtime of several hours wasn't a problem during the summer months, as the application is mainly focused on winter sports—quite a luxurious situation. We started the migration in the evening hours, with high hopes that it would not degenerate into a night shift. We kept the steps and the commands for migration in a file to copy and paste into the console window.

Then we started the migration by exporting the WordPress database. Here, too, we used the MigrateDB plug-in. Although the host name doesn't change in this case, the path where the WordPress installation is located does. After the export, the Apache configuration for the web server was disabled. From that point onward, the website, the map application, and the API were no longer accessible.

In the subsequent step, we started the `docker-compose` setup for production use (i.e., without the *override* file) and made sure the containers were running:

```
docker-compose -f docker-compose.yml ps

    Name                    Command                      State    [...]
----------------------------------------------------------------------
snowhow_api_1           node /src/server.js               Up     [...]
snowhow_mariadb_1       docker-entrypoint.sh mysqld       Up     [...]
snowhow_memcached_1     docker-entrypoint.sh memcached    Up     [...]
snowhow_mongo_1         docker-entrypoint.sh mongod       Up     [...]
snowhow_web_1           nginx -g daemon off;              Up     [...]
snowhow_wordpress_1     docker-php-entrypoint php-fpm     Up     [...]
```

The server couldn't be reached from the outside yet because the corresponding configuration in the upstream reverse proxy server hadn't been activated. This was just as well because neither the MariaDB nor the Mongo database were populated at this point. To populate the WordPress database, we used the compressed database dump and imported it using the following command:

```
zcat snowhowinfo-migrate-20190510103700.sql.gz | \
  docker-compose -f docker-compose.yml exec -T mariadb mysql \
  -u root -ptopsecret snowhow
```

The compressed SQL dump was unpacked by zcat and sent to the input channel of mysql. docker-compose again had to be called with the -T option; otherwise, compose-compose would have emulated a terminal that isn't available.

After the successful import, we copied the files that had been uploaded to WordPress to the volume created for this purpose. The files were all located in the *wp-content/uploads* folder and were copied using docker cp:

```
docker cp /home/snowhow/cms/wp-content/uploads/ \
  snowhow_wordpress_1:/var/www/html/cms/wp-content/
```

```
docker-compose exec wordpress chown -R www-data:www-data \
  /var/www/html/cms/wp-content/uploads/
```

The first command copied the uploads from the *old* path to the Docker volume we had mounted in the WordPress container. Note that for the destination path, the *uploads* directory doesn't have to be specified again.

The second command sets the owner of the directory and all subdirectories to the www-data user, under which the Nginx web server runs. This step was necessary so that files could be uploaded and edited via the WordPress web interface. The WordPress part of the site was already working correctly at that point.

The last step involved importing the Mongo database. For this purpose, we created a Mongo dump in the current directory, copied it to the MongoDB container, and restored it there:

```
mongodump -o snowhowdump
```

```
docker cp snowhowdump snowhow_mongo_1:/
```

```
docker-compose exec mongo mongorestore

  using default 'dump' directory
  preparing collections to[...]
  reading metadata for sno[...]
  [...]
```

```
restoring indexes for co[...]
finished restoring snowh[...]
done
```

If everything goes smoothly, the configuration for the reverse proxy can now be acti-vated, and the new application is online. With a bit of luck, this limits the downtime to a few minutes, which should be acceptable even for sites with higher traffic.

15.5 Updates

As mentioned earlier, the ability to easily apply updates was an important reason for switching to Docker. The procedure for a bug fix or a new feature after that was as fol-lows:

- On the developer system:
  - Updating the development environment and starting it locally
  - Implementing a feature or fix bug
  - Rebuilding Docker images (`docker-compose build`)
  - Pushing Docker images to the private registry (`docker-compose push`)
- On the production system:
  - Updating Docker images (`docker-compose pull`)
  - Recreating containers for modified images (`docker-compose up -d`)

This was a big step forward, as updating the existing application used to be a tricky issue: There was one small dark spot concerning the use of WordPress. Theoretically, it would be possible to make changes to the CMS locally and prepare and import the changes to the production system using the MigrateDB plug-in; however, we didn't want to risk that. This is because if a new user registers in the meantime, that user will be overwritten during the database import. Thus, the rule remains that changes to the CMS are only to be made online on the production system.

This limitation is no big deal because the development only takes place in the API or in the map application. When using PHP-FPM, however, there's still a small problem with the updates: for the PHP files to be interpreted correctly by WordPress, they must be accessible by both the web server and the FPM server. The Docker solution for this is a shared volume, in our case `wpdata`.

Unfortunately, however, there are still some PHP files in the map application that don't access the databases via the API. These files are made available to both containers in the `mapdata` volume. When an update is made to the map application, these files are modi-fied and stored in the updated image. After updating the image on the server, the `docker-compose up` command creates a new container, but the data in the volume remains untouched. (This is intentional with `docker-compose` to avoid data loss.)

Our—admittedly not very elegant—solution was to delete the volume before the restart, resulting in the update history looking like the following:

```
docker-compose pull

  Pulling wordpress ... done
  Pulling web       ... done
  Pulling mariadb   ... done
  Pulling api       ... done
  Pulling mongo     ... done
  Pulling memcached ... done
docker-compose stop wordpress web

  Stopping snowhow_web_1       ... done
  Stopping snowhow_wordpress_1 ... done

docker volume rm snowhow_mapdata

  snowhow_mapdata

docker-compose up -d

  Creating volume "snowhow_mapdata" with default driver
  snowhow_api_1 is up-to-date
  Starting snowhow_wordpress_1 ...
  snowhow_mapdev_1 is up-to-date
  snowhow_memcached_1 is up-to-date
  snowhow_mariadb_1 is up-to-date
  Starting snowhow_wordpress_1 ... done
  Starting snowhow_web_1       ... done
```

15.6   Tips for the Transition

As part of the transition, we tried to install all versions of the software with the same state in the Docker setup that they were running on our current production system, if possible. There were enough changes to the code anyway that were only necessitated by the new setup (e.g., host names and ports).

In addition, it was convenient to start right away with a Git repository (or another version control of your choice) and commit small steps. During the transition, many files had to be opened, and small changes had to be made (adjustment of host names, port, or paths). Modern code editors suggest small improvements for automatic correction right here. If you accept, test, and commit these changes, you can easily improve the code without risking bugs in a huge change to the entire transition.

The more components involved, the greater the risk that something will end up working incorrectly. In our project, this affected the PHP cookie component, which was correctly stored in the Memcached server but couldn't be read there by the map application. Automatic tests would have been the decisive help here, but unfortunately these weren't available at the time of the transition. This experience led us to set up a basic set of tests later that can now be started manually if needed.

15.7   Results

The transition of this particular project was prepared in just a few days and went more or less smoothly. Of course, we created and tested several backups up front. There was also always the possibility of returning to the existing system if there had been major problems.

Because the application's workload fluctuates from season to season, we were able to perform the migration at a time when the short downtime during the database migration had no negative impact.

Docker achieved the major goals of the transition: First, we were able to update the server running the project to the new Ubuntu release in the meantime. Second, because the Docker variant has been up and running, we've been able to make updates to the code much more straightforward and without any bad feelings. In addition, the Docker setup facilitates further maintenance. This should ensure that our project doesn't end up in the graveyard of forgotten web projects in a few years.

15

Chapter 16
GitLab

In this chapter, we'll introduce a Docker setup that allows you to manage small or large projects as a team and at the same time provides you with the greatest possible convenience when developing and testing your applications. A requirement of this setup was that all components were able to run on their own hardware (on premises) and that no external cloud services were needed for this.

With Microsoft's acquisition of GitHub in June 2018, it once again became clear that cloud services and thus also the data stored there can quickly change hands. In addition, a public cloud solution for very sensitive data often isn't legally permissible. GitLab is a very powerful tool that you can install on your own server.

Git as a Prerequisite

For this chapter, we assume that you already have experience with the Git version management tool. If you're just getting started with Git, we recommend reading the first three chapters of the free Git book as well as the Git online tutorial:

- *https://git-scm.com/book/en/v2*
- *https://git-scm.com/docs/gittutorial*

Of course, we don't want to hide the fact that we also wrote a Git book:

- *https://kofler.info/buecher/git* (in German)
- *www.rheinwerk-computing.com/5555*

The core component of this setup is *GitLab*, an application for managing software projects based on the Git version management system. GitLab provides the following features:

- Project management with wiki and a ticket system
- Web interface for source code
- Docker image registry
- Pipelines for testing and building projects
- Statistics on the course of the project

GitLab has been available for download under the free MIT license since 2011. In 2014, the project was split into a *Community Edition* and an *Enterprise Edition*, with the Community Edition still freely available. The Enterprise Edition includes features typically needed in large enterprises, such as the integration of multiple Active Directory or Lightweight Directory Access Protocol (LDAP) servers.

GitLab Inc., the Silicon Valley company behind GitLab, offers both cloud-based installations and self-hosted installations in a variety of flavors. For a current overview, visit *https://about.gitlab.com/pricing*. In this chapter, we'll use the free Core package for self-installation.

The setup contains the following:

- GitLab as a web frontend for your Git repositories (see Figure 16.1)
- A modern ticket system with milestones and boards
- A wiki with Markdown syntax for additional documentation
- A private Docker registry
- Mattermost as a team communication platform (optional)

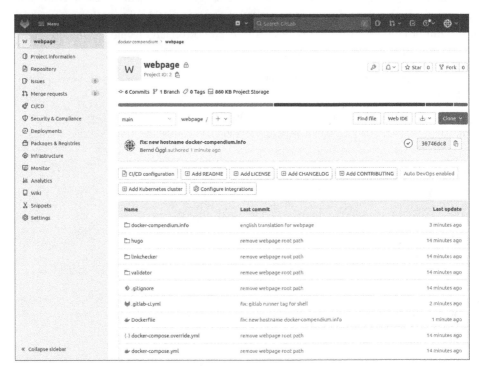

Figure 16.1 Overview of a GitLab Project

All parts of this environment are available as open-source code. The licenses are also open for commercial use.

16.1   GitLab Quick Start

To get a first impression of GitLab, you can simply start a GitLab container locally and try out the web interface. Note that all settings and all content created in the test mode will be lost.

```
docker run -e GITLAB_ROOT_PASSWORD="StrictlySecret" \
  --name gitlab -p 8888:80 gitlab/gitlab-ce
```

-p 8888:80 connects the local port 8888 for access to the web interface. Initializing the database for the first time can take up to five minutes, depending on the performance of your computer.

Because we didn't start the container in the background, you'll see the log output in the terminal. When the message gitlab Reconfigured! appears among the messages, you can open your browser with the address *http://localhost:8888* and enter the user name root and the password specified under ROOT_PW. Then you can create your first project (see Figure 16.2).

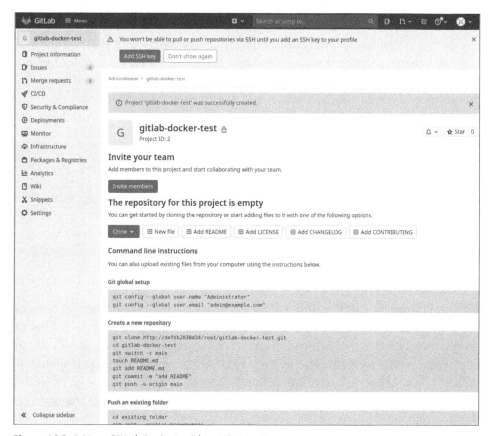

Figure 16.2 A New GitLab Project without Content

The overview page provides useful tips on how to import an existing Git repository or check out this project in a new folder on your computer. You could also create files directly there, which is also very convenient with the recently introduced Web IDE, but is still an unusual way. Typically, locally installed editors such as Atom, Visual Studio Code (VS Code), Vim, or Emacs are used for developing projects.

To use GitLab in production, you'll need to adjust some parameters to ensure that your data is stored securely, that encryption works, and that you can enable other features of this impressive program. The following sections provide more information about this.

16.2   GitLab Web Installation

GitLab is a modern web application that consists of various components in different programming languages. Installing from the source code isn't recommended because it's very time-consuming and requires various libraries on the system (including Ruby, Go, Node.js, PostgreSQL, and Redis). While there are packages for different operating systems, the more elegant way is to install it with Docker.

The official Docker image from GitLab doesn't fully comply with the concept of a microservices architecture because databases and program code are packed in the same image and several processes run there in parallel. Because GitLab itself maintains this image very consistently, updates and the greatest possible compatibility are ensured. We'll also use this image for our setup, but we've swapped out the databases (Redis and especially PostgreSQL) to separate containers.

Alternate Setup
Of course, you can also launch the GitLab image as a container running PostgreSQL and Redis alongside the application code. This will give you the highest possible degree of compatibility, as GitLab will undoubtedly test the components extensively in the versions installed there. We'll describe a distributed setup here to illustrate how straightforward Docker can be to manage various services.

For the following descriptions, it's necessary that you install GitLab on a server that can be accessed through the internet with a valid domain name. For communication to work smoothly between GitLab, the integrated Docker registry, and *GitLab Runner*—an outsourced service for builds and tests—it must be encrypted. Although it should be possible to use self-signed certificates for this purpose, our attempts weren't successful. We'll therefore use official certificates from Let's Encrypt, which are managed on the upstream reverse proxy.

We'll use the following host names for the example:

- *gitlab.dockerbuch.info*
- *registry.dockerbuch.info*
- *mattermost.dockerbuch.info* (optional)

Although we only launch one container, we'll use `docker-compose` to clearly store the launch parameters in a file. We'll install GitLab on a server that already has other websites running on HTTPS port 443 using the setup with Nginx as a reverse proxy described in Chapter 9, Section 9.3 (see Figure 16.3).

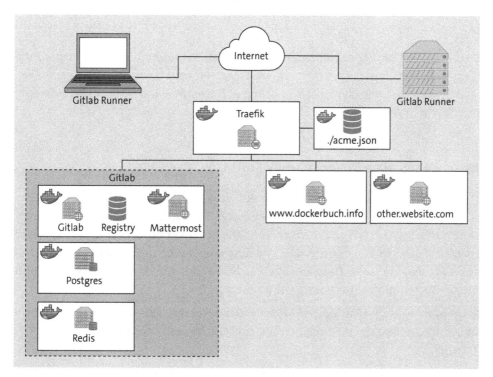

Figure 16.3 Network Setup with Traefik as the Terminating Proxy (Traefik Container Encrypts to the Internet via HTTPS)

All customizations for the GitLab configuration can be done using the `GITLAB_OMNIBUS_CONFIG` environment variable. The advantage of this type of configuration is that no external file needs to be included. GitLab reads the configuration from this environment variable before consulting the actual configuration file */etc/gitlab/gitlab.rb*. In the default installation, this file contains only lines that have been commented out, so only the values of the environment variables apply.

In the *YAML Ain't Markup Language* (YAML) syntax of the *docker-compose* file, the corresponding excerpt looks like the following (the | pipe character indicates the multi-line entry):

```
# in file gitlab/docker-compose.yml
environment:
  GITLAB_OMNIBUS_CONFIG: |
    external_url 'https://gitlab.dockerbuch.info/'
    nginx['listen_port'] = 80
    nginx['listen_https'] = false
    nginx['proxy_set_headers'] = {
```

```
    "X-Forwarded-Proto" => "https",
    "X-Forwarded-Ssl" => "on"
  }
[...]
```

To prevent the further explanations of the GitLab configuration from becoming too confusing, we've distributed the various aspects (reverse proxy, email, Secure Shell [SSH], etc.) across several sections. A listing of the entire *docker-compose.yml* file will then follow in Section 16.8.

16.3   HTTPS via a Reverse Proxy Setup

The internal Nginx server runs on port 80. HTTPS is turned off, so the *terminating proxy* is responsible for managing the certificates. For the Docker registry, we use a separate host name: `registry.dockerbuch.info`. The benefit of this is that we don't need to enable a separate port in the firewalls, and the configuration in the upstream proxy can be set in the same way as from a web server. In the container, the registry runs on port 5000; HTTPS is disabled as it is for the web server.

It's important to specify the `external_url` and the `registry_external_url` because these values are displayed in the web interface, and GitLab can't determine these values on its own.

As mentioned earlier, we'll use an upstream reverse proxy to connect to the internet, which also manages the Secure Sockets Layer (SSL) certificates from Let's Encrypt (see Chapter 9, Section 9.6). Both the GitLab server and the Docker registry server are served by the proxy server and controlled by the `labels` statements in the *docker-compose.yml* file.

16.4   Email Dispatch

GitLab provides for email notifications by default, which can be a pretty cool feature. For the email dispatch to work, either a locally installed `sendmail` variant is used or the dispatch is carried out via an external Simple Mail Transfer Protocol (SMTP) server. The latter usually has the advantage that any spam filters present at the recipient's end are more likely to trust the SMTP server than a local dispatch.

GitLab's official Docker image doesn't support the local `sendmail` variant, which leaves only the SMTP variant. The GitLab documentation includes examples for more than 30 major email providers, including GMX, Gmail, Office 365, Yahoo, Hetzner, and many more. Details can be found on the GitLab help page:

https://docs.gitlab.com/omnibus/settings/smtp.html

16.4.1 Sending Emails with Your Own Exim Mail Server

Another minimal configuration with a separate Exim mail server allows you to send email via SMTP. Exim, of course, runs in its own Docker container.

> **Incorrect Spam Detection**
>
> Note that email notifications with the variant shown here can very easily end up in the recipient's spam filter or not be delivered at all. The preferred approach is to use an external SMTP server as described earlier.

There's no official Docker image for the Exim mail server, but it's very easy to create an image based on Alpine Linux. In the following *Dockerfile*, the server gets installed and started:

```
# File gitlab/exim/Dockerfile
FROM alpine:3.14
RUN apk --no-cache add exim
COPY docker-exim.conf /etc/exim/exim.conf
EXPOSE 25
ENTRYPOINT ["/usr/sbin/exim"]
CMD ["-bdf", "-q15m"]
```

The -bdf parameter starts the Exim server as a daemon, but it doesn't run in the background; instead, it remains connected to the Docker container as a foreground process. The second parameter, -q15m, starts a *queue runner* every 15 minutes that tries to send remaining emails.

In the Exim configuration file (*exim.conf*), which is copied to the image via COPY (see the preceding listing), we changed only two lines to the default configuration:

```
# File: gitlab/exim/docker-exim.conf
keep_environment = RELAY_FROM
hostlist relay_from_hosts = ${env{RELAY_FROM}{$value} fail}
[...]
```

By default, the mail server only accepts mail from localhost, whereas all others are rejected with the message **550 relay not permitted**. There's a good reason for this, as otherwise countless mail servers on the internet would be easy prey for spam mail senders. In our Exim configuration, we want to replace the value for relay_from_hosts with a variable that we populate in the *docker-compose* file using the environment directive.

To use environment variables in the Exim configuration file, they must first be marked as *valid* (keep_environment). Then the value can be inserted with the somewhat unfamiliar syntax ${env{RELAY_FROM}{$value} fail}. If the value of the RELAY_FROM variable is

16

empty, `fail` gets called, causing the mail server to produce a corresponding error message.

16.4.2   Integration into the GitLab Configuration

Finally, the following entries must be added to the central `docker-compose` configuration file of GitLab:

```
# in file gitlab/docker-compose.yml
services:
  exim:
    build: exim/
    environment:
      - RELAY_FROM=gitlab_gitlab_1.gitlab_default
      [...]
    environment:
      GITLAB_OMNIBUS_CONFIG: |
        gitlab_rails['smtp_enable'] = true
        gitlab_rails['smtp_openssl_verify_mode'] = 'none'
        gitlab_rails['smtp_address'] = "exim"
        gitlab_rails['smtp_port'] = 25
        gitlab_rails['gitlab_email_from'] = 'gitlab@dockerbuc...
        [...]
```

The Exim image is created from the *Dockerfile* in the *exim* subfolder, filling the `RELAY_FROM` environment variable with the value `gitlab_gitlab_1.gitlab_default` to start. This value reflects the host and network name of the GitLab container in the `docker-compose` network (we're working in the *gitlab* directory). Exim therefore accepts emails from our GitLab container without authentication. The GitLab variable `GITLAB_OMNIBUS_CONFIG` is extended to include the SMTP entries. Verify Mode must be disabled for OpenSSL because the Exim container works with self-signed certificates.

To test whether emails can actually be sent, you want to start a shell in the GitLab container and connect to the `gitlab-rails` console:

```
docker-compose exec gitlab bash

  root@gitlab:/# gitlab-rails console

  Ruby:         ruby 2.7.2p137 (2020-10-01 revision 5445e04352)
  GitLab:       14.0.1 (76b84b42f64) FOSS
  GitLab Shell: 13.19.0
  PostgreSQL:   12.7
```

```
Loading production environment (Rails 6.1.3.2)
irb(main):001:0> Notify.test_email('bernd@dockerbuch.info', \
irb(main):002:1* 'Test message', \
irb(main):003:1* 'Here comes the test message.').deliver_now
...
Delivered mail 60df238146262_fcf5a8c20989@gitlab.dockerbuc...
```

The test message should arrive in the mailbox of *bernd@dockerbuch.info* after a short time. Here you can see the message in the source code (shortened for space reasons):

```
Return-Path: <gitlab@dockerbuch.info>
[...]
Received: from gitlab_gitlab_1.gitlab_default ([172.24.0.5]
  helo=localhost.localdomain) by 0bbe5e1c6c75 with esmtps
  (TLS1.3) tls TLS_AES_256_GCM_SHA384
  (Exim 4.94.2)
  (envelope-from <gitlab@dockerbuch.info>)
  id 1lzKDZ-00001T-Dv
  for bernd@dockerbuch.info; Fri, 02 Jul 2021 14:32:33 +0000
From: GitLab <gitlab@dockerbuch.info>
Reply-To: GitLab <gitlab@dockerbuch.info>
To: bernd@dockerbuch.info
Message-ID: <60df238146262_fcf5a8c20989@gitlab.dockerbuch.info...
Subject: Test message
[...]
X-Auto-Response-Suppress: All

<!DOCTYPE html PUBLIC "-//W3C//DTD HTML 4.0 Transitional//EN" ...
<head>
<meta http-equiv="Content-Type" content="text/html; charset=ut...
<body><p>Hier comes the test message..</p></body></html>
```

Attention—Spam!

GitLab also has a feature called *Incoming Email*, which is disabled by default. If the function is activated, it's possible to reply to notifications by email and create new tickets by email.

There are different ways to configure this function. In any case, you need to set up a public email address that can receive these emails. However, the associated issue of spam emails (and spam messages in GitLab) poses a problem, as your ticket system could be flooded with automated messages. For this reason, we won't describe this configuration variant any further.

16.5   Secure Shell Access

GitLab provides the option to access your repositories with HTTPS or via SSH. We've already configured the HTTPS access. However, SSH has the additional advantage that you can store a key in GitLab, which makes logging in more secure and easier.

If you install GitLab on a Linux server that you also use for other services, there's a good chance that SSH is already in use. We want to avoid a conflict between the Docker installation and the existing server, so we connect the SSH port of the GitLab container (22) to a free port on the server, in our case, that's 2222. If a firewall is installed upstream of your server, you must release this port.

The corresponding entries in the *docker-compose* file are as follows:

```
# in file gitlab/docker-compose.yml
...
    environment:
      GITLAB_OMNIBUS_CONFIG: |
        gitlab_rails['gitlab_shell_ssh_port'] = 2222
      ...
    ports:
      - "2222:22"
```

The `gitlab_rails['gitlab_shell_ssh_port']` entry in the configuration variable causes GitLab to correctly display the practical information about cloning the repositories.

As long as you haven't yet stored an SSH key in GitLab, a note will be displayed in the web interface stating that it's not yet possible to *push* or *pull* code directly via SSH. If you don't have an SSH key yet, you can create one via the following command:

```
ssh-keygen -t rsa -C "info@dockerbuch.info" -b 4096
```

The command generates a key pair consisting of a private and a public key and then asks for the location and an optional password. If you accept the suggested answers, the keys will be stored without a password in your SSH configuration directory (*$HOME/ .ssh/*). Then you need to copy the contents of the public key file (the file ends with *.pub*) into the **User Settings/SSH Keys** text box provided in GitLab: *https://gitlab.docker-buch.info/profile/keys*.

16.6   Volumes and Backup

For the GitLab container, we use three named volumes: `config`, `logs`, and `data`. This way, backups can be created easily, and file permissions are managed by GitLab within the Docker container.

```
# in file gitlab/docker-compose.yml
...
volumes:
  - config:/etc/gitlab
  - logs:/var/log/gitlab
  - data:/var/opt/gitlab
```

In any case, you should back up the data volume as this is where all your Git repositories and associated wikis reside. If you ever want to switch to a platform other than GitLab, you can find your source code here as *bare repositories*. Combined with the export function of the entries in the ticket system, the risk that you'll reach a dead end with GitLab is very low.

16.6.1 Backing Up GitLab Application Files

Backing up the data volume is the first step, but you don't save the application data (e.g., the GitLab user data) with it. However, GitLab has taken precautions and integrated its own backup script into the system. The script creates a database dump and compresses all other files related to GitLab into a TAR file:

```
docker-compose exec gitlab gitlab-rake gitlab:backup:create
```

This file is located in /var/opt/gitlab/backups, and the file name includes the current timestamp, a readable date, and the GitLab version number. For example, in our case, the backup file is named *1625405719_2021_07_04_14.0.2_gitlab_backup.tar*.

Note that the backup process uses the pg_dump command to back up the database, which works only if the server and client have the same version. Currently, GitLab uses PostgreSQL version 12 as a client, so our docker-compose setup also uses the PostgreSQL 12 server.

> **Note**
> If you use GitLab in a production environment, it's definitely advisable to back up the backup directory to an external server. GitLab has preconfigured settings for Amazon S3, Google Cloud Storage, and locally mounted paths (e.g., via Network File System [NFS] or Samba).

16.6.2 Restore

Creating a backup is one thing; restoring it is another. To import the backup just described into a new GitLab instance, you first need to start an *empty* working GitLab instance, which should be easy with the Docker setup described here. Then you must copy the backup file to the container:

```
docker cp 1625405719_2021_07_04_14.0.2_gitlab_backup.tar \
  gitlab_gitlab_1:/var/opt/gitlab/backups
```

After that, you need to stop the unicorn and sidekiq processes in the gitlab container:

```
docker-compose exec gitlab gitlab-ctl stop puma
docker-compose exec gitlab gitlab-ctl stop sidekiq
```

In the current version of GitLab, you still need to adjust the file permissions of the backup directory to be able to import the backup correctly:

```
docker-compose exec gitlab chmod -R 775 /var/opt/gitlab/backups
```

Once that has been done, nothing stands in the way of a restore:

```
docker-compose exec gitlab gitlab-rake gitlab:backup:restore \
  BACKUP=1625405719_2021_07_04_14.0.2
```

You'll be asked during the restore process if you really want to delete the entire database (including those tables that aren't related to the GitLab installation). After that, GitLab will import the backup, and you can restart the system:

```
docker-compose exec gitlab gitlab-ctl start
```

Finally, you want to start a check if the software versions and file permissions are correct:

```
docker-compose exec gitlab gitlab-rake gitlab:check \
  SANITIZE=true
```

In our tests, the check didn't reveal any errors, and the previously deleted GitLab instance was operational again. A small problem occurred a little later when we tried to upload a new Docker image to the registry (see Section 16.7).

The file system permissions for the registry weren't adjusted accordingly, which prevented the image from being created. The problem is known and could possibly have been fixed by the time you read this book:

https://gitlab.com/gitlab-org/gitlab-ce/issues/19936

If not, simply enter the following command:

```
docker-compose exec gitlab chown -R registry:registry \
  /var/opt/gitlab/gitlab-rails/shared/registry/docker/
```

16.7   Custom Docker Registry for GitLab

While it's also very easy to start a private registry with Docker (you just need to start a container from the `registry:2` image), GitLab's built-in registry provides some advantages (see Figure 16.4):

- GitLab user management
- Clear graphical user interface (GUI)
- Images assigned to projects
- Images included in the backup of GitLab

The integration with GitLab is so well done that users no longer even notice that they are dealing with a separate component.

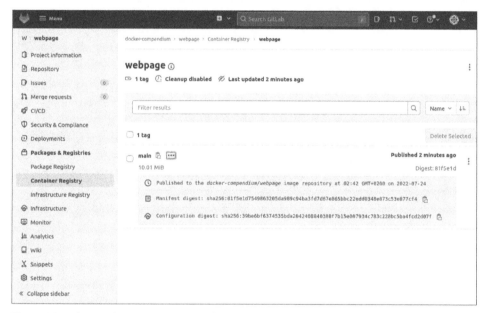

Figure 16.4 The Docker Registry in GitLab

To enable the registry in GitLab, a few entries in the environment variable `GITLAB_OMNI-BUS_CONFIG` are sufficient:

```
# in file gitlab/docker-compose.yml
...
registry_external_url 'https://registry.dockerbuch.info'
registry['registry_http_addr'] = "0.0.0.0:5000"
registry_nginx['enable'] = false
```

Similar to the GitLab application, we set a `registry_external_url`, the address that will be correctly displayed in the web interface. The specification of `registry_http_addr` is needed to specify the port for the registry server (5000) and also to make the server reachable from outside the container (by default it binds only to the local IP address 127.0.0.1, which isn't useful inside a container). The third parameter `registry_nginx` `['enable']` must be set to `false` so that the Nginx server running in the container doesn't attempt to look up SSL certificates for the registry server. In our example, this task is performed by the upstream Traefik proxy server.

16.8   The Complete docker-compose File

The entire *docker-compose* file for the GitLab instance thus looks like the following:

```
# File: gitlab/docker-compose.yml
version: '3'
services:
  gitlab:
    hostname: gitlab.dockerbuch.info
    image: gitlab/gitlab-ce:latest
    environment:
      GITLAB_ROOT_PASSWORD: StrictlySecretStrictly
      GITLAB_OMNIBUS_CONFIG: |
        external_url 'https://gitlab.dockerbuch.info/'
        nginx['listen_port'] = 80
        nginx['listen_https'] = false
        nginx['proxy_set_headers'] = {
          "X-Forwarded-Proto" => "https",
          "X-Forwarded-Ssl" => "on"
        }
        postgresql['enable'] = false
        gitlab_rails['db_host'] = 'postgresql'
        gitlab_rails['db_port'] = '5432'
        gitlab_rails['db_username'] = 'gitlab'
        gitlab_rails['db_password'] = 'ief6baehohQu'
        gitlab_rails['db_database'] = 'gitlab_prod'
        gitlab_rails['db_adapter'] = 'postgresql'
        gitlab_rails['db_encoding'] = 'utf8'
        redis['enable'] = false
        gitlab_rails['redis_host'] = 'redis'
        gitlab_rails['redis_port'] = '6379'
        gitlab_rails['gitlab_shell_ssh_port'] = 2222
```

```
            gitlab_rails['smtp_enable'] = true
            gitlab_rails['smtp_openssl_verify_mode'] = 'none'
            gitlab_rails['smtp_address'] = 'exim'
            gitlab_rails['smtp_port'] = 25
            gitlab_rails['gitlab_email_from'] = 'gl@dockerbuch.info'
            registry_external_url 'https://registry.dockerbuch.info'
            registry['registry_http_addr'] = "0.0.0.0:5000"
            registry_nginx['enable'] = false
    ports:
      - "2222:22"
    restart: always
    volumes:
      - config:/etc/gitlab
      - logs:/var/log/gitlab
      - data:/var/opt/gitlab
    networks:
      - web
      - default
    labels:
      - traefik.enable=true
      - traefik.http.routers.gitlab.rule=Host( \
              `gitlab.dockerbuch.info`)
      - traefik.http.routers.gitlab.tls=true
      - traefik.http.routers.gitlab.tls.certresolver=lets-encrypt
      - traefik.http.services.gitlab.loadbalancer.server.port=80
      - traefik.http.routers.gitlab.service=gitlab
      - traefik.http.routers.reg.rule=Host( \
              `registry.dockerbuch.info`)
      - traefik.http.routers.reg.tls=true
      - traefik.http.routers.reg.tls.certresolver=lets-encrypt
      - traefik.http.routers.reg.service=gl-rg
      - traefik.http.services.gl-rg.loadbalancer.server.port=5000
  redis:
    image: redis:6
  postgresql:
    image: postgres:12
    environment:
      - POSTGRES_USER=gitlab
      - POSTGRES_PASSWORD=ief6baehohQu
      - POSTGRES_DB=gitlab_prod
    volumes:
      - pgdata:/var/lib/postgresql
```

```
  exim:
    build: exim/
    environment:
      - RELAY_FROM=gitlab_gitlab2_1.gitlab_default
volumes:
  config:
  logs:
  data:
  pgdata:

networks:
  web:
    external: true
```

For your own tests, you can download a sample of this file here:

https://github.com/docbuc/gitlab

Once *docker-compse.yml* is complete, you can start the setup as usual via docker-compose up -d.

16.9   Using GitLab

After successfully launching your Docker setup, it may well take several minutes for GitLab to initialize the databases and for you to reach the web interface. When you access the web interface for the first time, you must set a password for the administrator account. After that, you'll be redirected to the login and can log in as root user with the password you just set.

> **Online Documentation**
>
> We don't want to go into too much detail about the GitLab user interface (UI) here, as you'll certainly find your way around there quickly. In the following sections, we'll briefly deal with a few highlights of GitLab to give you an idea of the system. A comprehensive user manual for GitLab can be found here:
>
> *https://gitlab.com/help*

In the current version of GitLab, you'll find a hamburger (three-bar) icon in the top toolbar that shows a submenu for global settings (**Admin**) and is only visible to administrators. On the far right, there is a dropdown menu for settings related to your profile (name, email, SSH keys, etc.).

16.9.1 User

A default setting of GitLab provides that users can sign up at the system with their email address. If you want to change this setting so that only administrators can create new users, you can find the setting under **Admin Area · Settings · Sign-Up Restrictions** or at the following address:

https://<your-gitlab-url>/admin/application_settings

For our setup, we created a separate user with administrator rights (under **Admin Area · Overview · Users**) and stored the public SSH key for this user (see Figure 16.5).

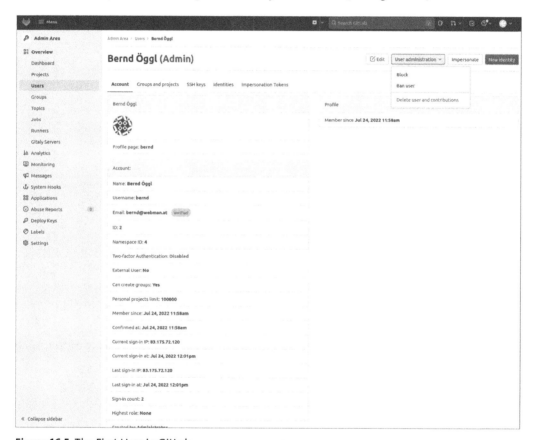

Figure 16.5 The First User in GitLab

In your profile settings, you can also change the preferred language of the web interface. Multilanguage support is currently listed as an experimental feature, and translations aren't yet complete. We'll therefore stick with English as the language (see Figure 16.6).

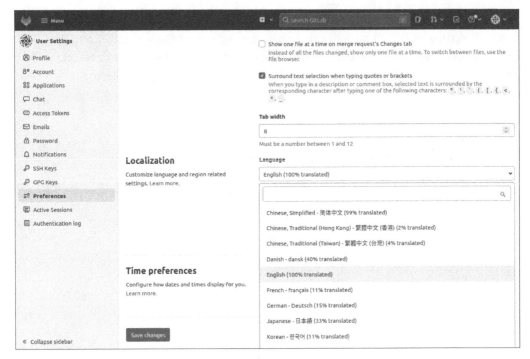

Figure 16.6 User Profile Settings in GitLab

16.9.2   Projects

When creating a new project, you have the option to build on one of the existing templates (GitLab will then create a typical directory structure, e.g., for a project using Node.js or Ruby), import a project from an existing service, or start an empty project. An important decision concerns the path to your repository.

If you collaborate with several people, it's usually recommended to create a group and assign the project to that group.

Finally, there's the option to declare the project as *private*, *internal*, or *public*:

- **Private**
  Private access requires you to manually add users or groups to the project

- **Internal**
  access allows all users logged in to your GitLab instance to view the project.

- **Public**
  Public access causes the project to appear in the list at *https://your-gitlab-domain/ public*, and users who aren't logged in to the system can also clone the project.

However, to get write access to a project, you must add the users or groups manually in any case.

16.9.3   Wiki

Each project also includes a wiki by default. Using the web interface, you can create and edit pages there in Markdown, RDoc, or AsciiDoc format, as well as upload and link files.

The special thing about this wiki is that texts and attachments are stored in a separate Git repository that you can edit without the interface. The name of the repository corresponds to the name of the project with the extension .*wiki*.

16.9.4   Tickets and Issues

In modern software development with multiple people involved, an *issue tracking* or *bug tracking* system is considered an absolute must. As early as 1998, the Mozilla software project put Bugzilla, a program for this purpose, on the internet for free download. Today, you can choose from a variety of open-source projects (e.g., Redmine, Trac, Mantis) and commercial products (e.g., Jira from Atlassian) for ticket management.

GitLab includes its own issue tracking system, which brings integration advantages, including making it very easy to link tickets with commit messages or with texts from the wiki (see Figure 16.7).

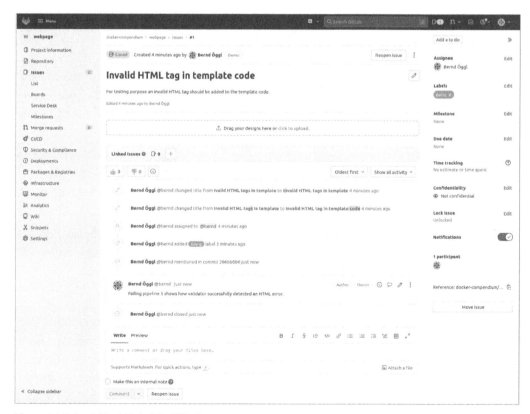

Figure 16.7 An Edited Ticket in GitLab

In daily use, *boards* are a popular way to manage tickets. Tasks can be edited and delegated using drag and drop. In addition, the arrangement looks very tidy (see Figure 16.8).

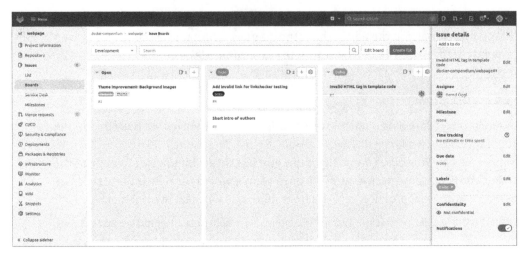

Figure 16.8 A GitLab Board with Open Tickets

16.10   GitLab Runner

In Chapter 17, we'll use the concept of a continuous integration (CI)/continuous delivery (CD) pipeline. In the process, different jobs are processed that test the source code for errors and, if necessary, also produce a new version of the software at the same time.

GitLab handles the management of such pipelines, but swaps out the execution to external programs called *GitLab Runners*. A runner typically runs on one of your servers or in a cloud environment. If you use the widely used Jenkins build server, you'll know this concept as *distributed builds* or *build slaves*.

A GitLab Runner communicates with the GitLab instance encrypted over the internet and therefore doesn't need to run on the same server. It's even possible to install a runner on your laptop, for example, to test a new setup.

16.10.1   Installation

GitLab Runners are available as executable binaries for all major platforms. On Linux, you can also take the easier way and import a runner from the package sources of your distribution. GitLab also provides the latest stable version as its own package source. For all Debian-based distributions (Debian, Ubuntu, Mint), a call like the following is sufficient:

```
curl -L "https://packages.gitlab.com/install/repositories/runner/
gitlab-runner/script.deb.sh" | sudo bash
```

The call installs the appropriate package source for your system. You can then install the package using `apt install gitlab-runner`. For detailed instructions on how to install a GitLab Runner for your operating system, see the following web page:

https://docs.gitlab.com/runner/install/index.html

> **GitLab Runner as Docker Image**
>
> You may be wondering why we don't start the GitLab Runner in a container, when we run everything in containers as much as possible in this book. In this case, however, it's easier to start with a runner that doesn't run as a container: When running the CI/CD pipelines, Docker is also often used to create images; if the runner itself is already running in Docker, there are limitations.

After the successful installation, you need to register the runner with your GitLab instance. Calling `gitlab-runner register` will take you through the following dialogue, which has been shortened a bit here for space reasons:

```
Enter the GitLab instance URL (for example, https://gitlab.com/):
  https://gitlab.dockerbuch.info/

Enter the registration token:
  pyXXXXXXXXXXXXXXXXXy

Enter a description for the runner:
  [almanarre]: my-laptop

Enter tags for the runner (comma-separated):
  shell,linux

Registering runner... succeeded
runner=pyakWJUR
Enter an executor: docker, shell, ssh, docker-ssh+machine,
kubernetes, custom, docker-ssh, parallels, virtualbox,
docker+machine:
  shell

Runner registered successfully. Feel free to start it, but if ...
```

If you started the runner as `root` user, then the runner is now ready for use and can be activated by the GitLab server at any time. However, you can also register a runner as an unprivileged user, but then you need to activate the runner manually. You'll be notified of this during setup with the following lines:

```
WARNING: Running in user-mode.
WARNING: The user-mode requires you to manually start builds
processing:
WARNING: $ gitlab-runner run
WARNING: Use sudo for system-mode:
WARNING: $ sudo gitlab-runner...
```

You can read the gitlab-ci token in the web interface under **Admin • Runners**. The final question about the executor for this runner is important.

GitLab provides several methods of how a runner works. We'll focus on three types in the following sections: the *Shell Executor*, the *Docker Executor*, and the *Kubernetes Executor*. More information about the GitLab Runner types can be found here:

https://docs.gitlab.com/runner/executors

16.10.2 The Shell Executor

We'll use shell here, which runs the job on the operating system with the privileges of the gitlab-runner user (created during installation, unless you chose user-mode during registration, in which case, it runs under your user ID). Because we use Docker in our example, you need to give the user the appropriate permissions to run Docker (usually you need to assign them the docker group).

With the Shell Executor, the user runs the CI pipeline jobs in the home directory. You can trace the individual steps there under the *build* folder, which facilitates debugging. All docker commands can draw on the locally installed images. All instructions in the CI pipeline can call the programs installed on the computer where the runner is running.

> **Accessing Project Files**
> The good news is that each shell runner keeps the current state of your project in the working directory (via git clone). You can use these files in the CI/CD pipeline.

If the steps described previously were successful, you'll see in the web interface under **Admin Area • Runners** that the runner has logged in. Here you can also configure the runner by assigning it to a specific project or adding a description and tags to it.

16.10.3 The Docker Executor

Things are a little different when the runner uses the Docker Executor. We're not talking about the GitLab Runner running as a Docker container here, we're talking about the natively running runner using the Docker service to process the CI pipeline.

This results in certain limitations compared to the Shell Executor. Jobs are run in the context of a Docker image. In the configuration file, you can set whether the same image should be used for all jobs in the pipeline or whether each job should use its own image. The runner can either use the official Docker registry or images from the private registry.

Unfortunately, it's not straightforward to call `docker` directly because we're already working in the context of a container. While it's theoretically possible to use the Docker-in-Docker image (`docker:dind`), this requires the runner to start Docker in Privileged Mode, which undermines all security mechanisms and is therefore not recommended.

Project Files in Docker Executor

Unlike the Shell Executor, the project files in the Docker Executor can be accessed at `/builds/<namespace>/<project-name>`.

16.10.4   The Kubernetes Executor

The Kubernetes Executor works very similarly to the Docker Executor just described, except that the container and associated services run in a *Kubernetes pod* within a Kubernetes cluster.

Kubernetes

Kubernetes (aka k8s) is a platform developed by Google to efficiently manage containers. See Chapter 20 for more information on using Kubernetes.

We won't go into the details of setting up a Kubernetes cluster here, but we'll use the *Google Kubernetes Engine* (GKE) GitLab integration.

The requirements for this are a Google account and a login to the Google Cloud Platform. Currently, Google grants a 90-day trial period with a bonus of around $250. That's definitely sufficient for our experiments. So, if you try the examples in this book with the Google Cloud, you shouldn't incur any additional costs (see Figure 16.9).

To initialize the GKE integration, you must first configure the OmniAuth Google OAuth2 provider. To do this, you need to create a new project in Google Cloud Console and generate OAuth credentials (an OAuth2 client ID) for a web application there (you can find the menu for this under **APIs and Services** and **Credentials**). The addresses for the **Authorized Redirect URIs** are listed here:

- *https://<your-gitlab-domain>/users/auth/google_oauth2/callback*
- *https://<your-gitlab-domain>/-/google_api/auth/callback*

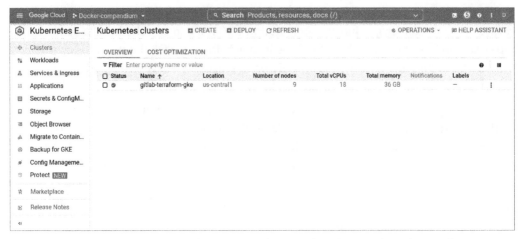

Figure 16.9 The Kubernetes Cluster Created by GitLab in the Google Web Console

Under **APIs & Services** in Google Cloud Platform, you now need to enable the following APIs for your project:

- Google Kubernetes Engine API
- Cloud Billing API
- Cloud Resource Manager API

Google OAuth2 Configuration

For precise step-by-step instructions on how to connect your Google account to GitLab, visit the following web page:

https://docs.gitlab.com/ee/integration/google.html

Then add the credentials to the GITLAB_OMNIBUS_CONFIG variable in the *docker-compose.yml* file, and restart the Docker setup via docker-compose up -d:

```
# File: gitlab/docker-compose.yml (excerpt)
...
gitlab_rails['omniauth_providers'] = [
  {
    "name" => "google_oauth2",
    "app_id" => "4444444444444-xyzxyzxyzxyzxyzxyzyxzxyzxyzx...",
    "app_secret" => "ongaineefohtoon9Shei6ais",
    "args" => { "access_type" => "offline",
      "approval_prompt" => ''
    }
  }
]
```

If all the information is correct, after restarting, you'll find the option to also log in via Google on the login screen (see Figure 16.10).

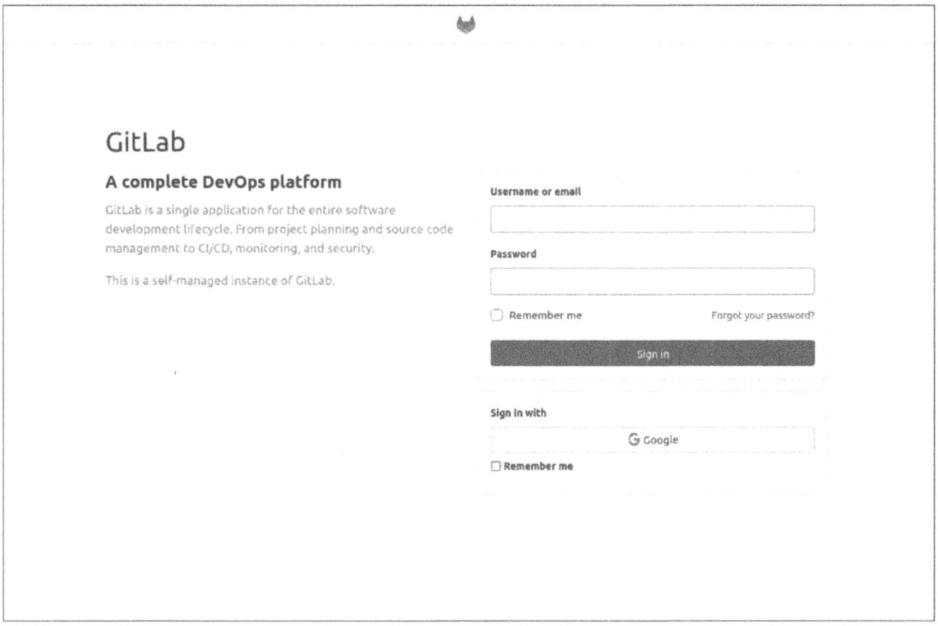

Figure 16.10 Option to Log In via a Google Account

You can now create the cluster in the administration menu under **Kubernetes**. To do this, click the **Integrate with a Cluster Certificate** button and fill in the necessary parameters in the dialog that opens (see Figure 16.11). This process takes several minutes because virtual machines are installed and configured for you there.

If you've followed us this far and all steps have been implemented successfully, then your Kubernetes cluster is now running, but there's no GitLab Runner there yet. Up to version 14, you could install some useful programs called *GitLab Managed Apps* via the web interface in Kubernetes. Those included the GitLab Runner. However, this approach has now been marked as deprecated and is no longer supported. Instead, you must now create your own GitLab project where you manage the applications you want to run in your Kubernetes cluster by default.

This sounds more complicated than it actually is. When creating the project, you use the GitLab Cluster Management template, which already contains all the settings. The only thing you need to do is amend lines two and three in the file *applications/gitlab-runner/values.yaml*:

```
## REQUIRED VALUES
gitlabUrl: "https://gitlab.dockerbuch.info/"
runnerRegistrationToken: "pyXXXXXXXXXXXXXXXXoy"
```

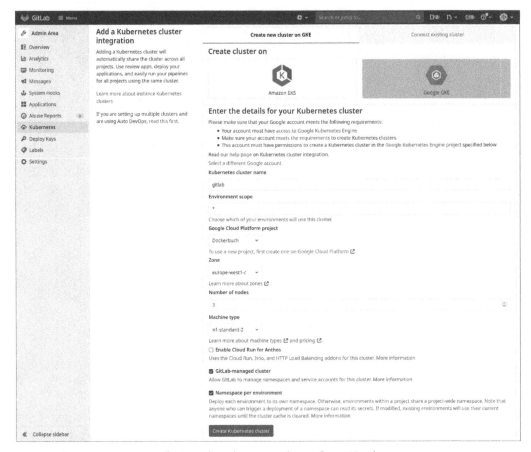

Figure 16.11 Creating the Google Kubernetes Cluster from GitLab

Finally, you want to remove the comment character for the GitLab Runner in the *helm-file.yaml* file. Once you've committed the changes, the CI process will deploy the application to your Kubernetes cluster (see Chapter 17).

The runner will be automatically added to your project, which you can check via **Settings • CI/CD • Runner Settings** in your GitLab project. Table 16.1 contains a brief comparison of the three runner types described here.

Executor	Shell	Docker	Kubernetes
New environment per job	No	Yes	Yes
Parallel execution uncomplicated	No	Yes	Yes
Debugging	Simple	Complicated	Complicated

Table 16.1 Comparison of Three Types of GitLab Runners

16.11 Mattermost

The developers of Mattermost have set out to establish a free alternative to the very popular cloud service called Slack (*https://slack.com*), which has set new standards in terms of team communication. Whether on the desktop, in the app for mobile devices, or in the browser, the UI is intuitive and fun to use. The information, divided into *channels*, can be quickly viewed and commented on as needed. Especially in teams with many developers at different locations, the communication process is often more efficient than via email.

The Mattermost developers have taken this concept as a model and created a great open-source product that's convincing in many areas. Especially for teams that don't want to handle their communication via a cloud provider, Mattermost is the tool of choice to enable modern team communication. Due to the free license model (the server can be used for commercial and noncommercial projects without any charges) and the easy installation, nothing stands in the way of using it in your own company network (i.e., on premise).

The developers of GitLab obviously appreciate the Mattermost server as well because the GitLab Docker image contains a slightly customized Mattermost version.

Without an External Database

The docker compose setup we've presented in this chapter uses an external PostgreSQL database. In the current version of GitLab, the Mattermost integration doesn't use this setting. This may change again in the future, of course, but with version 14 of GitLab, we had to switch to the integrated PostgreSQL version.

To enable Mattermost, all we need is four lines in the environment section of the *docker-compose.yml* file:

```
mattermost_external_url 'https://mattermost.dockerbuch.info'
mattermost_nginx['enable'] = false
mattermost['service_address'] = "0.0.0.0"
mattermost['service_port'] = "8065"
```

As with the Docker registry, we need to turn off the upstream Nginx server for Mattermost because the SSL certificates are taken care of by the Traefik proxy. To make port 8065 accessible from the proxy, we set the service_address to 0.0.0.0.

The settings for the Traefik proxy server can be found in the labels section of the *docker-compose.yml* file:

```
- traefik.http.routers.mm.rule=Host(`mattermost.dockerbuch.info`)
- traefik.http.routers.mm.tls=true
- traefik.http.routers.mm.tls.certresolver=lets-encrypt
- traefik.http.routers.mm.service=mm
- traefik.http.services.mm.loadbalancer.server.port=8065
```

This completes the configuration of Mattermost. You can start the setup with docker-compose up -d.

If you want to transfer the existing users of the GitLab instance to Mattermost, you can include GitLab as a Single Sign-On (SSO) provider. Again, all you need to do that is a few lines in the *docker-compose.yml* file:

```
mattermost['gitlab_auth_endpoint'] =
    "http://gitlab.dockerbuch.info/oauth/authorize"
mattermost['gitlab_token_endpoint'] =
    "http://gitlab.dockerbuch.info/oauth/token"
mattermost['gitlab_user_api_endpoint'] =
    "http://gitlab.dockerbuch.info/api/v4/user"
```

Note that we don't use https here, but http. The reason for this is that both servers—GitLab and Mattermost—are running in the same Docker container where the DNS name for gitlab.dockerbuch.info doesn't resolve to the external, official IP address, but to the internal Docker IP address. Because GitLab is running there without the upstream Traefik proxy that manages the SSL certificates, we have to use unencrypted communication via http. In terms of security, this is irrelevant because the connection doesn't leave the Docker container at all. After restarting the GitLab container, the SSO button on the Mattermost login screen works without a problem (see Figure 16.12).

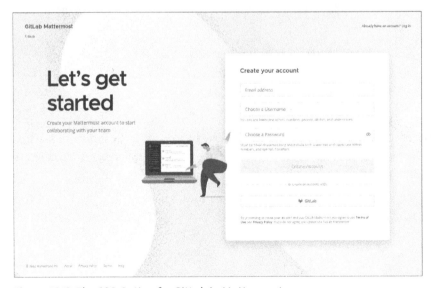

Figure 16.12 The SSO Option for GitLab in Mattermost

16.11.1 Connecting to GitLab

The connection between Mattermost and GitLab refers to two areas:

- Incoming webhooks
- Slash commands

Via incoming webhooks, notifications from GitLab can be displayed directly in a Mattermost channel (see Figure 16.13). These notifications include the following:

- Git push
- Changes to tickets
- Status change of a CI/CD pipeline
- Changes in the wiki

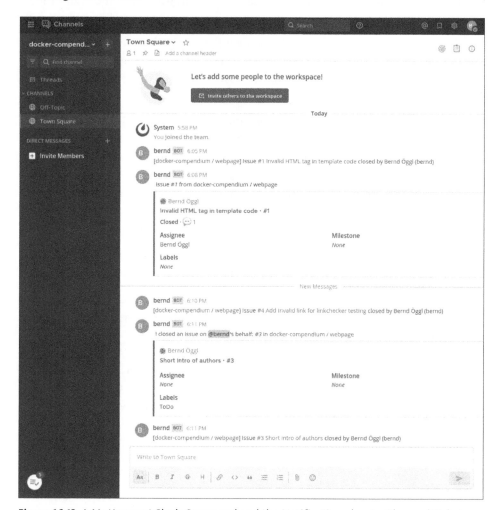

Figure 16.13 A Mattermost Slash Command and the Notification about a Changed Ticket

Slash commands, on the other hand, let you actively start a GitLab action in the Mattermost system. All you need to do is start a message with a *slash* and use the corresponding keyword. The actions you can perform include searching for tickets, viewing tickets, or creating new tickets. You can also start the deploy operation of a CD pipeline, but we won't describe that any further here.

To enable viewing GitLab notifications, you need to open the **Settings** menu in Mattermost, and select the **Integrations** item. There you should create an **Incoming Webhook** named **GitLab** and a **Town Square Channel**. Mattermost will then show you a URL that you need to enter in GitLab as a webhook URL.

To do this, open the **Admin Area** in GitLab, and look for the **Mattermost Notifications** entry under **Settings Integrations**. At the bottom of that page, you need to fill in the **Webhook** text box with the URL you just mentioned. This will enable the notifications.

Unlike notifications, which can be set up for the entire GitLab instance, slash commands refer to a project. To enable them, open the **Integrations** item in the **Settings** menu in your GitLab project, and select **Mattermost Slash Commands** from the list. In the dialog that opens, click the **Add to Mattermost** button, and the integration is almost done.

For our Docker setup, you need to make one more adjustment: GitLab has entered the settings correctly in the Mattermost configuration, but when the Mattermost server tries to reach the GitLab server with the address *https://gitlab.dockerbuch.info*, the connection fails. As with the SSO configuration described earlier, the two servers communicate here in the container and not via the upstream Traefik proxy server. For this reason, you need to edit the entry in the Mattermost settings under **Integrations** at the **Slash Commands** item and change the https address to http (see Figure 16.14).

The first time you call a slash command in Mattermost, you'll be prompted to grant permission for this action. Once you've confirmed that, Mattermost and GitLab communicate via the web API.

App and Desktop Client

Mattermost provides a well-designed web interface, but there's also an app for cell phones with Android or iOS available in the corresponding stores. In addition, there's a desktop application based on the Electron runtime for Windows, Mac, and Linux. To learn more about the mobile and desktop apps, go to the following web page:

https://about.mattermost.com/download

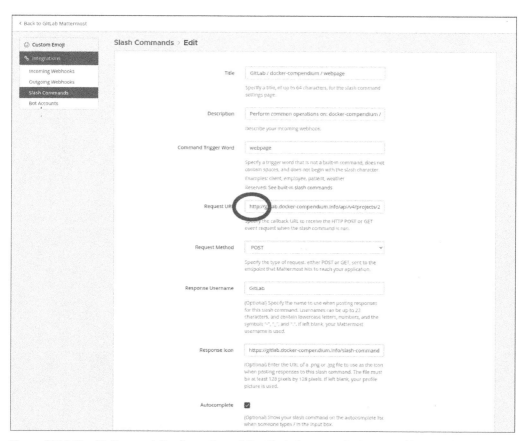

Figure 16.14 The Mattermost Configuration of the Slash Commands Generated by GitLab

16

Chapter 17
Continuous Integration and Continuous Delivery

Continuous integration (CI) and *continuous delivery* (CD) are two concepts often described in conjunction with the DevOps model. *DevOps* stands for a modern workflow in which the development team and the operations team no longer operate separately and one and the same person is often responsible for both areas.

CI describes a way of working in which developers check in even small changes to code into a central repository. CI is intended to prevent major problems when merging disparate pieces of code.

CD describes the continuation of this technique when a new version is automatically deployed following successful tests (see Figure 17.1).

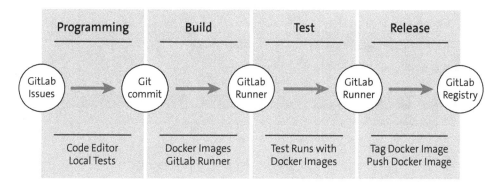

Figure 17.1 CI or CD Pipeline

Anyone who has worked on projects with a functioning CI/CD pipeline probably wouldn't want to miss this feature. The automatic tests with the subsequent release provide additional security during development.

GitLab as a Prerequisite

In this chapter, we'll use an example to describe a CD pipeline with Docker. The control and execution of this pipeline is handled by GitLab, which we introduced in detail in Chapter 16. For a better understanding of the processes, we recommend you read that chapter first, if you haven't done so yet.

As in Chapter 16, the prerequisite here is that you already have experience with the Git version management tool.

17.1 The dockerbuch.info Website with gohugo.io

As a sample project for CI/CD, we'll now describe how we implemented the website for the book and processed it in a CD pipeline. For the predominantly static content of the *https://dockerbuch.info* website, we didn't want to use a content management system with a database and programming language. A static website generator was sufficient and even has security advantages because SQL injections or attacks on the program framework simply don't occur.

The workflow is as follows:

1. Adding/modifying the Markdown file, live preview in the browser
2. Checking in changes to Git
3. CI pipeline launches (see Figure 17.2):
   - Production build of the website
   - Docker image of the website
   - Test 1: All links on the website checked
   - Test 2: HTML checked for validity
   - Tidying up
   - The Docker image marked as the new *latest* version
4. Manual deployment of the new Docker image

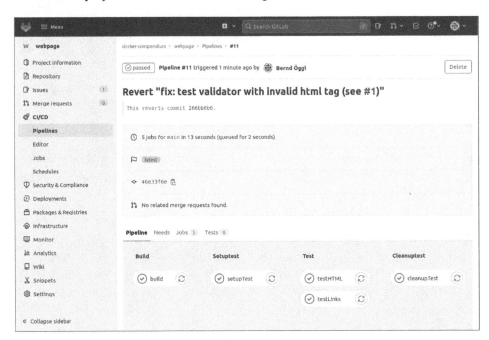

Figure 17.2 A Successful CI Pipeline in GitLab

For the static website generator, we use Hugo, a freely available program written in the Go programming language that generates a structure of HTML pages with navigation and menus based on the Markdown syntax. Because we also wrote this book in Markdown syntax, this format seemed very appropriate.

17.1.1   Running Hugo as a Docker Container

The easiest way to obtain Hugo is to download it from GitHub:

https://github.com/gohugoio/hugo/releases

Hugo is provided as a *static binary*, which means that all necessary libraries are already included in the executable file (about 17 MB). All you have to do is unpack the archive and copy the executable file to a folder in your search path.

However, you can also build a Docker image for Hugo. A variant based on Alpine Linux is only slightly larger than the original:

```
# File: cicd/hugo/Dockerfile (docbuc/hugo)
FROM alpine:3.14
ENV HUGO_VERSION=0.85.0
WORKDIR /tmp
RUN wget https://github.com/gohugoio/hugo/releases/download/v$HU
GO_VERSION/hugo_${HUGO_VERSION}_Linux-64bit.tar.gz \
  -O /tmp/hugo.tar.gz && \
  tar xf /tmp/hugo.tar.gz && \
  mv /tmp/hugo /usr/local/bin && \
  rm /tmp/hugo.tar.gz
WORKDIR /src
EXPOSE 1313
ENTRYPOINT ["hugo"]
```

If you want to upgrade to a new version of Hugo, you only need to adjust the environment variable, HUGO_VERSION.

> **Note**
>
> The URL for the RUN wget statement must be written in one line and has been spread across two lines here only for space reasons.)

By downloading, unpacking, and removing the archive in one layer (RUN), the resulting image consumes only 21 MB:

```
docker build -t docbuc/hugo .
docker run --rm docbuc/hugo version
  hugo v0.85.0-724D5DB5 linux/amd64 BuildDate=2021-07-05T1...
```

Because Hugo creates and reads files on your hard drive, it's best to use the Docker container with a bind mount volume (-v option) for the current directory:

```
docker run --rm -v ${PWD}:/src docbuc/hugo
```

Unfortunately, the application becomes a bit more complex if you want to use Hugo in the Docker container. Because the container runs as the root user, the files created in the local folder also belong to root. For this reason, you can't edit these files locally as an ordinary user. One possible workaround is to start docker with your own user ID (UID) and group ID (GID):

```
docker run --rm -v ${PWD}:/src -u $UID:$GID \
  docbuc/hugo version
```

Another stumbling block appears as soon as you start Hugo's extremely useful developer server. Here, you need to start Hugo with the bind address 0.0.0.0, as otherwise the server would be limited to localhost and only accessible within the container. You also need to add the port redirection from the container to the host (option -p 1313:1313). The complete call for the server looks like the following:

```
docker run --rm -v ${PWD}:/src -u $UID:$GID \
  -p 1313:1313 docbuc/hugo server --bind 0.0.0.0
```

For daily use, it makes sense to create an alias here so that you don't always have to type the long command line. And for all our love of Docker, using Hugo's static binary is arguably a bit more straightforward.

17.1.2   Hugo Quick Start

You may have already noticed that we're big friends of the command line. This is where it comes in handy that Hugo can also be controlled by commands. With just a few commands, you can create a new web page. To do this, you need to get started in a new directory. Let's call it webpage. The following procedure roughly corresponds to the instructions from *http://gohugo.io/getting-started/quick-start*:

```
hugo new site dockerbuch.info
  Congratulations! Your new Hugo site is created in
  /src/dockerbuch.info.

  ...
cd dockerbuch.info
cd themes && git clone \
  https://github.com/alanorth/hugo-theme-bootstrap4-blog.git
rm -rf hugo-theme-bootstrap4-blog/.git
cd ..
echo 'theme = "hugo-theme-bootstrap4-blog"' >> config.toml
hugo -D server
```

Hugo creates a directory with the name of the new website, here: *dockerbuch.info*. Change to the directory, and initialize a new Git repository there. (The entire website is stored in a Git repository.)

For Hugo to work, you must install a graphical template (theme). The *bootstrap4-blog* theme is based on the well-known Bootstrap library and provides good readability and a responsive design. Then remove the *.git/* directory in the repository you just downloaded. This way, changes to the theme you might implement later can be saved more easily to your Git repository.

Finally, we save the theme in the *config.toml* file, the central configuration file for the website. The Hugo development team has chosen TOML as the default format for configuration settings, but you can also use YAML Ain't Markup Language (YAML) or JavaScript Object Notation (JSON).

TOML vs. YAML vs. JSON

The TOML file format used here works very similar to the already known YAML format. A short overview of the differences between the two data formats and to JSON can be found here:

https://gohugohq.com/howto/toml-json-yaml-comparison

Calling `hugo -D server` starts the developer server with the option to also display content marked as *draft*. Now open your web browser with the URL *http://localhost:1313*. You should then see the home page of your web presence (see Figure 17.3).

Change the title of the website, and set the `baseUrl` to the value "/" in the *config.toml* file. After that, you need to add one more new post:

```
hugo new posts/first-post.md
```

This creates the *content/posts/first-post.md* file, which contains the following headers (with your current date, of course):

```
---
title: "First Post"
date: 2019-11-19T15:26:27+01:00
draft: true
---
```

Now when you make changes to the file and save them, your browser will automatically update and you'll see the new content. We won't go further into how Hugo works here. Just one more thing if you're interested in Hugo: many themes, like the bootstrap4-blog used here, include a sample page. A look into the *config.toml* file contained there usually makes it much easier to get started.

17

Figure 17.3 An Empty Website Created with Hugo and the bootstrap4-blog Theme

Hugo Themes

If you're interested in Hugo and its graphical design capabilities, we recommend you try out different themes of Hugo:

https://themes.gohugo.io

We still need the Git repository to trigger the CI pipeline in GitLab. Later you'll integrate it into a GitLab project. For this purpose, you want to change to the *webpage* directory; there you should see the subfolder created for you by Hugo.

```
git init
git add .
git commit -m "Website created with Hugo and the theme bootstrap4-blog".
```

These three commands enable you to first initialize a new Git repository, then add all files and all folders in the current directory, and save the first commit. We're going to create the connection to GitLab later.

17.2   Docker Images for the CI/CD Pipeline

Following the Docker philosophy of "one container for one job," we use multiple Docker images in the CI/CD pipeline:

- Web server image with the finished dockerbuch website
- Link checker image for testing the linked documents
- HTML validator image to test whether the HTML code conforms to the specification

17.2.1   Web Server Docker Image

Our goal is to create a complete container with web server and all needed files that is executable without any dependencies. We derive the Docker image required for this from the Nginx web server that will provide the HTML files:

```
# File: cicd/webpage/Dockerfile
FROM alpine:3.14 AS build
ENV HUGO_VERSION=0.85.0
WORKDIR /tmp
RUN wget https://github.com/gohugoio/hugo/releases/download/v$HU
GO_VERSION/hugo_${HUGO_VERSION}_Linux-64bit.tar.gz \
  -O /tmp/hugo.tar.gz && \
  tar xf /tmp/hugo.tar.gz && \
  mv /tmp/hugo /usr/local/bin && \
  rm /tmp/hugo.tar.gz
WORKDIR /src
COPY dockerbuch.info/ /src/
RUN hugo

FROM nginx:1-alpine
COPY --from=build /src/public/ /usr/share/nginx/html/
VOLUME ["/usr/share/nginx/html/"]
```

We also use the technique of multistage builds in the *Dockerfile*, which you already know. In the first step, we create the *developer image* that contains a current Hugo version and can run the developer server when creating the web pages. This part is largely similar to the image from the first section of this chapter. In the end, the source code of the web page (the Markdown files and the theme) gets copied into the image and translated into the finished web page by calling hugo.

The second section in the *Dockerfile* builds on the Alpine variant of the nginx image and copies the previously translated web page to the location in the file system where Nginx looks for the HTML files in the default configuration. This means your entire website has been packaged and is ready to run in a Docker container.

The final VOLUME statement allows for an easy backup of the entire site if needed. Although we can always regenerate the content from the Git repository, backing up the generated content won't do any harm either—better safe than sorry.

17.2.2   Link Checker

The first test for the website checks if all links are valid. For this purpose, we use the linkchecker program from the Debian distribution. You should now save the *Dockerfile* to a subfolder in the *webpage* directory and name this folder *linkchecker*. The *Dockerfile* itself is structured very clearly:

```
# File: cicd/webpage/linkchecker/Dockerfile (docbuc/linkchecker)
FROM debian:buster

RUN apt-get update && apt-get install -y \
      linkchecker \
    && rm -rf /var/lib/apt/lists/*
RUN useradd -ms /bin/bash linkchecker
USER linkchecker
WORKDIR /home/linkchecker
ENTRYPOINT ["linkchecker"]
CMD ["-h"]
```

To avoid running the container as root user, we first create a new user named linkchecker and then set the working directory (*WORKDIR*) to the newly created home
directory of this user. The combination of ENTRYPOINT and CMD causes the image to output the help for the program when started without parameters:

```
docker build -t linkchecker linkchecker/ && \
    docker run linkchecker
  Sending build context to Docker daemon  2.048kB
  Step 1/7 : FROM debian:buster
  [...]
  Step 7/7 : CMD ["-h"]
   ---> Running in 6cc0c3741da0
  Removing intermediate container 6cc0c3741da0
   ---> a4db81449f89
  Successfully built a4db81449f89
  Successfully tagged linkchecker:latest
  usage: linkchecker [-h] [-f FILENAME] [-t NUMBER] [-V] [--li...
```

Now this Docker image has been completely prepared. We'll use it later in the CI pipeline.

17.2.3   HTML Validator

Another test is supposed to make sure that the HTML syntax is correct everywhere by
using the HTML validator, which is available for download on GitHub. The code is programmed in Java and requires the Java runtime, which is why we use the OpenJDK
image as a basis:

```
# File: cicd/webpage/validator/Dockerfile (docbuc/validator)
FROM openjdk:13-alpine
ENV VALIDATOR_VERSION=18.11.5
WORKDIR /src
```

```
RUN wget "https://github.com/validator/validator/releases/\
download/$VALIDATOR_VERSION/vnu.jar_$VALIDATOR_VERSION.zip" \
  -O /src/vnu.jar.zip \
  && unzip /src/vnu.jar.zip \
  && rm /src/vnu.jar.zip

EXPOSE 8888
RUN adduser -S validator
USER validator
WORKDIR /home/validator
ENTRYPOINT ["java", "-jar", "/src/dist/vnu.jar" ]
CMD ["--help"]
```

You should also save this *Dockerfile* in a subfolder below the *webpage* directory (we use validator). As with the link checker image, we create a new user; note that in Alpine Linux, the command isn't called useradd but adduser. Again, the combination of ENTRY-POINT and CMD helps you to open the validator help when called. Create the image, and launch a container from it:

```
docker build -t validator .
```

```
  Sending build context to Docker daemon  2.048kB
  Step 1/10 : FROM openjdk:16-alpine
   ---> 2aa8569968b8
  Step 2/10 : ENV VALIDATOR_VERSION=20.6.30
  ...
  Step 10/10 : CMD ["--help"]
   ---> Running in a7947e66d5d6
  Removing intermediate container a7947e66d5d6
   ---> 6eccc2ced7c3
  Successfully built 6eccc2ced7c3
  Successfully tagged validator:latest
```

```
docker run --rm validator
```

```
  # The Nu Html Checker (v.Nu) [![Chat room][1]][2] [![Downlo...
   [1]: https://goo.gl/1kHqwI
   [2]: https://gitter.im/validator/validator
   [3]: https://goo.gl/3PC2Qn
   [4]: https://github.com/validator/validator/releases/latest
  The Nu Html Checker (v.Nu) helps you [catch unintended mista...
  [...]
```

17.3   The CI/CD Pipeline

GitLab evaluates the contents of the *.gitlab-ci.yml* file in the root directory of a project to build the instructions for the CI pipeline. This YAML file contains the description of the jobs to be executed within the pipeline. The names of the jobs can be freely chosen, except for the following reserved words:

- image
- services
- stages
- types
- before_script
- after_script
- variables
- cache

The structure of the *.gitlab-ci.yml* file and the definition of the individual jobs depend on which GitLab Runner (see Chapter 16, Section 16.10) is running the process. We'll show you two variants next, the first running with the shell runner and the second with the Docker runner.

17.3.1   CI/CD with the GitLab Shell Runner

As with *Dockerfiles* in the previous sections, it's recommended to work with variables here as well. If you move to another system, only the corresponding variables must then be adjusted.

```
# File: cicd/webpage/.gitlab-ci.yml
variables:
  REGISTRY: registry.dockerbuch.info
  TEST_IMAGE: $REGISTRY/dockerbuch/webpage:$CI_COMMIT_REF_NAME
  TEST_NETWORK: testnet
  RELEASE_IMAGE: $REGISTRY/dockerbuch/webpage:latest
  TEST_CONTAINER_NAME: dockerbuch
  LINK_CHECKER: $REGISTRY/dockerbuch/webpage/linkchecker
  VALIDATOR: $REGISTRY/dockerbuch/webpage/validator
```

Stages define the flow of the pipeline. One or more jobs can be assigned to each stage. The next entry in line won't be executed until the previous one was successful. By grouping multiple jobs in a stage, tests can run in parallel (refer to Figure 17.2):

```
# File: cicd/webpage/.gitlab-ci.yml (continued)
stages:
  - build
```

```
    - setupTest
    - test
    - cleanupTest
    - release

before_script:
    - docker login -u gitlab-ci-token -p $CI_JOB_TOKEN $REGISTRY
```

The before_script gets executed before all jobs. In this case, we log in to the Docker registry (docker login) using the special user gitlab-ci-token with the password from the $CI_JOB_TOKEN variable. GitLab creates this user specifically for this purpose and makes the variable available in the test environment.

In the build section, we create the required Docker images and copy them to the registry:

```
# File: cicd/webpage/.gitlab-ci.yml (continued)
build:
  stage: build
  script:
    - docker build -t $TEST_IMAGE .
    - docker push $TEST_IMAGE
    - docker build -t $LINK_CHECKER linkchecker/
    - docker push $LINK_CHECKER
    - docker build -t $VALIDATOR validator/
    - docker push $VALIDATOR
```

The $TEST_IMAGE contains the Nginx server, Hugo, and HTML code; $LINK_CHECKER and $VALIDATOR contain the images just described for testing. All of them are newly created and placed in the private Docker registry (push). In the next step, setupTest, we obtain the image to be tested from the registry, create our own network, and start the Nginx container:

```
# File: cicd/webpage/.gitlab-ci.yml (continued)
setupTest:
  stage: setupTest
  script:
    - docker pull $TEST_IMAGE
    - docker network create $TEST_NETWORK
    - docker run -d --network $TEST_NETWORK
        --name $TEST_CONTAINER_NAME $TEST_IMAGE
```

At this point, the web server with the updated website is running in the test environment. The link checker, which is started in the testLinks job, accesses the web page via HTTP and tries to validate all links:

```
# File: cicd/webpage/.gitlab-ci.yml (continued)
testLinks:
  stage: test
  script:
    - docker ps
    - docker run --rm --network $TEST_NETWORK $LINK_CHECKER
        http://$TEST_CONTAINER_NAME/ --check-extern
```

It's important that this container also runs in the specially created network because only then can the name resolution to the $TEST_CONTAINER_NAME work. You can follow the result of the test in the browser during a test run, but you can also call it up later at any time (see Figure 17.4).

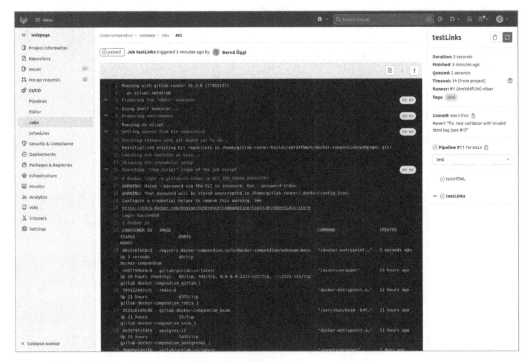

Figure 17.4 Result of the Link Checker Test

The HTML test accesses and crawls the files on the web server:

```
# File: cicd/webpage/.gitlab-ci.yml (continued)
testHTML:
  stage: test
  script:
    - docker run --rm --volumes-from $TEST_CONTAINER_NAME
        $VALIDATOR --verbose --skip-non-html
        /usr/share/nginx/html/
```

Because the testHTML and testLinks jobs are in the same stage, they run concurrently (refer to Figure 17.2). In the cleanupTest section, the test container and the test network are deleted:

```
# File: cicd/webpage/.gitlab-ci.yml (continued)
cleanupTest:
  stage: cleanupTest
  script:
    - docker stop $TEST_CONTAINER_NAME
        && docker rm $TEST_CONTAINER_NAME
    - docker network rm $TEST_NETWORK
  when: always
```

The preceding section from the *.gitlab-ci.yml* file shows one more special feature: the when: always setting indicates that this job should be executed even if previously running jobs haven't been successful. So we definitely want to clean up the test environment.

The final step involves the release job. Here the successfully tested image is tagged with the appropriate tag (in this case, latest) and copied to the registry. The special aspect about this job is that it won't be executed until the commit has been checked in on the master branch of the Git repository.

```
# File: webpage/.gitlab-ci.yml (continued)
release:
  stage: release
  script:
    - docker pull $TEST_IMAGE
    - docker tag $TEST_IMAGE $RELEASE_IMAGE
    - docker push $RELEASE_IMAGE
  only:
    - master
```

Your setup is now complete, and it's time for the first tests. To do this, you must first connect the Git repository you created in Section 17.1 to a new project in your GitLab instance. For this purpose, GitLab provides the instructions on the new blank project page. Currently, your project directory should look something like this (the entries in the *.git* directory have been shortened):

```
|-- dockerbuch.info
|   |-- archetypes
|   |-- config.toml
|   |-- content
|   |-- .gitignore
|   `-- themes
```

```
|-- docker-compose.yml
|-- Dockerfile
|-- .git
|    |-- [...]
|-- .gitlab-ci.yml
|-- hugo
|    `-- Dockerfile
|-- linkchecker
|    `-- Dockerfile
`-- validator
     `-- Dockerfile
```

To connect the new GitLab project to the existing directory, you need to run the following commands in the root directory:

```
git remote add origin \
  https://gitlab.dockerbuch.info/dockerbuch/webpage.git
git push -u origin master
```

The URL for the remote repository will of course be different for you. If you've set everything correctly, the CI/CD pipeline should start after the successful push. Open the **CI/CD** menu item in your GitLab project, and follow the process.

Troubleshooting

It's not uncommon for the pipeline to fail on the first few attempts. There are many components involved, and one small mistake is enough to stop the execution.

Most of the time, you'll find enough hints in the web interface regarding why an error occurred. For bugs that aren't related to the source code, you also have the option in the interface to restart a test without Git commit and Git push.

17.3.2   Testing the Pipeline

In the following section, we want to include an erroneous HTML construct in the website template to verify that the HTML validator detects the error. A simple HTML error is the incorrect nesting of tags. For example, the <p> tag mustn't appear inside the <span> tag, but we'll now insert exactly that into the template.

To do this, you need to edit the *layouts/_default/single.html* file in the theme directory (*themes/hugo-theme-bootstrap4-blog*), and add the following line wherever you like:

```
<span>Hello <p>World</p></span>
```

Then save, commit, and push the changes, which will start the CI pipeline. Because the test for valid HTML will now fail (error: element "p" not allowed as child of element "span"), the pipeline will terminate. The CleanupTest step will still be executed because it contains the entry when: always (see Figure 17.5).

If the test container and the test network weren't deleted, an error would occur in the setupTest job during the next pipeline run because it wasn't possible to create the network with the same name.

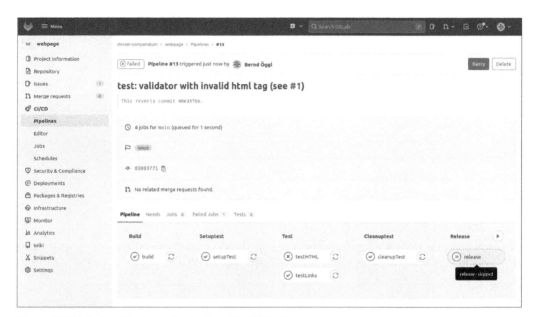

Figure 17.5 Failed CI Pipeline with the Invalid HTML Structure

17.3.3 CI with the GitLab Docker Runner

If you use a docker type GitLab Runner, the possible jobs in the CI pipeline will change. While the shell runner executes commands directly on the runner computer, the Docker runner runs everything inside a Docker container. You need to specify the associated Docker image in the *.gitlab-ci.yml* file:

```
# File: cicd/webpage/.gitlab-ci.yml (at git-branch docker-ci)
image:
  name: "registry.dockerbuch.info/dockerbuch/webpage/testimage"
  entrypoint: [""]
```

If you want to try the Docker runner example with your existing files, you can just create a branch in the Git repository, as follows:

```
git checkout -b docker-ci
```

This creates the new docker-ci branch after which Git immediately moves to it.

For our tests, we'll build our own Docker image that has the link checker as well as the validator and Hugo on board. We'll store the image named `testimage` in the private Docker registry in GitLab at the `webpage` project.

The *Dockerfile* for the `testimage` looks like this (the download links for `curl` are located in separate lines):

```
# File: webpage/testimage/Dockerfile
FROM debian:buster
ENV VALIDATOR_VERSION=20.6.30
ENV HUGO_VERSION=0.85.0

RUN apt-get update && apt-get -y install \
    curl \
    openjdk-11-jre \
    unzip \
    linkchecker \
    && rm -rf /var/lib/apt/lists/*

WORKDIR /tmp
RUN curl -SL https://github.com/gohugoio/hugo/releases/download/
v$HUGO_VERSION/hugo_${HUGO_VERSION}_Linux-64bit.tar.gz \
  | tar xzC /tmp && \
  mv /tmp/hugo /usr/local/bin

RUN curl -SL https://github.com/validator/validator/releases/dow
nload/$VALIDATOR_VERSION/vnu.jar_$VALIDATOR_VERSION.zip \
  -o /tmp/vnu.jar.zip \
  && unzip -d /opt /tmp/vnu.jar.zip \
  && rm /tmp/vnu.jar.zip
RUN useradd -ms /bin/bash linkchecker
USER linkchecker
WORKDIR /home/linkchecker
ENTRYPOINT ["/bin/bash"]
```

We use the current Debian version as a base image and then install a Java runtime (for the HTML validator), the link checker, and `curl` and `unzip` to download and extract the software, respectively.

Again, the *.gitlab-ci.yml* file specifies which tests will run inside the container:

```
# File: cicd/webpage/.gitlab-ci.yml (docker-ci, continued)
stages:
  - test
```

```
before_script:
  - cd dockerbuch.info && hugo -d dockerbuch-out

testHTML:
  stage: test
  tags:
    - validator
    - dockerRunner
  script:
    - pwd
    - /usr/bin/java -jar /opt/dist/vnu.jar
        dockerbuch-out/index.html

testLinks:
  stage: test
  services:
    - name: registry.dockerbuch.info/dockerbuch/webpage/testweb
      alias: webserver
tags:
  - dockerRunner
script:
  - linkchecker http://webserver/
```

Unlike the shell runner, the configuration file now contains only one stage, namely, the test runs. As we already described in Chapter 16, Section 16.10, the GitLab Docker executor can't call the docker program because the entire execution takes place inside a container. For this reason, there's no way to build the final Docker image. The pipeline presented here covers only the CI part and no longer the delivery part.

In the before_script, Hugo is started in the *dockerbuch.info* folder, and the finished website is saved in the *dockerbuch-out* subfolder. This works because we're in the project folder while the pipeline is running. In the testHTML job, we display this *pwd* directory. *pwd* stands for *print working directory* and is a part of the standard Unix shell. The call is only for information about where the script is executed. The second entry in the script section then starts the HTML validator for the generated website under dockerbuch-out.

The testLinks job has one more extension compared to the testHTML job. The services section can list one or more Docker images that are available during job execution. For example, for integration tests of more complex programs, a database can be started here that temporarily stores data required for the test execution. In our example, we start a container with the Nginx web server that serves the generated website. We derive the *Dockerfile* for this from the official Nginx image. Then we copy an appropriate configuration file into the image:

```
FROM nginx:1
COPY default.conf /etc/nginx/conf.d/
```

In the *default.conf* file, only the line with the root statement was changed from the default configuration:

```
location / {
 root /builds/dockerbuch/webpage/dockerbuch.info/dockerbuch-out;
 index  index.html index.htm;
}
```

Just like the default image where the pipeline is run, all services have the project directory mounted below the */builds* folder. The root directory for the Nginx server just needs to be set to the correct path, and the website is accessible within the pipeline. Because the host name within the Docker network is derived from the name of the image, which in our case is a rather long name, we also assign the alias name webserver for the service in the service section. This makes the call linkchecker http://webserver/ work with the correct name resolution (see Figure 17.6).

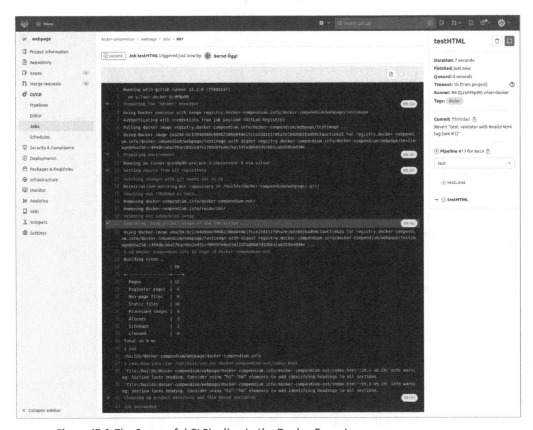

Figure 17.6 The Successful CI Pipeline in the Docker Executor

17.3.4 CI/CD with Kubernetes in the Google Cloud

The Kubernetes runner is very useful if your CI/CD pipeline runs multiple times in parallel. First, each runner gets a clean build environment, and second, the Google Kubernetes Engine (GKE) can automatically scale to quickly process the pipelines.

As in Chapter 16, Section 16.10, we'll use the Kubernetes runner in the GKE (see Figure 17.7). The runner runs in Privileged Mode, which involves the aforementioned security issues, but we can use the Docker-in-Docker image here and map the entire CI/CD pipeline.

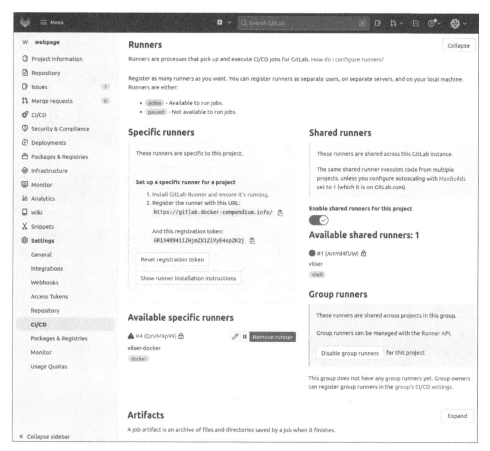

Figure 17.7 The Kubernetes Runner in the Web Page Project

Again, you need to create a new branch in your Git repository; we'll call it kubernetes-runner. Because the flow of the pipeline will be very similar to the shell runner, it's best to derive the branch from the master:

```
git checkout master
git checkout -b kubernetes-runner
```

For the Docker-in-Docker setup to work, you need to make the following changes to the *.gitlab-ci.yml* file:

```
# File: cicd/webpage/.gitlab-ci.yml (branch kubernetes-runner)
variables:
  REGISTRY: registry.dockerbuch.info
  [...]
  DOCKER_DRIVER: overlay
  DOCKER_HOST: tcp://localhost:2375

image: docker:dind
services:
  - docker:dind
```

Unlike the shell runner, the Kubernetes runner runs each job in a container. For this to work, you must specify in the configuration file from which image the container is derived. For the Docker-in-Docker image, this must also be specified as a service, and the two variables DOCKER_DRIVER and DOCKER_HOST must be defined in the variables section.

By being able to start the docker program in the container, the rest of the process should remain the same as with the shell runner; unfortunately, that doesn't quite work. The configuration with the shell runner had a job that started the test environment (the web server with the website), which the other jobs had access to. Because the Kubernetes runner starts containers in new environments, you need to set up the test environment for each job. This means that the jobs setupTest and cleanupTest are irrelevant.

```
# File: cicd/webpage/.gitlab-ci.yml (kubernetes-runner)
[...]
testLinks:
  stage: test
  tags:
    - kubernetes
  script:
    - docker network create $TEST_NETWORK
    - docker run -d --name $TEST_CONTAINER_NAME
        --network $TEST_NETWORK $TEST_IMAGE
    - docker run --rm --network $TEST_NETWORK $LINK_CHECKER
        --check-extern http://$TEST_CONTAINER_NAME/
testHTML:
  stage: test
  tags:
    - kubernetes
```

```
  script:
    - docker run -d --name $TEST_CONTAINER_NAME $TEST_IMAGE
    - docker run --volumes-from $TEST_CONTAINER_NAME $VALIDATOR
        --rm --errors-only --skip-non-html /usr/share/nginx/html/
[...]
```

Jobs are assigned the kubernetes tag, which causes them to run only one runner that is either configured for all jobs or has that very tag. GitLab's auto-generated Kubernetes runner has this tag set (see Figure 17.7).

In the testLinks job, a Docker network is created first; then both containers (the web server and the link checker) are started in this network. This gives the link checker access to the web server via $TEST_CONTAINER_NAME.

The testHTML job also starts the test container but only to access the volume where the generated HTML files are located. Then the HTML validator starts and examines these files for any invalid HTML syntax.

17

Chapter 18
Security

Aside from the application development and deployment benefits, when used correctly, containers provide better protection against attacks than applications that don't run in containers:

- On the one hand, depending on the platform or distribution, security measures are active by default that prevent certain attacks when containers are executed. You can find more information on this in Section 18.7 and Section 18.8.

- On the other hand, containers are separated from the operating system by *namespaces*. This compartmentalization can be further enhanced by *user namespaces* (Section 18.5).

Because Docker covers the range from operating systems to applications, we can only scratch the surface in this chapter without going into greater detail. However, we'd like to introduce you to Docker's basic security mechanisms and share some *best practices*. In this context, we'll focus on Linux as a Docker host because Linux is the most widely used platform in terms of deployment (irrespective of the operating system you're developing on).

> **Additional Information**
>
> If you want to dig deeper into container security, we recommend Jessie Frazelle's blog at *https://blog.jessfraz.com*. She was instrumental in introducing secure computing mode and AppArmor support as standard security measures in Docker.

18.1 Software Installation

Independently of Docker, we want to spend a little time talking about installing external programs in advance because we describe such installations several times in this book. In the container environment, the Go programming language is extremely popular. Programs in this language can be easily compiled for different platforms and distributed as a statically linked binary. `kubectl`, `helm`, and `hcloud` arae such examples. In terms of installation, it's sufficient to download the program with `curl`, make it executable (on Linux and macOS), and copy it to the search path.

Unlike installing programs with your operating system's package manager, there's no digital signature verification here. Thus, you can't tell if the binary on the server has been exchanged by an attacker. Your trust in the program is based on the identity of the web server from which you download the program using `curl`. This identity is confirmed by the Secure Sockets Layer (SSL) certificate. So, you should never use the -k or --insecure options of curl for such a download because that would bypass the certificate verification.

The same applies to the installation of programs using the following command:

```
# potentially dangerous!
curl -fsSL get.docker.com | sudo sh
```

The *https://get.docker.com* page provides a shell script that performs the Docker installation for different operating systems. This call is problematic in several respects: First, you don't explicitly connect to the SSL-secured server but connect unencrypted on port 80. The -L parameter of curl enables an automatic redirection, which in this case, really leads to the encrypted page *https://get.docker.com* and thus to the desired result. However, a man-in-the-middle attack would be very easy to carry out here because the first connection is unencrypted.

Another risk originates from downloading and running the script at the same time. A failure in the network connection during the download could lead to a very unpleasant situation. Just think of a construct like the following:

```
TEMPDIR="delete_me"
rm -rf $HOME/$TEMPDIR
```

If the network connection were to be terminated after the /, the command would only be rm -rf $HOME/, which wouldn't lead to the desired result. Admittedly, this is a somewhat contrived example, but you can see the problem. With a little more typing, however, the problem can be significantly mitigated:

```
curl https://get.docker.com/ -o docker-install.sh
# check if it's really the installation script:
vi docker-install.sh
chmod +x docker-install.sh
./docker-install.sh
```

18.2   Origin of Docker Images

All Docker images you see in this book can be derived from other images. This will save you a lot of work. Furthermore, in most cases, the images are maintained by the software developers themselves and are therefore optimized for the respective software.

Except for Chapter 16, we always use the official Docker image repository, Docker Hub, in this book. Docker Inc. provides this service for public images free of charge. Any registered user can upload images, which will then become available to all Docker users under the <username>/<image> identifier. There's no warranty whatsoever for these images. If a *Dockerfile* is publicly visible, it's a good idea to take a look at it. Without access to a *Dockerfile*, you should make sure to get the address to the image from a secure source.

As a registered user in Docker Hub with a paid subscription model, you have the option to have your own images automatically scanned for known security gaps (see Figure 18.1). Docker has outsourced this business to Snyk (*https://snyk.io*). Snyk isn't limited to scanning Docker images; you can also include your other projects from GitHub or GitLab there.

As of July 2021, we couldn't find any specific information on whether the official images in Docker Hub are automatically scanned for security issues. Official images are marked as *Official Repository* on Docker's website, and they aren't prefixed with a user name. On the Docker Hub website, you can recognize such images by the fact that they are preceded by an underscore in the URL; for example, the URL for the official Node.js image is *https://hub.docker.com/_/node*. Before Docker partnered with Snyk, these images were always scanned automatically.

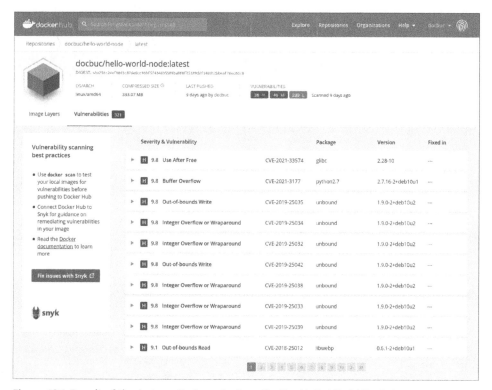

Figure 18.1 Result of the Automatic Security Scan for the Hello World Node Image

18.2.1   External Registries

Major IT service providers such as Google, Microsoft, and Amazon also offer container registries in their cloud portfolios. If you decide to use one of those platforms to run your containers, reaching for the respective registry certainly makes sense. Images have short transfer times and are billed to the existing account.

Security controls aren't yet as tightly integrated there as they are in Docker Hub for the official images. With Azure, you can enable the paid Azure Defender, which handles container image scanning, among other services.

Google has an integrated service that can currently search for security issues in images based on Ubuntu, Debian, Alpine Linux, and Red Hat. In Amazon's Elastic Container Registry, you also have the option to have Docker images scanned automatically. Amazon uses the open-source Clair scanner for this, which you can find on GitHub at *https://github.com/quay/clair*.

Another commercial provider of a container registry is Quay (*https://quay.io*). In the Enterprise Edition, your images are also automatically scanned for security issues, and the results are displayed in the web interface. The scanner even provides suggested solutions through package updates of the distribution (see Figure 18.2). Quay was developed as a registry for the container-optimized CoreOS operating system, which was acquired by Linux distributor Red Hat in early 2018.

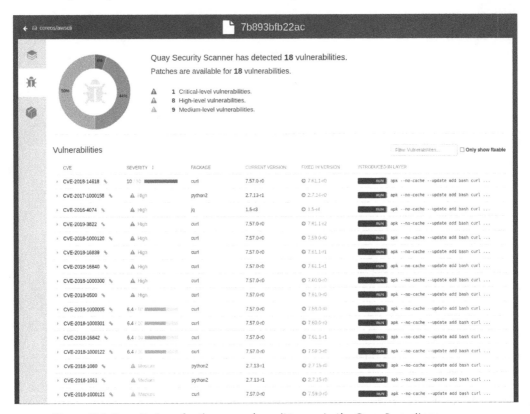

Figure 18.2 Security Scan for the coreos/awscli Image in the Quay Repository

Wherever you store your images, it's important that you can trust all the layers in your image. Automatic scanning in the registry definitely increases image security.

18.3   "root" in Docker Images

Administrator (root) access to Unix systems used to be very strictly regulated. *Regular* users always worked with limited rights, and changes to the system had to be requested from the administrator. From this time originates the rule that network ports below 1024 may only be opened by the root user. Users who connected to the server through one of these ports knew that the administrator had checked the application. The standard ports of all common servers (mail, web, FTP, etc.) are below this limit.

In software development, it has always been clear that a server service running under the root user ID constitutes a problem from a security point of view. For this reason, functions were built into the source code that relinquish root privileges after connecting to the privileged port and continue running under a different user ID.

You can check this very easily in a Docker container. To do this, start the Apache web server in a container and display the processes with the corresponding user ID:

```
docker run -d --name apache httpd:alpine
docker exec apache ps xau
PID   USER      TIME  COMMAND
    1 root       0:00 httpd -DFOREGROUND
    8 daemon     0:00 httpd -DFOREGROUND
    9 daemon     0:00 httpd -DFOREGROUND
   10 daemon     0:00 httpd -DFOREGROUND
   97 root       0:00 ps xau
```

As you can see, the process with process ID 1 runs as root user, while the other httpd processes run as daemon users.

18.3.1   Nginx Web Server without "root" Privileges

The Nginx web server also uses this technique:

```
docker run -d --name nginx nginx:alpine
docker exec nginx ps xau

PID   USER      TIME  COMMAND
   1  root       0:00 nginx: master process nginx -g daemon off;
   6  nginx      0:00 nginx: worker process
   7  root       0:00 ps xau
```

Here you can also see the user change: the *master* process runs as root with process ID 1, whereas the *worker* process runs under the nginx user ID. If you try to start the container as nginx user, you'll receive the error message Permission denied because the user doesn't have write permissions in the */var/cache/nginx* directory:

```
docker run -d --user=nginx --name nginx nginx:alpine
docker logs nginx

  2021/07/24 15:57:13 [emerg] 1#1: mkdir()
    "/var/cache/nginx/client_temp" failed (13: Permission denied)
  nginx: [emerg] mkdir() "/var/cache/nginx/client_temp" failed...
```

But that's not the only problem with write permissions in the system. When the server starts, a file with the process ID gets created in the */var/run* folder. A simple solution to these problems is to create the file and folder as root in your *Dockerfile*, and then change the permissions so that the file is owned by the nginx user. The *Dockerfile* may then look like the following:

```
FROM nginx:alpine
RUN touch /var/run/nginx.pid \
   && chown -R nginx:nginx /var/run/nginx.pid \
   && chown -R nginx:nginx /var/cache/nginx
```

However, although the write permission problem has been solved now, the container still won't start. The new error message reads:

```
docker run -d --name nginx docbuc/nginx:nonroot
docker logs nginx

  2021/07/24 16:17:16 [emerg] 1#1: bind() to 0.0.0.0:80 failed
    (13: Permission denied)
```

This is where the problem with privileged port 80 comes into play. But in the container, you usually don't need to use port 80 at all because there's another intermediate layer for access from the outside. If your container runs behind a reverse proxy setup, there'll be no problem anyway because you set internal port redirection in the proxy server. If you connect the container directly to the internet using the Docker daemon, you can specify the port assignment with the -p parameter when starting the container.

To start the Nginx server without root privileges on port 8080, you must change the listen entry in the Nginx configuration file:

```
# File: /etc/nginx/conf.d/default.conf (excerpt)
server {
    listen        8080;
```

With this, Nginx no longer tries to connect to the privileged port 80 at startup and thus doesn't need any root privileges. You still need to copy the modified configuration file to your new Nginx image. In addition, you can display the port used (EXPOSE) and specify the user under which the container is to be run (this way you can do without the --user parameter at startup). Here's the finished *Dockerfile*:

```
# File: security/nginx/Dockerfile (docbuc/nginx:nonroot)
FROM nginx:alpine

RUN touch /var/run/nginx.pid \
  && chown -R nginx:nginx /var/run/nginx.pid \
  && chown -R nginx:nginx /var/cache/nginx
COPY default.conf /etc/nginx/conf.d/
EXPOSE 8080
USER nginx
```

If you start a container from this image and call ps xau in it, all processes will run under the nginx user ID.

You've probably noticed it already: without root privileges, traditional Unix servers don't really work in the container without any tricks. For other servers, you'll need to make further adjustments (often this involves write permissions in subfolders of */var*).

18.4   The Docker Daemon

When you run the docker program in the command line, it contacts a Docker daemon. By default, communication is handled through Unix socket, /var/run/docker.sock; you can also use environment variable DOCKER_HOST to access a Docker daemon accessible over the network. The problem with the Docker daemon is that it has to run with root privileges. And here, of course, the alarm bells are ringing because a bug in the Docker daemon code can result in an attacker gaining root privileges on the host system.

Another problem that arises from this situation is that users who have access to the Docker daemon (i.e., those who are allowed to use Docker) have quasi-root privileges in the host system. Let's demonstrate this with a simple example. The */etc/shadow* file on a Linux system contains the encrypted passwords of the local user accounts. For security reasons, the file isn't readable for normal users:

```
cat /etc/shadow
```

```
  cat: /etc/shadow: Permission denied
```

With a Docker container, the same unprivileged user can read the file:

```
docker run -it --rm -v /:/host alpine cat /host/etc/shadow

  root:!:17779:0:99999:7:::
  daemon:*:17779:0:99999:7:::
  bin:*:17779:0:99999:7:::
  sys:*:17779:0:99999:7:::
  [...]
```

You simply need to mount the root directory of the host computer into the container and thus have root access to the entire file system. You could have also run rm -rf /host, but then your computer would have stopped working in no time. Of course, an attacker can use this trick not only to spy on your system but also to replace a program with a corrupted version or encrypt your hard drive.

As we described in Chapter 6, Section 6.6, it's a common practice to add your user account to the docker group. You can then start the docker program without the sudo call, which is very convenient for frequent calls. From a security point of view, however, this isn't recommendable and is acceptable at best for development computers. However, an attacker who wants to plant a piece of executable code on you doesn't need a password to become root on your system!

18.4.1   Rootless Docker

The problem of one service having full access to the entire system has now been addressed by the developers of Docker. After all, it was one of the big criticisms of Docker and arguably prompted the development of alternatives (see Appendix A), among other things.

Since Docker version 20.10, the *rootless mode* has been considered stable and can be installed very easily (more on this in Chapter 2). If you're interested in how this technique exactly works, you'll find more information in the next section.

18.5   User Namespaces

We also outlined the functionality of namespaces, the technology that separates containers from each other and from the host, in Chapter 6, Section 6.6. The *user namespaces* presented in this section go one step further.

User namespaces are especially recommended if you need to work as the root user in your containers. We've already pointed out in Section 18.3 how you can use the USER statement to avoid running the process in the container with root privileges. However, this approach isn't always possible. In such cases, thanks to user namespaces, you can still use root in the container; however, this user ID doesn't get converted to root on the host. Rootless Docker takes advantage of this very feature, mapping the `root` user in the container to an unprivileged user on the system.

18.5.1   Functionality

With user namespaces, the Linux kernel provides you with the ability to manage user IDs (UID, the numeric identifier of a user account) in a namespace independent of the host computer. Within the namespace (i.e., within the container in Docker), this doesn't change anything: `root` retains UID 0. However, if the `root` user in the container accesses a file mounted by the host, the access rights of an unknown user will be applied to the accessing user.

If you use rootless Docker, you don't need to bother about the other settings because the unprivileged Docker daemon handles these settings for you. If you want to switch a system-wide Docker installation to user namespaces, you have different options. If you installed Docker on Ubuntu Linux 21.04 using the installation script from *https://get.docker.com*, you can simply create the */etc/docker/daemon.json* file with the following content:

```
{
  "userns-remap": "default"
}
```

Then you must restart the Docker server with `systemctl restart docker`. Docker created the `dockremap` user on the host during the reboot. There's also an entry in the */etc/subuid* file for this user:

```
cat /etc/subuid
```

```
lxd:100000:65536
root:100000:65536
dockerbuch:165536:65536
dockremap:231072:65536
```

The file contains the user name, the start ID for user IDs in a container, and the number of possible users in the container. This means that `root` with UID 0 in the container is mapped to UID 231072 on the host. A user in the container with UID 1001 gets UID 232073 on the host. We then logged on to the host as user `dockerbuch` and started the program `top` in a container with Alpine Linux:

```
docker run -it --rm -v /:/host alpine top
```

The following listing of processes on the host shows the user ID, the process ID, and the command that was executed:

```
USER       PID COMMAND
  root       998 /usr/bin/containerd
  root     23615 /usr/bin/containerd-shim-runc-v2 --namespace ...
  231072   23642  \_ top
  [...]
  dockerb+ 21998        \_ bash
  dockerb+ 23582                \_ sudo docker run -it --rm -v /:/ho...
```

As you can see, the bash and the docker run commands run under user ID dockerbook. The user in the top command in the container is displayed only with the numeric UID 231072 because there's no equivalent on the host here (in */etc/passwd*, to be precise). The UID is calculated (as described earlier) from the entry in the */etc/subuid* file and the UID of the container user. In this case, it's 0 because the top program was started as root user.

The root user within the container can now no longer write or modify files in the host system:

```
docker run -it --rm -v /:/host alpine touch /host/abc.txt

/host/abc.txt: Permission denied
```

> **Limitations**
>
> The Docker documentation refers to user namespaces as an advanced feature, probably implying that not all features have been tested to the last detail with this configuration. For example, drivers for external storage media are mentioned, which can cause problems with user namespaces. In addition, the network mode --network=host doesn't work. Please refer to the Docker documentation for more configuration options for user namespaces:
>
> *https://docs.docker.com/engine/security/userns-remap*

18.6   Control Groups

Control groups (*cgroups*) have been an integral part of the Linux kernel for many years. They enable you to limit the resource consumption of processes. The security aspect here is to prevent a potential denial-of-service attack: Because a container has full access to the host computer's memory and CPU(s) by default, a single container can also utilize the computer to 100% capacity.

Let's take a look at a short example to demonstrate how easily cgroups work with Docker. For this purpose, you need to use the two Linux programs—stress and htop—and install them in a Docker image:

```
# File: security/cgroups/Dockerfile
FROM debian:buster
RUN apt-get update && apt-get install -y \
  stress \
  htop \
  && rm -rf /var/lib/apt/lists/*
CMD [ "stress" ]
```

The stress program allows you to easily create load on your system, whether for CPU, I/O, or memory. Create the image and run it with the CPU load parameter:

```
docker build -t docbuc/stress .
docker run --rm docbuc/stress stress -t 10s --cpu 8
```

The stress test takes 10 seconds and loads all 8 CPUs in our test device to 100%. Then, open a second console window and start the htop program, which displays the load on your computer:

```
docker run -it --rm docbuc/stress htop
```

Because htop also runs in a container, only one process gets displayed, but the CPU usage is correctly represented by all CPUs. Now start the stress container with the cgroups restriction to 2.5 CPUs (--cpus=2.5), and you'll see that the utilization on all CPUs increases to about one-third (see Figure 18.3).

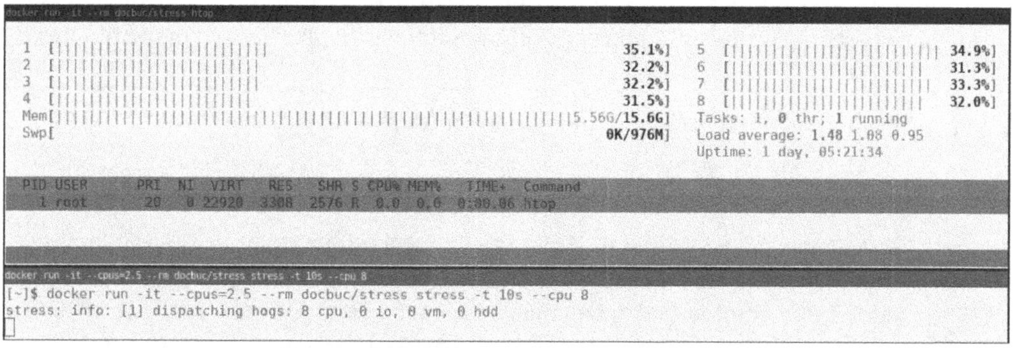

Figure 18.3 CPU Usage during a Stress Test in the Container with the "cgroups" Constraint

---

macOS, Windows, and Cloud

In addition, as described in Chapter 6, Section 6.6, on Windows and macOS, you can limit the overall performance of the Docker Engine.

When you run your containers in the cloud, the server is usually virtualized. This allows you to dynamically adjust the resources (see Chapter 19, Section 19.2, and Chapter 20).

18.7   Secure Computing Mode

Another Linux kernel feature for restricting processes is *Secure Computing Mode* (*seccomp*). This technique can prevent the execution of selected system calls in the kernel. However, indiscriminate blocking naturally doesn't lead to the goal: before you block one of the many calls, you need to understand its exact task.

Each Docker container starts with a default list of seccomp settings. This blocks about 44 out of more than 300 possible system calls. The default list for containers can be found on GitHub:

https://github.com/moby/moby/blob/master/profiles/seccomp/default.json

You can use the `--security-opt seccomp=my_profile.json` parameter to pass your own seccomp list in the `docker run` call. However, the creation and associated debugging of such a list can be very time-consuming and nerve-racking, as Jessie Frazelle has documented in her blog:

https://blog.jessfraz.com/post/how-to-use-new-docker-seccomp-profiles

Without deep kernel knowledge, you can only rely on the expertise of Docker developers at this point.

18.8   AppArmor Security Profiles

AppArmor is another Linux kernel security feature that can be used to restrict or even just record the actions of a process. Common actions involve file and network access.

> **Security-Enhanced Linux (SELinux) as an AppArmor Alternative**
>
> Unfortunately, AppArmor is only available in a few Linux distributions, especially Ubuntu and openSUSE.
>
> Linux distributions from the Red Hat environment, in particular Red Hat Enterprise Linux (RHEL), Fedora, Oracle Linux, and others, rely on a different security technology with SELinux. You can find background information on the interaction between SELinux and Docker here: *https://access.redhat.com/documentation/en-us/red_hat_enterprise_linux_atomic_host/7/html/container_security_guide/docker_selinux_security_policy*

18.8.1   AppArmor Profile for Docker

While configuration files for AppArmor aren't quite as complex as the previously mentioned seccomp profiles, creating a complete AppArmor profile is certainly no piece of cake either.

AppArmor settings apply to Docker for the running containers, not for the Docker Engine. Under Ubuntu, a default profile is dynamically created for each container at startup, which essentially disallows writing to /proc and /sys and using mount. Here's an excerpt from that profile:

```
# docker-default apparmor-policy (excerpt)
  deny mount,
  deny /sys/[^f]*/** wklx,
  deny /sys/f[^s]*/** wklx,
  deny /sys/fs/[^c]*/** wklx,
  deny /sys/fs/c[^g]*/** wklx,
  deny /sys/fs/cg[^r]*/** wklx,
  deny /sys/firmware/** rwklx,
  deny /sys/kernel/security/** rwklx,
```

For more information on the syntax of AppArmor profiles, refer to the AppArmor wiki:

https://gitlab.com/apparmor/apparmor/wikis/QuickProfileLanguage

18.8.2   Custom AppArmor Rules

Finally, we want to demonstrate the use of a custom AppArmor profile on the basis of a short example. The profile should prevent and log all write accesses below the */usr* directory. All other write accesses in the container should also be logged. Create a file with the following content:

```
# File security/apparmor/ro-usr
profile ro-usr flags=(attach_disconnected,mediate_deleted) {
  file,
  audit deny /usr/** w,
  audit /** w,
}
```

The profile named ro-usr contains only a few lines. The flags statement must be set like this for containers. Then the rules for the /usr/** and /** paths are set. Create the profile using the following command:

```
sudo apparmor_parser -r -W ro-usr
```

Then start a container with the profile, and use the touch command to try and create a file in the container under /usr:

```
docker run --security-opt "apparmor=ro-usr" -it alpine

  touch /123
    (OK)
```

```
touch /usr/123
  touch: /usr/123: Permission denied
```

While creating the file under the root directory works, the second call fails with the error message `Permission denied`. You can find the logs in the output of `dmesg` on the host (slightly shortened here):

```
apparmor="AUDIT" operation="open" profile="ro-usr"
  name="/root/.ash_history" pid=3117 comm="sh"
  requested_mask="ac" fsuid=0 ouid=0
apparmor="AUDIT" operation="file_perm" profile="ro-usr"
  name="/root/.ash_history" pid=3117 comm="sh"
  requested_mask="w" fsuid=0 ouid=0
apparmor="DENIED" operation="mknod" profile="ro-usr"
  name="/usr/123" pid=3278 comm="touch" requested_mask="c"
  denied_mask="c" fsuid=0 ouid=0
```

Note, however, that with this minimal profile you'll lose the useful defaults of the standard Docker profile!

Chapter 19
Swarm and Amazon Elastic Container Service

The trend to outsource services to the *cloud* is unbroken. Many companies see potential savings in this because their own hardware and possibly also the IT department can be reduced. Whether a public cloud is the right solution for your project, you still have to decide on a case-by-case basis.

So far in this book, we've mainly used Docker for development and installations on a computer or server. In this context, Docker was able to impress with numerous functions. But another major strength of Docker is its ability to run containers in a cloud environment.

The magic word in cloud computing is *scalability*. While monolithic applications eventually reach the limits of the hardware, the following theory applies to microservices: if a service reaches the limit of its capacity, you can simply start a new service on another host that can take on the additional load. In the Docker environment, this means "start a new container with this service." This sounds logical and simple; however, whether it works in practice as promised in theory depends heavily on the service it provides.

The load of containers that operate *statelessly*, that is, don't require a persistent connection with the counterpart and complete a work step, can be scaled very well. For a web application, for example, this would be a container that provides a REST interface.

Databases are generally less suitable for automatic scaling. The requirement that data be stored in a consistent state in one place doesn't allow different database processes to write to it at the same time. NoSQL databases have an advantage here because it's easier to split up the data set (*sharding*) and distribute the queries via an upstream database router. In the world of relational databases, this concept also exists, but it becomes much more complicated when individual tables are involved. You've already noticed that with databases, there's no simple solution that fits everything.

19.1   Swarm versus Kubernetes

There are several ways to bring Docker containers to cloud environments in an easily scalable way. In this and the following chapter, we'll focus on the two most popular variants:

- **Swarm**
  Since 2016, Docker Swarm has been integrated into Docker in its current form and can be controlled using the `swarm`, `service`, `node`, and `stack` commands. Docker's built-in orchestration is notable for its ease of use: you create a swarm (`swarm init`),

join (`swarm join`) additional nodes (machines running Docker), and launch your Docker compose setup (`stack deploy`). Swarm takes care of the initial distribution of containers and starts new containers when a node fails. The nodes communicate encrypted via Transport Layer Security (TLS), of course.

- **Kubernetes**
Kubernetes builds on years of preliminary work by Google, which needed a management tool that was flexible and scalable for very large clusters. In 2014, Google introduced Kubernetes as an open-source project on the internet and soon welcomed major partners (Microsoft, IBM, Red Hat, Docker) to the Kubernetes community.

When Google transferred the project into the hands of the Cloud Native Computing Foundation a rapid development process began. In November 2019, Amazon, Microsoft, and Google itself offered Kubernetes clusters on a rental basis. Managing and using a Kubernetes cluster is significantly more complex than a Docker Swarm cluster. Kubernetes makes up for these difficulties, however, with a large community, many good tools, and sophisticated technical documentation.

The specific implementation of an app in the cloud depends not only on the process used but also on which commercial cloud offering you choose. Of course, it's impossible to go into detail about all providers at this point. However, the examples in this and the next chapter exemplify the interaction with the following providers:

- Hetzner Cloud (with Docker Swarm)
- Amazon Elastic Container Service (ECS)
- Amazon Elastic Container Service for Kubernetes (EKS)
- Microsoft Azure Kubernetes Service (AKS)
- Google Kubernetes Engine (GKE)

As sample applications, we'll use the JavaScript program presented in Chapter 13 and the setup shown in Chapter 14. You don't need to understand these programs to the very last detail to follow the descriptions in those two chapters. However, it's certainly a good idea to skim through the chapters at least once before reading on here.

19.2   Docker Swarm

In many of the previous examples, we used `docker compose` to run multiple containers in a federated fashion. `docker compose` creates its own network and names the containers and volumes so that you can easily find them again.

However, scaling is especially useful when the load is distributed across multiple computers. This is where Docker's *orchestration* tools come into play. When Swarm tools for controlling distributed containers were added to the Docker core in 2016, four principles were at the forefront:

- Simple and powerful
- Fail-safe
- Secure
- Expandable

Docker Swarm (or just *Swarm*) is based on a model of one or more manager nodes and any number of worker nodes. A basic requirement for interaction is a current Docker version. In addition, of course, the nodes must be able to communicate over the network.

The communication is encrypted with TLS. Fortunately, you don't need to bother about that: Docker takes care of the certificate management on its own.

The swarm achieves resilience through constant communication among nodes; services from a node that's no longer available will automatically be taken over by another node (*self-healing*). In the following sections, we'll show you how easy Docker Swarm is to install and use.

19.2.1   Swarm Quick Start

The developers of Docker Swarm were keen to be able to control the management of a cluster with just a few commands. As you'll see momentarily, corresponding commands docker swarm <command> are wonderfully simple to use!

For the first attempt with Swarm, you can create a setup according to the following pattern: For this purpose, you need to start three computers on the local network. All computers must be reachable via Secure Shell (SSH), and all computers must have an up-to-date Docker version installed. You could also use virtual machines on your computer; however, the distribution will be better visualized if you use real hardware. If you run Docker Swarm on CentOS/Red Hat Enterprise Linux (RHEL), you must open port 2376 in the firewall configuration, which isn't the case by default.

In our trial, it was a laptop running Ubuntu Linux, an old PC running CoreOS, and another laptop running an older version of Ubuntu. The host names were t480s, core, and almanarre. Now you should initialize Docker Swarm on one of the devices (we use the laptop named almanarre) via the following command (the long tokens have been shortened to [...]):

```
almanarre$ docker swarm init --advertise-addr 192.168.11.56

  Swarm initialized: current node (qascapb[...]) is now a
  manager.

  To add a worker to this swarm, run the following command:
  docker swarm join --token SWMTKN-1-3[...] 192.168.11.50:2377
```

19

```
   To add a manager to this swarm, run 'docker swarm join-token
   manager' and follow the instructions.
```

The IP address passed to the `--advertise-addr` parameter is assigned to the Ethernet interface on the local computer. Now log in to another computer using SSH, and execute the `docker swarm join` command specified in the preceding code. (SSH is useful here because you can copy and paste the long tokens into the SSH window.) Then, repeat the procedure on the third computer. After that, the cluster is ready and waiting for tasks:

```
core$ docker swarm join --token SWMTKN-1-3xw27lp0a7d[...]
   This node joined a swarm as a worker.
```

Make sure that the worker nodes are all successfully registered in the swarm:

```
almanarre$ docker node ls --format \
    '{{.Hostname}}\t{{.Status}}\t
    {{.Availability}}\t{{.ManagerStatus}}'

   almanarre  Ready    Active    Leader
   t480s      Ready    Active
   core       Ready    Active
```

So, the three hosts almanarre, t480s, and core are now part of a swarm and ready to run commands and containers.

19.2.2   "Hello World" in the Swarm

As a first task, you need to provide the cluster with an adapted version of the Hello World example that you know from Chapter 1, Section 1.3. For this purpose, you want to add a line to the output where you output the host name and the version of the operating system (Linux kernel). The full server code is as follows:

```
// File: swarm/hello-swarm/server.js
const http = require("http"),
  os = require("os");
http.createServer((req, res) => {
  const dateTime = new Date(),
    load = os.loadavg(),
    net = os.networkInterfaces();
  let ips = [];
  for (const key of Object.keys(net)) {
    for (const iface of net[key]) {
      if (iface.internal === false) {
        ips.push(iface.address);
      }
```

```
      }
    }
    ips.sort();
    const doc = `<!DOCTYPE html>
<html>
  <head>
    <title>Hello swarm</title>
    <meta charset="utf-8" />
  </head>
  <body>
    <h1>Hello swarm!</h1>
    Swarm node: ${os.hostname()}, ver. ${os.release()}<br />
    Server time: ${dateTime}<br />
    Uptime: ${os.uptime()/60/60} hours<br />
    Network: ${ips.join(',')}<br />
    Server utilization (load): ${load[0]}
  </body>
</html>`
    res.setHeader('Content type', 'text/html');
    res.end(doc);
}).listen(8080);
```

You can tell which node in the cluster is responding to the request by the output of os.hostname() and os.release(). The associated *Dockerfile* doesn't get changed:

```
# File: swarm/hello-swarm/Dockerfile
FROM node:16
ENV TZ="Europe/Amsterdam"
COPY server.js /src/
EXPOSE 8080
USER node
CMD ["node", "/src/server.js"]
```

Although we'll start only one service, we'll use a *docker-compose.yml* file as before:

```
# File: swarm/hello-swarm/docker-compose.yml
version: '3'
services:
  web:
    image: docbuc/hello-swarm
    build: hello-swarm/
    ports:
      - "8080:8080"
```

19

To start the service in our private cluster, a single call is sufficient:

```
almanarre$ docker stack deploy -c docker-compose.yml helloswarm

  Ignoring unsupported options: build
  Creating network helloswarm_default
  Creating service helloswarm_web
```

The docker stack deploy command requires you to specify a configuration file (-c) and a name for the stack (helloswarm). All services in *docker-compose.yml* (in this case, it's only one, web) are created as service, with the specified name prepended to the service name. The listing of the services spread over several lines here for space reasons shows whether everything worked correctly:

```
almanarre$ docker service ls

  ID              NAME             MODE         REPLICAS
  r22vhnd7my90    helloswarm_web   replicated   1/1

  IMAGE                        PORTS
  docbuc/hello-swarm:latest    *:8080->8080/tcp
```

Currently, exactly one container is running in the cluster. Now you can scale up the application to three containers, deploying all nodes in the cluster:

```
almanarre$ docker service scale helloswarm_web=3

  helloswarm_web scaled to 3
  overall progress: 3 out of 3 tasks
  1/3: running
  2/3: running
  3/3: running
  verify: Service converged
```

If you now call the web page *92.168.11.50:8080*, the responses will come from a different container each time (see Figure 19.1). Call the web page with curl or wget to check the output in the command line:

```
$ curl -s http://192.168.11.50:8080 | egrep '(Swarm|Netzw)'
    Swarm node: a10811bb4d8f, ver. 5.11.0-22-generic<br />
    Network: 10.0.0.16,10.0.5.21,192.168.96.3<br />

$ curl -s http://192.168.11.50:8080 | egrep '(Swarm|Netzw)'
    Swarm node: 990827f484ae, ver. 5.11.0-22-generic<br />
    Network: 10.0.0.6,10.0.5.5,192.168.96.5<br />
```

```
$ curl -s http://192.168.11.50:8080 | egrep '(Swarm|Netzw)'
    Swarm node: c3f5dac2fd28, ver. 4.15.0-48-generic<br />
    Network: 10.0.0.14,10.255.0.25,172.21.0.3<br />
```

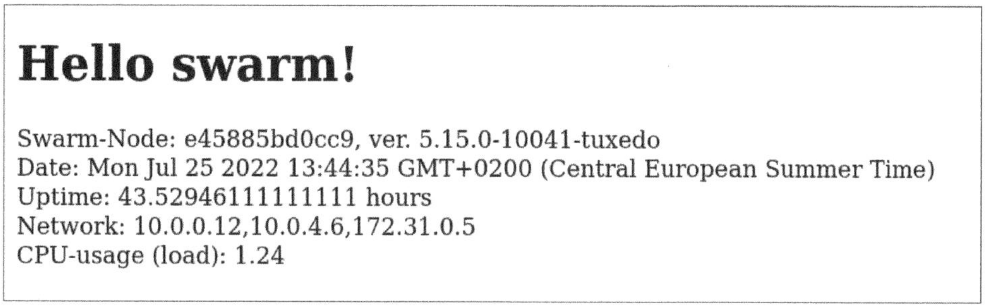

Hello swarm!

Swarm-Node: e45885bd0cc9, ver. 5.15.0-10041-tuxedo
Date: Mon Jul 25 2022 13:44:35 GMT+0200 (Central European Summer Time)
Uptime: 43.52946111111111 hours
Network: 10.0.0.12,10.0.4.6,172.31.0.5
CPU-usage (load): 1.24

Figure 19.1 The Hello Swarm Application in the Browser

The question as to which process is running on which node can be answered by the `docker stack` command:

```
almanarre$ docker stack ps helloswarm --format \
        '{{.Name}}\t{{.Node}}\t{{.CurrentState}}'

  helloswarm_web.1   almanarre  Running 23 minutes ago
  helloswarm_web.2   t480s      Running 2 minutes ago
  helloswarm_web.3   core       Running about a minute ago
```

Docker Swarm delivers what it promises: in no time, you can launch and scale an application across a cluster of multiple computers.

19.3   Docker Swarm in the Hetzner Cloud

In this section, we'll launch and scale the program you already know from Chapter 13 in a Docker swarm. This time, however, the swarm won't run in a test environment but will be accessible to the whole world on the internet. The remainder of this chapter then contains instructions related to the cloud offerings from Amazon, Google, and Microsoft. At this point, however, we want to show a solution that doesn't require the very large companies of the IT world.

Hetzner (*www.hetzner.com*) has been offering a very flexible cloud solution at reasonable prices since 2018. The costs for the smallest virtual machines currently start at $3.91 per month, and billing is by the hour, so you can start your cloud experiments here without the risk of exploding costs. To create new cloud servers, you can either use the well-structured web interface (see Figure 19.2) or the command-line program `hcloud` provided by Hetzner. In the remaining sections of this chapter, we'll use `hcloud`.

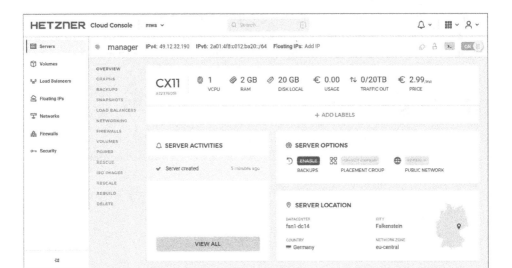

Figure 19.2 Web Interface of the Hetzner Cloud

19.3.1   CLI Installation and Configuration with "hcloud"

To install the hcloud program on your computer, you should download the latest binary package from GitHub (*https://github.com/hetznercloud/cli/releases*) and copy the program in the *bin* directory of the zip file to the search path of your computer.

Before you can start with the command-line program, you must create a new project in the Hetzner Cloud Console. To do this, log in to *https://console.hetzner.cloud*, and add the project, mwa. Then select the project and create a new access token with read and write permission under **Security • API Tokens**. You need to copy the token right now because you can't look up the string later.

Then start the hcloud program in the command line and create a context. When prompted for the token, copy the 64-character string into the console window.

```
hcloud context create mwa

  Token: ShiRiHah[...]
  Context mwa created and activated
```

The program is now ready for use; you can display the list of available data centers with the following command:

```
hcloud datacenter list

  ID   NAME       DESCRIPTION       LOCATION
  2    nbg1-dc3   Nuremberg 1 DC 3  nbg1
  3    hel1-dc2   Helsinki 1 DC 2   hel1
  4    fsn1-dc14  Falkenstein 1 DC14 fsn1
```

If you work on Linux or on a Mac, you'll certainly want to use the very handy autocompletion of commands with the [Tab] key. We've already introduced you to this feature in Chapter 3, Section 3.3, for the docker command. The hcloud program also contains a function that passes statements to the shell for completion. You can start it via the following:

```
source <(hcloud completion bash)
```

Or alternatively you can start it using zsh instead of bash if you use the more modern zsh as your shell. After that, you'll get the possible options suggested or prefilled with the [Tab] key at each position in the command.

To gain access to the cloud servers, it's advisable to store an SSH key. You can either create a new key or use an existing one and upload the public part using the following command:

```
hcloud ssh-key create --name hetzner-cloud-key \
  --public-key-from-file ~/.ssh/id_rsa_hetzner.pub
```

19.3.2   Installing Docker with "cloud-init"

You can now start your first cloud server with Hetzner. Hetzner currently offers Ubuntu, Fedora, Debian, or CentOS as operating systems. To create a Docker swarm, the underlying operating system isn't that critical—what's important is that a current Docker version is installed.

We used Ubuntu for our tests and installed Docker during the initialization of the server. The server operating systems support cloud-init for this purpose. This package provides a cross-distribution quasi-standard for customizing Linux systems in cloud applications.

19

---

cloud-init

The cloud-init system is very powerful and supports a variety of ways to customize a Linux system during the initial boot. At this point, we'll only describe a very simple configuration variant to install the docker-ce package. For more information about cloud-init, visit the following:

- *http://cloudinit.readthedocs.io*
- *https://help.ubuntu.com/community/CloudInit*

Create a cloud-init configuration file with the following content. Note that the first line must start exactly like this!

```
#cloud-config
# File: swarm/hetzner-cloud/manager.cfg
package_upgrade: true
```

```
packages: ['docker-ce']
apt:
  preserve_sources_list: true
  sources:
    docker-ppa.list:
      source: "deb [arch=amd64] \
              https://download.docker.com/linux/ubuntu \
              $RELEASE stable"
      keyid: 0EBFCD88
runcmd:
  - "docker swarm init"
  - "docker swarm join-token worker > /token.txt"
```

You certainly recognized the syntax right away: Cloud-init also uses the YAML Ain't Markup Language (YAML) format (see Chapter 5, Section 5.3). The entries in the apt section cause new file */etc/apt/sources.list.d/docker-ppa.list* to be created with a reference to the package sources of the Docker Community Edition.

The entries under runcmd will be executed after a successful start. In this case, a Docker swarm is initialized and the join-join-token for additional members is stored in a */token.txt* file. Strictly speaking, the second step wouldn't be necessary; however, it's useful to quickly see whether the previous steps were successful.

19.3.3   Creating Cloud Instances

Now you should create the server of type cx11 (the smallest server type) at the Hetzner site, Falkenstein (fsn1):

```
hcloud server create --name manager \
    --type cx11 \
    --location fsn1 \
    --image ubuntu-20.04 \
    --user-data-from-file ./manager.cfg \
    --ssh-key hetzner-cloud-key

  4.541s ... 100%
  Server 13104107 created
  IPv4: 78.46.XXX.YYY
```

The server is ready for use after just a few seconds, which is an impressive performance. By specifying --user-data-from-file and the cloud-init configuration described previously, the server runs as a manager in Docker Swarm. You can now connect to the server via the following command:

```
hcloud server ssh manager
```

After confirming the SSH fingerprint, you're logged in as the root user on your cloud server. There you'll find the */token.txt* file, which contains the Docker command to connect to the swarm.

If you're prompted for a password when logging in, that's probably because your local configuration didn't send the correct SSH key (the private one for the previously stored public key). You can specify the key with the SSH command; use the IPv4 address output by the server create command:

```
ssh -i ~/.ssh/id_rsa_hetzner  root@78.46.yyy.xxx
```

Now you need to start two more servers with a slightly modified cloud-init configuration. You've probably expected it already: instead of running docker swarm init, cloud-init is now supposed to run docker swarm join with the appropriate token. Name the servers worker1 and worker2 (see Figure 19.3).

Figure 19.3 Web View of the Running Servers in the Hetzner Cloud

The cloud-init configuration for the two *worker* servers is identical (the long token and the apt configuration have been shortened again):

```
#cloud-config
# File: swarm/hetzner-cloud/worker.cfg
package_upgrade: true
packages: ['docker-ce']
apt:
  [as before ...]
runcmd:
  - "docker swarm join --token SWMTKN-[...] 78.46.XXX.YYY:2377"
```

Now create the servers with the following command:

```
for i in {1..2}
do
  hcloud server create --name worker$i \
    --type cx11 \
    --location fsn1 \
    --image ubuntu-20.04 \
    --user-data-from-file ./worker.cfg \
    --ssh-key hetzner-cloud-key
done
  5s ... 100%
  Server 13104398 created
  5s ... 100%
  Server 13104398 created
```

Instead of the for loop, you can of course just type the command twice in a row with the parameters --name worker1 and --name worker2.

Note that the manager server must be fully operational for that; in other words, the package updates must have been applied, the docker-ce package must have been installed, and the swarm must have been initialized.

The output of the hcloud server list command should then look something like this (the IP addresses have been changed):

```
hcloud server list
```

ID	NAME	STATUS	IPV4	IPV6	DATACENTER
3693267	manager	running	168.119.x	xxxx::/64	fsn1-dc14
3693302	worker1	running	168.119.y	yyyy::/64	fsn1-dc14
3693303	worker2	running	49.12.x.z	zzzz::/64	fsn1-dc14

19.3.4   Launching the Diary App in Docker Swarm

Now that Swarm is ready, you can copy the *docker-compose.yml* file from Chapter 13 to the manager instance and start the application via the following command:

```
docker stack deploy -c docker-compose.yml mwa
```

Give the containers some time to start. Docker must first load the images from Docker Hub and then derive the containers from them. You can monitor the process using docker service ls. When all services have reached their desired replicas (you can see this in the REPLICAS column), the first command you run is the MongoDB initialization. (The container name will be slightly different for you.)

```
docker exec mwa_mongo1.1.4u0840u5bfgjqebs3yje0iqai mongo --eval '
rs.initiate( {
  _id : "rs0",
```

```
  members: [
    { _id: 0, host: "mongo1:27017" },
    { _id: 1, host: "mongo2:27017" },
    { _id: 2, host: "mongo3:27017" }
  ]
})
'
```

MongoDB Replication versus Docker Replication

Don't let yourself get confused by the same names: Mongo database replication has nothing to do with Docker services replication. For MongoDB replication, you need to start three containers that aren't replicated by Docker. The MongoDB containers have a fixed mapping to the Docker volumes where the database is stored. The configuration file stores the host names of the three containers that are part of the MongoDB replica set. Automatic scaling via docker service scale doesn't work here.

Now the MongoDB replica set is ready, and the application should run as desired. Because the frontend service has a default placement (constraints: [node.role == manager]), you know exactly which IP address the Nginx frontend server is running on. Find the IPv4 address for the manager from the list generated via hcloud server list, and enter this address in your web browser. You should then see the home screen of the diary app.

If you want to get an overview of which server is running which container, you can use the docker stack ps command:

```
docker stack ps mwa -f desired-state=running \
    --format '{{.Name}}\t{{.Node}}' | sort
```

```
mwa_api.1        manager
mwa_frontend.1   worker2
mwa_mongo1.1     worker2
mwa_mongo2.1     worker1
mwa_mongo3.1     manager
mwa_redis.1      worker1
```

19.3.5   Secure Sockets Layer Certificates

A serious web application in this day and age needs an SSL certificate. Thanks to *Let's Encrypt*, this is both free of charge and not complicated at all. We want to adapt the setup analogously to the description in Chapter 9, Section 9.3.

"root" Privileges for the Frontend Service

To use the certificates in the frontend service, the container must be started with root privileges. The easiest way to do this is to remove the USER statement in the second section of the Dockerfile (see Chapter 13, Section 13.2.2).

For this purpose, you need to create a *le.yml* file with the following content:

```
# File: swarm/hetzner-cloud/le.yml
version: '3.4'
services:
  frontend:
    volumes:
      - lecerts:/etc/letsencrypt
      - ledata:/data/letsencrypt
      - ./default.conf:/etc/nginx/conf.d/default.conf
    ports:
      - "443:443"
volumes:
  lecerts:
  ledata:
```

You're going to use this file along with the *docker-compose.yml* file shown next and update the existing Docker stack. In the frontend service, this will mount the Docker volumes lecerts and ledata, which will later store the certificates and the data for verifying your domain, respectively. In addition, the default port for https, 443, will be released to the outside world. With the bind mount volume for the Nginx configuration file, you overwrite the existing file in the image. Extend the *default.conf* file with the following entry:

```
# in default.conf
[...]
  location ^~ /.well-known {
    allow all;
    root  /data/letsencrypt/;
  }
```

You need this entry to make the Nginx server on the frontend work correctly with the certbot program. certbot will store a file here and retrieve it via the web server to verify that the Domain Name System (DNS) entry also references the correct server.

To update the running Docker stack, you want to restart docker stack deploy on the manager server:

```
docker stack deploy -c docker-compose.yml -c le.yml mwa

  Updating service mwa_api (id: jc05tm6t3cic6d45d12m2h59e)
  Updating service mwa_frontend (id: jp7612kehveahdsynztiw6w47)
  Updating service mwa_mongo1 (id: j74cit761xxcwgovgm1nkoo15)
  ...
```

Docker merges the entries in the two YAML files and updates the services. Take a look at the newly included directories:

```
docker exec mwa_frontend.1.6s4c61kcevn1drgvz79gmyrmp ls /data

  letsencrypt
```

For Nginx to apply the configuration changes, you need to restart the container once (docker restart mwa_frontend.1.wv....). Then you can apply for the first certificate to be issued:

```
docker run -it --rm \
    -v mwa_lecerts:/etc/letsencrypt \
    -v mwa_ledata:/data/letsencrypt \
    certbot/certbot \
    certonly \
    --webroot --webroot-path=/data/letsencrypt \
    -d swarm-diary.dockerbuch.info
```

Of course, before you launch this Docker call, you need to register the domain (we use swarm-diary.dockerbuch.info) with your provider and configure a DNS-A entry for the corresponding IP address. You could use the IP address from your manager server for this, but it makes more sense to reserve a *floating IP* address from Hetzner, which you can bind very flexibly to one of your servers. The easiest way to perform this step is in the web interface; however, the hcloud command also handles all operations on floating IP addresses. (This can be helpful if you want to start another script-driven manager server.). To use a floating IP address on the server, you must adjust the network configuration (*https://wiki.hetzner.de/index.php/Cloud_floating_IP_persistent*).

When everything is ready and the certificate has been issued successfully, the extension is still missing, which will ensure that the Nginx server will also use the certificates. For this reason, you need to add the following lines to the *default.conf* file. The ssl_ciphers have been shortened; you can get the current values from the Certbot GitHub page at *https://github.com/certbot/certbot*.

```
# in default.conf
listen 443 ssl;
ssl_certificate
 /etc/letsencrypt/live/swarm-diary.dockerbuch.info/fullchain.pem;
```

19

```
ssl_certificate_key
 /etc/letsencrypt/live/swarm-diary.dockerbuch.info/privkey.pem;
if ($scheme != "https") {
  return 301 https://$host$request_uri;
}
ssl_session_cache shared:le_nginx_SSL:1m;
ssl_session_timeout 1440m;
ssl_protocols TLSv1.3;
ssl_prefer_server_ciphers on;
ssl_ciphers "ssl_ciphers ECDHE-ECDSA-AES128-GCM-SHA256:ECDH[...]"
```

After another container restart, your application will run with SSL certificates from Let's Encrypt. Concerning certificate renewal, refer to Chapter 9, Section 9.3.

19.3.6   Simulating a Server Failure

With the setup running, you can now simulate the failure of a server. To do this, simply turn off the server with the hcloud program. Before that, you can still obtain an overview of the containers that are currently running on the server:

```
docker node ps -f desired-state=running \
      --format '{{.Name}}\t{{.Image}}' worker2

  mwa_api.1      docbuc/mwaapi:3.3
  mwa_mongo3.1   mongo:4
  mwa_redis.1    redis:6-alpine
```

Switching off can be done via the poweroff subcommand of the hcloud program:

```
hcloud server poweroff worker2
```

After a few seconds, the server will disappear from the swarm cluster, and the remaining nodes will take over the services. Any existing active login in the browser will no longer be valid after this failure. The reason for this is that on the worker2 node that was just deactivated, the Redis database with the session information was also active. Because Redis is configured without replication, the login is no longer valid. Of course, MongoDB isn't affected by this.

When you restart the server after the simulated failure (poweron), it will automatically reconnect to the swarm cluster. However, the current containers won't be allocated anew. In discussions about this on GitHub, the reason given is that *healthy* containers would have to be stopped in the process. If you want to start splitting containers manually, the following command will help:

```
for i in $(docker service ls -q)
do
  docker service update $i --force
done
```

The service ls -q command lists the IDs of all services. In the for loop, each service gets updated with the --force option, resulting in the new distribution among the existing nodes.

19.3.7 Security

Setting up the servers and launching the diary app in Docker Swarm is very straightforward. Unfortunately, the advantage doesn't come without a disadvantage: unlike solutions from Amazon, Google, and Microsoft, each cloud server automatically receives a globally valid IP address (IPv4 and IPv6). This makes it easy to connect to the server—but unfortunately not just for the owners. Once docker swarm has been started, the ports for managing the swarm cluster are externally accessible to all machines on the internet.

You can implement a little more security with a firewall on each of your servers. However, you would need to enable the ports necessary for Docker Swarm (TCP 2377, TCP and UDP 7946, and UDP 4789) for the IP address range of the IP addresses used by Hetzner. This would be another configuration setting for cloud-init or the new firewall function in the Hetzner cloud, which is currently still in beta (see Figure 19.4).

Figure 19.4 A Firewall for the Docker Swarm Servers in the Hetzner Cloud

However, there's one aspect about this setup you can't entirely do without: not only do you have to bother about Docker Swarm and your Docker images, but you also need to worry about the servers running Swarm. The cloud products in the next section and in the following Chapter 20 try to take some of that burden off your shoulders.

19.4   Amazon Elastic Container Service

Amazon is undoubtedly assuming a pioneering role in cloud computing. Under the name *Amazon Web Services (AWS)*, the IT giant has been providing various IT services for paying customers since 2002. Amazon was adept at renting idle hardware capacity flexibly and at attractive prices. Application Programming Interfaces (APIs), command-line tools, and a web interface make managing services convenient.

Two main pillars in the multitude of services offered by Amazon are Elastic Compute Cloud (EC2) and Simple Storage Service (S3). In EC2, customers can start and stop virtual machines at will, dynamically adjusting computing power. S3 is a quasi-unlimited storage location with high availability. Unlike traditional computers, the system isn't designed with files and folders but consists of *buckets*, which are containers, and *objects* contained there, which represent the actual data.

An easy way to launch a Docker container in the Amazon cloud is to launch a virtual Linux machine in EC2 and install Docker there. This will run your Docker host, and you can run any Docker containers on it. You'll then have a setup like the one we described in the previous section. However, the cloud computing part is limited to the underlying virtual machine. For this reason, it's necessary to update the operating system components of this machine and, of course, the Docker daemon itself. Using `docker swarm`, you could build your own container cloud on this basis and scale it via the command line.

But it would be much nicer if the cloud infrastructure took care of the underpinnings itself, was highly available, and still scaled automatically to meet the needs of your application. Amazon is trying to do exactly this work for you with the *Elastic Container Service (ECS)*. The following section provides an introduction to using this service.

19.4.1   Quick Start: Launching a Container in the AWS Cloud

For the first example, you need an Amazon AWS account. When registering, a cell phone number is currently mandatory, as Amazon has interposed an automatic control call with PIN entry here. Once this hurdle has been cleared, you can access the ECS from the **Service** menu in the AWS console (*https://console.aws.amazon.com*). Use the **Get Started** button, which guides you through a simple ECS configuration in three steps.

A very helpful tool for understanding Amazon terminology is the superimposed graphic that illustrates the current configuration level in each step (see Figure 19.5).

The required components are as follows:

- Container and task definition
- Service
- Cluster

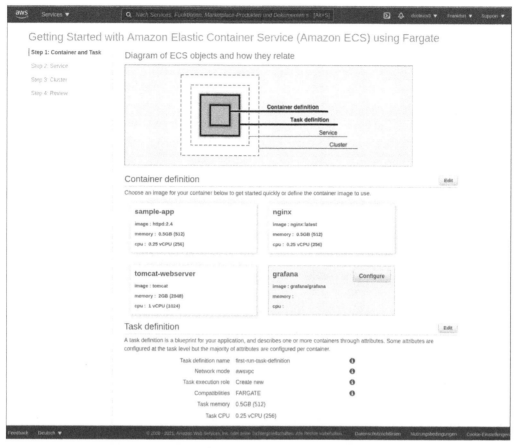

Figure 19.5 The Useful Quick Start with Amazon ECS

When defining a container, you can choose from three preconfigured web servers or specify an image yourself from which to launch a container. For example, you can use the Grafana image we described in Chapter 14.

ECS resolves to the familiar Docker naming convention for images here. The grafana/ grafana image can be downloaded from the official Docker Hub. In the container settings, you can specify port mapping for the Grafana Image 3000. Unlike docker run, where the container port and the host port can be different, only one port must be specified here.

Advanced settings for networking and logging are correctly preset for our purposes in the **Getting Started** configuration.

The second step is to create a service with a task (the Grafana container). A **Security Group** gets created so that the service can be accessed from the internet. The **Load Balancer** can remain disabled for this test.

The third and final step is to set up the cluster on which the service will run. The default setting for **VPC ID** and **Subnets** is **Automatically Create New**, which should work correctly for the test. This completes the definition, and you can start the container via **Create**.

After creating the components (a process that takes several minutes), you can find the cluster on the Amazon ECS home page. If you then click on the current job in the **Tasks** tab, you'll find the **Public IP** address of your cluster under **Network** (see Figure 19.6). As expected, the Grafana login page appears when you enter this IP address with port 3000 in your browser.

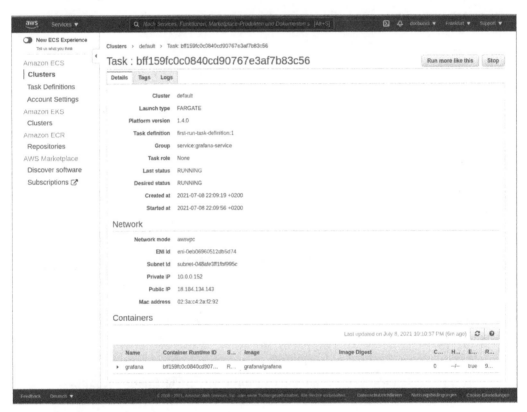

Figure 19.6 The Public IP Address of Your Amazon Cluster

The useful wizard has done a few things for you. Via the command-line tool `ecs-cli`, you can configure these steps in detail and execute them manually. In the next section, we'll show you exactly what was done in these steps and how you can even use them to launch a slightly modified `docker compose` configuration.

19.4.2   Amazon Elastic Container Service with "docker compose"

A key difference between the *old* docker-compose and the new compose subcommand (see Chapter 5) is that the new version can launch existing compose setups in an Amazon or Microsoft cloud infrastructure. Starting a Docker Compose setup in ECS has really become a walk in the park. With just two commands, your existing setup will run in the cloud.

First, you need to create a Docker Context of type ecs named ecsgrafana:

```
docker context create ecs ecsgrafana
```

```
? Create a Docker context using: AWS secret and token credentials
  Retrieve or create AWS Access Key and Secret on
  https://console.aws.amazon.com/iam/home?#security_credential
? AWS Access Key ID: BCDAKKDJSKDJ8BBNAWQR
? Enter AWS Secret Access Key ********************************
? Region eu-west-1
Successfully created ecs context "ecsgrafana"
```

If you've used Amazon's aws-cli command-line tool before, you can select an existing profile when creating the context; if not, you should enter the Access Key ID and Secret Access Key as in the preceding listing. Then you can start the Docker Compose setup with the reference to the context:

```
docker --context ecsgrafana compose up
```

```
x grafana                      CreateInProgress User Initiated
x Cluster                      CreateComplete
x LogGroup                     CreateComplete
x GrafanaTCP3000TargetGroup    CreateComplete
x CloudMap                     CreateComplete
x TelegrafTaskExecutionRole    CreateComplete
x InfluxTaskExecutionRole      CreateComplete
x GrafanaTaskExecutionRole     CreateComplete
x LoadBalancer                 CreateComplete
[...]
```

If you're used to docker compose from your local machine or a server, you'll now have to wait a little longer. Here, a cluster is created first; followed by roles, services, and listeners; and finally the three containers get started (see Figure 19.7).

19

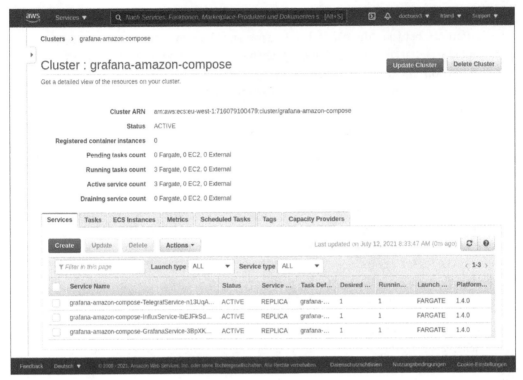

Figure 19.7 The Automatically Generated AWS Fargate Cluster with the Three Active Services

In our test, it took about 10 minutes until it was really time and we could access the Grafana instance. The quickest way to find out the public IP address is to use docker compose:

```
docker --context ecsgrafana compose ps
```

```
NAME                               SERVICE   STATUS    PORTS
task/grafana-amazon-compose/1d...  influx    Running
task/grafana-amazon-compose/24...  grafana   Running   gr...
task/grafana-amazon-compose/78...  telegraf  Running
```

We had to shorten the somewhat overlong container names and ports for better readability. In our case, the PORTS output at the grafana service was grafa-LoadB-A9JOOIW-MO4TJ-89ac444864fad7b9.elb.eu-west-1.amazonaws.com:3000, which we could enter directly as the address in the browser. There, to our great joy, the working Grafana setup presented itself (see Figure 19.8).

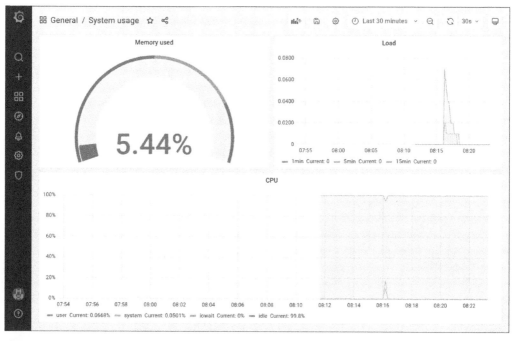

Figure 19.8 The Grafana Telegraf InfluxDB Setup in Amazon ECS

We were a bit surprised by the very successful integration of ECS with Docker. The compose subcommand is still in an early phase of development, so you should be cautious
about running such services on production systems currently. It's also questionable
whether the automatic scaling measures in the cluster will work well for your application. In any case, it will be exciting to continue to observe the development. More information about the integration of ECS and also Microsoft Azure Container Instances
(ACI) can be found here:

- *https://docs.docker.com/cloud/ecs-integration*
- *https://docs.docker.com/cloud/aci-integration*

433

Chapter 20
Kubernetes

In this chapter, we'll take a look at Docker containers in the Kubernetes network. The software package, developed by Google and available as open source since 2014, enables you to flexibly manage container-based applications. Kubernetes (also known as k8s) isn't limited to Docker as a container format but can also run other container runtimes (e.g., *rkt* or *runc*).

We'll provide a brief overview of Kubernetes here so you can get a feel for what Kubernetes is and how it works. We'll briefly explain some new concepts and terms in context.

A Kubernetes network consists of one or more *nodes*, which can be either physical computers or virtual machines. At least three services run on each of these nodes:

- **kubelet**
  coordinates the execution of *pods* in which containers are running.
- **Container runtime**
  Runs the containers.
- **Kube proxy**
  Manages network rules for the node.

Unlike Docker, Kubernetes has another layer of abstraction between the operating system and the individual processes: *pods*. One or more containers can run in a pod. Containers within a pod share an IP address and can communicate with each other via `localhost`. In many cases, however, only one container runs in a pod. You can then think of the pod as another layer around the container that's needed in the Kubernetes world.

All nodes have one or more *Kubernetes masters*. A master contains the following services:

- **API server**
  Central connection point for nodes. All requests from nodes are intercepted here.
- **etcd**
  A key-value store that stores the state of the cluster.
- **scheduler**
  Distributes new work packages.
- **Kube** and **cloud controller manager**
  These managers take care of the state of the nodes in Kubernetes. Due to the separation into two areas, cloud providers can easily bring in customized solutions without changing the core of Kubernetes.

20

Workloads are handed over as *deployments* to a Kubernetes cluster. The master component takes care of the distribution of these tasks according to the deployment specifications. Not until these specifications are met will the controller managers of the master try to meet them. The same applies in the event of a node failure: if pods are lost in the process that are intended in the current deployment, the controllers cause a pod to be re-created on a node in the cluster.

Because setting up your own Kubernetes infrastructure is beyond the scope of the DevOps activity we're going to check in with the major cloud providers on the internet in the following sections.

20.1   Minikube

You don't need to get out your credit card just yet to get acquainted with Kubernetes. *Minikube* is a small program that simulates a single-node Kubernetes cluster on your computer. For this purpose, only virtualization software (VirtualBox or Kernel-based Virtual Machine [KVM]) must be installed on the PC. Installation packages for all major operating systems can be found on the following GitHub page: *https://github.com/kubernetes/minikube/releases*.

The packages for Windows were marked as experimental for a long time, but since version 1.4 from September 2019, this build is also considered stable. For Linux and on the Mac, it's sufficient to download the binary and copy it to the search path. To install the current version on Linux, you need to run the following two commands:

```
curl -LO https://storage.googleapis.com/minikube/releases/latest/
   minikube-linux-amd64
sudo install minikube-linux-amd64 /usr/local/bin/minikube
```

Start the Kubernetes cluster with the following command:

```
minkube start
```

```
minikube v1.22.0 on Ubuntu 21.04
Automatically selected the docker driver. Other choices: vir...
Starting control plane node minikube in cluster minikube
Pulling base image ...
Downloading Kubernetes v1.21.2 preload ...
> preloaded-images-k8s-v11-v1...: 502.14 MiB / 502.14 MiB    ...
> gcr.io/k8s-minikube/kicbase...: 361.09 MiB / 361.09 MiB    ...
Creating docker container (CPUs=2, Memory=3900MB) ...

Preparing Kubernetes v1.21.2 on Docker 20.10.7 ...
x Generating certificates and keys ...
```

```
x Booting up control plane ...
x Configuring RBAC rules ...
Verifying Kubernetes components...
x Using image gcr.io/k8s-minikube/storage-provisioner:v5
Enabled addons: storage-provisioner, default-storageclass
Done! kubectl is now configured to use "minikube" cluster and
"default" namespace by default
```

During startup, you'll be notified that kubectl has been configured for you. If the command-line program hasn't been installed yet on your computer, you can do that now.

As with Minikube, the executable binary is sufficient for kubectl, but you can also install the program via the package manager of common Linux distributions. You can also find more options on the Kubernetes installation page:

https://kubernetes.io/docs/tasks/tools/install-kubectl

Use the following commands to install the current binary on Linux. (The HTTPS addresses, each spread over two lines, are to be joined without \ characters.)

```
KVER=$(curl -s https://storage.googleapis.com/kubernetes-release\
              /release/stable.txt)
curl -LO https://storage.googleapis.com/kubernetes-release\
          /release/$KVER/bin/linux/amd64/kubectl
chmod +x ./kubectl
sudo mv kubectl /usr/local/bin/kubectl
```

"kubectl" Version

Always install the latest version of kubectl to avoid communication issues with the Kubernetes cluster. Newer versions of kubectl work correctly with older Kubernetes cluster versions, but the reverse isn't guaranteed.

One of the steps Minikube performed at startup was to create a configuration file for kubectl. The *.kube/config* file within your home directory contains the certificates for encrypted communication in addition to the server address. Check the connection using the following command:

```
kubectl cluster-info
```

```
Kubernetes control plane is running at https://192.168.49.2:...
CoreDNS is running at https://192.168.49.2:8443/api/v1/names...
```

You can display the versions of client and server via `kubectl version` (shortened here):

```
kubectl version

  Client Version: version.Info{Major:"1", Minor:"21",
    GitVersion:"v1.21.2", GitCommit:"092fbfbf53427de67cac1e9f..."
  Server Version: version.Info{Major:"1", Minor:"21",
    GitVersion:"v1.21.2", GitCommit:"092fbfbf53427de67cac1e9f..."
```

20.1.1   Autocompletion for "kubectl"

Because you'll be using the `kubectl` command a lot when working with Kubernetes, it's worth enabling the useful autocompletion feature. To do this, you need to add the following line to your `~/.bashrc` configuration file:

```
source <(kubectl completion bash)
```

The completion is thus dynamically generated each time the shell gets started. If you use the more modern `zsh` with the Oh-My-Zsh extension (*https://ohmyz.sh*), you can also enable the `kubectl` plug-in, which generates some handy shortcuts as `alias`, for example, the following:

```
k=kubectl
kaf='k apply -f'
kdd='k describe deployment'
kdp='k describe pods'
kds='k describe svc'
keti='k exec -ti'
kgd='k get deployment'
kgi='k get ingress'
kgp='k get pods'
kgrs='k get rs'
```

Autocompletion works in `zsh` even when you use an `alias`. For example, if you press the ⌜Tab⌝ key after the `keti` command (the alias for `kubectl exec` is similar to `docker exec`), all active pods will be listed for selection, which is a huge relief when you type.

20.1.2   The First Deployment in Minikube

Start a web server for the first attempt with Minikube:

```
kubectl create deployment nginx --image nginx
  deployment.apps/nginx created
```

You can use `kubectl get` to find out the status of your deployment:

```
kubectl get deployment
```

```
NAME    READY   UP-TO-DATE   AVAILABLE   AGE
nginx   1/1     1            1           39s
```

```
kubectl get pod
```

```
NAME                     READY   STATUS    RESTARTS   AGE
nginx-755464dd6c-hzhx4   1/1     Running   0          64s
```

Both the `nginx` deployment and the `nginx-56f766d96f-9mrs5` pod run as desired. To reach the web server, you still need to create a service that opens port 80 of your deployment to the outside world:

```
kubectl expose deployment nginx --type=NodePort --port 80
```

Now when you list the active services, you'll find the `nginx` service with the corresponding port redirection:

```
kubectl get service
```

```
NAME         TYPE        CLUSTER-IP    ...   PORT(S)        AGE
kubernetes   ClusterIP   10.96.0.1     ...   443/TCP        16m
nginx        NodePort    10.98.236.44  ...   80:31681/TCP   8s
```

However, the internal IP address (CLUSTER-IP) isn't routed for access from your PC. Now you should run the `minikube` program again to determine the URL for the Nginx server:

```
minikube service list
```

```
NAMESPACE     NAME         URL
default       kubernetes   No node port
default       nginx        http://192.168.49.2:31681
kube-system   kube-dns     No node port
```

When you enter the URL "92.168.49.2:31681" in your browser, you should then see the Nginx home page you already know. Another service that was enabled by default in previous versions of Minikube is the Kubernetes dashboard. In the current version, you need to enable the dashboard as an add-on:

```
minikube addons enable dashboard
[...]
  The 'dashboard' addon is enabled
```

20

```
minikube dashboard

    Verifying dashboard health ...
    Launching proxy ...
    Verifying proxy health ...
    Opening http://127.0.0.1:35937/api/v1/namespaces/kubernetes-...
```

The second command should open your browser and display the Kubernetes web interface, which provides a good overview of the cluster (see Figure 20.1).

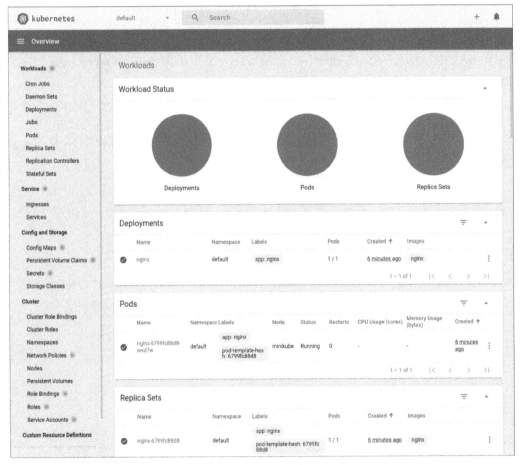

Figure 20.1 The Kubernetes Dashboard of the Local Minikube Cluster

The web interface is just another deployment running in the Minikube cluster. It's separated from your deployment in the `default` namespace by the `kube-system` namespace.

The method of creating a deployment and service via the command line shown here is rather uncommon in the Kubernetes environment. While you can very quickly try out containers in the cluster this way, it remains difficult to track which steps you applied. It's much more common to create files that describe deployments and services.

20.1.3   Object Configuration in Files

Deployments and services are two examples of *objects* managed by Kubernetes. Using the kubectl run command in the previous section, you created a deployment object in Kubernetes without knowing it. In the object definition of this deployment, an instance (replica) of the Nginx image is specified.

The Kubernetes application programming interface (API) expects object configurations in JavaScript Online Notation (JSON) format. Because writing JSON is a bit complex, kubectl can also read the YAML Ain't Markup Language (YAML) syntax, translate it to JSON format, and send the JSON string to the API. You could store the Nginx deployment that resulted from the kubectl run command in a YAML file as follows:

```
# File: k8s/minikube/nginx/nginx.yml
apiVersion: apps/v1
kind: Deployment
metadata:
  name: nginx
spec:
  replicas: 1
  selector:
    matchLabels:
      run: nginx
  template:
    metadata:
      labels:
        run: nginx
    spec:
      containers:
      - image: nginx
        name: nginx
        ports:
        - containerPort: 80
          protocol: TCP
```

Let's take a closer look at the object definition just shown. The following keys are mandatory:

- **apiVersion**
  Each object needs a version number of the Kubernetes API to be used.
- **kind**
  Defines the type of object.

- **metadata**
  At least the name of the object must be defined here.

- **spec**
  The object specification is different for each object. In the case of a deployment, enter the list of containers to be launched under `template-spec-containers`—in our case, that's the Docker image `nginx`. The `containerPort` entry opens the specified port on the pod. In addition, the template for creating new pods includes the `run: nginx` label, to which we'll come back later in this chapter.

`kubectl` can also display existing objects in the Kubernetes cluster in YAML syntax. For this purpose, you just need to place the parameter `-o yaml` after the command:

```
kubectl get deployment nginx -o yaml
```

```
apiVersion: apps/v1
kind: Deployment
metadata:
  annotations:
    deployment.kubernetes.io/revision: "1"
  creationTimestamp: "2021-07-08T22:42:29Z"
  generation: 1
  labels:
    app: nginx
  name: nginx
  namespace: default
[...]
```

As you probably already expected, you can use `-o json` to output the object in JSON format. If you view the active deployment in YAML syntax, you'll find one more entry at the lowest level: `status`. Kubernetes stores the current state of this object in this structure.

To create an object based on a YAML file, you should use the `create` command of `kubectl`:

```
kubectl create -f nginx.yml
  deployment.apps "nginx" created
```

Once you create an object in Kubernetes, the Kubernetes system attempts to create that object according to the included description.

Using the `kubectl expose` command, you've already created another object at the start. It's of type *Service* and enables communication within the Kubernetes network. The communication differs from that in the Docker network in several ways. The networking concept of Kubernetes is that all containers (actually pods) can communicate with each other via the internet protocol, regardless of which computer they are running on. Services defining a connection were introduced as a level of abstraction.

The YAML notation for the previously created `nginx` service might look something like this:

```
# File: k8s/minikube/nginx/nginx-service.yml
apiVersion: v1
kind: Service
metadata:
  name: nginx
spec:
  ports:
  - port: 80
    protocol: TCP
  selector:
    run: nginx
  type: NodePort
```

The service specification connects to port 80 on all pods that have the `run: nginx` label (defined in the `selector` section). In our example, only one pod is running with this label, so the service will redirect requests only to this pod. However, if you scale up the `nginx` deployment to three pods, the service automatically acts as a load balancer and distributes requests to the running pods.

Using this service, pods in the Kubernetes network can communicate with the Nginx pod on port 80. The default type for a service is `ClusterIP`. Such services are only accessible within the Kubernetes network. Because we use the entry `type: NodePort` in this example, the service is externally accessible on all nodes. The behavior is similar to `docker run -P`, which results in all published ports of a container being connected to random ports on the host. To find out which port on the node is connected to service port 80, you want to use the `minikube service list` command.

20.1.4   Kubernetes as a Cloud Platform

You've likely already noticed that a new world is opening up here. While there are similarities to the instructions in a *docker-compose.yml* file, the Kubernetes implementation is much more generic and thus more complex.

The position that Kubernetes has in the environment of cloud providers shouldn't be underestimated. As we've already shown (see Chapter 19, Section 19.3), Docker container solutions currently need to be adapted for different cloud providers to run productively there.

Kubernetes, on the other hand, has managed to become the quasi-standard for distributed container applications within a very short time: Microsoft, Amazon, Google, and

20

Red Hat offer Kubernetes clusters on a rental basis. Provided your configuration files are prepared for Kubernetes syntax, you can switch cloud providers with relative ease and without running the risk of a *vendor lock-in*.

The fact that the development was assigned to a nonprofit consortium, the Cloud Native Computing Foundation, has certainly also contributed to the widespread use of Kubernetes. This gives the community the assurance that Kubernetes can't be sold overnight and become pay-as-you-go software.

Describing all the features of Kubernetes is beyond the scope of this book; for this reason, we want to give you an insight into this world based on a few examples without exploring every detail of Kubernetes.

20.1.5   Grafana Setup in Minikube

We'll now launch the Grafana setup we previously launched in the Amazon Elastic Container Service (ECS) in the Minikube environment. A great help in moving from a Docker Compose setup to Kubernetes configuration files is the kompose command-line utility:

https://github.com/kubernetes/kompose

It's part of the Kubernetes infrastructure and, like minikube and kubectl, can be downloaded and installed as a binary from GitHub. (The HTTPS address is separated in the following listing only for space reasons; you must put it together without the \ character.)

```
curl -L https://github.com/kubernetes/kompose/releases\
        /download/v1.22.0/kompose-linux-amd64 -o kompose
chmod +x kompose
sudo mv ./kompose /usr/local/bin/kompose
```

Other installation variants are described on the following web page:

https://kompose.io/installation

Let's recall the *docker-compose.yml* file for the Grafana setup from Chapter 14:

```
# File: k8s/grafana/docker-compose.yml
version: '3'
services:
  grafana:
    image: docbuc/grafana:2
    restart: always
    ports:
      - 3000:3000
    environment:
      - GF_SECURITY_ADMIN_PASSWORD=secret
```

```
telegraf:
  image: docbuc/telegraf:2
  restart: always
influx:
  image: influxdb
  restart: always
  ports:
    - 8086:8086
  environment:
    - INFLUXDB_USER=telegraf
    - INFLUXDB_USER_PASSWORD=iijineeZ9iet
    - INFLUXDB_DB=telegraf
```

To convert *docker-compose.yml* to the syntax required for Kubernetes, you need to run `kompose convert` in the Grafana installation directory:

```
kompose convert
```

```
INFO Kubernetes file "grafana-service.yaml" created
INFO Kubernetes file "influx-service.yaml" created
INFO Kubernetes file "grafana-deployment.yaml" created
INFO Kubernetes file "influx-deployment.yaml" created
INFO Kubernetes file "telegraf-deployment.yaml" created
```

The `kompose` program has created a separate YAML file for each required service and deployment. Let's take a look at the *influx-deployment.yaml* file to see an example:

```
apiVersion: apps/v1
kind: Deployment
metadata:
  annotations:
    kompose.cmd: kompose convert
    kompose.version: 1.22.0 (955b78124)
  creationTimestamp: null
  labels:
    io.kompose.service: influx
  name: influx
spec:
  replicas: 1
  selector:
    matchLabels:
      io.kompose.service: influx
  strategy: {}
  template:
    metadata:
```

20

```
      annotations:
        kompose.cmd: kompose convert
        kompose.version: 1.22.0 (955b78124)
      creationTimestamp: null
      labels:
        io.kompose.service: influx
    spec:
      containers:
        - env:
            - name: INFLUXDB_DB
              value: telegraf
            - name: INFLUXDB_USER
              value: telegraf
            - name: INFLUXDB_USER_PASSWORD
              value: iijineeZ9iet
          image: influxdb
          name: influx
          ports:
            - containerPort: 8086
          resources: {}
      restartPolicy: Always
status: {}
```

All the details from the *docker-compose.yml* file were copied to the `template` statement
of the Kubernetes configuration file. You can use these files to start the Grafana setup
in your Kubernetes cluster.

After these adjustments, you can start the Grafana setup:

```
kubectl create -f grafana-deployment.yaml \
              -f grafana-service.yaml \
              -f influx-deployment.yaml \
              -f influx-service.yaml \
              -f telegraf-deployment.yaml
```

What's still missing now is the service that provides access to the web interface:

```
kubectl expose deployment grafana --type=NodePort --name=grafexp
  service/grafexp exposed
```

Now you should request the address for the Grafana web interface:

```
minikube service grafexp --url
  http://192.168.49.2:31855
```

Then you can open the Grafana application you already know or view the state of your deployment in the Kubernetes web interface (see Figure 20.2).

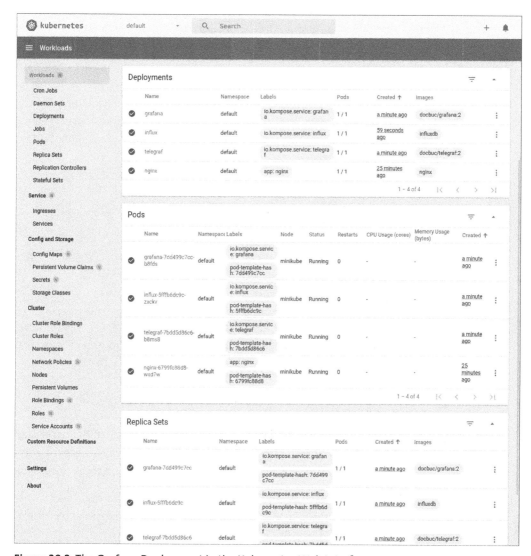

Figure 20.2 The Grafana Deployment in the Kubernetes Web Interface

20.2   Amazon Elastic Kubernetes Service

The major cloud providers have been working flat out to integrate the most user-friendly Kubernetes infrastructure possible into their portfolios. At Amazon, this service is called *Elastic Kubernetes Service (EKS)* and has been generally available since June 2018.

AWS Command-Line Interface

If you want to try the example in this section yourself, you must have the AWS command-line utility installed in addition to your Amazon account. Instructions for installation can be found on the following website: *https://docs.aws.amazon.com/cli/latest/userguide/cli-chap-install.html*.

Like many other AWS services, you start EKS in a specific Amazon data center. Before you decide on a data center, however, it's first worth taking a look at the table of regions in the Amazon web interface: *https://aws.amazon.com/de/about-aws/global-infra-structure/regional-product-services*.

Here you can see which data center provides which services. To change the default setting for the data center, you can run the aws command-line utility:

```
aws configure
  AWS Access Key ID [****************T3WA]:
  AWS Secret Access Key [****************FiXR]:
  Default region name [us-west-2]: eu-west-1
  Default output format [json]:
```

You can use the default settings for the Access Key ID and the Secret Access Key because your Amazon account is valid worldwide at all data centers. Then choose as region, for example, eu-west-1 and json as output format.

20.2.1 Creating Clusters with "eksctl"

Amazon has developed a command-line utility that carries out many of the necessary steps to set up a Kubernetes cluster with Amazon for you. Starting with roles for your account and creating a *virtual private cloud* configuration with subnets and security groups, the installer helps a lot here.

Like many other tools in the cloud environment, you can download a static binary from GitHub and copy it into the search path:

```
curl -sL "https://github.com/weaveworks/eksctl/releases/latest/\
  download/eksctl_$(uname -s)_amd64.tar.gz" | tar xz -C /tmp
sudo install /tmp/eksctl /usr/local/bin
```

To access the virtual servers (*nodes*) of your cluster via Secure Shell (SSH) at a later point, you must first deposit an SSH key with Amazon. You can find settings for servers in Amazon under **EC2**. There you import your personal SSH key under **Key Pairs** (see Figure 20.3).

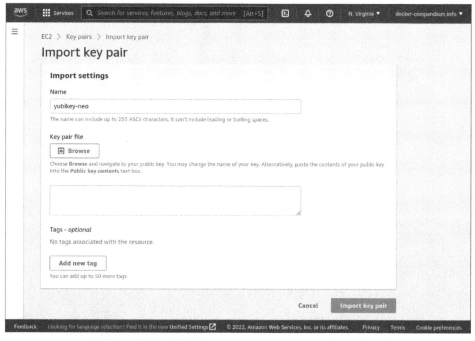

Figure 20.3 SSH Key Import into Amazon EC2

Now you can create the Kubernetes cluster. Amazon currently offers version 1.20.0 of Kubernetes:

```
eksctl create cluster --name mwa --version 1.20 --with-oidc \
  --without-nodegroup

2021-07-09 10:28:50 [i]  eksctl version 0.55.0
2021-07-09 10:28:50 [i]  using region eu-west-1
2021-07-09 10:28:50 [i]  setting availability zones to [eu-w...
2021-07-09 10:28:50 [i]  subnets for eu-west-1c - public:192...
[...]
2021-07-09 10:46:34 [i]  no tasks
2021-07-09 10:46:34 [x]  all EKS cluster resources for "mwa"...
2021-07-09 10:48:37 [i]  kubectl command should work with
  "/home/bernd/.kube/config", try 'kubectl get nodes'
2021-07-09 10:48:37 [x]  EKS cluster "mwa" in "eu-west-1"
  region is ready
```

The program ran for more than 15 minutes during our tests but was able to complete all tasks successfully. The local kubectl configuration has been adjusted so that you can now communicate directly with the cluster. But the suggested call of kubectl get nodes returns no results:

```
kubectl get nodes
  No resources found
```

For your Kubernetes cluster to work, you still need to add these nodes. Fortunately, the eksctl program has a command for this as well:

```
eksctl create nodegroup --cluster mwa --name mwa-nodes \
  --node-type t3.medium --nodes 3 --nodes-min 1 --nodes-max 4 \
  --ssh-access --ssh-public-key yubikey-4 --managed

  2021-07-09 11:08:27 [i]  eksctl version 0.55.0
  2021-07-09 11:08:27 [i]  using region eu-west-1
  2021-07-09 11:08:27 [i]  will use version 1.20 for new nodeg...
  2021-07-09 11:08:32 [i]  nodegroup "mwa-nodes" will use
    [AmazonLinux2/1.20]
  ...
  2021-07-09 11:13:00 [x]  created 1 managed nodegroup(s) in c...
  2021-07-09 11:13:00 [i]  checking security group configurati...
  2021-07-09 11:13:00 [i]  all nodegroups have up-to-date conf...
```

The nodegroup you create here should consist of three servers of type t3.medium and should have enabled SSH access. You can use ssh-public-key to reference the SSH key you previously imported in the web interface.

After a few minutes, your Kubernetes cluster is ready, and you can query your nodes via kubectl:

```
kubectl get nodes
  NAME                  STATUS   ROLES    AGE      VERSION
  ip-192-[...]te.internal  Ready    <none>   4m27s    v1.20.4-...
  ip-192-[...]te.internal  Ready    <none>   5m8s     v1.20.4-...
  ip-192-[...]te.internal  Ready    <none>   5m9s     v1.20.4-...
```

Now the time has really come, and you can start an application in the cluster:

```
kubectl apply -f grafana-deployment.yaml \
              -f grafana-service.yaml \
              -f influx-deployment.yaml \
              -f influx-service.yaml \
              -f telegraf-deployment.yaml

  deployment.apps/grafana created
  service/grafana created
  deployment.apps/influx created
  service/influx created
  deployment.apps/telegraf created
```

The Grafana setup with InfluxDB and Telegraf runs in Amazon's Kubernetes cloud. To get access to the web interface of your application, you still need to start a load balancer service:

```
kubectl expose deployment grafana \
    --type LoadBalancer --name grafexp

  service/grafexp exposed
```

To find out which host name has been assigned to your load balancer, you need to call kubectl again:

```
kubectl get services grafexp -o yaml
```

```
  apiVersion: v1
  kind: Service
  metadata:
    creationTimestamp: "2021-07-09T09:22:07Z"
    finalizers:
    - service.kubernetes.io/load-balancer-cleanup
    labels:
      io.kompose.service: grafana
    name: grafexp
    namespace: default
    resourceVersion: "5248"
    uid: f041c9f7-78b0-4ede-874e-65b7ac4ecef2
  spec:
    clusterIP: 10.100.211.75
    clusterIPs:
    - 10.100.211.75
    externalTrafficPolicy: Cluster
    ports:
    - nodePort: 31829
      port: 3000
      protocol: TCP
      targetPort: 3000
    selector:
      io.kompose.service: grafana
    sessionAffinity: None
    type: LoadBalancer
  status:
    loadBalancer:
      ingress:
      - hostname: af041c9f778b04ede874e65b7ac4ecef-319538918.e...
```

20

Now open your browser with the (rather long) entry under hostname on port 3000, and you'll see the start screen of Grafana.

Thanks to the eksctl program, the effort to create a Kubernetes cluster with Amazon has become very manageable. However, if you work in a production environment on the Amazon platform, then sooner or later, you'll have to deal with the numerous settings options of the AWS resources.

20.2.2   Deleting Data Clusters

If you've finished experimenting and may still be considering another platform for Kubernetes, don't forget to delete your resources from Amazon. Even though the cost of resources per hour isn't high, at the end of the month, you'll be surprised how much the unused cluster has cost. First delete the virtual servers using the following command:

```
eksctl --cluster mwa delete nodegroup --name mwa-nodes
  ...
  2021-07-09 11:36:39 [x]  deleted 1 nodegroup(s) from cluster...
```

Finally, you must remove the cluster itself:

```
eksctl delete cluster --name mwa
  ...
  2021-07-09 11:42:52 [i]  will delete stack "eksctl-mwa-cluster"
  2021-07-09 11:42:52 [x]  all cluster resources were deleted
```

20.3   Microsoft Azure Kubernetes Service

Even though the effort to start a Kubernetes cluster on Amazon EKS wasn't much thanks to the eksctl program, you'll see that it's even easier in Azure. Of course, you'll also need to register with Microsoft and provide your credit card information. Microsoft will provide you with server services for approximately $200 to get started. This is perfectly adequate for the first steps.

Similar to Amazon, Microsoft also provides a handy command-line utility that allows you to manage the services you can rent in the Azure Cloud. In particular, we want to mention the well-designed web interface here (*https://portal.azure.com*, see Figure 20.4): we've been amazed to notice that it displays flawlessly even on non-Microsoft platforms—a fact that could not be taken for granted a few years ago.

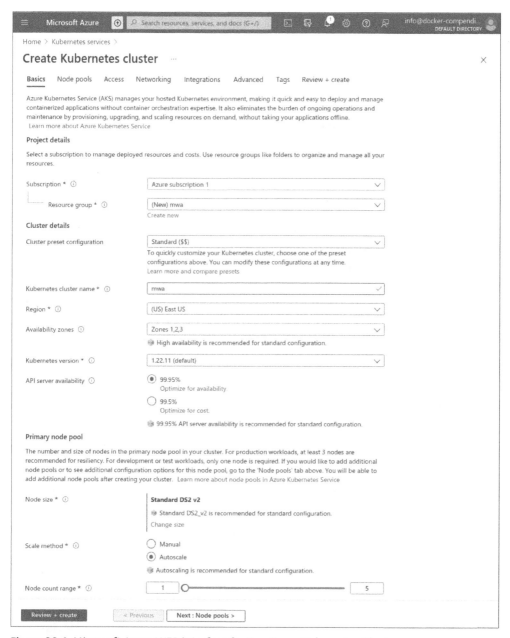

Figure 20.4 Microsoft Azure WEB interface for Creating a Kubernetes Cluster

20.3.1   Creating Clusters

The easiest way to create your Kubernetes cluster is right from the web interface. For this purpose, you select **Create Resource** from the main menu, and then search for "Kubernetes". The **Kubernetes Service** list entry takes you to the **Create Kubernetes cluster** form (refer to Figure 20.4).

Here you only need to fill in two fields:

- **Resource group**: "mwa"
- **Kubernetes cluster name**: "mwa"

You can leave all other settings unchanged. Azure will create a cluster of three nodes, each with 7 GB of RAM and two virtual CPUs. The cluster creation can take up to 15 minutes, depending on the workload.

To manage your Kubernetes cluster, you should use the `kubectl` program again. However, you can only get the `kubectl` configuration file for your AKS cluster using the Azure command-line utility. Installation packages are available for all major operating systems, and the instructions can be found at the following address:

https://docs.microsoft.com/en-us/cli/azure/install-azure-cli

To perform short tasks in the shell, however, the *cloud shell* provides access to a Linux system in the Azure cloud, which of course conveniently already has the Azure command-line utility installed.

Click the shell button in the web interface (see Figure 20.5), and enter the following command in the emulated terminal in the browser:

```
az aks get-credentials -n mwa -g mwa -f -

  apiVersion: v1
  clusters:
  - cluster:
  [...]
```

The call of the `get-credentials` subcommand requires the name of the cluster (`-n`) and the name of the resource group (`-g`) as parameters. Usually, the settings are stored in a file, and the `-f -` parameter redirects the output to the console.

You can now copy and paste the YAML construct into a *~/.kube/config-aks* file on your computer and then save it to the KUBECONFIG environment variable as in the previous section:

```
export KUBECONFIG=~/.kube/config-aks
```

Now your local `kubectl` installation should have access to the new Kubernetes cluster in Azure:

```
kubectl cluster-info

  Kubernetes control plane is running at https://mwa-dns-c2107...
  healthmodel-replicaset-service is running at https://mwa-dns...
  CoreDNS is running at https://mwa-dns-c2107bd2.hcp.westeurop...
  Metrics-server is running at https://mwa-dns-c2107bd2.hcp.we...
```

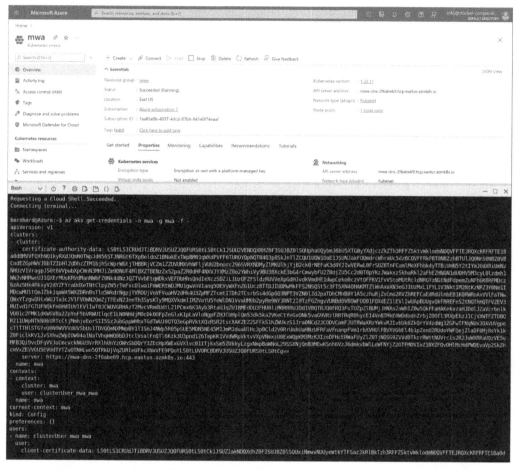

Figure 20.5 Azure Cloud Shell in the Browser

20.3.2   Installing an Application

In the next step, you'll install the web application from Chapter 13 in your Kubernetes cluster. To do this, you need to convert the *docker-compose.yml* file to Kubernetes format using the kompose program (Section 20.1, and Section 20.1.5). In doing so, you package each Docker container into a Kubernetes pod in your cluster.

Because all pods in Kubernetes explicitly require a service to open a port, you need to slightly modify the *docker-compose.yml* file before converting it. While in the Docker network, it isn't necessary to reopen ports that are used by a container and that the container has marked with EXPOSE in the configuration file, kompose needs this hint in *docker-compose.yml*. For this reason, you need to extend the three MongoDB services and the Redis service with the ports entry:

```
# in mwa/docker-compose.yml
  mongo1:
    image: mongo:4
    command: --replSet "rs0"
    volumes:
      - mongovol1:/data/db
    ports:
      - 27017
  [...]
  redis:
    image: redis:6-alpine
    ports:
      - 6379
```

The frontend and API services have already defined the port opening anyway. To make port 80 on the frontend accessible from the internet, you can use another trick from the kompose application: add a label to the frontend that sets the service type to LoadBalancer:

```
# in mwa/docker-compose.yml
  frontend:
    restart: always
    image: docbuc/mwafe:latest
    depends_on:
      - api
    ports:
      - "80:80"
    labels:
      kompose.service.type: LoadBalancer
```

The kompose program uses the specified type on the Kubernetes service object, which results in a public IP address being reserved for that service and port 80 from the frontend pod being connected to that IP address.

The output of kompose writes each service, deployment, and the volumes used (in Kubernetes, a PersistentVolumeClaim) to a separate file. In the case of the diary application from Chapter 13, that's a total of 15 files ending up in the directory. The -o kube.yaml parameter combines all Kubernetes objects into a *kube.yaml* file, which is a Kubernetes object of type List. You can start the conversion of the configuration using the following command:

```
kompose convert -f docker-compose.yml -o kube.yaml
```

20.3.3 Starting the Application

After the conversion, you can start the services using the following command:

```
kubectl apply -f kube.yaml
```

```
service/api created
service/frontend created
service/mongo1 created
[...]
deployment.apps/api created
deployment.apps/frontend created
deployment.apps/mongo1 created
persistentvolumeclaim/mongovol1 created
[...]
deployment.apps/redis created
```

In addition to the deployments and services, kompose also created volumes for the Mon-goDB deployments. With volumes, unfortunately, the Kubernetes configuration also becomes a bit more complicated than you know from Docker. The Kubernetes object for a database volume looks like the following example:

```
apiVersion: v1
kind: PersistentVolumeClaim
metadata:
  creationTimestamp: null
  labels:
    io.kompose.service: mongovol1
  name: mongovol1
spec:
  accessModes:
    - ReadWriteOnce
  resources:
    requests:
      storage: 100Mi
```

This means you don't create a volume directly but request a *persistent volume* (*claim*). If a requested volume is already present, it will be connected to the pod; if none is present, it will be created according to the specifications provided. In this case, it should have a minimum size of 100 MB and the ReadWriteOnce access right, which means that only one pod has read and write access to the volume. Size specifications are made in bytes but can also be set with the familiar abbreviations (e.g., M, G, and T) or the power-of-two specifications Mi, Gi, and Ti used here. You can view a PersistentVolumeClaim (often abbreviated *PVC* in Kubernetes) via the following command:

20

```
kubectl describe pvc mongovol1

   Name:          mongovol1
   Namespace:     default
   StorageClass:  default
   Status:        Bound
   Volume:        pvc-8317e1c0-0e05-11ea-8544-2a2601c97f54
   Labels:        io.kompose.service=mongovol1
   [...]
   Capacity:      1Gi
   Access Modes:  RWO
```

You'll see a Volume entry in the listing and should also request the description of this object to display:

```
kubectl describe persistentvolume pvc-8317e1c0-0e05-11ea-854[...]

   Name:              pvc-8317e1c0-0e05-11ea-8544-2a2601c97f54
   Labels:            failure-domain.beta.kubernetes.io/region=we...
   [...]
   Source:
     Type:            AzureDisk (an Azure Data Disk mount on
                      the host and bind mount to the pod)
     DiskName:        kubernetes-dynamic-pvc-8317e1c0-0e05-11ea-[...]
     DiskURI:         /subscriptions/809758a4-ad84-436a-9164-7b1[...]
```

With Kubernetes, you no longer need to worry about the details of storage. Your cloud provider, in this case Azure (i.e., Microsoft), will provide the infrastructure (AzureDisk) and mount the mass storage on your cluster nodes accordingly.

The diary application should now be running in your Azure Kubernetes cluster. Finally, you should start the MongoDB replication on one of the running mongo pods:

```
kubectl get pods

NAME                        READY   STATUS    RESTARTS   AGE
api-f95c5cc47-jxwbl         1/1     Running   5          7m25s
frontend-77b4669694-961sk   1/1     Running   0          7m25s
mongo1-5548c49448-7wkr6     1/1     Running   0          7m9s
mongo2-64c7478db7-n8zk7     1/1     Running   0          7m9s
mongo3-688955759d-gz2cn     1/1     Running   0          7m21s
redis-b69f7bd88-r655f       1/1     Running   0          7m23s

kubectl exec mongo1-5548c49448-7wkr6 -- mongo --eval '
```

```
rs.initiate( {
  _id : "rs0",
  members: [
     { _id: 0, host: "mongo1:27017" },
     { _id: 1, host: "mongo2:27017" },
     { _id: 2, host: "mongo3:27017" }
  ]
})
'
```

Note the syntax when running the command in a pod with kubectl: after specifying the pod name, the command must be separated with two hyphens (--). The mongo command is identical to the one in Chapter 13, Section 13.4.

You can find the public IP address of your load balancer service using Kubernetes command get service:

```
kubectl get service

  NAME      TYPE          CLUSTER-IP    EXTERNAL-IP    PORT(S)
  api       ClusterIP     10.0.217.50   <none>         3000/TCP
  frontend  LoadBalancer  10.0.67.4     20.86.229.150  80:30925/TCP
[...]
```

20.3.4   First Test

You can now open your web browser with the address *20.86.229.150*, and you'll see the home page of the diary application. (Before logging in, you still need to add a user, see Chapter 13, Section 13.4).

Because the web application is designed so that both the frontend and the api deployment can scale independently, one command is sufficient to scale up the API to three pods, for example:

```
kubectl scale --replicas=3 deployment api

  deployment.extensions/api scaled
```

Microsoft omits the Kubernetes dashboard in the default installation and replicates the corresponding views in the web interface at *https://portal.azure.com*. For a quick overview of the running pods, you can search for "mwa" and select the **Kubernetes** service. In the menu on the left, click on **Workloads** (see Figure 20.6).

Figure 20.6 Azure Dashboard with the Running Diary Application

20.3.5   Tidying Up

Even if you delete the services and pods created in Kubernetes, your cluster will continue to run and, once your initial credit from Microsoft has been used up, will also cost you money. You can delete services and pods using the `kubectl delete -f kube.yml` command in the command line.

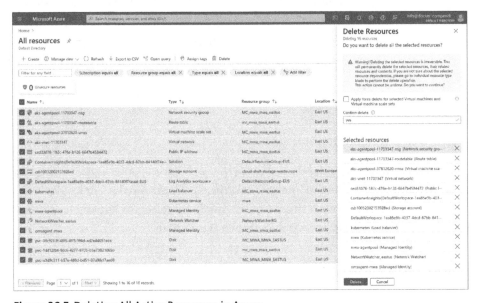

Figure 20.7 Deleting All Active Resources in Azure

However, to delete all resources, Microsoft provides a very simple way via the web interface. In the overview of all resources, you can select all elements and also delete them permanently using **Delete** (and another confirmation), which won't cause any further costs for this project (see Figure 20.7).

20.4 Google Kubernetes Engine

Finally, as a third example of a managed Kubernetes cluster, let's introduce the service provided by the original Kubernetes creator: Google. At *https://cloud.google.com*, the IT giant provides a number of services, including the Google Kubernetes Engine (GKE). When you first sign up for Google Cloud Platform, you'll get a credit of about $300 USD for 90 days, which is enough to experiment with.

20.4.1 Creating a Project and Cluster

If you tried the example in Chapter 16, Section 16.10, your Google account is already activated, and you've also already created a project. Otherwise, you need to log in via the web interface and create your first project there. In this project, we also want to launch the diary example from Chapter 13 in Kubernetes, so we'll name the project k8s-diary (see Figure 20.8).

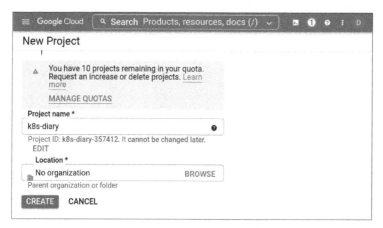

Figure 20.8 A New Project in the Google Cloud Platform

Now create a *container cluster* in your project. The easiest way to do this is to use the web interface and search for "Kubernetes Engine" in your project. Before you can create the cluster, you still need to enable the GKE for your project. When creating the cluster, you have the choice between standard mode and autopilot. While in standard mode, you have full control over your cluster's computing power (you decide how many virtual servers run and with what equipment); in autopilot mode, Google does that for you.

We chose the standard mode, in which the cluster consists of three computers (*nodes*) of type e2-medium, each with two virtual CPUs, 4 GB of RAM, and 100 GB of disk space (see Figure 20.9). The nodes run a special Linux variant of Google, **Container-Optimized OS**, but you don't need to worry about those details anymore with the Kubernetes cluster. As of July 2021, Google uses version 1.19.9 of Kubernetes.

Figure 20.9 A New Cluster in the Google Cloud Platform

20.4.2   The "gcloud" Command

If you want to work more intensively with Google Cloud, we recommend installing the gcloud command-line tool locally. Although Google also provides a cloud shell that works well in the browser (see Figure 20.10) and in which the gcloud command is of course already installed and configured, the local shell is more convenient for frequent use.

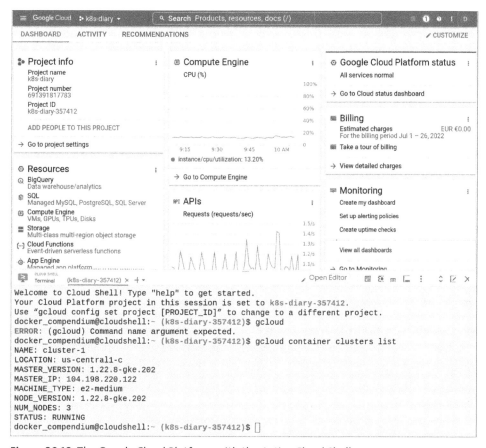

Figure 20.10 The Google Cloud Platform with the Active Cloud Shell

As you can expect from Google, the installation of the Cloud SDK isn't complicated. The instructions for Linux, macOS, and Windows can be found at the following address:

https://cloud.google.com/sdk/docs/quickstarts

For Linux and macOS, you need to extract a compressed archive to your hard drive after downloading. The installer searches for a matching Python version on your computer and then extends your shell's search path to include the newly created folder. The automatic command completion for gcloud gets activated in the process as well. On Linux, this happened automatically for us; on macOS, we had to manually enter the corresponding source commands into the ~/.bashrc file. On Windows, a wizard guides you through the setup program.

First, you should start gcloud using the init command. The program first tests the Internet connection and then launches your web browser with Google's login page. After confirming that gcloud gets access to the Google account, the program is ready.

If you already have more than one project set up in your Google account, you can now select the project you want to access by default. Finally, you can select the zone in which you want your virtual machines to run. (We chose europe-west1-b.)

The gcloud command has automatically saved the credentials for the cluster in your *~/.kube/config* configuration file at the end and set them as the default value. If you want to retrieve settings on another computer, you can use the following command:

```
gcloud container clusters get-credentials k8s-cluster
```

```
  Fetching cluster endpoint and auth data.
  kubeconfig entry generated for k8s-cluster.
```

If you haven't installed kubectl yet, you can perform this step very easily now using command gcloud components install kubectl. Google includes a version in the Cloud SDK.

20.4.3   The Diary Application in the Google Kubernetes Engine

Now you need to start the diary example from Chapter 13. We've already shown how you can convert the *docker-compose.yml* file into a Kubernetes configuration file in the previous section. Because you're going to run the application with SSL certificates in this example, you need to customize the kompose.service.type in the *docker-compose.yml* file:

```
# in k8s/google/docker-compose.yml
  frontend:
    restart: always
    image: docbuc/mwafe:2
    ports:
      "80:8080"
    labels:
      kompose.service.type: nodeport
```

Later, we'll use a special ingress-type load balancer that can terminate SSL traffic, among other things. Now you must convert the modified *docker-compose.yml* file again using kompose and create the objects in your Kubernetes cluster:

```
kompose convert -f docker-compose.yml -o kube.yaml
kubectl apply -f kube.yaml
  service/api created
  service/frontend created
  service/mongo1 created
  [...]
```

Verify that all pods have been successfully launched and find one of the MongoDB pods:

```
kubectl get pods
```

```
NAME                          READY   STATUS    RESTARTS   AGE
api-695875bff-xgcvm           0/1     Error     1          1m
frontend-77669f6d6b-5xvj5     1/1     Running   0          1m
mongo1-77486cd98-sptq5        1/1     Running   0          1m
[...]
```

The api pod is in Error status because the database connection isn't working yet. Now initialize the database replication on the MongoDB pod:

```
kubectl exec mongo1-77486cd98-sptq5 -- mongo --eval '
rs.initiate( {
   _id : "rs0",
   members: [
       { _id: 0, host: "mongo1:27017" },
       { _id: 1, host: "mongo2:27017" },
       { _id: 2, host: "mongo3:27017" }
   ]
})
'
```

Finally, you need to create the ingress object that connects the application to a public IP address and makes it accessible on the internet. In the list of active services, you can see the frontend service of type NodePort:

```
kubectl get svc
```

```
NAME      TYPE        CLUSTER-IP    EXTERNAL-IP   PORT(S)
api       ClusterIP   10.0.4.82     <none>        3000/TCP
frontend  NodePort    10.0.11.221   <none>        80:30155/TCP
[...]
```

In the *ingress.yaml* file, you should define this frontend service as defaultBackend and connect it to port 80. Name the new object frontend-ingress:

```
# File: k8s/google/ingress.yaml
apiVersion: networking.k8s.io/v1
kind: Ingress
metadata:
  name: frontend-ingress
spec:
  defaultBackend:
```

```
service:
  name: frontend
  port:
    number: 80
```

After creating the object (kubectl apply -f ingress.yaml), you need to be patient for a while. It may take up to 10 minutes for Google to reserve a free IP address for you and assign it to the new frontend-ingress service. You can get information about the current status of the reservation using kubectl get ingress or in the web interface under **Kubernetes Engine · Services & Ingress** (see Figure 20.11). Once the IP address is available, you can enter it in the web browser and use the diary application.

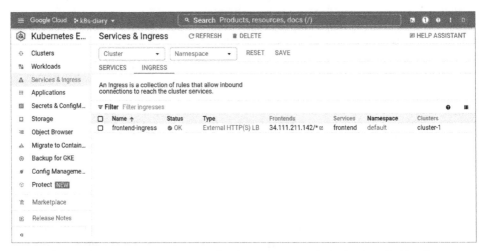

Figure 20.11 Kubernetes Ingress Services for the Diary Example in the Google Cloud

20.4.4   Using Secure Sockets Layer Certificates from Let's Encrypt

Finally, we want to extend the Kubernetes setup with the SSL certificates from Let's Encrypt. Unlike Docker Swarm, Kubernetes provides different ways to enable a built-in load balancer. The SSL certificates must of course work with the load balancer. Fortunately, other developers have already faced the same problem and have created a practical solution for that: cert-manager.

cert-manager is a Kubernetes controller that helps you create certificates from different issuers (including Let's Encrypt). The software is distributed as Helm-Chart, a packaging system for Kubernetes. To install Helm-Charts, you need to install the helm command-line program on your computer.

Like many other command-line programs from the cloud tools environment we've presented in this book, Helm is also available as a statically linked binary and can be downloaded and installed via a shell script from GitHub:

```
curl -fsSL -o get_helm.sh https://raw.githubusercontent.com/helm\
    /helm/master/scripts/get-helm-3
bash ./get_helm.sh
```

Now you need to add the repository where `cert-manager` is located to your Helm repositories and update the repositories:

```
helm repo add jetstack https://charts.jetstack.io

  "jetstack" has been added to your repositories

helm repo update

  [...]
  Update Complete.
```

Finally, the installation of the cert manager package follows. For this purpose, you should use the `cert-manager` namespace and set the `installCRDs` variable to `true` so that the custom resource definitions of the `cert-manager` package will work.

```
helm install \
  cert-manager jetstack/cert-manager \
  --namespace cert-manager \
  --create-namespace \
  --version v1.4.0 \
  --set installCRDs=true

  NAME: cert-manager
  LAST DEPLOYED: Fri Jul  9 14:07:07 2021
  ...
  cert-manager has been deployed successfully!
  ...
```

After installing `cert-manager`, you can create a Kubernetes object of type `ClusterIssuer` in which you configure the issuance of certificates. As with the other Let's Encrypt examples in this book, you should use the ACME protocol with the HTTP-01 mechanism. (This will create a file on your web server that will be queried by the ACME server at the specified domain.)

For the first attempts, the *staging* variant of Let's Encrypt is recommended because here the number of attempts for certificate creation isn't as strongly limited as with the production certificates. The process is identical to that for production certificates, but the root certificate for staging isn't stored in the web browsers. If you want to switch to valid Let's Encrypt certificates later, you only need to remove the `staging` from the configuration.

Kubernetes and "cert-manager"

The creation of the certificates has changed during the writing of this book in such a way that it also took us many attempts and a lot of time to do this successfully. What could actually be trivial, as we showed in Chapter 9, Section 9.6, can quickly become a waiting game with Kubernetes: the different versions of Kubernetes and cert-manager coupled with the almost endless configuration options provide plenty of scope for incompatibilities.

The configuration file for the ClusterIssuer with Let's Encrypt staging is as follows:

```
# File: k8s/google/clusterissuer.yaml
apiVersion: cert-manager.io/v1
kind: ClusterIssuer
metadata:
  name: letsencrypt-staging
spec:
  acme:
    email: v3@dockerbuch.info
    server: https://acme-staging-v02.api.letsencrypt.org/directory
    privateKeySecretRef:
      name: letsencrypt-staging
    solvers:
    - http01:
        ingress:
          class: nginx
```

Now you should create the object in the Kubernetes cluster:

```
kubectl apply -f clusterissuer.yaml
```

```
clusterissuer.cert-manager.io/letsencrypt-staging created
```

Make sure that the ClusterIssuer object was created correctly:

```
kubectl describe clusterissuer
```

```
...
Status:
...
  Message:               The ACME account was registered with
                         the ACME server
  Observed Generation:   1
  Reason:                ACMEAccountRegistered
```

```
Status:                 True
Type:                   Ready
```

To apply for a certificate, you must first assign the public IP address of the `frontend-ingress` service to a host name in your DNS management (*A entry* or *DNS A entry*). You can determine the IP address by calling `kubectl get ingress` under the ADDRESS entry. We use `k8s-diary.dockerbuch.info` as the host name in this example.

The current version of `cert-manager` has the feature to automatically request certificates if the appropriate annotations are present in the ingress configuration (you may recognize similarities with Traefik). In our attempts, that didn't work for a long time. Extensive internet research has revealed that the `cert-manager` in the GKE sometimes requires parameter `acme.cert-manager.io/http01-edit-in-place: "true"`.

Now you should add the lines needed for encryption to the ingress configuration. To do this, you copy the previously used *ingress.yaml* file to *ingress-tls.yaml*, and extend the file as follows:

```
# File: k8s/google/ingress-tls.yaml
apiVersion: networking.k8s.io/v1
kind: Ingress
metadata:
  name: frontend-ingress
 annotations:
   cert-manager.io/cluster-issuer: letsencrypt-staging
   acme.cert-manager.io/http01-edit-in-place: "true"
spec:
  tls:
  - hosts:
    - k8s-diary.dockerbuch.info
    secretName: k8s-diary-certificates
  defaultBackend:
    service:
      name: frontend
      port:
        number: 80
```

After activation (again with `kubectl apply -f ingress-tls.yaml`), you'll see that the ingress service is now enabled on port 80 and on port 443:

```
kubectl get ingress
```

```
NAME                HOSTS     ADDRESS           PORTS      AGE
frontend-ingress    *         35.244.138.87     80, 443    1h
```

Your application can now be accessed with SSL encryption at the address you use (see Figure 20.12).

Figure 20.12 Let's Encrypt Staging Certificate of "cert-manager"

Appendix A
Podman as a Docker Alternative

Docker is by no means the only container system. There are about a dozen alternatives available. One of them is *Podman*. Although this system was only released in 2019 with version number 1.0, it's currently gaining increasingly in importance as expressed by the rapid increase in version numbers to 4.0 in spring 2022. The success of Podman is primarily due to the fact that Red Hat stands behind the self-developed system with its entire market power in the professional Linux segment.

Only time will tell if Podman is just another example of the not-invented-here syndrome or if Red Hat (or ultimately IBM) will succeed in adding a profitable Kubernetes-related line of business to its own enterprise offerings with Podman.

From a technical perspective, Podman scores over Docker primarily because of its more modern and secure architecture. Containers are created and executed without root privileges by default. *Inside* the container, processes still run with root privileges, of course—otherwise most containers wouldn't work. But if you create a process list on the host machine with ps axu, you'll realize that processes of the container are actually assigned to your own account. User namespaces are responsible for this mechanism. This kernel feature is also used by Docker.

Podman uses the same image format as Docker and can therefore obtain images from Docker Hub as well as from other registries. The Podman website promises a completely straightforward switch from Docker to Podman (alias docker=podman and done). But as is so often the case, this is only half the truth.

- Podman is only available on Linux. Windows and macOS versions don't exist. Strictly speaking, although the podman command can be installed on Windows or macOS, the containers must be run on a Linux machine or a virtual machine, so it lacks the simplicity and convenience provided by Docker in this regard.

- The podman command performs the same functions as docker, but in detail, the compatibility occasionally reaches its limits.

- Docker has had time to establish itself as a de facto standard. Countless instructions and procedures are optimized for Docker. It's currently not foreseeable whether Podman (or another Docker alternative) will be able to catch up.

- For the docker compose command, which is enormously important in practice, Podman doesn't yet provide a usable equivalent counterpart. You have the choice to install the docker-compose command, which is familiar from the Docker world but doesn't work rootless in interaction with Podman, or to switch to podman-compose, which is developed separately from the official Podman project and has limited compatibility with the original.

Nevertheless, in this book, we want to provide at least an introduction to Podman. However, advanced functions such as Kubernetes have been left out. You can find more information about Podman here:

- *https://podman.io*
- *https://github.com/containers/libpod*

> **Standardization Efforts**
>
> The Open Container Initiative (OCI) (*https://opencontainers.org*) is trying to establish standards for dealing with containers. Docker is one of the founding members of OCI, and Red Hat is also an OCI member.

A.1   Docker versus Podman from a Technical Perspective

To understand the way Podman differs from Docker, you first need to understand the basic idea behind implementing Docker: the primary task of docker is to communicate with the two background processes, dockerd and containerd. These processes do the actual work; that is, they manage the container and image file systems, run containers, and so on.

Podman's way of working is fundamentally different as the podman command directly takes care of image management and container execution. There's no demon running in the background. The podman command thus performs all the tasks for which dockerd or containerd are responsible in the Docker universe. podman also uses other programs and libraries, of course, but not a central daemon. The Podman developers consider this the biggest advantage of their architecture because there's no *single point of failure*.

The security advantages of Podman over Docker described in the documentation sound plausible, but it's too early to make a final judgment on them.

It's currently unclear how far Podman's security depends on SELinux. In that case, all distributions without SELinux (especially Debian and Ubuntu) would have a security disadvantage. Red Hat has developed its own tool, *Udica*, to help set SELinux rules for containers of all types (including Podman):

www.redhat.com/en/blog/generate-selinux-policies-containers-with-udica

Last but not least, the much-advertised operation of containers without root privileges quickly reaches the limits of what is technically possible in practice. Whether you use Podman or Docker without root privileges, similar restrictions apply. For example, you can't create a network in which multiple containers communicate with each other, nor can you run the podman mount command, which is very handy in itself.

A.2 Installing Podman

Podman packages are available by default in current versions of most distributions. We performed our tests on Fedora 34, Oracle Linux 8, and Ubuntu 21.04. If Podman hasn't already been installed by default, a short command is sufficient to install it:

```
root# dnf install podman          # Fedora, RHEL and Clones
root# apt install podman          # Debian >=11, Ubuntu >=20.10
root# zypper install podman       # openSUSE
```

On RHEL 8 and compatible distributions, the Podman packages are located in the container-tools module. You can choose between different versions via dnf module enable -y container-tools:<stream>. More or less recent versions (but often still significantly older than those provided by Fedora) are contained in the rhel8 (RHEL and CentOS) or ol8 (Oracle Linux) stream:

```
root# dnf module list container-tools

  Oracle Linux 8 Application Stream (x86_64)

  Name              Stream    Summary
  container-tools   ol8       Rolling versions of podman ...
  container-tools   1.0       Stable versions of podman 1.0 ...
  container-tools   2.0       Stable versions of podman 1.6 ...
root# dnf module enable container-tools:ol8
root# dnf install podman
```

No Parallel Installation

Due to package conflicts, it's impossible to install Docker and Podman in parallel at the system level. However, it's possible (though probably rarely useful) to combine a system-wide Podman installation with a local installation of rootless Docker.

A.3 Container Registries

When you use Docker, the question of image provenance doesn't arise as the docker command automatically downloads images from the world's largest public container repository, Docker Hub. With Podman, the situation is different as the */etc/containers/registries.conf* file decides from which sources (registries) the containers are downloaded.

In most distributions, *registries.conf* already contains sensible default settings after installation. The following lines show the configuration that's valid in Fedora:

```
# File /etc/containers/registries.conf
unqualified-search-registries = ["registry.fedoraproject.org",
                                 "registry.access.redhat.com",
                                 "docker.io", "quay.io"]
```

According to this, Podman first accesses two registries from Fedora and RHEL. Fedora and Red Hat each operate their own "marketplaces" for containers. If the desired container can't be found there, Podman uses Docker Hub or the Quay.io registry. (This project is also part of the Red Hat cosmos.)

What at first glance appears to be a large registry selection quickly turns out to be a sham. The offering in Fedora's registry is extremely scarce. Red Hat's registry makes a much better impression but requires authentication as is common with the other commercial RHEL offerings. Thus, Podman mostly uses Docker Hub in the default configuration.

It's to be expected that in the future more and more companies or open-source organizations will provide their own registries, which you can then easily add to *registries.conf* as needed.

The following links reference some established registries:

- *https://aws.amazon.com/de/ecr*
- *https://registry.fedoraproject.org*
- *https://container-registry.oracle.com*
- *https://catalog.redhat.com/software/containers/explore*

A.4   Hello World!

The following command enables you to run Alpine Linux as a container. Thanks to --rm, the container gets automatically deleted as soon as you end the interactive use via exit.

> **Note**
> To make it clear which commands you can execute as an ordinary user, we give a prompt in each of the following examples. user$ means that you can execute the command on the host machine as an ordinary user. root# accordingly indicates that you need root privileges for this command.

```
user$ podman run -it --rm alpine:latest
  Trying to pull container-registry.oracle.com/alpine:latest ...
    unable to retrieve auth token: invalid username/password:
    unauthorized: authentication required
  Trying to pull docker.io/library/alpine:latest ...
```

```
   ...

/ # cat /etc/os-release
  NAME="Alpine Linux"
  VERSION_ID=3.13.5

   ...

/ # ip a
  1: lo: <LOOPBACK,UP,LOWER_UP> ...
      inet 127.0.0.1/8 scope host lo ...
  2: tap0: <BROADCAST,UP,LOWER_UP> ...
      inet 10.0.2.100/24 brd 10.0.2.255 ...

/ # exit
```

Two things are noteworthy about this example:

- First, you don't need `root` privileges to run the `podman` command, nor does your account need to be associated with a group that a daemon running with privileged rights also uses for container execution. Podman works quite similar to rootless Docker in this regard. One major difference is that the operation without `root` privileges isn't a special case but the default method.

- Secondly, `podman` first tries to get in touch with its own registries. (We performed the preceding test on Oracle Linux. Accordingly, in *registries.conf*, the package offer from Oracle was in the first place.)

  Registry access often fails because of the required authentication or because the desired image isn't available there at all. Then, `podman` accesses Docker Hub in the subsequent step.

  In newer versions, you need to select the registry explicitly with the cursor keys. Alternatively, you can prepend the name of the desired registry:

  ```
  podman run ... docker.io/mariadb
  ```

A.5   Storage Location for Containers and Images

If the `podman` command is executed with ordinary user rights, then images, containers, and so on will also be stored in the user account in the following directory: */home/<accountname>/.local/share/containers*.

If you run `podman` with `root` privileges (which is still allowed, of course), the OCI-compliant directory */var/lib/containers* will be used. Accordingly, this directory performs the same function as */var/lib/docker*.

> **Note**
>
> These two directories are completely separate from each other. Thus, if you down-loaded an image to launch a container without root privileges and then discover that you actually do need root privileges, you must download the image a second time.

Podman thus doesn't provide for mixed operation with/without root. As a rule, follow-ing the Podman philosophy, you'll initially try to get along without root privileges. If you hit an insurmountable limit, then this means "back to start." You need to execute all podman commands again and establish your setup again, this time with root privi-leges.

A.6   Compatibility of the "podman" Command

The podman command was designed to be as compatible as possible with docker. How-ever, there's no central reference as to which docker commands are supported or not supported with which options. If necessary, you need to take a look at the manual page (i.e., man podman). There you'll find a list of all subcommands. Detailed information can be found on subordinate manual pages whose name is composed of podman and the subcommand (e.g., man podman images or man podman run).

We've tried to follow the examples in Chapter 3 and Chapter 4 with podman, and, or the most part, it worked well.

The biggest exception were all examples where multiple containers should communi-cate with each other over their own network. podman network create and the associated commands require root privileges on the one hand, which contradicts the Podman phi-losophy; on the other hand, name resolution fails within the Podman network. In con-trast to Docker, containers can't communicate with each other via their host names. Pods provide help in this context (details will follow shortly), but there's nothing left of the frequently invoked compatibility between Docker and Podman in this aspect.

An inconspicuous but decidedly practical extension to the podman syntax compared to docker is the --all option. It extends the effect of various commands to all similar objects. docker stop --all stops all containers, docker images rm --all deletes all images, and so on.

After all, the podman command knows some subcommands that docker doesn't. In the following paragraphs, we'll introduce podman mount and podman pod in particular.

A.7   No "ping"

As with rootless Docker, `ping` also causes an error message in containers run by Podman. You can solve this by allowing the host to run `ping` for the user ID (UID) range reserved by Podman (see /etc/subuid):

```
root# sysctl -w "net.ipv4.ping_group_range=0 2000000"
```

For this change to be permanent, you must include the setting for `ping_group_range` in */etc/sysctl.conf*. You can read this tip and some other instructions on how to fix common problems here:

https://github.com/containers/podman/blob/master/troubleshooting.md

A.8   Volumes

Podman supports volumes in the same way as Docker. The familiar flag `:z` or `:Z` from Docker to establish SELinux compatibility is also required. The following example sets up a MariaDB container that stores its databases in the local *varlibmysql* directory:

```
user$ podman run -d --name mariadb-test  \
  -e MYSQL_ROOT_PASSWORD=secret   \
  -v myvolume:/var/lib/mysql mariadb
```

Inside the container, the files are assigned to the user and the group `mysql`:

```
user$ podman exec -it mariadb-test /bin/bash

root@eb541f4bc934:/# ls -l /var/lib/mysql/
  ... mysql mysql    32768 Nov 17 11:34 aria_log.00000001
  ... mysql mysql       52 Nov 17 11:34 aria_log_control
  ... mysql mysql     6176 Nov 17 11:34 ib_buffer_pool
  ...
root@eb541f4bc934:/# exit
```

However, a look at the directory on the host computer shows that the files are actually assigned to completely different UIDs and group IDs (GIDs):

```
user$ podman volume inspect myvolume
  ...
  "Mountpoint": "/home/user/.local/share/containers/\
                storage/volumes/myvolume/_data",
  ...
```

```
user$ cd /home/user/.local/share/containers/storage/volumes/\
        myvolume/_data

user$ ls -l
  ... 100998 100998    32768 17. Nov 12:34 aria_log.00000001
  ... 100998 100998       52 17. Nov 12:34 aria_log_control
  ... 100998 100998     6176 17. Nov 12:34 ib_buffer_pool
  ...
```

Like rootless Docker, Podman uses UIDs and GIDs beyond 100000, that is, numbers that are typically not used in normal Linux operations. The */etc/subuid* and */etc/subgid* files are responsible for assigning UIDs and GIDs, respectively, to a particular user. They contain, line by line, the user name, a start ID, and a number. So, the following output means that UIDs/GIDs between 100000 and 165535 are reserved for the user user.

```
user$ cat /etc/subuid
  user:100000:65536
user$ cat /etc/subgid
  user:100000:65536
```

Subordinate UIDs/GIDs

Subordinate UIDs/GIDs are based on a mechanism that was introduced in Linux as early as kernel version 3.12: the procedure allows users to be assigned a range of UIDs/ GIDs for their own management.

The configuration files subuid and subgid belong to the shadow utilities; their syntax is described in the man pages of the same name.

A.9   "podman secret"

Secrets are data (often passwords) that should be exchanged between containers without appearing in plain text in the process list or in too many configuration files. Docker supports secrets both through docker compose and in the Docker Swarm configuration but not for individual containers. You'll then receive the following error message: **This node is not a swarm manager.**

The corresponding podman secret command is much more flexible in this respect. It works independently of the context and does exactly what you would actually expect from docker secret.

A.10   Access to Container File Systems ("podman mount"/"umount")

While a container's access to a host directory is a procedure familiar from Docker, you can directly access a container's file system in Podman. To do this, you must first use pod mount <containername> to determine the location of the mount directory. However, you can't execute this command as a normal user—this will only result in an error message. You must rather first run podman unshare to change to the namespace used by Podman. All other commands are executed in this environment. They are preceded by the # character.

In the following example, you'll start a container with the Apache web server. While the container is running, you'll run podman mount <containername>. The command returns a rather long string with the mount directory. Usually, it's convenient to store this string in a variable, so you can view the contents of this directory and even make changes. When you're done, you can exit the namespace environment using exit or ⌈Ctrl⌉+⌈D⌉.

```
user$ podman run --name myapache -d -p 8080:80 httpd
  ...
user$ podman unshare

# podman mount myapache
  /home/kofler/.local/share/containers/storage/.../merged

# mountdir=$(podman unshare podman mount myapache)

# ls -l $mountdir
  ... root root 4096 21. Oct 15:39 bin
  ... root root 4096 21. Oct 15:39 boot
  ... root root 4096 18. Nov 08:16 dev

# exit
```

By default, you have read and write permissions to the mount directory. So, for example, you can run a script on the host machine that makes changes to the container's file system.

podman mount without parameters lists all container file systems currently mounted in the host directory tree. Using podman mount --latest, you can apply the command to the last started container, which often saves typing.

If you want to execute only a single command (and not, as in the previous example, a whole group of statements), it's sufficient to type the podman unshare <command>:

```
user$ podman unshare podman mount --latest
  /home/user/.local/share/containers/storage/overlay/.../merged
```

A.11   Managing Pods ("podman pod")

Have you ever wondered where the name Podman comes from? It's a short form of *Pod Manager*. According to this, podman is a command for managing pods. But what are pods? The term *pods*, coined by Kubernetes, refers to a group of related containers.

Because running individual containers in their own Podman network (podman network) comes with fundamental limitations compared to Docker, you need to get familiar with pods when you want multiple containers to work together.

The following example shows how you can set up the mypod pod with port redirection from port 80 (container) to 8080 (host). Strictly speaking, podman pod create also creates a container that's paused continuously. Its primary task is to keep the container group alive as long as there are no other containers in it.

The pod now runs a MariaDB database server and the phpMyAdmin administration tool. For the two run commands, the --pod mypod option is crucial. To the phpMyAdmin container, you pass either the name of the MariaDB container or the name of the pod (here, mypod) via PMA_HOST. Note that all containers in a pod use the same IP address internally!

```
user$ podman pod create -p 8080:80  -n mypod
user$ podman run -d --name mariadb-test --pod mypod \
        -e MYSQL_ROOT_PASSWORD=secret \
        -v myvolume:/var/lib/mysql \
        mariadb
user$ podman run -d --name pma --pod mypod \
        -e PMA_HOST=mariadb-test phpmyadmin/phpmyadmin
```

On the host computer, you can now access the phpMyAdmin web server in the web browser using *http://localhost:8080* and log in to the MariaDB server as root with the password secret.

The approach outlined here looks a little different from a comparable setup in Docker, but it's just as easy to set up. podman pod knows a lot of other subcommands besides create:

- podman pod ps or podman pod list lists all pods.
- podman pod top <podname> returns a list of all processes from all containers running in the specified pod.
- podman pod stop <podname> terminates all containers of the specified pod. As usual, you can also specify the --all option instead of the pod name to terminate the containers of all active pods.
- podman pod start <podname> starts all containers of a pod.
- podman pod pause <podname> or podman pod unpause <podname> pauses or resumes the execution of a pod's container.

- `podman pod rm <podname>` deletes the pod if it doesn't contain any containers. To delete a pod along with its containers, you should use `podman pod rm --force <podname>`. Running containers are stopped before deletion.

- `podman pod prune [--force]` deletes all pods that aren't currently running.

A.12   Creating Images ("podman build", "buildah")

`podman build -t <imgname> .` reads the *Dockerfile* or *containerfile* file from the local directory and creates an image from it. Here, the syntax described in Chapter 4 applies.

Behind the scenes, `podman build` draws on *Buildah*, which is a separate image build tool from the Podman family (see also *https://buildah.io*). Instead of `podman build`, you can also run the `buildah` command directly. This requires the installation of the package of the same name and then provides various additional functions:

https://developers.redhat.com/blog/2019/02/21/podman-and-buildah-for-docker-users

A.13   Running "docker-compose" in Podman

In current versions of `docker`, the `compose` subcommand is integrated. This extremely useful command is unfortunately missing in Podman. After all, since version 3.0, Podman can be configured relatively straightforwardly to be compatible with the standalone `docker-compose` command.

We performed the following tests on Fedora 34. Essentially, all you need to do is install two add-on packages, enable Podman as a background service at the system level, and modify *registries.conf*:

```
dnf install podman-docker
dnf install docker-compose
systemctl enable --now podman.socket
<editor> /etc/containers/registries.conf
```

The following explains each of these commands in more detail:

- The `podman-docker` package provides the `/usr/bin/docker` script, which simply calls `podman`. The script is required because `docker-compose` assumes that the container management command is called `docker` and not `podman`.

- With `dnf install docker-compose`, a not-quite-current version of the standalone command `docker-compose` is installed. (Strictly speaking, this is a Python script.)

- `systemctl enable --now podman.socket` enables an API through which `docker-compose` can "talk" to Podman. In the introduction, we told you that Podman usually avoids this Docker concept, but to make it compatible with `docker-compose`, Podman needs to be rebuilt a little.

- Finally, you must remove from /etc/containers/registries.conf all the registries enumerated via the unqualified-search-registries keyword except docker.io. As long as there are multiple registries, the resulting queries will lead to errors. (Of course, you can specify the address of another registry instead of docker.io if it has all the images you need for your setup. What matters is that it's a registry.)

After this preparatory work, sudo docker-compose should work as in a Docker installation. This was the case in our tests. Note, however, that the resulting containers now also operate with root privileges. Accordingly, manual access to containers, images, volumes, and so on must also be done with sudo podman.

We haven't been able to combine Podman in rootless mode with docker-compose. This is strange because docker-compose is quite compatible with rootless Docker.

A.14   "podman-compose" Instead of "docker-compose"

Instead of docker-compose, you can use the Python script, podman-compose. The installation is very simple and doesn't require root privileges:

```
pip3 install podman-compose
```

In addition, in use, the biggest advantage of podman-compose over the original is that it gets along very well with Podman and, unlike docker-compose, doesn't require a central Podman service or other compatibility bridges. podman-compose uses pods instead of networks to get multiple containers to work together.

However, our tests unfortunately showed that podman-compose has limited compatibility with docker-compose and, for example, has fundamental problems with volumes. Even with relatively simple setups like the introductory examples from Chapter 5, errors occurred.

What's perhaps even more critical is the fact that the project, while not dead of late, seemed largely dormant. The GitHub page shows only a few current commits, but a lot of unresolved issues/bugs and open pull requests (i.e., extensions intended for integration). The project is currently not an official part of Podman: *https://github.com/containers/podman-compose*.

Appendix B
The Authors

Bernd Öggl is an experienced system administrator and web developer. Since 2001, he has been creating websites for customers, implementing individual development projects, and passing on his knowledge at conferences and in publications.

Michael Kofler studied telematics at Graz University of Technology and is one of the most successful German-language IT specialist authors. In addition to Linux, his areas of expertise include IT security, Python, Swift, Java, and Raspberry Pi. He is a developer, advises companies, and works as a lecturer.

Index

- Your complete guide to the Java Platform, Standard Edition 17

- Understand the Java langauge, from basic pricinples to advanced concepts

- Work with expressions, statements, classes, objects, and much more

Christian Ullenboom

Java

The Comprehensive Guide

This is the up-to-date, practical guide to Java you've been looking for! Whether you're a beginner, you're switching to Java from another language, or you're just looking to brush up on your Java skills, this is the only book you need. You'll get a thorough grounding in the basics of the Java language, including classes, objects, arrays, strings, and exceptions. You'll also learn about more advanced topics: threads, algorithms, XML, JUnit testing, and much more. This book belongs on every Java programmer's shelf!

1,126 pages, pub. 10/2022
E-Book: $54.99 | **Print:** $59.95 | **Bundle:** $69.99

www.rheinwerk-computing.com/5557

- The complete Python 3 handbook
- Learn basic Python principles and work with functions, methods, data types, and more
- Walk through GUIs, network programming, debugging, optimization, and other advanced topics

Johannes Ernesti, Peter Kaiser

Python 3

The Comprehensive Guide

Ready to master Python? Learn to write effective code, whether you're a beginner or a professional programmer. Review core Python concepts, including functions, modularization, and object orientation and walk through the available data types. Then dive into more advanced topics, such as using Django and working with GUIs. With plenty of code examples throughout, this hands-on reference guide has everything you need to become proficient in Python!

1,036 pages, pub. 09/2022
E-Book: $54.99 | **Print:** $59.95 | **Bundle:** $69.99

www.rheinwerk-computing.com/5566